McCRAE'S BATTALION

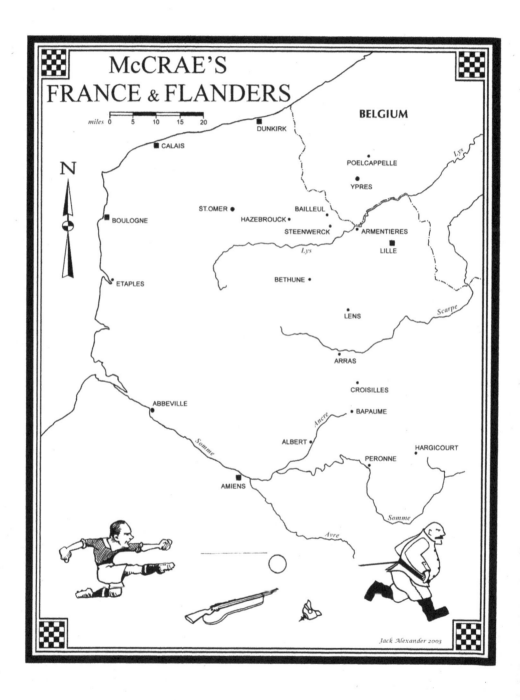

McCRAE'S BATTALION
THE STORY OF THE 16TH ROYAL SCOTS

Jack Alexander

MAINSTREAM
PUBLISHING
EDINBURGH AND LONDON

This edition, 2004

First published in Great Britain in 2003 by
MAINSTREAM PUBLISHING COMPANY (EDINBURGH) LTD
7 Albany Street
Edinburgh EH1 3UG

ISBN 978 1 84018 932 2

Reprinted 2003 (twice), 2007, 2010,2011

All picture section photographs from *McCrae's Battalion* collection
(Jack Alexander) except where stated

A catalogue record for this book is available from the British Library

Typeset in Cheltenham and Van Dijck
Printed in Great Britain by
Clays Ltd, St Ives plc

This book is dedicated with all my love to
MARGARET CLARK ALEXANDER
1926–2003
Who made everything possible.

Goodnight, Mum.

THE GREATER GAME.

MR. PUNCH (*to Professional Association Player*). "NO DOUBT YOU CAN MAKE MONEY IN THIS FIELD, MY FRIEND, BUT THERE'S ONLY ONE FIELD TO-DAY WHERE YOU CAN GET HONOUR."

[The Council of the Football Association apparently proposes to carry out the full programme of the Cup Competition, just as if the country did not need the services of all its athletes for the serious business of War.]

Contents

List of Abbreviations		10
Introductory		11
Chapter One	'This veritable curse'	13
Chapter Two	'Auld Reekie, wale o ilka town!'	28
Chapter Three	'White Feathers of Midlothian'	54
Chapter Four	'If it's football that you're wanting . . .'	73
Chapter Five	'Marching wi Geordie'	91
Chapter Six	'An awful biz'	117
Chapter Seven	'My little all to Mother, with best love'	133
Chapter Eight	'A tall, grey-haired soldier'	155
Chapter Nine	'Such a wall of steel and shell'	180
Chapter Ten	'The Offensive Spirit'	200
Chapter Eleven	'Flowers o the Forest'	232
Chapter Twelve	'A great life out there, after all'	257
Postscript and Acknowledgements		282
Appendices		288
Notes		299
Select Bibliography		312
Index		317

16th (Service) Bn. The Royal Scots
December, 1915

* indicates pre-war service in the Regular Army
❖ indicates pre-war service with Volunteer or Territorial Force

COMMANDING OFFICER
Lieut-Col. Sir George McCrae, VD ❖
(civil servant)

SECOND-IN-COMMAND
Major Herbert Warden ❖
(solicitor)

THIRD-IN-COMMAND
Major Richard Lauder ❖
(porridge magnate)

ADJUTANT/ORDERLY ROOM
Capt. William Robertson
(manager, linen factory)

CHAPLAINS
Capt. James Black ❖
Capt. John Crotty

MEDICAL OFFICER
Capt. George Adams
(physician)

PIPE BAND
Pipe-Major William Duguid *
(hospital porter)

ORCHESTRA
Sgt. Gerald Crawford
(consulting engineer)

FOOTBALL
Lt. Cuthbert Lodge
(Arts/Science student)

TRANSPORT OFFICER
Lt. Robert Husband ❖
(trainee stockbroker)
Sgt. Robert Stewart
(saddler)

SIGNALLING OFFICER
Lt. Jock Miller
(schoolmaster)
Sgt. Robert Davie
(joiner)

REGIMENTAL SERGEANT-MAJOR
R.S.M. Fred Muir *
(coal miner)

PROVOST SERGEANT

BOMBING OFFICER
Lt. James Davie
(Higher Grade student)
Sgt. John Duncan
(librarian)

QUARTERMASTER
Lt. Donald Munro ❖
(City Chamberlain's clerk)
R.Q.M.S. John Macrae ❖
(furniture salesman)

COOK SERGEANT
Sgt. John Brodie ❖
(hotelier)

SHOEMAKER SERGEANT
Sgt. William Littlejohn *
(shoemaker)

PIONEER SERGEANT

ARMOURER SERGEANT

N.C.O. TAILOR

MACHINE-GUN OFFICER
Lt. James Moir ❖
(spirit merchant's clerk)
2/Lt. Alastair MacLachlan
(Arts student)
Sgt. John Hamilton
(joiner)

TRENCH-MORTAR OFFICER
2/Lt. Leslie Kitton
(trainee civil servant)
Cpl. Hugh Porter
(coal miner)

SNIPING OFFICER
2/Lt. 'D.M.' Sutherland
(art college lecturer)
L/Cpl. David Gracie
(Higher Grade student)

WATER N.C.O.

STRETCHER BEARERS

GAS N.C.O.

SANITARY N.C.O.

'HQ' COMPANY

'A' COMPANY
C.S.M. William Scott
(railway engineer)
C.Q.M.S. Alex Ogilvie
(commercial clerk)

1 PLATOON
Capt. Peter Ross
(schoolmaster)
Sgt. John Jolly
(librarian)

2 PLATOON
2/Lt. John Stewart
(solicitor)
Sgt. David Lawson
(schoolmaster)

3 PLATOON
2/Lt. Norman Walker
(law apprentice)
Sgt. William Pillans
(bookseller's clerk)

4 PLATOON
2/Lt. Fraser MacLean ❖
(schoolmaster)
Sgt. Clarence Walker
(solicitor)

'B' COMPANY
C.S.M. John Muirhead *
(professional footballer)
C.Q.M.S. Charles Stirling
(commercial clerk)

5 PLATOON
Capt. Napier Armit
(advocate)
Sgt. James Martin
(stereotyper)

6 PLATOON
2/Lt. Russell Tod
(bank clerk)
Sgt. Robert Miller *
(commissionaire)

7 PLATOON
2/Lt. James Davie
(Higher Grade student)
Sgt. Sandy Lindsay
(apprentice draughtsman)

8 PLATOON
2/Lt. George Hamilton
(warehouse clerk)
Sgt. Angus Cameron ❖
(letterpress printer)

'C' COMPANY
C.S.M. Annan Ness *
(journalist)
C.Q.M.S. Donald Gunn
(provision merchant)

9 PLATOON
Capt. Lionel Coles *
(planter)
Sgt. Duncan Currie
(professional footballer)

10 PLATOON
2/Lt. Tommy Millar
(medical student)
Sgt. Cecil Neill *
(colliery labourer)

11 PLATOON
2/Lt. James Stevenson ❖
(Burgh Insurance clerk)
Sgt. George Anderson
(lithographer)

12 PLATOON
Lt. Cuthbert Lodge
(Arts/Science student)
Sgt. Sandy Yule *
(rubber-worker)

'D' COMPANY
C.S.M. Tom McManus *
(railway servant)
C.Q.M.S. Charles Robertson
(provision merchant)

13 PLATOON
Capt. James Hendry
(electrical engineer)
Sgt. Sandy Cormack *
(hotel cook)

14 PLATOON
Lt. Robert Martin
(manager, linen factory)
Sgt. William MacFarlane
(sheep farmer)

15 PLATOON
Lt. James MacKenzie
(solicitor)
Sgt. Ned Dempster
(paper maker)

16 PLATOON
Capt. Andrew Whyte ❖
(senior hospital clerk)
Sgt. Andrew Adams
(bookbinder)

'The Empires with whom we are at war have called to the Colours almost their entire male population. The principle which we on our part shall observe is this — that while their maximum force undergoes a steady diminution, the reinforcements we prepare shall steadily and increasingly flow out until we have an Army in the field which, in numbers not less than in quality, will not be unworthy of the power and responsibilities of the British Empire.'

Field-Marshal Rt. Hon. *Horatio Herbert* Earl *Kitchener of Khartoum,*
KG, KP, GCB, OM, GCSI, GCMG, GCIE,
Col. Commandant Royal Engineers,
Colonel Irish Guards.
Secretary of State for War.

'McCrae's. I like that battalion: it has a dash about it.'

Major-General Edward Charles Ingouville-Williams, CB, DSO
Commanding Officer,
34ᵗʰ Division, BEF

'I thought: if the Kaiser was looking for trouble, we were just the boys to give it to him.'

James Stirling Brown, Esquire.
Private 18982, C Company, 16th (Service) Bn. The Royal Scots,
apprentice gasfitter, five feet tall (at a stretch),
armed and occasionally dangerous.

List of Abbreviations

Lieutenant	Lt
Second Lieutenant	2/Lt
Regimental Sergeant-Major	RSM
Company Sergeant-Major	CSM
Regimental Quartermaster Sergeant	RQMS
Company Quartermaster Sergeant	CQMS
Sergeant	Sgt
Lance Sergeant	L/Sgt
Corporal	Cpl
Lance Corporal	L/Cpl
Private	Pte
Royal Scots	RS
Northumberland Fusiliers	NF
Scottish Rifles	SR
Highland Light Infantry	HLI
Royal Field Artillery	RFA
Royal Garrison Artillery	RGA
Royal Engineers	RE
Royal Flying Corps	RFC
Royal Army Medical Corps	RAMC
Machine Gun Corps	MGC

Introductory

From *The Scotsman*, Friday, 28 December 1928:

> McCRAE. – At *Torluish*, North Berwick, on 27th December, Colonel Sir George McCrae, D.S.O. Service in Lady Glenorchy's Established Church, Roxburgh Place, Edinburgh, on Saturday 29th December at 2 p.m.; thereafter funeral, with military honours, to Grange Cemetery. Those desirous of attending, kindly accept this (the only) intimation and invitation.

A great many people were 'desirous of attending' – as *friends*, mark you, not just respectful strangers. The turn-out for Sir George McCrae's funeral remains the largest ever seen in Scotland. Businesses closed, traffic was suspended, the streets of the capital's old southside were so crowded that in the words of one who was there, 'you might have thought the King had passed away'. Yet today the memory of the man, and of the brilliant battalion that he raised and later commanded on the Western Front, has dimmed to the point of extinction.

This, at long last, is their story.

16TH ROYAL SCOTS · THE ATTACK

1 JULY, 1916

0   500 yards

xxxx   barbed wire entanglements

✳   known machine-gun positions

Jack Alexander 2003

N

Keir's Redan

USNA HILL

TARA HILL

100

Dunfermline St.

Dalhousie St.

Pilcher's Street

Northumberland Ave.

Kinfauns St.

Berkshire Ave.

Pannure St.

Tanner St.

Methven St.

Atholl St.

Scone St.

Y Sap Crater

Moffat St.

Glory Hole

Mercier St.

Monteith St.

Kirriemuir St.

Lochnager St.

GERMAN FRONT LINE

80

Dundee Ave.

Ashdown St.

Kirkgate St.

Crater

Crater

Bun

Carnoustie St.

CHAPES SPUR

Arbroath Street

Montgomery St.

BECOURT WOOD

Aberdeen Ave.

BRITISH FRONT LINE

①

SAUSAGE VALLEY

LA BOISSELLE

120

100

21st Div Sap

Hedigund

KIPPER

BLOATER

120

WILLOW PATCH

Scott's Redoubt

new saps

new saps

WOOD ALLEY

Scott's Redoubt

new saps

HORSESHOE

FETLOCK TRENCH

TRENCH

THE DINGLE

ROUND WOOD

BIRCH TREE TRENCH

BIRCH TREE WOOD

SHELTER WOOD

PEAKE WOOD

BAILIFF WOOD

THE CRUCIFIX

SHELTER ALLEY

QUADRANGLE

CONTALMAISON

Château

100

TRENCH

PEARL ALLEY

BOTTOM WOOD

① Kitton's trench-mortar emplacement
② Millar's patrol (29th/30th June)
③ Arnott's command (1st/2nd July)
④ Lodge & Hamilton's command (3.30 a.m., 2nd July)
⑤ Buchanan's reconnaissance
⑥ Coke's command
⑦ Rawson wounded (8.45 a.m., 1st July)
⑧ Whyte (9.45 a.m.) & Pringle (9.30 a.m., 1st July)
⑨ Kelly's field
⑩ Russell's stand

CHAPTER ONE

'This veritable curse'

John George Lambton, 3rd Earl of Durham, was prepared to be blunt. 'I am almost hard-hearted enough,' he told a patriotic matinée at the Empire Theatre, 'to wish that the Germans would drop a shell among these footballers some Saturday afternoon. I really think it would be the best method of waking up the young men of Sunderland.'

It was Wednesday, 11 November 1914. That morning had brought the heaviest bombardment of the war, as Von Falkenhayn's artillery pounded the makeshift British line in front of Ypres. Close behind the cover of this murderous barrage advanced a field-grey mass of Prussian Guards, overwhelming the shallow fire-trenches north of the Menin road and rolling unopposed towards the town. They were halted by the crack of Enfield rifles. Through the mist and shell-smoke, it might have seemed like hundreds; in fact it was just four and forty men – Black Watch mainly, one or two Scots Guards – firing rapid, refusing to fall back, standing firm until their field-guns came to bear. By 2.45 p.m., even as Lord Lambton rose to speak, a shattered remnant of the 2nd Ox and Bucks was charging headlong into Nonne Boschen to repel the Hun at bayonet point.

No parade-ground soldiers these; no serried ranks of scarlet tunics. Tired, ragged, haggard and unshaven, Thomas Atkins had been continuously engaged for three bloody weeks. He was hardly fit to walk, never mind charge. Flanders mud had claimed his kit, the German guns his friends. His battalion, once a thousand strong, now barely mustered hundreds; his company had dwindled to the strength of a platoon. Only the thought of reinforcement sustained him in his trials: he was holding the line until help could arrive. 'Entrenching all night, fighting all day, holding on everywhere without relief is impossible,' observed *The Scotsman*,

13

Scotland's leading daily newspaper. 'Our troops have almost reached their limit.'

Reached and passed, in fact. Passed at Gheluvelt in the dying days of October. One of the journalists had been doing his sums. He counted the names in the War Office casualty returns (printed daily in the press to the growing consternation of the public) and produced a figure of 57,000 British casualties in the actions up to 1 November. Since the British Expeditionary Force – Field-Marshal French's 'contemptible little army' – had embarked for France in August with fewer than 90,000 men, the position on the Continent was grave. November's headlines – HOW THE GERMAN HORDES WERE KEPT AT BAY/GREAT FIGHT BY THE BRITISH AGAINST HEAVY ODDS/CHARGE AFTER CHARGE BROKEN – were hardly calculated to calm the fears of the nervous domestic observer; nor, indeed, were the numerous graphic letters from soldiers at the front, which left no one in any doubt that in spite of a steady infusion of fresh units, the old British Army was bleeding to death.

'Who will now take up the flag and save the world from *Kultur*?' asked a correspondent in *The Times*. The answer, for the moment, wasn't clear. There were the part-time soldiers of the Territorial Force, who had waived their right to serve at home and even now were being directed overseas; and the eager young volunteers of Lord Kitchener's 'New' Army, who would not be ready for service abroad until the following spring at the earliest. His Lordship's appeal struck a popular chord: the plight of little Belgium, the bravery of France, the vileness of the threat to Home and Empire. Thus the month of August saw men flocking to his side, some 300,000 in total. Through September the momentum was sustained; only in October did the numbers start to fall.[1] This was not due to some sudden moral collapse on the part of the unenlisted millions, but rather to the problems faced by those already joined. They were drilling with broomsticks: there were no tunics, no breeches and no proper boots. Frustration was the order of the day. 'Your Country Needs You' the poster should have read, '*but not just at the moment.*' If there were shortages of labour in the factories and mines, surely service as civilians had its merits.

But not in the opinion of the patriotic crank. The crank was offended by men standing in the street and saw it as his duty to report them – not to the police, who were powerless to act, but to local and national papers. 'It is nothing short of shameful,' was a typical complaint. 'If I was young, I would have been away.' No matter that most of the offenders were servicemen caught in civilian attire, or munition workers, or physically unsound, or under-aged, or over-aged, or the sole support of wives and widowed mothers. It was nothing short of shameful just the same. Elderly ex-soldiers who had tried to re-enlist, angry young ladies who wished they were men, jingoistic priests who thought the Kaiser was the Devil and a Christian was obliged to go and fight him. Open any journal and their voices seemed to cry out from the page: *Cowards! Shirkers! Have they no sense of Honour? Can thoughts of England truly leave them cold?*

Such questions were rhetorical, for the questioners were deaf to explanation. No reason was accepted as legitimate excuse, no job of any kind conceded vital. Like children counting soldiers in the safety of the playroom, they saw the matter simply: if Britain could muster more men than the Hun, then Britain would win, it was certain. And they were therefore certain: failure to enlist was almost tantamount to treason. There could be no one lower than a shirker.

Except, of course, a shirker with a football.

✖ ✖ ✖

On 4 August 1914, with the Kaiser's troops pouring across the border into neutral Belgium, Great Britain declared war on Germany. Two days later, Parliament sanctioned the raising of an additional 500,000 men for the Army, a measure that reflected the gravity of the situation in which the nation now found itself. Five days later still, and with the crisis no less grave, members of the Scottish Football Association (the SFA) convened in Glasgow to make the draw for the first round of the Qualifying Cup.

At the start of the proceedings letters were read out asking that the new season, due to begin on the following Saturday, be postponed until hostilities had ended. Mr Munro, the delegate from Inverness, agreed with this suggestion, saying it would be sacrilege to play football while soldiers might be dying at the front, and that postponement was indeed the only answer. He found little support in the room, however, and it was no surprise when the postponers – the 'stoppers', as they would soon become known – were defeated in the ensuing ballot. Emboldened by victory, the chairman, Duncan Campbell of Greenock Morton, concluded on behalf of his colleagues that 'we do not consider it expedient to take any action in the meantime. It might be necessary to take some action later in the season, but it would simply be giving in to general panic to do anything now.' A further motion, to call a special meeting to discuss the matter in greater depth, was also rejected. Football would go on despite the war.

Or would it? Influential figures in the Scottish game were appalled at the thought. Thomas Forsyth, chairman of Airdrieonians, was moved to speak out in the strongest of terms. 'I am much disappointed,' said the solicitor and Kirk elder, 'that in this present crisis no step has been taken by the SFA to lend their help to the country.' Arguing forcibly for postponement, he concluded that 'playing football while our men are fighting is repugnant, and unless some action is forthcoming soon, I will feel compelled to resign my position and take no further part in the game.'

On the following Saturday, however, the new season started off as planned, with the game of the day taking place at Tynecastle Park in Edinburgh, where champions and cup-holders Glasgow Celtic went down 2–0 to a fine young Heart of Midlothian side. That same afternoon saw golf, cricket and racing all continue much as before. In the last case the aristocratic Jockey Club had come out strongly against suspension because of the large number of people dependent on the sport for a living. Football was far from isolated. Nevertheless Forsyth duly tendered his resignation, placing his letter on the boardroom table, where it remained until his fellow directors persuaded him to change his mind. He would stay and fight on from within, encouraged by the prospect of a meeting called in London to discuss whether football might be stopped south of the border.

In England the new season was not due to start until September; it was therefore natural that the English authorities should come to address the question of the war somewhat later than their Scottish counterparts. On 20 August the English Football Association (the FA), the English Football League and the Southern League gathered to consider what they termed 'the national crisis'. Forsyth was well aware that if England voted for postponement the Scots would find it impossible not to follow suit. Again, however, he was disappointed, for the only successful resolutions committed clubs to subscribe to the various local and national relief funds, and to collect footballs for men serving at the front. 'It would be a mistake,' delegates decided, 'to give up the game. We must remain calm and give the public something to think about besides war.'

Then on 24 August the crisis deepened. Members of the tiny British Expeditionary Force (BEF), which only the previous day had held their ground so gallantly at Mons, were now retiring, dragged back by the French on their right, whose unheralded departure in the middle of the night had taken everybody by surprise. At home the ink was hardly dry on headlines that recorded a heroic stand; now the compositors were shuffling their letters to spell the word 'withdrawal'. The first British blood had been spilled. 'What is required now,' warned *The Times*, 'is that the young men of this nation should flock to the recruiting centres ready to enrol on the spot. There is no alternative to some such great voluntary movement but conscription.'

Conscription! Alone among the major European powers, Britain imposed no compulsory military service. The Regular Army – fewer than 250,000 strong and scattered across the surface of the globe – was made up of highly trained professional volunteers. Not a pressed man among them. To the ordinary citizen (who did not read Lord Northcliffe's *Times*), this was a matter of fierce national pride. Conscription was anathema; worse still, it was foreign. None the less, Northcliffe had his supporters – even in the Liberal heartland of the Scottish Borders. Writing to *The Scotsman* on 26 August, Dr Thomas Luke of Peebles stated that 'Football and race meetings should be stopped until we see a way out of the wood, and a strong hint of compulsion should be given to our young men that they owe it to their country to enlist.' The following morning in the same journal the Reverend Thomas Macauley of the United Free Church in Larbert suggested that 'the military would do well to commandeer all football fields; they would make excellent drilling grounds, while the grandstands, with but slight alteration, would afford excellent accommodation for the troops. This is not the time for well-developed youths to be kicking a leather ball with idle crowds looking on at them.'

Suddenly – and it was indeed quite sudden – football found itself being coupled with reluctance to enlist. In London on 29 August, 81-year-old Lord Roberts of Kandahar stirred the waters further, when, addressing the newly formed 7th Battalion of the Royal Fusiliers, he praised their fine example before damning by comparison 'another sort of fellow altogether, who goes about his football as if the future of the country were not at stake'. 'Bobs', awarded the Victoria Cross in 1858, was the hero of Afghanistan and saviour of South Africa. His courage was unquestioned and he always set his name to his opinions. The same could not be said for countless other critics of the game, who preferred to hide behind pseudonymous disguises. 'Teacher', writing to *The Scotsman*, demanded to know 'how anyone can read accounts of the Belgian losses without longing to arise and help them? Let those who do not feel this way refrain from flaunting their callousness in public, and let the public refrain from looking on at, and thus encouraging, this revolting spectacle.' 'Catholic Priest' (also in *The Scotsman*) complained 'that crowds of callous, thoughtless fools gather in their thousands to watch the awful farce of football. Has the country gone stark mad? Is the flag, under whose folds we enjoy glorious British freedom, of less importance now than a league flag or some other footballing trophy?' 'An Old Blue', writing the same day in *The Times*, wondered 'if games and sport are now the only things that stir the blood of our youth? Why are our football clubs arranging their fixtures as usual? What we want to see is not our athletes kicking a football about to amuse a crowd of idlers, but doing their best to kick the German Army out of Belgium and France.'

These letters echoed sentiments, in vogue before the war, that football somehow exerted a malevolent influence on the nation's youth. Football, so the argument went, had become an obsession, filling the dreams and daytime thoughts of men whose dreary lives offered no other distraction quite so thrilling. Scrounge yourself a sixpence and visit any ground. Here was drama, here was tension, here were gaudy strips and splendid goals; here, scandalously, was *professionalism*, spreading (some said) like a cancer into the noble world of sport, usurping every high ideal, corrupting the very foundation of Empire – 'Service for Service's sake'. Now, in the country's hour of need, all the darkest prophecies appeared to be fulfilled. Clearly football must be stopped for the duration.

But not so, said the War Office, where cooler heads apparently prevailed. When consulted by the FA, Harold Tennant, Liberal MP for Berwickshire and Under-Secretary of State for War, had said nothing about stoppage; indeed he had shown solicitous concern for every aspect of the game – not least its obvious potential as an instrument of recruiting. On 31 August FA chairman J.C. Clegg issued a statement confirming that 'War Office opinion is favourable to continuation.' He went on to announce the establishment of a standing committee to confer with the military authorities, and urged clubs to cancel the contract of any player who wanted to enlist. 'Calls for the suspension are mischievous,' he concluded. 'Football players and supporters are as patriotic as the next man. Why should football be singled out for such a slur?'

It was a fair question. Mr Clegg was a man of few, well-chosen words. In the face of unfounded abuse, he maintained both his calm and his dignity. The same could not be said for his counterparts on the Management Committee of the English Football League, who presently issued their own statement of defence – a document that appears to have been composed with the assistance of Uriah Heep:

> Thousands upon thousands of the flower of British manhood, who upon the playing fields of this country have acquired the splendid characteristics of the fearless warrior, are now, at the peril of their lives, fighting the battle of honour, honesty and uprightness against military despotism in the greatest struggle the world has ever known. From the decimated towns and villages and grievously-wronged yet heroic and sacrificing people of Belgium, comes the call for help. It is the call of patriotism, justice and redress, and we trust that in this hour of England's need every young man who can possibly do so will respond to his country's call.
>
> In considering the course to be adopted with reference to our great national winter game, we are not unmindful of the days of deep sorrow now with us and yet to come. To sit and mourn is to aggravate the nation's sorrow. Any national sport which can save the people at home from panic and undue depression is a great asset. Just as we look hour after hour for the latest news from the theatre

of war, our vast Army in the field will, week by week, look for papers from home, and in so far as their minds may be temporarily directed from the horrors of war, much will be done to give them fresh heart and a renewed vitality for the work before them.

At home our clubs are in a helpless position. Their contracts, entered into with all the formality of legal contracts, must be performed as far as possible. We feel that the advice offered by politicians, the Press and commercial authorities that business should be carried on as usual is sound, well considered and well seasoned. We therefore without the slightest reservation appeal to the clubs, the Press and the public that our great winter game shall pursue its normal course.

This was just inflammatory. Football's actions (they claimed) were restricted by the letter of the law. If a player walked out on his club in order to enlist, he would be in breach of contract; if the same club sacked that player in order to allow him to enlist, *it* would be in breach of contract. It was a cleft stick, they insisted; football was indeed helpless. In fact the Management Committee was busy digging a deep trench for itself. Whether it would prove at all tenable remained to be seen.

The next offensive round was fired by Northcliffe's London *Evening News*, suspending publication of its Saturday *Football Special*, which normally boasted an enormous sale. 'This is no time for football editions,' boomed the editorial. 'This is no time for football. The nation must occupy itself with more serious business. The young men who play football and those who look on have better work to do. They are summoned to leave their sport, and play their part in a greater game. That game is War, for life and death.' The same day 'A Bishop in the West Country' submitted the following letter to all major newspapers for immediate publication:

The trouble of the moment is that crowds of vigorous young men have as yet no perception of their country's need, nor of the great service they could immediately do for her. But why should not a 'Footballer's League for National Service' be at once enrolled? In almost every county in Great Britain a battalion might be raised, and some counties could contribute whole regiments of four battalions each. The following suggestions are offered:
1. Let such a force have the distinctive title of 'The Footballer's Legion'.
2. Let none but known footballers be enrolled.
3. Let commissions be given to well known footballers.
4. Let there be some distinctive mark on the uniform.

5. Let the enlistment and immediate training take place in the
county of origin.

The effect of such a movement on our young men may be far-
reaching; and I venture to urge that the suggestion is worth the
attention and support of all people who can help in carrying it into
effect.

Replying directly to the English League's statement, 'Colonel' of Coupar-
Angus asked (in a letter to *The Scotsman*): 'Could anything be more cynical?
Surely they have misinterpreted the situation and will change their minds.
Are there no old, or present, footballers who have the gift of eloquence to
carry round the fiery cross and gather the many who would be willing?
What regiments these young fellows would make! Would that I were young
again.'

Colonel's plea was answered in Glasgow on 1 September, when another
colonel, Stanley Paterson, who claimed to be an old footballer, but who was
now serving his time as the city's recruiting officer, met representatives of
the six local senior clubs (Celtic, Rangers, Partick Thistle, Clyde, Queen's
Park and Third Lanark) to propose the formation of a 'Glasgow Footballer's
Battalion'. Paterson gave an undertaking on behalf of the Army that if the
clubs combined their efforts to raise such a unit, then those men who
volunteered to serve in it would be permitted to remain together for the
duration. The offer was not well received. The clubs, it transpired,
favoured what they termed 'independent action' – the drilling of their
players, the use of their grounds for recruiting purposes, the display of
patriotic placards and the collection of funds for war relief. A battalion was
out of the question.

Meanwhile down in London Mr Clegg and his colleagues were trying to
repair some of the damage done by the English League's effusions. On 2
September the FA announced that in order to assist with recruiting, it had
placed its whole organisation and influence at the disposal of the War
Office. In effect, when the new season started the following Saturday, every
ground in England would have its own enlistment station. Arrangements
had been made for well-known public figures to address the crowds and for
the terms and conditions of military service to be brought to the attention
of every supporter. Four days later, the FA amplified their willingness to
cooperate with the authorities, when they issued an official poster to be
displayed at every ground:

The FA earnestly appeal to the patriotism of all who are interested
in the game to support the nation in the present emergency; and, to
those who are able to do so, to render personal service in the Army

20

or the Royal Navy, who are so gallantly upholding our national honour. Recruits for the Army are most urgently needed. Players and spectators who are physically fit and otherwise able are urged to join the Army at once.

Lord Kinnaird (President)

J.C. Clegg (Chairman)

F.J. Wall (Secretary)

Arthur Kinnaird was a Scottish international. On 8 March 1873 he had played at London's Oval in the inaugural away fixture against England. A pacy inside-forward, he was admired for his skill. Now 67, he would require all that skill, and more, to outwit the man who liked to bill himself as 'Football's Greatest Foe'.

The phenomenon in question was Frederick Nicholas Charrington, who nurtured such an unbridled hatred of the game that the press had lately dubbed him 'The Stop Football Fiend'. Before the war, from his mission in London's East End, this former brewery heir (who had renounced his substantial inheritance on moral grounds) directed his considerable energies towards the promotion of Christianity and temperance, scarcely mentioning professional sport, except in relation to these twin preoccupations. Since the outbreak of hostilities, however, he had come to see football as 'profoundly evil', and had repeatedly described the game's ruling bodies as 'the greatest hindrance to recruiting in the Kingdom'. Now he was exploiting his respected position as a protector of the poor in order to write presumptuous letters to anyone he pleased, demanding their support for his campaign. Even the King was not spared. George V received a telegram suggesting that he give up his patronage of the FA. When the cursory reply proved disappointing, the Fiend immediately sent a further wire, with identical results. Undaunted, he then telegraphed Lord Kinnaird, urging him to resign his FA presidency. Kinnaird responded politely, explaining that 'the case for continuation is too long for a letter'. The following day Charrington called unannounced at Kinnaird's London home 'to secure a more favourable pronouncement'. Kinnaird told him that all professional footballers should be released from their contracts if they wished to enlist, but that he saw no reason why the game should be suspended, since many players (including many professionals) had other work of national importance. Charrington was unimpressed.

On Saturday, 5 September he attended Fulham's home match against Clapton Orient in order to denounce continuation. The Fulham directors had offered to assist him in any way they could, and agreed to let him address the crowd at half-time, provided he said nothing to insult or inflame. Declining to give any such assurance, Charrington rose up at the

21

interval and took a deep breath to help him deliver his choicest invective. 'I am here,' he cried, 'to protest against the *foot* —' but nothing more was heard as two burly stewards covered his mouth, grabbed his arms, dragged him (he later said) along a gangway, and threw him down the stairs. Summonses were issued the following Monday, and in due course he continued his crusade at the West London Police Court.

While all this was happening, the SFA had not been idle. They sent a deputation down to London in order to reassure themselves that the FA had not misread Harold Tennant's position. Robert Campbell of St Johnstone and Tom Steen, SFA treasurer, were in favour of stoppage; Tom White, SFA vice-president, and John McDougall, SFA secretary, were undecided. Having left Scotland in order to place themselves 'unreservedly in the hands of the military authorities', they were received warmly at the War Office and informed that those authorities had 'no desire that the game be stopped, but rather that more help could be given in recruiting and in the relief of distress by its continuance'. Not surprisingly, they returned home unanimous that the game should go on. Within days a full meeting of the SFA Council endorsed their report, whereupon a set of recruiting measures similar to those adopted in England were introduced at Scottish grounds – or, at least, at those grounds where they had not already started.

Football was fighting back. It had the invaluable support of the War Office, but in any case it was becoming clear that contrary to the wildest statements of its critics, areas where interest in the game was strong – Liverpool and Glasgow, for example – were also areas where recruiting drives were most successful. Apparently oblivious of this fact, however, the stoppers maintained their offensive, drawing ammunition throughout September from the brutal bombardment of Rheims Cathedral and the subsequent sacking of that ancient industrial town. 'Are there no lengths to which the Prussian will not stoop?' asked 'Impatient' in *The Scotsman*. 'Perhaps now the footballer will see where his duty lies.' Mr A.G. Adamson of Kirkcaldy, a director of Raith Rovers, resigned his seat on the board in protest at the continuing continuation. 'I have been unhappy for weeks,' he told the press, 'but in view of recent events, I am ashamed.' FA secretary F.J. Wall produced a letter from the Army Council, confirming War Office support for the game in the plainest terms yet, but Charrington countered by announcing the recruitment of Lord Grenfell and Lord Methuen to the ranks of the stoppers. 'I hope in due course,' he added, 'to get General Baden-Powell as well.' And so it went on, each side trying to outmanœuvre the other – which was exactly what was happening in the real war.

After their advance on Paris was halted at the Marne in early September, the Germans had retired to a strong defensive position on the Chemin des Dames ridge behind the River Aisne. Having crossed the river on 13

September, the BEF tried to storm the ridge the following day, only to be beaten off by heavy artillery fire and well entrenched infantry. Forty-eight hours later, the Germans counter-attacked. For nine days the British held their ground, digging-in themselves and sowing the seed for the trench war yet to come. Each side now tried to end the deadlock by turning the other's northern flank, and on 29 September the British commander-in-chief, Sir John French, secured the approval of his French counterpart, General Joseph Joffre, to return the BEF to the Allied left, from where it could cover any German move on the Channel ports.

The original plan was for the British to concentrate just south of Lille, but the so-called 'Race to the Sea' was proceeding at such pace that when that city fell to the Germans on 12 October, the BEF was quickly redirected to Flanders in order to take up position between the northernmost French forces and the tiny Belgian Army on the coast. On 20 October the British I Corps, newly arrived from the Aisne under the command of Lieutenant-General Sir Douglas Haig, was ordered to advance north of Ypres, near the town of Langemarck, where it marched straight into two oncoming German corps with precisely the same instructions. Again bloody stalemate ensued, and the Germans resolved to shift the focus of their attack further south, to the British line between Messines and the Menin road, a brittle seven-mile front protecting the southern approaches to Ypres itself. If they could break the BEF here, then Calais and Dunkirk were theirs to keep. For a week the British held twice their numbers, then on 29 October, supported by more than 250 heavy guns, 16 German divisions attacked out of the morning fog. The line stretched and bent, but did not snap – until two days later at Gheluvelt, where the Germans forced a breach, all but wiping out the 1st Royal West Surreys in the process. By nightfall the strength of this battalion was two officers and twelve other ranks. The position had never been so grim. At length a heroic counter-attack by what was left of the 2nd Worcesters closed the gap, but the line was now perilously thin, all available reserves having been committed – right down to the wounded, the cooks and the quartermaster sergeants. On the same day 30,000 men visited Parkhead football ground in Glasgow to watch Celtic defeat Rangers by two goals to one in the first 'Old Firm' match of the season. The stoppers were beside themselves.

'A 30,000 crowd constitutes a poor compliment to those noble fellows who have gone to the front,' wrote 'Over 45' in the *Glasgow Herald* on 4 November. 'What does it matter about Rangers and Celtic when the greatest of all internationals is being played on the Continent?' The paper withheld its own opinion until the 10th, when it finally declared that 'the shame of football must be shared by all concerned – by shareholders who have displayed a keener instinct for dividends than for glory, by the players themselves, and by every youth who has looked on while they played'. This was to ignore evidence produced in the wake of the Old Firm match which indicated that the attendance was less than half the peacetime average for the fixture, that many supporters of both clubs had already enlisted, that a substantial proportion of the crowd was in uniform, and that most of the remainder were employed in munition works or shipyards. Subtract all those who were too young, too old, or the wrong sex to serve; subtract all those victims of lifelong malnutrition who were too small or too infirm, and there would surely have been few men left to label shirkers. The Report of the Ministry of National Service into the physical condition of men of military age was still four years away, but it would show that less than 60 per cent of them were fit for overseas service, and that not far short of half of *those* had some form of disability that would keep them out of the firing line – thus confirming the well-publicised results of numerous pre-war enquiries into the poor health of the working classes.[2] In spite of this, the *Glasgow Herald* concluded that football was 'a disease, an obsession encouraging lust for pleasure and undermining the capacity for self-sacrifice'. Even Mr Punch had entered the fray, depicted in his famous journal taunting a footballer with the words: 'No doubt you can make money in this field, my friend, but there's only one field where you can get any honour.'

By 11 November Charrington was claiming the support of Admiral Sir John Jellicoe, commander of the Grand Fleet, to whom he had dispatched the following wire: 'Am fighting professional football. Lord Roberts and Lord Grenfell both given pronouncements against it during war. Will you join protest?' Sir John's reply was non-committal, and brief to the point of brusqueness, but Charrington claimed his support anyway. On the same day, while Lord Lambton was delivering his speech to the young men of Sunderland (and conveniently ignoring his own deep involvement in the ongoing 'Sport of Kings'), the Germans again broke the British line in Flanders, only to be driven out at the last possible moment. Tales of selfless heroism, none of them exaggerated, immediately filled the pages of the press. *The Times* published an alarming column, headlined 'From the Front', in which an exhausted captain was quoted as saying, 'Oh! If only we had men now. I doubt whether people at home realise the wastage. We as a battalion have been lucky, but we have lost in killed and wounded 14 officers and just on 600 men; the sick raise the numbers still further, so every man is wanted, and a law should forbid a football being kicked.'[3]

Indeed, every man was wanted, but *The Scotsman* struck a blow for common sense when it pointed out that it would help if they were *trained*. To hear some of those who talked of shirking, you would think that a man had only to volunteer, whereupon he would be handed a rifle, hurried to the front, and positioned at his place on the fire-step. Reality was different: if every eligible man then outwith the Army had enlisted the following day, they would have overwhelmed an entirely inadequate recruiting machine and set back the country's cause by many months. In fact it would be months – if not a year – before any man enlisting the following day would even *see* the front. Yet all over Britain patriotic public speakers and opinionated letter-writers continued to link the shortage of replacements in Flanders to the size of the crowd at the latest local League game. Hour by hour their words became more spiteful; hour by hour football withdrew further behind its only defence, War Office approval. But even that was being worn down by bombardment, and on 14 November, unable any longer to withstand the constant strain, it cracked out loud and crumbled into dust.

Tom Forsyth it was who fired the fateful shot. Writing to the *Glasgow Herald*, he explained that in the wake of the SFA deputation's London visit in September, he had been reluctant to accept that the War Office would actually sanction continuation. So strange did it seem to him, in fact, that he had taken it upon himself to contact Harold Tennant personally in order to seek clarification. Tennant, a busy man, had only recently replied. 'No objection is taken to occasional recreation,' wrote the Under-Secretary for War. 'It is considered, however, that football does not come within that category. It is much more desirable that professional footballers should find employment in His Majesty's forces than in their old occupation.'

This was quite unexpected. The War Office had changed its position, yet there had been no formal announcement to that effect; indeed had Forsyth not published Tennant's reply the matter might never have come to light . . . unless, of course, Tennant had *intended* publication, thereby making the announcement indirectly. When they lent support to football in September the military authorities misjudged public opinion and greatly overestimated the recruiting power of the game. Since mid-October, therefore, they had been looking for some way to end what one critic had called their 'unsavoury alliance'. Simply to announce a withdrawal of support, however, would acknowledge that support had been given in the first place – an embarrassing admission now that football was synonymous with shirking. Better to suggest casually – through some unwitting third party – that the football associations, deliberately or otherwise, had misread the position.

Members of the SFA were outraged. Meeting in Glasgow on 17 November, they denied that there had been any misunderstanding or (worse) any misrepresentation. They were honourable men, they insisted, who had pledged themselves to abide by the wishes of the authorities and who remained bound by that pledge no matter how badly the War Office chose to conduct itself. 'Circumstances,' said the chairman, restraining himself admirably, 'have arisen that make it necessary to reconsider the future of the game.' To this end he called upon his counterparts in London to convene a meeting of the four national ruling bodies – English, Scottish, Irish and Welsh – without delay. Agreeing to this request, the FA issued a further appeal to players and spectators, pointing out that 'every man should know his duty', and asking them 'to enlist today to show that you are good sportsmen'. In the light of Forsyth's revelations, however, this was hardly sufficient to see off the stoppers. 'Parliament,' declared 'A Scot' in the *Glasgow Herald*, 'must step in now and send every professional footballer to the front without the option of refusal.' With charitable observations such as this flying at him from every corner, FA secretary Wall responded rather lamely that 'special recruiting measures' would be introduced at matches the following weekend. In making this announcement, he was placing a noose around his association's neck. Now it only wanted tightening.

Saturday dawned damp and very foggy. The previous morning Poet Laureate Robert Bridges had written against football in *The Times*, declining to employ verse, choosing instead some emotional prose. This morning, however, as the stoppers sharpened their sarcasm ready to belittle the English game's efforts, a poem was supplied by the novelist E. Phillips Oppenheim, courtesy of the *Daily Express*:

> For you who play football while others seek fame
> The knickers of sport are the garments of shame.

It set the mood quite nicely for the dreadful day to come.

On the stroke of half-time at every League match in England, prominent men rose up to speak. Many of them knew nothing of the game, save what they had read in the press or heard from the likes of Mr Charrington. They had come prepared to taunt, they had come prepared to shame the cowering shirker into acting like a man. But they had not expected *women*, they had not expected quite so many *old* men; above all, they had not expected khaki. There were convalescent wounded in the crowds. No one had said anything about convalescent wounded. No one had said anything, either, about the *size* of the crowds. It came as a shock to these prominent men to be told that where 20,000 supporters had stood before the war, less than half that number were standing now.[4] It came as a further shock to learn that the missing thousands were either working extra shifts in factories and mines, or drilling many miles away in military camps. Where, the speakers must surely have wondered, are the shirkers? Where were Mr Charrington's corrupted legions? Colonel Charles Burn, Unionist MP for Devonshire Torquay, arriving at Stamford Bridge, home of Chelsea, was amazed to discover that one-third of his audience was already in uniform.

'I have no need to speak to you,' he told his soldier comrades in embarrassed tones. 'I take my hat off to you.' To the remainder – and he had to search the enclosures for suitable targets – he delivered the moving speech he had written the previous night: 'I am here to ask if there is any young man without encumbrances who will join the forces. I don't say *Come*; I say *Come, for God's sake*! *You are needed*! I have given my son. He enlisted at the start of the war. He is now dead. I have given up my house as a shelter for the wounded. I say to you young men that if I had twelve sons, I would give them all, as well as my own life, for my country and my King.'[5] But not a single man stepped forward; the recruiting sergeants waiting by the exits returned home without blunting their pencils.

Elsewhere in England the response was mixed. At Birmingham, where (in the words of an observer) there were 'thousands of able-bodied young men present', no one enlisted. At Nottingham Forest, where a reserve battalion of the Sherwood Foresters marched around the pitch at half-time, no one enlisted – although Forest already had two players and a substantial number of supporters in khaki. At Everton, however, where the home side defeated Sunderland 7–1, scores of men came forward before, during and after the game. On Monday morning *The Times* reported that this fixture had produced only one recruit – a wicked misrepresentation, but quite consistent with the coverage offered by other papers. Across the land football's special measures were condemned as a failure, swelling the ranks of the stoppers with thousands of fair-minded people whose only fault was a tendency to believe what was printed in the pages of the press. 'How long,' demanded 'Zeno' in *The Scotsman* that same Monday, 'is this craze of football to remain with us? How long are we to permit this miserable exhibition of spectacular blackguardism to sap the intellect of our young men? Let us legislate for conscription without delay and so put an end to this veritable curse.'

There was venom in these words, but had Zeno been at Everton in person, would he (or, indeed, she) have still put pen to paper? Public opinion had been captured by the stoppers, captured and confined in heavy irons. That done, and done well, they now began to stalk the House of Commons. On Wednesday, 25 November, as *The Times* published its strongest statement yet against the game, it was announced that Sir John Lonsdale, Unionist MP for Mid Armagh and a Charrington supporter, would ask the prime minister in Parliament the following afternoon if 'in view of the failure of Saturday's recruiting meetings, he would introduce legislation taking powers to suppress all professional football matches during the continuance of the war'. With the mood of the country set so firm against the game, it would take a miracle to save it now.

A miracle. Or a tall, bewhiskered hatter from the Athens of the North.

CHAPTER TWO

'Auld Reekie, wale o ilka town!'

On 9 September 1513 James IV, Scotland's darling prince, together with 12,000 of his countrymen, was slain by the Earl of Surrey's victorious English army on Flodden Field in Northumberland. Edinburgh, James's capital, lay just 50 miles to the north; the town's provost, Sir Alexander Lauder, was among those who had fallen. When the dreadful news was broken, the surviving magistrates acted with commendable dispatch. A proclamation was issued, enjoining all menfolk to make ready their fencible gear and weapons of war in order to oppose any English attempt to seize the town; while womenfolk were advised to refrain from public displays of grief and to pray for the souls of the dead. The civic purse was examined in the council chamber and, after the moths had dispersed, sufficient funds were identified to form a body of trained guards. Amid great solemnity, in keeping with the gravity of the moment, 24 volunteers were sworn in. They would take it in turns with the sword.

The magistrates also made plans to enclose the town in a grand protective wall, which reassuring structure was begun early the following spring. Every man (it was said) who laid his hand to block or chisel was conscious of the awful urgency of his task. Some 40 years would come and go and still it wasn't finished.

The Flodden Wall proved an ineffective measure at the best of times. In 1745 Donald Cameron of Lochiel captured the town for Charles Edward Stuart by slipping through the main gate behind the council's own official coach. Indeed the wall was destined to play little part in war or insurrection; instead, for two centuries it served only to inhibit the town's expansion – so severely that speculators were obliged to build *upwards* in order to contain the raging population. There was but one substantial thoroughfare, the aptly named 'High Street', which rose steeply up the spine of a narrow, craggy, wind-tormented ridge until it reached the medieval castle. From there the drop was sheer. Continental visitors admired the street for its airy breadth, but there was little room for houses on the level. Great stone tenements, some 12 or 13 storeys, sprouted from its rocky shoulders in such density that there was scarcely room between them for two fat men to pass without a fight. A labyrinth of straitened, mirksome wynds fell quickly down on either side – into a sunken cow-track to the south, and a stinking man-made sewer to the north. The natives dubbed this last affront a 'loch'; journalist Daniel Defoe concluded that they took a strange delight in 'Nastiness and Stench'.

Defoe arrived incognito in 1706 and worked discreetly behind the scenes to bring about the great 'Union' of the following year. In return for certain English baubles, the three Estates of the ancient Scottish parliament voted themselves out of existence. Shorn of its regality in 1603, when James VI assumed the English crown and moved his Court to London, Edinburgh was now a capital without purpose. Only the Kirk and the law courts remained to call the town their home; these and a small but backward merchant class which struggled to survive its sudden plunge into the wider English pool. Slowly, however, Scotland began to adapt to her new circumstances – helped by the greatest legacy of the old discredited Estates, the principle of universal learning. Since the sixteenth century a succession of education acts had been passed, ensuring that almost every parish had its own school and every school its own well-educated master. By the beginning of the eighteenth century the nation characterised by southern opinion as primitive and stupid was in fact more literate than most, so that when improvers in agriculture and industry began to sow their seeds of wisdom, they found the soil both yielding and productive. With the failure of the '45 Rebellion, the violent past receded from the peaceful Lowland present and was replaced by more commercial confrontations.

Edinburgh was well-positioned to profit from these new opportunities. The historian Robert Chambers drew a nice analogy, comparing the town to 'a lady, who after long being content with a small and inconvenient house, is taught, by the money in her husband's pockets, that such a place is no longer to be put up with'.[1] As the merchant class expanded on the back of growing trade, so too did its revulsion at the town's decaying fabric. The North Loch was no less offensive to the sensibilities of the merchant's wife than to her poor, long-suffering nose. And it was no fit spot for grand financial dealings. At the behest of Provost George Drummond, a pamphlet was circulated proposing extensive 'Public Works'. Since one tenemented ruin had lately collapsed under the weight of time and dirt, it was suggested that a new Exchange for business might be erected in its stead.

Simultaneously new law courts and council chambers would be built, along with a home for the national archives.

The loch was duly drained and partly bridged, and in 1767 a Bill was passed to extend the burgh's boundaries. Meanwhile a competition to design a plan for these fragrant developments was won by a young architect, James Craig, whose simple grid of broad streets curtailed at either end by spacious squares was strangely reminiscent of the old town. George Street, down the centre, was the High Street; Princes Street, to the south, was the Cowgate; Queen Street, to the north, was the noisome track that ran beside the sewer. But where the buildings of the Old Town were high and wildly random, Craig's 'New Town' was uniform and low. And where the buildings of the Old Town were piled perilously close, the New Town was liberally spaced, a monument to progress and Hanoverian good taste. Marooned upon its ancient rock, 'Auld Reekie' gazed down meanly on the future.

James Craig had a famous uncle, the poet James Thomson, composer of the Unionist anthem 'Rule, Britannia'. Their proud old country was now a mere province of 'North Britain', Edinburgh its first city – home of the burgeoning 'Enlightenment', an unheralded flowering of philosophers and scientists, artists and authors, inventors and crackpots that left European observers looking on in disbelief and awe. Scotland had been sneezed on by the gods of Inspiration (who were surely headed elsewhere at the time).

This was the Edinburgh of David Hume and Adam Smith, of Adam Ferguson and Dugald Stewart, of Robert Burns and Allan Ramsay, and of the ill-fated law clerk Robert Fergusson, whose irreverent verse evoked the drunken heart that beat beneath respectable facades. The Edinburgh of Boswell and Johnson, and Joseph Black; the Edinburgh of Deacon William Brodie, master cabinet-maker by day, master burglar through the night; of Raeburn, Robert Adam, Smollett and Mackenzie; of the learned judge Lord Gardenstone, who encouraged his pet pig to sleep on his clothes to keep them warm and toasty for the morning. The Edinburgh of the equally learned Lord Monboddo, who believed we all once had tails, and of Robert Macqueen, Lord Braxfield, who condemned the errant Deacon to the gallows. The Edinburgh, too, in time, of the prodigious Walter Scott; and of James Hogg, the unschooled shepherd, whose astonishing third novel would turn up on a French hillside nine decades later, broken-spined and stained with human blood.

Something of the Flodden spirit was revived in 1803, when the failure of the Peace of Amiens led to renewed fear of invasion by the armies of Napoleon. Henry Cockburn, historian and jurist, recalled that Edinburgh became a military camp and remained so for 11 long years. 'We were all soldiers, one way or another,' he wrote. 'Professors wheeled in the College area; the side-arms and the uniform peeped from behind the gown at the Bar, and even on the Bench; and the parade and the review formed the staple of men's talk and thoughts.'[2]

Charles Hope, the Lord Justice-Clerk, served as a lieutenant-colonel in the Edinburgh Regiment of Gentleman Volunteers; as did his cousin, the lawyer James Hope, a classmate of Walter Scott's at the Royal High School. Scott overcame his lameness to serve as 'Paymaster, Quartermaster and Secretary' to the city's own regiment of volunteer cavalry, the Royal Corps of Edinburgh Light Dragoons. Cockburn was a captain in the Western Battalion of the Midlothian Volunteers; his fellow Whig lawyers, Francis Jeffrey, Henry Brougham and Francis Horner (founders of Constable's *Edinburgh Review* in 1802) served as private soldiers. 'Terror of the ballot for compulsory service in the regular militia was enough to fill the ranks,' Cockburn concluded; 'while duty, necessity, and especially the contagion of the times supplied sufficient officers. Any able-bodied man, of whatever rank, who was *not* a volunteer, or a member of the local militia, had to explain or apologise for his singularity.'

Napoleon never did make it to Edinburgh: he was detained at Waterloo and reluctantly curtailed his European tour. In the years after 1815, however, the city welcomed many Continental visitors who braved the bleak northern roads in order to view Scotland's 'Modern Athens'. Cockburn disliked the phrase, calling it 'foolish and sarcastic', but he approved mightily of the sudden influx of foreign influence and opinion. Edinburgh, he thought, had become too conservative, particularly with regard to its architecture. He looked on approvingly, therefore, when the odd pillar and portico began to appear, heralding a full-blown Scottish 'Greek Revival', led by William Playfair and Thomas Hamilton. Hamilton's High School was perhaps the jewel in the crown, but within 60 years Robert Louis Stevenson would write of 'buildings in almost every style upon the globe. Egyptian and Greek temples, Venetian palaces and Gothic spires, huddled over one another in the most admired disorder.'[3] This contagion from the Old Town could never be controlled: disorder has a tendency to spread.

Between 1775 and 1825 the population of the city more than doubled. Since the New Town was designed almost exclusively for the benefit of the professional and upper classes, most of the people – including a substantial minority of articulate and well-educated tradesmen – remained crowded into a crumbling, tenemented warren which had remained largely unaltered for 200 years. They had no vote and therefore no effective voice against a Tory council which Cockburn described as 'omnipotent, corrupt and impenetrable'. It was not just a local problem. Across the country aristocratic Whigs, middle-class intellectuals and working-class radicals now combined to create one concerted 'Liberal' movement for change. In 1832 the Scottish Reform Bill removed one layer of political patronage by abolishing the right of town councils to elect members of Parliament and introducing a direct franchise for property owners. This was followed in 1833 by the Burgh Reform Act, which abolished the old municipal constitution of Edinburgh and replaced it with a system of popular election by owners and occupiers of property within the burgh boundaries. In theory, at least, the City Chambers thus became home to a democratically elected, accountable local authority for the first time.

One of the first members of this Reform Town Council was the radical dissenter, Duncan McLaren. McLaren, born in Argyllshire in 1800, had no formal education; he was apprenticed at 12 to a draper in Dunbar, and arrived in Edinburgh at the age of 18 to work behind the counter of a wholesale establishment in the High Street. In the spirit of self-improvement, he enrolled in evening classes, including those of the anatomist Robert Knox, unwitting patron of the murderers William Burke and William Hare. In 1824 he entered business on his own account in a shop some doors away from his erstwhile employers and began (in *The Scotsman*'s inimitable words) 'to devote part of his surplus energies and talents to the public affairs of the city'.

In 1836 these talents saw him elected Treasurer, a position that had broken many lesser men. Put bluntly, Edinburgh was bankrupt. The origins of the debt could be traced back to 1589, when James VI married Princess Anne of Denmark. Edinburgh's share of the dowry amounted to £40,000 (Scots) plus a further £500 per month to defray the cost of a boat and royal travelling expenses from Norway. Since the city was already as poor as a kirk mouse, the money was borrowed at punitive rates of interest. In 1626 the city fathers, eager to show their support for the Stuarts, borrowed an additional £60,000 to loan to Charles I, followed by £14,000 in 1633 to help fund his belated Scottish coronation, and £60,000 more in 1640 to help maintain General Leslie's victorious anti-royalist force in the north of England. At no point were any sensible arrangements made to repay these (or many subsequent) sums, and by 1798 the total owed stood at a prodigious £170,000 (sterling), at which point old Hughie Buchan, City Chamberlain and chief finance officer for the previous 30 years, was living in denial. He claimed to know nothing of the matter, and professed himself 'surprised'. Indeed the single word 'bankrupt' was not really adequate to describe the situation; in 1833 the Commission on Municipal Corporations required several hundred words and still didn't quite get the point across as fully as they might have wished:

We have not found sufficient evidence to report that the disastrous state of the city affairs has been caused by actual embezzlement or fraudulent malversation. Exaggerated expectations of the increase of the city in prosperity and size may have led the Corporation into an expense far disproportioned to the real growth of the revenue. Officers were multiplied and salaries raised; a spirit of litigation prevailed, great profusion took place in the expenses of civic parades and entertainments, and extravagant sums were expended on public buildings. The closeness and irresponsibility of the Corporation could not alone account for continuance of such a system. The studied concealment of the affairs of the community for a long period, and the partial and confused statement of them that was afterwards made, probably kept the respectable members in ignorance of their financial embarrassment, and it is that ignorance which can alone save the city managers from a charge of fraud.[4]

It transpired that the Reform council had inherited a debt in excess of £400,000, including some paper liabilities dating back nearly 300 years. An Act of Parliament was passed sequestrating the revenues and property of the city on behalf of its creditors, while official Trustees were appointed to oversee repayment. McLaren was reportedly unfazed; he negotiated the terms of the Agreement Act of 1838, which issued proven claimants and their descendants with a promissory note. Under his stewardship the debt was defined and brought under control for the first time. As a measure of their gratitude, his fellow councillors presented him with a silver dinner service worth a hefty £500, the cost of which was (of course) borne by the city. In 1851 he was appointed Lord Provost, and in 1865 he was elected to Parliament, where he served as one of the most respected Liberal members until his 81st year. The 'Member for Scotland' died in April 1886, as old as the century and as wise (so they said) as a barn full of owls.

McLaren, like many Scots of his generation, was profoundly influenced by three books – King James's Bible, Adam Smith's *The Wealth of Nations* and Thomas Paine's *The Rights of Man*. He believed in free trade, a free Kirk, extension of the franchise, reform of the land laws, and simple common decency. His party, rooted in high principle, moral outrage and fierce patriotism, would dominate Scotland for a further 30 years. Lord Kitchener's Scottish volunteers of 1914 were steeped in this tradition, earnest young men remaining true to their King and their Country, but also to their fathers, their grandfathers and – perhaps most importantly – themselves.

In 1859 there was a taste of things to come – the Flodden spirit revived again, or something more portentous. During the Crimean conflict Great Britain and France were allies; three years after the peace they had fallen out once more. With the Army and the Royal Navy committed to the protection of Britain's overseas possessions, old concerns were raised over the vulnerability of the homeland to invasion – the 'Great Threat', as it became known. There was even a brief, unseemly panic until the Liberal ideal of mutual self-help came to the rescue in the form of the 'Volunteer' movement. Irregular units were formed all over the country, successors to the militia and yeomanry of earlier times. By the summer of 1860, 160,000 men had paid for the privilege of enlisting, many providing their own uniforms, boots and rifles. In Scotland the response was disproportionately high, not just among the middle and skilled classes, but also among the ranks of the unskilled working class. When the Threat subsided after 1861 these bodies were not disbanded, though in certain parts of the country they struggled to recruit sufficient members to remain viable. In Scotland, however, and particularly in Edinburgh, where recruitment was seldom a problem, they evolved into a curious social phenomenon, an alternative masonry, an additional source of comradeship and influence in a society where getting on was considered more important than simply getting by. Thus in 1865 several Volunteer companies, formed in the capital six years earlier, were remodelled as the First and Second Battalions of the 'Queen's Edinburgh Rifles', an elite and somewhat self-satisfied corps that drew inspiration from the knowledge that in their own domestic, dutiful and often inscrutable way they were emulating the great military heroes of an Empire on which the sun would surely never set. They attended weekly drill nights, arranged musketry competitons and field sports, and held annual summer camps in exotic border outposts like Peebles and Stobs.

In 1867 a further battalion appeared. The 'Third Edinburgh Volunteers' were raised and commanded by John Hope, a 60-year-old Edinburgh lawyer, eldest son of Walter Scott's High School contemporary and fellow Napoleonic skirmisher, James. Like his friend Duncan McLaren, Hope was an abstainer; as a captain in the Second City Battalion, he had chosen as his company's crest a lion's head with water gushing out of its mouth, signifying that every man in the ranks had pledged never to touch a drop of alcohol. The new battalion, affectionately known as the 'Edinburgh Water Rats', grew out of his old company (which transferred en masse) and hundreds of former members of the juvenile cadet force that he had formed at his own expense to spread the ideals of the Volunteer movement among the poorer classes of the Old Town. Hope was a philanthropic perfectionist, committed to excellence in all things, and in due course his scarlet-coated battalion was acknowledged the smartest in the city, if not the most socially advanced. Also by far and away the best shots, the best trained, the best marchers and the best equipped. In 1873 the more sporting members of the rank and file even furnished Edinburgh with its first Association Football team, playing some of their early fixtures in a field on the Powburn estate on the city's southern edge. Powburn was owned by Duncan McLaren, perhaps the first politician in the country to appreciate the benefits of not only supporting a popular working-class pastime, but also of being seen to do so. As it happened, he would not be the last.

In 1888 Edinburgh's Volunteer battalions were incorporated into an entirely new formation, the 'Queen's Rifle Volunteer Brigade, The Royal Scots'. Formed in 1633, the Royal Scots were Britain's oldest infantry regiment, the famous 'First of Foot', with a list of battle honours which included Malplaquet, Waterloo and Balaclava, and a finer opinion of themselves than any military unit in the world. By association, the Volunteers could now claim a little of the glory. The 'regulars' maintained two battalions (one of which served at home while the other was engaged on garrison duty overseas), plus a third 'depot' battalion near Edinburgh for training and reinforcement. When the reserve army was reorganised under the Territorial and Reserve Forces Act of 1907, the three capital Volunteer units were re-titled the 4th, 5th and 6th Royal Scots battalions of the new Territorial Force. They were joined by the Leith Volunteer battalion, which became the 7th Royal Scots, and two 'County' Volunteer battalions which became the 8th (Midlothian, Haddingtonshire and Peebleshire) and 10th (Linlithgowshire) Royal Scots. In 1900 the capital's community of exiled Highlanders had formed their own Volunteer corps as part of the Queen's Brigade; in 1908 they became the 9th Royal Scots with the distinction of being the only *kilted* battalion in the regiment.

The 'Dandy Ninth' (as they were known) were grouped together with the 4th, 5th, and 6th Battalions in the Lothian Brigade, which had its headquarters at 28 Rutland Street in Edinburgh. The battalions were structured on an eight-company basis, each company distinguished by some common bond among its members. Those of the 4th Battalion (for example) ran as follows: 'Citizens', 'Solicitors and Accountants', 'Bankers', 'Civil Service', and four 'Highland' companies, including one composed entirely of men with Caithness connections. The 5th Royal Scots, which claimed to have by some distance the best recruiting record in Britain, included three 'Artisan' companies, a 'Merchants' company, an 'Abstainers' company, and one dedicated to the Edinburgh High Constables. The competitive spirit that existed between and within these units gave the Brigade an *esprit de corps* unrivalled in the entire Territorial Force. Put simply, like their regular contemporaries, they considered themselves 'a cut above'.

Since only a limited number of commissions were available, the 'other' ranks of these battalions were an impressive lot. Lawyers, teachers, bank managers and academics served contentedly as privates alongside labourers, warehousemen and shop assistants. The Brigade represented Edinburgh's contribution to the defence of the Empire, but in a very real way it also represented the city, full stop. Here was history and tradition, a strange kind of *classlessness*; but here, too, was patronage and privilege and not a little smugness with the pride. Add 'complacency' and you had the capital in miniature.

Walter Scott would have kent Edwardian Edinburgh fine. The Old and New Towns still vied to embarrass each other in front of the guests, the one with its coarseness and squalor, the other with its astonishing conceit. The industries that had grown out of the age of Enlightenment – publishing, printing and financial services – continued to prosper alongside the ship-building and brewing of older times. Engineering and rubber-making, however, were relatively new, and construction had expanded greatly towards the end of the old century as the city stretched and slowly spread itself around. Stockbridge, Gorgie, Dalry, Merchiston, Morningside, Marchmont, Newington, St Leonard's, Abbeyhill and Easter Road were tenemented *villages*, each with its own peculiar identity; they satisfied the demand of the skilled and white-collar classes for decent housing, but in a town whose population had more than quadrupled in a hundred years, almost no new accommodation had been provided for the unskilled, poorly paid working class. People were drawn to the capital by the abundance of employment, but there was nowhere for them to live. In the worst of the ancient Old Town slums, around Tron Square or the Canongate, over-crowding was simply unimaginable, while the once-picturesque adjacent districts of the Pleasance and the Dumbiedykes were now considered amongst the most dangerous places in Scotland for a stranger to venture after dark. Everyone agreed it was a scandal, but the so-called 'Housing Question' (which sounded almost as insubstantial as the 'Balkan Question' when expressed with such politic brevity) remained the one challenge that proved intractable to even the most energetic of Liberal reformers.

In 1914, Edinburgh was resting on the laurels of a glorious past. The merchant's wife had grown comfortable and perhaps a little sleepy; the town council, meanwhile, was positively comatose. Unionist Provost, Robert Kirk Inches, had not endeared himself to the *Evening News*. 'His municipal reign,' went the editorial in July, 'will be remembered as three years of quietness decidedly, dullness maybe, semi-stagnation possibly. Lord Provost Inches desires nothing more than that during the next year and a quarter things should remain as they are . . .'

Inches held a unique Royal Warrant: 'Clockmaker, Keeper and Dresser of His Majesty's clocks, watches and pendulums in His said Kingdom of Scotland'. He had established his Princes Street business in 1886, and spent every night for the first two years curled up under the counter with a heavy club, arguing that it was cheaper than employing a watchman. Three weeks before war broke out, the King and Queen arrived at Waverley Station for an informal break at the Palace of Holyroodhouse. Inches and his fellow councillors were on the platform to present their Majesties with the keys to the city. George and Mary's visit was a huge success. Relieved that everything had gone well, Edinburgh entered into the holiday spirit. Another George – the popular English comedian, George Robey – was appearing at the Empire Theatre and there was speculation that the town's favourite performer, the 'Tramp Juggler', W.C. Fields, might soon be making a welcome return from his American travels. The death was reported of the great Imperial champion, Joe Chamberlain, who had infuriated Liberal free-traders in 1903 with his proposals for tariff reform, and (in so doing) helped fuel the rise of the Young Scots Society. This organisation, originally little more than a protest group set up to oppose the Boer War, was now seldom out of the news. Its founder, James Hogge, was Liberal MP for East Edinburgh; its honorary president, John Gulland, was Liberal MP for Dumfries Burghs; its secretary, Frank Robertson, represented the Dalry Ward on Edinburgh Town Council. Another member, now a respected Edinburgh minister, had spent a night in the Glasgow cells in 1901 after disagreeing with a constable on the subject of concentration camps. He was a Divinity student at the time, which was something in his favour: he will turn up again in due course.

The Young Scots had rejuvenated the Liberal party north of the border. Prospective MPs were now likely to be university-educated lawyers or teachers rather than businessmen like Duncan McLaren. They were still reformers, but now the Land Laws (rather than the Corn Laws) were their target. Their aim was an end to landed privilege, the beginning of Home Rule for Scotland, and the continued extension of the franchise. These issues were endlessly debated in the pages of the press, alongside more parochial concerns such as harvest prospects, trade wages, football signings and the recently published love letters of Jane Welsh and Thomas Carlyle. The main topic, however, towards the end of that sweltering July was the imminence of civil war in Ireland. It served as a distraction from developments elsewhere.

❋ ❋ ❋

On 28 June 1914 Archduke Franz Ferdinand, heir presumptive to the Habsburg monarchy of Austria-Hungary, and his wife Sophie, were shot dead in Sarajevo. It was the anniversary of their wedding day. The assassin, who was apprehended immediately, was a young Serb nationalist called

Gavrilo Princip. Sarajevo was the capital of Bosnia, a minor province of the Austrian Empire since 1908. The Bosnians, late subjects of the ailing Turkish Empire (which considered them too troublesome to keep), were a dangerous mixture of Slav, Serb and Croat, many of whom resented such despotic annexation. Had they been asked, they would have chosen to join the neighbouring independent state of Serbia. In protest, therefore, over the next few years periodic attempts were made on the life of Habsburg officials; Princip's, by accident rather than design, was the first to succeed.

Twelve hundred miles away, the Edinburgh papers were largely unimpressed. The possibility of Serbian complicity in the murders, of a Balkan *conspiracy*, however, received a little more attention. It was like one of Dr Conan Doyle's mysteries: a problem that required no end of pipes. There were alleged confessions, and claims that darker forces were at work. The Austrian Foreign Minister, Count Berchtold, had spent the week before the assassination secretly treating against Serbia by seeking German support for an alliance with Bulgaria and Turkey that would isolate the tiny state completely.

On 5 July Berchtold sent an emissary to Berlin in the hope of persuading Germany that Serbia had sponsored the murders and calling for 'its elimination as a power factor in the Balkans'. Austria, he said, would act if Germany assented: Kaiser Wilhelm duly gave his approval and promised German backing if Russia, self-appointed guardian of the local Slav minorities, threatened to support Serbia. On 23 July a ten-point Austrian ultimatum was dispatched to the Serbian capital, Belgrade, demanding that Serbia immediately suppress all nationalist societies within her borders and initiate a full investigation (to be supervised by Austrian officials) into the origins of the assassination plot. This was deliberately provocative: Austria was spoiling for a fight. To everyone's surprise, it looked as if the Serbs were about to give in; however, at the last moment pride got the better of them and they added certain reservations to their reply. Austria broke off diplomatic relations and on 28 July declared war. Two days later, Russia mobilised. Archie Primrose, Lord Rosebery, the respected former Liberal prime minister, was deeply concerned. 'Never,' he said, 'have I seen the political horizon, both in Great Britain and Europe, so charged with clouds pregnant with thunder.' Rosebery, honorary colonel of the 7th Royal Scots, had been one of the few politicians in the country to oppose Britain's 1904 *entente* with France, arguing that sooner or later it would draw the Empire into a bloody confrontation with Germany.

On 31 July Germany announced itself in the 'State of Danger of War', a bureaucratic resting place on the road to full mobilisation. A dispatch to this effect was sent to St Petersburg, warning that mobilisation would follow unless Russia suspended 'all war measures against ourselves and

Austria-Hungary'. A further dispatch (a thinly veiled warning, in fact) was sent to France – Russia's ally since 1894 – demanding a declaration of neutrality in the event of any Russo–German hostilities. Russia refused to back down and on 1 August Germany declared war.

'Germany has drawn the sword from the scabbard,' announced the *Evening News*. 'Before the weapon is sheathed history will be written deeply in blood.' Now the sword was turned on France. War again. The French invoked the British *entente*, and Rosebery's worst nightmare was realised. On 2 August Germany delivered its final ultimatum, this time to Belgium, demanding territorial access during the course of operations in the west, and threatening dire consequences in the event of refusal. They were advancing across the border even as the telegram arrived. By treaty of 1839 Britain was Belgium's protector; on 4 August, therefore, London intervened, demanding an end to Germany's violation of the Belgian frontier. 'The Napoleon of Berlin', as the *Evening News* had dubbed the Kaiser, did not reply. War again by midnight: Great Britain and the Empire stood to arms.

The mood in Edinburgh was quiet. Contempt for Germany was tempered by the fact that no one much cared for the Russians or the French. Or (especially) the Serbians, of invidious repute. Little Belgium, however, was being bullied, and that struck a chord with some innate British sense of fair play. The Kaiser would get his desserts: there was a touching confidence in the nation's editorials. An Imperial crusade was underway.

On the morning of 5 August the Territorial Force was mobilised. By chance the Lothian Brigade was still in summer camp – at Stobs, near Hawick, in the Borders. All ranks were invited to waive their right to insist on home service; almost no one refused. It was a stirring example. Across the country Army reservists were called up; the response was so complete that even some deserters reappeared. As normal life continued, *The Scotsman* reported a curious sidelight: Edinburgh's senior First Division football club, Heart of Midlothian, would now be without two of their players for the opening of the new season. Neil Moreland, a young centre-forward, and George Sinclair, the Scottish international winger, were already soldiers. Moreland, who came from Tarbrax in Lanarkshire, was a member of his local Territorial battalion, the 8th Highland Light Infantry; Sinclair, a former regular, had rejoined his Field Artillery battery in accordance with the commitment he gave when his term of service expired in 1905. The playing squad, however, was deemed large enough to cope: Edinburgh's assault on the championship would not be unduly compromised.

That evening it was announced that Britain had appointed a new Secretary of State for War, Field-Marshal *Rt. Hon.* Horatio Herbert, *Earl* Kitchener of Khartoum. The conqueror of the Sudan and South Africa, now 64, was a popular choice. 'It was unthinkable,' declared *The Times* on 6 August, 'that so great a military asset should be wasted. In the huge task of equipping and dispatching our land forces, as well as perfecting the measures for protecting these shores, Lord Kitchener's services will be invaluable.' Kitchener was currently Britain's representative in Egypt; he had returned home on leave at the end of June, and only narrowly missed escaping on the boat train from Dover, when Prime Minister Asquith personally ordered his immediate return to London. The breezy assertion, repeated ad nauseam at every street corner as well as in the pages of the press, that the war would be over by Christmas, had even infected the Cabinet. At their first meeting, Kitchener startled his new colleagues with the opinion that it would take much longer to defeat the Central Powers. It would also take an army several times greater than even the gloomiest pessimist had predicted. Mention was made of 1,000,000 men. Accordingly, on 6 August, Parliament authorised an increase in the Army of half that figure. Tellingly, the terms of service were 'three years, or until the war is concluded'. Meantime the voluntary principle would continue to apply. The Germans conscripted their youths, the Austrians too; Russia and France were enthusiastic members of the club. That was no reason, however, for Britain to join; indeed, for some, it was more than sufficient reason not to.

The 'First Hundred Thousand' volunteers were obtained within the month. Kitchener, who had previously concealed an unsuspected flair for publicity, was everywhere, peering out of papers and plastered in his poster on 100,000 walls. 'Your Country Needs You!' he insisted, and few would have the nerve to disagree. Since no national machine existed to mount such an unprecedented campaign, it was mainly conducted at local level. In 1907, when the reserve forces were reorganised, each city or county in the country was given its own Territorial Force Association, an administrative body composed of indigenous military, 'representative' (i.e. town council) and university members. While retaining responsibility for the control and enlargement of their own Territorial units, the TFAs now also lent their authority and their offices to Lord Kitchener's appeal. Their efforts were augmented by the formation of many ad hoc local recruiting committees, made up of the great and the good, who endeavoured on behalf of the War Office to raise Kitchener units around a particular town, district or occupation. The resulting 'Pals' battalions were a peculiarly British response to adversity: each comprised a thousand (or more) officers and men, each of whom drew comfort from the thought that whatever lay in wait, they would meet it with their friends.

The Pals appeared most commonly in the northern and middle counties of England. Scotland, for the most part, favoured a less homogenous approach. Thus, early in the war, the strength of the Royal Scots was increased by two new Kitchener (or 'Service') battalions, numbered 11th and 12th, which were raised randomly from members of the daily queue outside Edinburgh's regular Army recruiting office in Cockburn Street. This was a former shop, small, cramped and utterly unsuited to its suddenly expanded role. Behind the counter (although it seemed at times more like a breastwork) stood the city's own recruiting officer, Captain William Robertson of the Gordon Highlanders, who had been awarded the Victoria Cross in October 1899 for his gallant conduct in the ranks during the Battle of Elandslaagte, near Ladysmith, in the Natal province of South Africa. Robertson was assisted by two stout sergeants, beribboned veterans of Omdurman and Paardeberg, who performed heroics processing the vast number of additional applicants crowding through the door.[5] One particular morning (the captain told a visiting journalist) had been a wee bit like Rorke's Drift. When asked if he wanted anything, he replied, 'Aye, my old rifle, a good bayonet, and a box o' .303.' He was probably joking.[6]

A further battalion – the 13th Royal Scots – followed soon after; then on 10 September Provost Inches, stirred by the recent example of (among others) Liverpool, Manchester and Sheffield, announced that recruiting would shortly begin for a dedicated 'City of Edinburgh Battalion', a unit which (he had decided) would be distinguished by the quality of its members. He didn't say what quality he had in mind, but let us assume that it was decent. This was by no means a new idea. In fact it dated back to early August, two days after Parliament endorsed the expansion of the Army, when Harry Rawson, chairman of the Edinburgh TFA, received a personal letter from King George, asking if he would do all in his power to assist Lord Kitchener's appeal for recruits.

Rawson was born in Halifax, Yorkshire, in 1862; he arrived in Edinburgh at the age of 23 with £100 borrowed from his brother and vague hopes of making a bit of money. In 1886 he purchased the old established business of James Robertson & Co. in York Place. Robertsons manufactured aerated water, supplying both the retail and catering trade in much of central Scotland. In 1891 Rawson bought out the famous St Ronan's Wells Mineral Water Company of Innerleithen and extended his markets into England. In 1906, having made his fortune with something to spare, he was elected to serve as an 'independent' on the Broughton Ward of the town council. Six years later, he was voted off when he loudly opposed the council's proposals for ten o' clock closing of public houses. 'The proposed closing time,' he observed, 'would be imposed on the majority by a bench of magistrates. Those same magistrates and their kind have no intention themselves of abiding by any such limit.' A little too blunt, perhaps, for Edinburgh's liking: no matter, by the way, that it was true.

Rawson was also a fine billiard player and the man credited with saving the Scottish deerhound from extinction. His membership of the TFA dated from its inception; he had succeeded to the chair in 1914 when the military members moved off to more bellicose duties. His response to the King's letter was immediate: he told his Majesty that the matter was already well in hand. Having consulted his Association colleagues, including its esteemed President (who happened at that moment to be Provost Inches), he then publicly announced that pending War Office approval, a City of Edinburgh Battalion would be formed at once – to which end a special recruiting office was being set up in Parliament Square. Everything was ready, he concluded; a single word from Whitehall and recruiting could begin.

But the single word from Whitehall did not come. One week passed, then another. And another. Rawson disliked procrastination: it occurred to him that the nationwide success of Lord Kitchener's appeal may have rendered the Association's help unnecessary. Cockburn Street was awash with flat-capped youths, one of whom had absconded with William Robertson's solid brass megaphone, which was kept on a hook inside the door. The good captain was quickly becoming something of an Edinburgh character: 'You can't trust anyone these days,' he told the press.

Certainly not in nearby Portobello – not far from Harry Rawson's home – where attention was being drawn to extensive building work lately carried out on the factory premises of the Continental Chocolate Company, whose elderly owner, one William Schulze (renamed 'Wilhelm' in the interests of clarity) was a naturalised Briton of German extraction. The factory's foundations, claimed some neighbours in the know, had been strengthened *not* to support new and expensive machinery (as wily old Wilhelm was claiming), but rather to receive the Kaiser's heavy guns, which, following the expected invasion, would pound Leith Docks and the east coast railway line to rubble, leaving Edinburgh at the mercy of the Hun.[7]

This was too much for the Provost: 'Edinburgh will fight!' he insisted. When Rawson told him that the Association had decided to abandon its plans for a City Battalion, he pointed out that Glasgow (of all places) was on the point of raising a third such unit, while the city of Salford had already added another to the list. Was the capital of Scotland to be outdone? On 10 September, therefore, Inches announced that recruiting for the Edinburgh Battalion would begin immediately *without* War Office approval – which (he added rather sourly) should never have been waited on in the first place, since it was bound to be forthcoming in the long run, and that was the same as having it at present. At 74 he had no intention of going anywhere; none the less he appealed for a thousand young men from the business and professional classes to 'join' him, naming solicitors, stockbrokers and advocates as his preferred applicants, although students (he said) would be welcome as well – along with time-served craftsmen of the highest order. Warehousemen and clerks would be fine at a pinch, but labourers were not to be encouraged. One week, he submitted, was all it would take before the city would present Lord Kitchener with a battalion of which he could indeed be proud.

Harry Rawson was appalled. It was wrong, he said, to enlist men without official approval, and the TFA would have nothing to do with it. Alarmed by this rebuff, Inches replied that he was not proposing to enlist men; he was proposing to 'enrol' them, taking their names and addresses until the day that official approval came through, when they would be summoned to some central location and formally sworn in.

Nonsense, countered Rawson: you couldn't ask men to sign up on such terms. Where would they stand if War Office approval was not forthcoming? They would be hostages to fortune, condemned thereafter to serve in any unit that the military authorities thought fit. It was a good point, but the Provost wasn't listening: on 11 September his enrolment went ahead. There was no recruiting office as such; instead applicants were invited to present themselves at one of several law practices in the New Town, where clerks had been appointed to record their particulars. One such office belonged to Herbert Warden, respected solicitor and formerly a captain in the 4th Royal Scots. Warden was 37; in early August he had founded the Edinburgh Military Training Association, a body (now over 40 companies strong) intended to teach unenlisted men the basics of drill and soldierly discipline. He supported the idea of an Edinburgh battalion, but, like Harry Rawson, harboured doubts as to whether it could succeed under the present conditions – doubts confirmed when after a fortnight's hard campaigning, the Provost could boast barely 500 men. Worse: with the battalion growing only slowly, and nothing heard from Whitehall, there were murmurings among those who had enrolled – mainly students from the University at this stage – that they might ask to be released from their commitment in order to try their luck elsewhere.

Finally, on 25 September, a telegraph message was received from the War Office intimating that approval had been granted for a City of Edinburgh Battalion to be raised as part of Lord Kitchener's Army. The Provost was beside himself. 'Now,' he remarked at a meeting called that very afternoon, 'we shall see.' Despite a heartening rise in applications over the following two days, however, there was no great rush to enlist. It was as if the battalion had been tainted by the weeks of inaction. In the end, just when it looked as if recruiting might drag on until November, the city's face was saved by the arrival at Waverley Station of 417 Lancashire 'Scots', who, having failed to convince the War Office of the need for a 'Manchester

Scottish' battalion, opted instead to join the first real Scottish unit that would take them as a group. Thanks largely to these men, therefore, the 'Provost's Battalion' (as it was provisionally titled) was completed on 10 October, uniformed in navy-blue 'emergency serge' and billeted in the grand – if somewhat Spartan – surroundings of Edinburgh Castle.

The new unit's commanding officer was Sir Robert Cranston, who took great satisfaction (he told everyone) from appearing about a decade younger than his full 71 years. This was, of course, a matter of opinion. Cranston was a veteran of the siege of Paris, where he had been studying in 1870 when the Germans invaded. He returned to Edinburgh the following year and became a partner in the North Bridge drapery and house-furnishing firm of Cranston & Elliot. The business prospered and moved down to Princes Street, where he also established the first of his famous Temperance hotels. He was elected to the Council, served as Treasurer and Provost, and enjoyed one of the longest Volunteering careers in the history of the movement. Starting out as a gunner in the Midlothian Coast Artillery, he had been commissioned in the Queen's Edinburgh Rifles in 1871, succeeding at length to the command of the Second Battalion. He was knighted in 1903. The Edinburgh-born lawyer, Richard Haldane, former Secretary of State for War and architect of the Territorial and Reserve Forces Act, appointed him to his advisory committee during the drafting of the Bill.

In late October Sir Robert, who was immensely proud of his Lancashire contingent, was obliged to defend them in the press against unfounded accusations that their behaviour had been causing offence in the town. Their language, apparently, was less restrained than that of their Scottish comrades. Cranston denied the charges, pointed out that the men in question were far from home, and that Edinburgh families might do well to 'adopt' one in the meantime as a gesture of good will. He also took the opportunity to criticise a curious local phenomenon, the 'League of the White Feather', whose female members had undertaken to go about at all times equipped with the means to embarrass any passing shirker. Feathers might be acquired (they advised) from a reputable butcher, or (in an emergency) from any available pillow, and should be preserved in an envelope to be carried in the hand. Their efforts, Cranston concluded dismissively, would be better directed elsewhere.

But where though? Perhaps towards the 'Women's Moral Patrol', whose members had grown alarmed at the number of enterprising young ladies who were arriving in Edinburgh from all over the country, eager to service the city's mushrooming military population. 'One young woman,' complained a correspondent in the *Evening Dispatch*, 'has earned sufficient funds to open a respectable business.' The staid old capital was going quietly mad. One evening in early November Mr Alexander Sibbald, 74, was arrested by the police for discharging both barrels of a borrowed shotgun on the back green of his Tollcross tenement. As he was being led away, the prisoner protested that he had simply been trying to 'disable' an unfamiliar pigeon, which (he was certain) was acting in the service of the local German spy.

In fairness to Mr Sibbald, it must be conceded that such patriotic concern over the threat posed by pigeons was by no means confined to Tollcross. Newcastle, Leeds, Birmingham, Plymouth, Southampton and Dover were all equally vigilant, while, as early as 24 August, Max Wilhelm Nagel and Charles King of Ashford had been found guilty at Feltham of unlawful possession of 60 'strong fliers'. Tellingly, it emerged during the trial that this was not Mr King's first disagreement with the Crown: he had also appeared on the wrong side in South Africa. Edinburgh, however, had always been an uncommonly suspicious place – which might explain why agents of the Central Powers were thought to have descended on the city in such sinister profusion. It was widely believed that there was at least one in every stair, and that they were able to communicate through the clever use of coloured handkerchiefs. You could tell them by their bowling-bags, in which they kept their bombs, and (one is forced to conclude) by their baskets, in which they kept their pigeons. They favoured names like 'Smith' and 'Brown' and spoke in perfect English, seasoned rather shrewdly with a sprinkling of 'Och ayes'.

They stood, it seems, a little on the short side – like Charles Inglis, the friendly American gentleman who had visited the city at the end of August. Mind you, his name wasn't Inglis, he wasn't an American, and he wasn't particularly friendly. He was, in fact, *Oberleutnant* Carl Hans Lody of the Imperial German Naval Reserve, and he had lately been tried by court martial at the Middlesex Guildhall, found guilty of war treason, and sentenced to be shot. During his fateful month in Edinburgh he had shifted addresses several times, hired a bicycle, and (in the words of *The Scotsman*) 'visited various places in the neighbourhood'. These various places included the Forth Bridge, Rosyth Naval Base, Leith Docks and the capital's stately New Town, which he perambulated daily, making notes. As he strolled along George Street, passing number 125, headquarters of the Local Government Board for Scotland, it is unlikely that his trained observer's eye would have missed the tall, straight figure, immaculately dressed, who arrived every morning prompt at nine. Discreet enquiry here and there would soon reveal his name. *Everybody* knew him: he was the famous George McCrae. Leaving Mr Inglis to find his own way to the firing-squad, we must now introduce ourselves to the Colonel.

※ ※ ※

There would come a time when the press would describe him as a native of Edinburgh. It was a truth universally accepted; he was the city's favourite son. But McCrae had a secret: he was born in Aberdeen – 82 Bon Accord Street, to be precise – on 29 August 1861. He was also illegitimate – George *Buchan*, by rights – the son of Jane Buchan, who was employed as a resident housemaid in the home of James Nicol, Professor of Natural History at Aberdeen University. Jane Buchan was unmarried; when registering the birth she named the father as 'George McCrae, mason'. There is no evidence that such a gentleman ever existed.

Dismissed from her position, Jane carried the child to Edinburgh, where a younger brother, John, already lived. John Buchan (who *was* a stonemason) rented a single-roomed house in a stair at 41 Arthur Street, a steeply sloping terrace on the edge of the notorious Dumbiedykes. Across the valley to the west rose Salisbury Crags, surrounded by the ancient wilderness of the Queen's Park, where plague bodies were said to be buried, along with some of Willie Brodie's swag. Walter Scott had set his greatest novel here, a tale of riot and romance: we will hear more of it quite soon.

The neighbourhood was like a Highland village, densely packed with exiles from the north: shoe-makers, bonnet-makers, stay-makers, feather-trimmers, carpet sewers, envelope folders, students, tailors and bookbinders. Families with four or five children were common. Jane found work as a laundress and a room of her own just up the hill; George remained with John and his young wife, Margaret, to be brought up with their children as an 'orphan' cousin. Clearly Jane was his uncle's sister: the boy was encouraged to believe, therefore, that she was also no more than a trusted and affectionate *aunt*. He would learn the truth in later years, but we cannot venture when.

McCrae recalled an early life of 'honest poverty'. In the winter his uncle would place a saucer of water on the window sill every evening: if it was frozen in the morning, there would be no work. He shared a bed with his two young cousins but was not resented. There is no doubt that it was a happy and loving household. When the Buchans' third child was born in 1871, he was unaware that Margaret was pregnant. He awoke from a deep sleep to find that the birth had taken place without waking him. John Buchan spent the night walking around the Queen's Park until the sparrows brought him home.[8]

George was educated at the Lancastrian School in Davie Street; he left, not quite aged ten, to take up employment as a message-boy to a South Bridge boot-maker.[9] 'I felt a strong impulse,' he later wrote, 'to add to the household resources.' Soon afterwards he was apprenticed to Robert Nicol, a Dunfermline hatter, whose Edinburgh branch was situated at 57 Cockburn Street. Trading hours were 'nine till nine' Monday to Friday and 'nine till late' at weekends: on a Saturday he would leave the shop around midnight. He was small for his age, and unable to see over the counter. In August 1872, when he attempted to join John Hope's Water Rats, he was turned down for this very reason.

The following year he began to grow rapidly; he was promoted to salesman and rewarded with a substantial rise. By the age of 16, he was 5 ft 9 in. and looked (so he said) 21. Events, as he tells it, now took a 'startling' turn:

> Incessant bickerings between father and son resulted in their partnership being dissolved. The son immediately opened a rival establishment on the other side of Dunfermline High Street. My employer was nearly distraint. Apart from the worry and unpleasantness of a family quarrel, the continued success of both the Edinburgh and Dunfermline branches was at stake. He was sore worried because he had ceased to take an active part in the business. Our Edinburgh manager was an elderly gentleman of great experience, but not over fond of work. The lion's share of running the business [therefore] fell upon me.[10]

It is plain that Nicol was initially unaware of this situation; when it was pointed out to him, however, he lit upon a solution to his problems. McCrae was transferred to the main shop in Dunfermline and placed in complete charge of the establishment. He was some weeks short of his 17th birthday. Nicol had given him a free hand, so he restructured the business, updated the premises and increased the turnover to unprecedented levels during the first year. Meanwhile he found time to reach an important decision: commercial success notwithstanding, he was going to join the Army.

McCrae later wrote of his failed attempt to join John Hope's cadets: 'My real inclinations were towards soldiering. Even at 12, I was burning with military ardour.' At 17 he was still alight. He had taken a fancy to enlist as a trooper in the Royal Scots Greys. There is reason to believe that he was on the very point of signing up, when something unexpected happened: he fell in love. There was a girl on his staff, Lizzie Russell, 'an attractive, unassuming maiden, who drew me like a magnet'. Complications now ensued. Nicol, it appears, had been trying to dispose of his three (ageing) spinster daughters, and had young George in mind as one potential *disposee*. 'Matters,' he tells us, 'were getting a little strained,' so when his employer offered him the opportunity of returning to Edinburgh to take over the Cockburn Street shop, he jumped at it. This was the spring of 1878; he was not yet 18.

He now re-applied to John Hope and was accepted as a private in No. 1

Company of the Third Edinburgh Rifle Volunteer Battalion. In 1879 he was promoted to sergeant, and in January 1880 he left Robert Nicol's employ to set up business on his own account at 42 Grassmarket as a hatter and hosier. He moved into new lodgings at 1 Rankeillor Place, and canvassed during March on behalf of Duncan McLaren in the general election. McCrae's political awakening appears to have coincided with Gladstone's stirring 'Midlothian Campaign' of November 1879. The former Liberal prime minister was returned to Parliament after a gruelling series of platform speeches that had electrified the country. McCrae's membership of the party dates from that December; McLaren sponsored his application, so they were likely well-acquainted before then. Clearly the old man had spotted a possible successor; McCrae credited him as both an inspiration and a friend. There were 60 years between them.

In July of 1880 he married Lizzie in the front room of her parental home at New Row in Dunfermline. A son, William, was born the following year. In 1882 he moved his business to 37 Cockburn Street, just down the hill from his former employer's establishment. If this was a tactical move, then Duncan McLaren may well have been behind it: the Member for Scotland had done the same thing himself in 1824. Robert Nicol surrendered the field, retiring at once to his stronghold in Fife.

The McCraes now moved to 5 Gladstone Terrace, a broad and airy spot, just off the Meadows. These early (frequent) changes of address reveal a pattern. Each successive house is clearly better than the last: George was leaving his past – and the Pleasance in particular – far behind. Two further children, Kate and little George, appeared. He was commissioned lieutenant in his battalion. The prodigious young hatter now began to attract wider attention by introducing certain innovations to the promotion of his business. On one occasion he contrived to manufacture a giant pair of gloves. Hiring a wagon, he then drove them round the town over a banner stating, 'Made to Measure by McCrae!' On another occasion an outsized bowler hat was seen strolling up the High Street. He stocked a greater range of goods, and styled himself 'Purveyor of the Latest London Fashions'. A further move – to 3 Dick Place – followed in 1887. It was a handsome little property in the leafy and somewhat select district of the Grange. Arthur Street was just a mile away: it might have been a thousand.

In 1888 the Third Edinburgh Rifle Volunteers were renamed the Fourth (Volunteer) Battalion, the Royal Scots. McCrae was promoted captain and succeeded to command of his company; he was now a part-time member of the oldest infantry regiment in the British Army. Another son, Kenneth, was born. The business continued to prosper. The following year he stood as a candidate in the municipal election for St Leonard's Ward, which included a large portion of his old neighbourhood. His campaign (said *The Scotsman*) 'was conducted with great enthusiasm and drive'. He was a fine public speaker, quick-witted and clever in debate. He defeated the sitting councillor by more than 600 votes and made a stunning impact at his first meeting in the City Chambers. An official of the Cleaning and Lighting Committee had delivered his report. McCrae rose up – he had grasped the situation immediately – and proceeded both to list the shortcomings of the operation and suggest a more sensible alternative. His reforms, which were introduced at once, turned out to be a vast improvement.

In 1891, still not yet 30, he was unanimously elected treasurer of the city. Duncan McLaren's various successors had basked a little in the reflected glory of the great man's achievements. McCrae, however, saw that his mentor's work had only been a start. He therefore spent the next three years preparing the hugely complicated Corporation Stock Act with the help of City Chamberlain Robert Paton. The act (which was passed in 1894) consolidated the remaining city debt by converting it into new stock. The scheme earned the city an immediate premium of £120,000, and saved huge amounts in interest and legal expenses. Effectively, the debt was written off.[11] Under his careful stewardship, the city acquired the tramway network, installed electric street lighting, and funded the reconstruction of the crumbling North Bridge, which connected the southern residential suburbs with the New Town business quarter. On 25 May 1896 he laid the foundation stone. Continuing his personal expansion, he purchased 39 Cockburn Street, employed more staff, and produced three further daughters, Gladys, Flora and Eliza. In 1897, Stock Act notwithstanding, he was denied the Provostship by a single, casting vote. It was the first major disappointment of his career. In 1898 he opened a new (main) branch at 113 Princes Street and moved his family to 8 Whitehouse Loan, a house he named *Torluish*. That same year 'little George', now 14, enlisted as a bugler in his father's battalion.

In 1899, following the sudden death of Dr Robert Wallace, Liberal MP for East Edinburgh, McCrae was invited to stand for Parliament. After some hesitation, he resigned from the council and accepted. He held the seat by a majority of 1,930 over his Tory rival and impressed everyone with the eloquence of his maiden speech at Westminster. He was appointed to Parliamentary committees dealing with Private Legislation for Scotland, and to the Royal Commission on Physical Education, which addressed the problem of physical deterioration and malnutrition among children of the poor. He shone in debate and his financial expertise was acknowledged on several occasions by the Unionist Chancellor, Sir Michael Hicks-Beach. His early admirers included the Liberal leader Henry Campbell-Bannerman, and the former Home Secretary, Herbert Henry Asquith. Asquith's former assistant private secretary, Harold Tennant, the Eton-educated, Liberal MP for Berwickshire, sat on several of McCrae's committees.

In September 1900, with Britain's prospects in South Africa apparently improving, Prime Minister Salisbury dissolved Parliament and called the 'Khaki election'. McCrae retained his seat and was promoted soon afterwards to the rank of major. In September 1901 he became an honorary lieutenant-colonel and spoke in the House on the subject of the reserve forces. He was invited to join a War Office committee on Volunteer Transport and ended up composing the report himself. The newspapers, speculating on the possibility of a Liberal government, began to mention his name in connection with the post of Parliamentary Private Secretary to the Treasury. McCrae himself coveted the position of Chief Whip, and seems to have anticipated an immediate appointment. At the last moment he was overlooked.

In 1904 he continued his domestic advancement by moving a short distance down Grange Road to 2 Cumin Place. There was another baby (Hector) now, and Lizzie needed the extra accommodation. They took the name *Torluish* with them. In early 1905 he was promoted full colonel and finally appointed to command of the Fourth. That December the Unionist Prime Minister, Arthur Balfour, resigned, and, following the January general election, Campbell-Bannerman formed a Liberal administration. McCrae was returned with an increased majority and had high hopes of a place on the front bench. Again he was disappointed; there was some consolation, however, when the new Secretary for War, Richard Haldane, began to consult him regularly during the composition of his Territorial Forces Bill. McCrae's contribution to the creation of the Territorial Force cannot be overstated – not simply in the detail of the Bill itself, but also (and perhaps more importantly) in defusing the opposition of the old Volunteering interests. As the most respected Volunteer officer in the country, he was a persuasive advocate for change.

With the passage of the Act in 1907, the Fourth (Volunteer) Battalion became the 6th Battalion Royal Scots (TF) – celebrated in verse that July by an anonymous sergeant:

> The 6th Territorial Royal Scots
> Are known as "McCrae's Fighting Cocks".
> They are able and willing
> Their duties fulfilling,
> And knock other regiments to spots.[12]

The last line was no idle boast. At a succession of military manœuvres over the years, the Fourth Battalion had proved itself the smartest and most efficient unit in the field. McCrae had matched and then surpassed John Hope's high standards. His services to Volunteering and to Edinburgh were finally recognised in 1908, when he was knighted in London by King Edward, who invited him to tea at Windsor. The shop girl from Dunfermline was now 'Lady McCrae'. That same year, incidentally, Sir George was appointed as a military member to the Edinburgh TFA, which is where he first became friendly with a certain Harry Rawson.

Following Campbell-Bannerman's resignation through ill health in April 1908, Asquith had become Prime Minister. In order to continue the intended Liberal programme of reform, he needed to overcome the opposition of a number of fiercely conservative institutions such as the Civil Service and the House of Lords. In Scotland nothing could be done in public health or housing without the cooperation of the Local Government Board. When the Board's chairman stood down in 1909, Asquith invited McCrae to assume control. Reluctantly, for he still harboured hopes of a place in government, Sir George accepted. Little George (now a strapping six-footer) took over as managing director of McCrae's Ltd in Princes Street, while William ran the Cockburn Street establishment. Kenneth, who had itchier feet, was bound for Buenos Aires and a job with the London and River Plate Bank.

The McCraes now left Cumin Place for a suitably grand house at 61 Grange Loan – *Torluish* the third. Sir George laid out a tennis court in the garden, where, to the consternation of the neighbours, he also practised his golf swing. In June 1913 he unexpectedly resigned command of his battalion; on 26 December Lizzie died of cancer. They had known it was coming for two years. She was buried across the Loan in Grange Cemetery: he used to visit her grave every evening.

Haldane's successor at the War Office, meanwhile, was concerned about Territorial recruiting. Numbers were down and it was thought that conditions of service might be to blame. Since McCrae's opinions on this very point had been ignored during the drafting of the 1907 Act, John Seely now solicited the Colonel's current views.

> We are having a stiff time as regards recruiting in Edinburgh [replied McCrae]. I feel that the middle-class man is shirking his duty and that we are becoming more and more dependent on the artisan to keep the numbers up. The middle-class fellow gets his fortnight's holiday – at least his pay is not stopped. By attending camp, he therefore sacrifices only his leisure or convenience. The artisan is in a much worse position. He gets only a week's holiday, during which his pay stops.[13]

Sir George's answer was an extra shilling a day for the second week in camp, along with a free pair of boots and payment of employees' National

Insurance contributions while they were unable to work. He also recommended the granting of a £10 'bounty' to officers who chose to remain for the full fortnight. 'The time has come,' he concluded, 'when we must boldly face this situation, if the voluntary system for Home Defence is to have a fair trial.'[14] But events now conspired to frustrate him again. Seely, whom Haldane considered incompetent, was forced to resign in March 1914 over an incident at the Curragh, near Dublin, when the commanding officer of the 3rd Cavalry Brigade and 56 of his officers opted for dismissal rather than use force against Ulster Unionists. The other head that rolled was that of Sir John French, Chief of the Imperial General Staff and soon-to-be commander of the British Expeditionary Force. Seely's departure left a vacancy, which was filled temporarily by Asquith until the honorary colonel of the 6th Royal Scots – Lord Kitchener himself – took over in August.

Within days of the outbreak of hostilities a fund for the relief of wartime distress was established under the patronage of the Prince of Wales. Sir George was appointed chairman of the Scottish committee, charged with the task of setting up a nationwide network of sub-committees and offices. As his honorary secretary and principal assistant, he chose an old friend and golfing companion, Sir Richard Lodge, Professor of History at the University of Edinburgh. Lodge, now 71, was considered to be the finest academic lecturer of his generation. Like McCrae, he had his own limerick:

> There was a professor, R.L.,
> Who never would stop for the bell.
> When his class showed their ire,
> He said, 'How can you tire,
> When I lecture so awfully well?'

The Professor had once been one of Rosebery's Liberal Imperialists. In 1910, however, he split with the party over Asquith's attempts to curb the power of the House of Lords and now considered himself an independent. He was one of the few public figures in Scotland to express reservations about the wisdom of Lord Kitchener's recruiting campaign. Although he was a staunch believer in the voluntary principle in peacetime, the demographer in him could see that the New Army was being filled by the brightest and the best. When these units were blooded, the cost would be great. Conscription, he thought, might have been a better course for the country to follow – not (like *The Times*) out of belligerent spite but rather in the spirit of simple common sense.

In September two of Lodge's sons enlisted in the 4th Royal Scots. Wilfred, the eldest, a graduate of Edinburgh and Oxford, was a teacher; Cuthbert, the youngest, was an undergraduate in the Science faculty at Edinburgh and was hoping to pursue a career in forestry. He was 6 ft 8 in. tall, with a weak heart and lungs. It is likely that his considerable charm was the only thing that got him through the medical. In October Wilfred took a commission in the Provost's Battalion; Cuthbert was biding his time.

Sir George's sons were also in khaki. William was a lieutenant in the Lowland (City of Edinburgh) Battery of the Royal Garrison Artillery; George, now a captain and married with his own home, was a company commander in the 6th Royal Scots; while Kenneth had returned from South America and taken a commission in the 7th Cameron Highlanders, an Inverness-based Service battalion, which had been recruiting aggressively in the Edinburgh area. McCrae remained a civilian, and, although undoubtedly busy with the Prince of Wales's Fund, he was conspicuous by his absence from any military platform. The news from the front was not good. Gheluvelt, then Neuve Chapelle: bloody stands and dreadful bloody odds. On Friday, 6 November, the Colonel had a long discussion with his second daughter, Gladys, then sat down to write a letter to Harold Tennant at the War Office.

CHAPTER THREE

'White Feathers of Midlothian'

There was another letter on its way to London that evening. It was addressed to Mr Charrington. The author, a senior Scottish advocate, lately appointed to the Bench, had written to complain about the Fiend's most recent statements against football. Andrew Macbeth Anderson, Lord Anderson, was the former Solicitor-General for Scotland. He was also a former player, having represented Edinburgh University while he was studying for the law. Now 52, his sporting activities were limited to curling, fishing and golf; he remained, however, a keen supporter of the game. The particular object of his affections was an Edinburgh club with an extraordinary name, the famous 'Heart of Midlothian' – foreshortened by some philistine to 'Hearts'.

We don't know the precise contents of Anderson's letter, but it's likely he pointed out that two members of the playing staff were already soldiers, that their colleagues were attending weekly sessions of military drill, and that the club had been the first sporting body in Britain to introduce regular collections at home games for the Prince of Wales's Relief Fund – whose respected chairman, moreover, was a prominent shareholder.

Hearts were founded in the autumn of 1873 at Washing Green Court in the South Back of the Canongate on the southern edge of the Old Town. Sir George's home in Arthur Street was a short walk away through the Dumbiedykes. The court was less than ten years old at that time, built by the Corporation to accommodate part of the overspill from the crowded tenements nearby. Bounded on the east by the Edinburgh Gas Light Company's new gasometer, it was a sorely squashed square, entered through a narrow pend and containing perhaps seventy cramped houses on two, three or four storeys. At ground level several small businesses were already established – among them a tannery, a ropeworks, a brass foundry, a cork factory and a malt barn. There were stables and a coach-house, and (on the street-front) a drysalter, a dairy and two rival provision merchants. The locals, mostly tenants, were coopers, joiners, draymen, cartwrights, painters, asphalters, glassblowers, shoe-makers, tailors and brewer's servants. William Cormack, a police constable, lived at number 30. Next door, drawing his clientele from all across the Old Town, James Crighton, self-styled 'Professor and Teacher of Swimming', operated a swimming pool. Had he bothered to consult the Valuation Roll, he would have found himself described as a 'Baths Attendant'.

Next door to Mr Crighton was a 'public steam wash-house', run by Mrs Robertson; next door to her were Mrs Cormack's Refreshment Rooms, the neighbourhood's main social focus. Mrs Cormack offered dancing in the evenings and catered cheerfully for weddings, christenings, funerals, and maybe the occasional divorce. The rooms also provided a convenient base for several of Mr Crighton's customers, who had formed themselves into a sporting club and were currently experimenting with the latest western craze of 'football' – although they hadn't quite mastered the rules, and their fevered exertions still resembled nothing so much as a dozen angry men pursuing a drunken piglet. One of their number, Thomas Purdie, an 18-year-old rubberworker, suggested naming their team 'The Heart of Mid-lothian' after the famous novel by Sir Walter Scott. Scott's masterpiece, first published in 1818, was set largely in the St Leonard's/Pleasance/Dumbiedykes quarter and opened with a dramatic account of the storming of the town's Tolbooth (or prison) by a mob intent upon hanging John Porteous, Captain of the City Guard. The author took his title from the Tolbooth's common name, and Purdie passed the burden on to Hearts. This was not, perhaps, surprising, for Thomas was a nephew (of sorts) of Sir Walter's most trusted servant. The original Thomas Purdie was a poacher from Ashestiel, near Selkirk. In 1804, when Scott was serving as the local Sheriff, Purdie had appeared before the Bench charged with the latest in a long line of petty offences, and (according to Lockhart) 'gave such a touching account of his circumstances – a wife, and I do not know how many children, depending on his exertions – work scarce and grouse abundant – and all this with a mixture of odd, sly humour . . .'[1] that the novelist was moved to offer him a job instead of jail. Purdie became his shepherd, his servant and his companion for 22 years. He died in 1829 and is buried at Melrose Abbey under a modest stone erected by Sir Walter – 'Thomas Purdie, Wood-Forester at Abbotsford . . . a humble but sincere friend'. The footballing Tom, born to these traditions, was evidently able to persuade his colleagues that the name 'Heart of Mid-lothian' was less ridiculous than they initially thought. The proposal is said to have been carried unopposed, although the hyphen disappeared before too long.[2]

In December 1873 a group of 'missionaries' from Glasgow's Queen's Park and Clydesdale clubs (who had recently qualified to contest that season's Scottish Cup final) staged an exhibition match at Raimes Park in Bonnington, on the north side of Edinburgh, in order to demonstrate the 'new football', as played under approved 'Association' rules. Among the spectators were several members of the Hearts, who resolved at once to become official. Their early matches, little more than informal kickabouts, were played on public ground at the East Meadows. In due course they accepted challenges from other aspiring clubs, and it became necessary to form a committee in order to arrange fixtures. Tom Purdie was elected as the first captain.

One of Purdie's teammates was the brother of Marion Anderson, widow of a local spirit merchant, Aaron Anderson, who had drunk himself to death in August 1874. Marion, then a portly 39, took over the licence from her late husband and allowed Heart of Midlothian FC the use of her home at 19 West Crosscauseway, directly above the pub, as a changing-room and general headquarters. West Crosscauseway was handy for the East Meadows and a short step from Percival King's Cricket and Football Warehouse in Lothian Street, where the club members purchased their equipment. In August 1875 Hearts (with 45 members now) joined the Scottish Football Association, which had been formed in Glasgow the previous year with the purpose of inaugurating a Challenge Cup competition. Their registered 'uniform' was a white shirt with a maroon heart stitched to the chest. This was replaced in due course by a shirt composed of red, white and blue hoops. When this was boiled in Mrs Robertson's steamie, the wash came out a deep maroon. White breeches were added, and the Hearts had found their famous colours.

The same year they became founder members of the Edinburgh Football Association, which purchased its own challenge cup and entered into negotiations with Duncan McLaren for the use of a large empty field on his Powburn estate. Powburn was no more than a small cluster of houses and an old tannery on the Liberton road. The area, mainly used for grazing, was awaiting development; the ground was flat, coarse, and needed constant rolling. No pitches were marked out and there were no goalposts; it was effectively an open meadow. In 1878 Hearts won their first trophy here, defeating local rivals Hibernian in the Edinburgh FA Cup final. 'Hibs' were a year younger than Hearts, but they came from the same part of town. They were formed at a meeting of the Young Men's Catholic Association, which rented a committee room in St Mary's Street hall, just around the corner from the South Back. The rivalry was keen but friendly: after their matches in the Meadows both sets of players would retire to Mrs Anderson's establishment and toast each other until the police joined in.

Around 1878 Hearts began to take the sport more seriously, moving their base a short distance away to Tom Mackenzie's athletic outfitting shop at 4 Chapel Street. With perhaps a dozen clubs using the East Meadows now, they moved permanently to Powburn, securing a corner of the field for use as their first 'home' ground. Initially they stored their goalposts in the yard behind Mackenzie's shop but moved them in due course to Duncan Street School. Two founder members, brothers Charlie and Willie Ross, used to carry them down the hill to Powburn for every fixture, then carry them back up the hill on the way home. Charlie was 6 ft 2 in. tall, Willie a good 10 inches shorter.

Around 1879 they moved again. There were around 120 members by now, so they could afford to rent a proper ground at Powderhall. The stay did not last long, however, for in February 1881 they acquired a field in the developing district of Gorgie with sufficient space for two pitches, named it after the neighbourhood, and erected a small pavilion. 'Tynecastle Park' was opened that April amid great local fanfare; Tom Purdie's wife, Annie, cut the ribbon on the stand.

During the following decade Hibs were Edinburgh's dominant side. Hearts seem to have had the better players, but suffered badly from the southern drift to England, where professionalism was legalised in 1885. As an amateur team, paying only legitimate expenses, Hearts could not afford to compete. When they tried to (in 1884), they were caught making illegal payments to two of their players and expelled from the SFA. Restored six weeks later, with an entirely new committee, they were suitably contrite: there is evidence, however, to suggest that the old practices thereafter were simply much more artfully concealed.

In 1886 the club moved again – across Gorgie Road, this time, to *New* Tynecastle, a vacant plot 'one field's width' from an old distillery. Once more, two pitches was the model. They ran from east to west, the first team using the northern one for their home fixtures.[3] Bolton Wanderers were the inaugural visitors; they returned to Lancashire lamenting a 4–1 defeat. The season ended with a win over Hibs at Powderhall in the final of a charity competition sponsored by Lord Rosebery, whose long association with Edinburgh football can be dated from this period.

In November 1887 Celtic Football Club was formed in Glasgow with the purpose of raising funds for Catholic charities. From the start Celtic defied the game's authorities by adopting a deliberately professional approach to their affairs. The SFA was stubbornly of the opinion that payment (whether for entry or for player) would serve only to undermine the essence of the game. *Scottish Sport*, a contemporary journal, observed that 'the feeling is strong among those who have the best interests of football at heart, that the way to maintain the tone of the game is not to make it a trade. True sporting spirit aims at elevating the game to a higher platform than pounds, shillings and pence; it seeks to purify and enoble, to rear and produce, not procure and pay.'

Mr Charrington couldn't have put it better. Celtic, on the other hand, were 'reared on breaches of the professional law'.' They set out to lure the best Irish players in Scotland, most of whom apparently had agreements with Hibernian. In 1888 six members of Hibs' first team defected; the Edinburgh club's fortunes declined accordingly, and in 1891 they were expelled from the SFA for failure to pay their subscriptions. They re-emerged officially two seasons later, re-joined the Association, and resumed their local rivalries. It would take them a while, however, to pick up the pace.

In Hibs' absence the Scottish League was formed. The 11 founder members in 1890 included Celtic, Rangers and Hearts. Celtic were the prime movers: fundamentally it was an effort to rationalise the fixture list in order to produce a regular, guaranteed income. The existing system – a mixture of friendlies, local competitions and the Scottish Challenge Cup – was haphazard and increasingly unworkable. *Amateur*, in fact. In 1893, again at Celtic's instigation, professionalism was legalised in Scotland.

On 7 February 1891 Hearts won the Scottish Cup for the first time, defeating Dumbarton 1–0 at Hampden Park in Glasgow. In 1895 they won the League, beating Celtic into second place. In recognition of their achievement they received a handsome commemorative trophy from the serving Treasurer of Edinburgh Corporation, one Bailie George McCrae. It was a personal gift – the Town Council gave them nothing – and was presented with the suggestion that the club organise a competition and win it every season. In 1896, therefore, they took the McCrae Cup for the first time and the Scottish Cup for the second, beating a resurgent Hibs 3–1 at Logie Green in the only final ever played outside Glasgow.

This was the year that Lord Rosebery resigned the Liberal leadership. The former prime minister's patronage of the game had inspired several clubs to use his family name in their titles. In April Hearts signed a young inside-forward called Robert Walker from local juvenile side, Dalry Primrose. It was a providential moment. Bobby Walker would shortly emerge as the finest footballer in the world, and (remarkably) show no inclination to leave Tynecastle during the entire course of his long career. In 1897 Hearts won the League again; in 1899 they were runners-up to Rangers. In 1901, with Walker in the team, they won the Cup for the third time, defeating Celtic 4–3 at Ibrox Park. He was an international now, having won his first cap against England 12 months earlier. The most striking characteristic of his play was a mesmerising dribble, which left even the sharpest opponent looking foolish. He had no pace and no physical presence beyond a certain portly charm; his feet, however, were the quickest in the game. He would draw defenders to him like a magnet, then appear from the crush with the ball fastened firmly to his boot. He was a magician, 'The Houdini of Dalry', the only footballer in history to have a style of play named after him – *Walkerism*. Crowned heads of Europe made the pilgrimage to Gorgie just to shake him by the hand. He remained unimpressed. King Haakon of Norway, for example, was favoured with a tug of the cap and a slight breeze as Bobby rushed off for a pint with his pals.[5]

Attendances at Tynecastle, which by now boasted its own cycle track and a seated pavilion, increased greatly during Walker's ascendancy. Encouraged by this success, the organising committee decided in 1903 to reconstitute itself as a board and float the club as a limited company. It was a disaster from the outset. By the end of season 1904–5 Hearts were nearly £2,000 in the red and close to total collapse. A new company was incorporated to 'acquire and take over as a going concern the undertaking and all or any of the assets and liabilities of Heart of Midlothian Football Club Limited'.[6] To generate sufficient capital to cover old debts and re-launch the business 5,000 £1 shares were issued. Robert Wilson, proprietor of the *Evening News*, was the brain behind the scheme. Football, after all, sold newspapers. He reported early difficulty in finding subscribers, but eventually recruited four local businessmen to serve on the board, expressing the hope that 'under the new regime more business-like methods will be imported into the control of the club'. One of the recruits was Harry Rawson.

McCrae took up 100 shares: a substantial investment for a man with such a family to support. Another prominent subscriber was his friend James Leishman, newly elected Liberal councillor for the city's George Square Ward. Leishman, like Sir George, was self-invented. He was born in West Linton in 1864, and took his name from his mother, Jane, a domestic servant on one of the local estates. He received only a rudimentary schooling before arriving in Edinburgh alone and unsupported around 1881. He found employment with the Post Office and attended night classes in History and English Literature at Heriot-Watt Training College. In 1885 he enrolled for a shorthand course organised by the Scottish Phonographic Association and came first in a class of 200. He had found his calling. He applied for membership and over the next few years served the Association as librarian, instructor and examiner. He also offered private tuition. In the meantime he set up on his own account as a typewriter salesman and 'phonographic practitioner' – a business that would grow into the largest independent typing and shorthand agency in Scotland.

As a strong believer in the value of a sound education, Leishman made several unsuccessful attempts during this period to join the Edinburgh School Board. In 1903, however, he managed to secure the consent of the Hearts committee to leaflet the Tynecastle crowds in order to gather support for his campaign. He was criticised locally for bringing football into the schools debate but he got his votes and was duly elected. The committee even issued a circular singing his praises. His personal response to the 1905 flotation was therefore something of a debt repaid. Although he turned down a seat on the board, he did agree to act as a financial consultant to the new administration. There was, however, one condition. The club, in return, would have to start listening to their young auditor, whose warnings about the imminent collapse of the original limited company had been completely ignored. The auditor's name was Elias Henry Fürst.

Elias Fürst was born in Russia in 1873. He was the eldest son of Jacob Fürst, minister of Edinburgh's growing Hebrew congregation, who had brought his family to Britain around 1874 to escape the pogroms of St Petersburg. Following a short stay in Middlesbrough, the Fürsts arrived in Edinburgh in 1879 and settled into a small flat above the city's synagogue at Park Place in the district of Bristo, not far from the East Meadows and Tom Mackenzie's sports shop in Chapel Street. Elias grew up with the club: Jacob carried him to matches. The old man encouraged all his charges to engage as fully as possible in the life of their new home town. Becoming Scots, he said, did not imply betrayal of their past: it was merely good manners towards a generous host. His eldest son acquired a strong Scottish accent, the skills of a watch-maker, and a mind for business that might have put Sir George himself to shame. At the age of 17 he became Hearts' youngest subscribing member and began to bombard the committee with gratuitous financial advice, most of which went unheeded. He organised a brake-club to travel to 'away' fixtures and dragged his entire family through to Glasgow to see the 1901 Cup victory at Ibrox.

He was appointed club auditor around 1902 and expressed grave concerns about the following year's public flotation. When his fears were confirmed, he was one of the first to offer his services to Robert Wilson. The 1905 Memorandum and Articles of Association are largely his work: there is an inherent recognition that the new board was setting out upon a business enterprise as well as a sporting one. Football was no longer just a game. When the relaunched Hearts won the Scottish Cup for the fourth time in 1906, Fürst travelled to the match as a guest of the board. Leishman's condition was therefore agreed, and in 1907, some months after Harry Rawson left to take up his seat on the council, Elias was invited to become a director. 'I did not storm the castle,' he later said. 'I crept inside one night when someone left the door unlocked.'

Harry Rawson's departure seems to have been followed by a certain amount of financial slippage. The new director discovered that the club was once more being run from a tin box in the boardroom. No receipts were kept and players were paid on demand, often direct from gate money on match days. The *Evening News* announced that Fürst had instituted immediate accounting changes – which implied that there had been some accounting in the first place. The club finished ninth in the League. It was a poor year.

Season 1907–8 was worse: they finished 11th and the manager, Willie Waugh, was sacked. Waugh's replacement, James McGhee, lasted only two years: another 11th, followed by a dreadful start to season 1909–10, saw him flee to Philadelphia. Fürst was vice-chairman now, sufficiently powerful to bring in his own man. On 19 January 1910 John McCartney arrived from St Mirren FC to take up the post of manager and secretary at Tynecastle Park.

McCartney came to Edinburgh with a substantial reputation. He was fiercely independent, a *builder* of teams rather than an inheritor. The playing staff knew there would be changes. The directors too, it would seem. On his first day in charge he found a framed notice above the door to the boardroom: 'YOU MUST ALWAYS CUT YOUR COAT ACCORDING TO YOUR CLOTH!' It was probably Fürst's, and it may have been intended as ironic. Whatever, the new manager tore it down and replaced it with a paper scroll of his own design: 'YOU MUST ALWAYS GIVE THE PUBLIC WHAT THE PUBLIC WANTS!' It would stay up there for nine momentous years.[7]

John McCartney was born in Mauchline, Ayrshire, in 1866.[8] Around 1875 he shifted to Mearns in Renfrewshire, when his father William, a land steward, took a position at one of the local big houses. John recalled that his parents were affectionate but strict. They intended him for a scholastic career, passing on their love of literature and (it would seem) their troublesome, inquiring minds.

In 1881 William McCartney was appointed steward of the Eaglesham Estate in Renfrewshire. John was 15. The family moved to a cottage near the village of Busby, where William became an elder of the parish church and a strong supporter of the local 'Reading and Recreation Club'. In the course of his work with the club, he made a field available to the local football team, Busby Cartvale. Under no circumstances, though, would he or his wife Margaret countenance John taking up the game. McCartney junior, for his part, was smitten at his first sight of the ball. In spite of parental objections he regularly went without his Saturday lunch in order to attend the weekly match. In due course he took the fateful step of joining in . . . 'no amount of chastisement, however severe, could keep me out of it'. By the age of 16 he was a regular in the side, and 'purloined' his mother's boots on one occasion in order to be properly turned out. 'The ruin I wrought brought upon me the maternal ire in an acute form,' he later wrote. The local newspaper described him as a 'fearless, fighting full-back', the last line of defence. It was a position he would fill until they placed him in his coffin.

McCartney admitted that his parents' desire for him to become a teacher had been 'shattered by my unquenchable love for the game'. He did not, however, neglect his studies. Having found work locally as a clerk with the Caledonian Railway Company, he attended evening classes in bookkeeping and shorthand. He also read voraciously. In time he would be recognised as an authority on the work of Robert Burns (whom he quoted constantly), but he was equally fond of Scott, Hogg, Stevenson, Dostoevsky and Charles Dickens. Anyone with whom he disagreed, in public or in private, was likely to find himself compared to some suitable Dickensian grotesque – especially Pecksniff, Stiggins or Gradgrind. His early submissions to the press were peppered with such references: his letters were knowledgeable, entertaining and provocative. In 1882 he was appointed Renfrewshire football correspondent for the *Hamilton Advertiser*: it was the start of a third career. A fourth, if you include tutoring part-time in the local school.

Cartvale were a tough side. 'It was customary,' wrote McCartney, 'to have at least one exponent of the art of self-defence in case of emergency – such as speeding out of neighbouring villages carrying our ordinary clothes under our arms.' Another phrase he used was 'fistic prowess': by the age of 19 he stood 5 ft 8 in., weighed a muscular 16 st and was captain of the finest team in Cartvale's short-lived history. In 1885 he was poached by Glasgow Thistle and in 1886 he signed for Rangers, going on to captain them, playing in the first match at the original Ibrox Park and breaking his jaw in Edinburgh against Hibs. In 1888 he left Rangers for Cowlairs, the biggest club in the Springburn district of Glasgow. Cowlairs' team was composed mainly of internationals: McCartney was the only uncapped player. He was appointed captain, however, and featured that year in their first match against the newly formed Celtic. He also helped to christen New Tynecastle in September 1890, helping his side to a deserved 4–0 defeat.

One Saturday, against Glasgow Thistle at Beechwood Park, Cowlairs needed an emergency centre-forward. McCartney volunteered, scored eight in a 10–0 victory and had to flee the ground pursued by an angry mob. Trouble followed him around. In a Glasgow Cup-tie against Rangers there were four draws before the last, decisive, game. At the end of the second match (at Ibrox) the Cowlairs players were imprisoned in their dressing-room for two hours while the local constabulary tried to quell a riot. 'I had a strong presentiment,' he later recalled, 'that my neck was about to be stretched.'

McCartney retired from the game in 1891, frustrated by his inability to earn anything more than expenses. He had married three years earlier and was looking for a more conventional career. His bride, a formidable young woman, was Jane Struthers, of Jackton, near East Kilbride. 'My Bonnie Jean', as he called her, was the niece of John's old dominie, John Struthers, later to become *Sir* John Struthers, Secretary of the Scottish Board of Education. Again teaching was suggested, and he was on the point of setting out on that very course, when Manchester's Newton Heath FC offered him the chance to turn legitimately professional. He accepted at once and remained in Manchester for three years. Newton Heath's directors, however, forbade the players from taking any employment outside the game. With a growing family, McCartney needed all the cash he could get, so in 1894 he moved to Luton Town, whose impecunious board positively encouraged its players to supplement their sporting incomes by any means available. As a result, he had several employers during his spell in the town. He departed over money. A fine young Luton side, he later wrote, broke up because the locals didn't support their team in sufficient numbers to allow the directors to offer a competitive wage. Barnsley was his final stop, in 1897. He captained the side for four seasons until a knee injury against Blackpool in 1901 ended his playing career for good.

The Barnsley boss was Arthur Fairclough. He told his board that he would stand down on condition that McCartney was offered the opportunity to replace him. A contract was agreed and the new manager was instructed to build a team that could look after itself on the park. There was no money for signings, but the directors were adamant. McCartney responded by selling a bundle of season tickets door-to-door around the town until he had raised ten pounds, with which he then went off to 'explore the north-east'. He returned with 14 players, one of whom, George Wall, went on to play for England. The 'Ten Pound Team' won the Midland League Championship and McCartney's reputation as a talent-spotter was established. It was the happiest time of his career and he always maintained that he would have remained in Yorkshire for the rest of his days, had his son not intervened. Young Willie spotted an advert in the local paper announcing that St Mirren FC of Paisley were looking for a manager. McCartney recalled that 'there was no domestic peace until I applied for the post'. The application was successful and he left Barnsley 'with a solid reputation as Cup fighters and £700 on deposit'. In return the board gave him a marble clock, a mahogany roll-top desk and a grand dinner. The entire town turned out to see him off to Scotland.

St Mirren were in dire financial straits; McCartney's brief was to restructure the business from top to bottom. Against strong local opposition he decided to float the club as a limited company and took to the streets again to hawk his shares until almost the entire issue had been taken up. When he arrived, St Mirren were selling off their players to cover debts; on his departure the board owned its ground and had a substantial bank account. His fine young team had even reached the Cup final. He had created a model of modern football club organisation: when Elias Fürst pinched him for the Hearts, therefore, he was nipping in before a pack of greedy English suitors.

McCartney's predecessor at Tynecastle, James McGhee, had promised much but delivered little. He made some good signings, but was unable to get along with his senior players. He suspended Bobby Walker for infringing club discipline and was in constant conflict with the board. In return for leaving St Mirren, McCartney had demanded an entirely free hand. Fürst persuaded his fellow directors to relinquish their day-to-day control over the business side of things and their unwelcome interest in the playing side. There was resentment, and it would fester for several years. By the time that McCartney had pinned up his scroll, however, he and Fürst were fast friends.

The end of season 1909–10 found Hearts 12th in the League. It was still McGhee's team. McCartney examined his players, declared them 'somewhat ancient' and decided that 'they needed a good kick up the backside'. It was 'urgently imperative,' he later wrote, 'to bring in younger men'. In fact the position of the club was much bleaker than anyone suspected, and he recalled a struggle raising the money needed to keep Hearts going over the summer. He had Walker, of course, who had been at Tynecastle for 14 years. But only three other lads had impressed him; the rest would have to go. George Sinclair was the first of the lucky ones; he was one of the best wingers in the country. The half-back, Peter Nellies, was another. Nellies was born in the 'Hearts village' of Kingseat, near Dunfermline, and had grown up supporting the club. When his parents took him to Douglas Water in Lanarkshire at the age of 11, he continued to travel through to Edinburgh for home games. He was miner to trade, and served his time at Douglas Colliery while playing football at the weekends for Douglas Water Thistle. A Junior international and much in demand, he picked Hearts ahead of Rangers for the chance to learn from Walker.

McCartney's final choice was Robert Mercer, a 21-year-old centre-half from Avonbridge in Stirlingshire. Mercer was the best young defender in Scotland, fast, skilful and intelligent – everything, in fact, that the traditional centre-half was never intended to be. In an age when defenders were instructed only to 'clear their lines' by booting the ball as far as possible (and, preferably, into touch), Mercer preferred to keep it well in play. Strong in the air, tactically astute, a deadly passer and a gifted dribbler, he was 60 years ahead of his time and the rock on which the manager would build.[9]

The rest of the players seem to have been retained on sufferance until McCartney could generate sufficient funds to replace them. Season 1910–11 finished with Hearts 14th in the League and the supporters distinctly unhappy. McCartney had used his southern contacts to import several Englishmen, and the critics loudly bemoaned the 'betrayal of the old Hearts'. The manager was unimpressed: 'If an albino piccaninny with one leg longer than the other can play the game better than one of the men already here [he wrote], then I will sign him. If he comes from Bacup rather than Newtongrange, it will make not one jot of difference.' He expanded this view in his next contribution to the *Evening News*, responding to 'Montpelier', a regular correspondent who had suggested native-only qualification for participation in the Scottish Cup:

> One of these days, when the game has developed more in some of the Continental countries, we will have Danes and Belgians, Germans and Frenchmen, Hungarians and Russians, and Turks and Bulgarians coming over to take part in our football. It may still be a long way off, but the day may come when an effort will be made in that direction, and even those who may be inclined to laugh at the idea as fantastical will surely admit that it would be a good thing if it could be carried out.

Some supporters, however, continued to question the commitment of the English acquisitions. Two men in particular, Lawrence Abrams and David Taylor, suffered badly at the hands of terracing hecklers. Taylor tended to respond in kind and thus made himself even more unpopular. The press labelled him an 'abnormal shouter'; he did not stay long. McCartney was constantly changing the side, looking for the perfect combination. Many years later he set out his thoughts on constructing a team:

> Several points are essential, chief amongst which is the securing of carefully selected, well-built lads whose play indicates the brain at work in unison with the feet. It takes time and patience to blend and perfect, but in due course a real football-playing team is the outcome. There is no room for the individualist in such a team, even if he gets goals. His inclusion prevents the moulding process and stultifies the growth of collective force. A young team, like a growing plant, has to be carefully tended and malformation prevented. Any appearance of selfishness or weakness in the formation must at once be remedied.

The governing theory behind McCartney's tactical approach was 'the quick movement of a collective body'. Most teams of this period (with the possible exception of Willie Maley's irresistible Celtic side) tended to separate the functions of defence and attack. For a defender to become involved in an attacking move was simply bad manners. Under the prevailing system, the game tended to be characterised by intense individual bursts, largely unsupported by any predetermined plan. McCartney and Mercer (whom he had appointed captain), introduced such a plan and then set about finding the men who might put it into practice. 'Build young,' he advised, 'carefully noting the mentality of your players. They must fit in socially and personally, as well as in the team.'

McCartney travelled constantly during this period. In 1911 he signed the bustling centre-forward Percy Dawson at Jarrow Station after watching him play for North Shields Athletic. The fee was £100, and he beat scouts from Sheffield Wednesday, Arsenal and Manchester City, all of whom were waiting till the morning. Dawson was then tried out in every position before McCartney restored him to his rightful jersey. He scored goals for fun: he was Tynecastle's new hero and the first of the manager's successes. At the close of season 1911–12 Hearts were fourth in the League.

In keeping with his theories of social compatibility and the development of team spirit, McCartney now led the club on its first overseas tour. It was Elias Fürst's idea: the newly elected chairman used his Continental contacts to arrange challenge matches in Norway and Denmark during the close season. He arranged also for their hosts to pay for the trip, so that Hearts returned to Edinburgh with a tidy profit. The manager's purse was hardly overflowing, but it was a welcome addition. By the end of the following season Hearts were *third*. The good news, however, was tempered by the sudden retirement of Bobby Walker. As the country entered a period of mourning, McCartney remained unexpectedly cheerful. He had already found a worthy successor. In his first-team debut at Tynecastle against Rangers, Harry Wattie ran the game and scored two winning goals. It was an astonishing display. Walker himself was watching from the stand. 'I think the boss has found a good 'un,' he told a reporter.

Wattie was an Edinburgh lad, born at 8 Livingstone Place in 1891. Educated at Boroughmuir, he supported Hearts and had played for several Junior sides before McCartney signed him from Tranent in 1913. His sister, Alice, was engaged to one of the manager's earliest signings, a charismatic young right-back called Patrick James Crossan. Crossan, who came from the Midlothian shale village of Addiewell, was the same age as Harry. The two were best friends. If Wattie was quick, then Crossan was explosive. Patrick – known as 'Paddy' by the press, but 'Pat' to his pals – was wont to supplement his summer income by joining the professional sprinting circuit, employing a number of curious pseudonyms in order to confound observers and keep his winnings private. Journalists who monitored such things believed he was the quickest man in Scotland over 100 yards. He was 5 ft 9 in. and exceptionally powerful. Also (so he claimed) exceptionally good-looking, attributing Hearts' large female support solely to his presence in the side. His mates, in the spirit of teasing, had taken to calling him the 'handsomest man in the world'. Harry would later inform a journalist: 'Pat can maybe pass the ball, but he couldn't pass a mirror if he tried!'[10]

Wattie lived with his parents at 12 Marchmont Road; Crossan lodged with the Wilson family at 10 Ogilvie Terrace in Merchiston. Willie Wilson, a son of the house, was another of McCartney's chosen sons. He had signed for Hearts in 1912 from Arniston Rangers and, until the appearance of Wattie, was being groomed to take Walker's place in the team. The manager preferred him as a winger, so it was all working out for the best. Wilson was born in McLeod Street, right beside Tynecastle; he was, as they say, Hearts daft. His first side was Walker's old team, Dalry Primrose; and he worked as a tinsmith for Alder & Mackay in Stewart Terrace, the same shop where Bobby learned his trade. He had a trick shoulder, which was always slipping out: he cursed it as a nuisance, never suspecting that one day it would likely save his life.

Sinclair, Wattie, Dawson and Wilson were four gifted forwards, in search of a decent inside-left. McCartney found him in Fife, turning out for Kirkcaldy's Raith Rovers – an asthmatic dental student by the name of Harry Graham. Graham, an Edinburgh-born Hearts supporter, had played in the same Junior international team as Peter Nellies. Quick, mobile and deceptive, he packed a powerful shot in both feet. Previous Tynecastle regimes had overlooked him, citing the asthma as a barrier to progress. Again McCartney was unimpressed. 'If the lad can play, then he plays for Hearts,' he told the press.

Neil Moreland, a stocky centre-forward, arrived from Pumpherston Rangers as back-up for Dawson. Significantly, their style of play was almost identical. The manager was planning an extended assault on Celtic's dominance of the Scottish game, and told the *Evening News* that he wanted 'a good understudy for every position, a man who can come in and play his part according to the script'. While watching Wattie weave his magic for Tranent, McCartney had spotted Jimmy Speedie, a 20-year-old winger, who had already had a Tynecastle trial under James McGhee. McGhee thought he lacked confidence and sent the boy away; McCartney saw something he liked and offered him a contract. Speedie, another Boroughmuir graduate, worked as an insurance clerk. He disliked the idea of turning professional and signed on amateur terms. Some observers sneered, but as Edinburgh would shortly discover, Jimmy was a principled young man.

Jamie Low, a young Agriculture undergraduate, was also added to the squad. Born in Ayrshire in 1894, he was educated in Elgin after his parents moved up there at the turn of the century. A utility forward with pace and skill, McCartney found him playing for Edinburgh University. He was an incurable prankster. On one occasion he told several of the players that he had arranged a slap-up meal for them at the Caledonian Hotel. They should just go in and order what they wanted: he might be a wee bit late, but not to worry because he had settled with the management already. It was an affecting gesture, made in the spirit of true friendship. The players turned up and ordered the best meals in the house, only later to discover that the establishment had never heard of their host. Low tried something similar at the other end of Princes Street, where the North British Hotel had a large revolving door. Peter Nellies takes up the story:

> Jamie sang out, 'Come along in boys.' The others thought it much too flash a place for them, and said so, but Jamie persisted and led the way in. Imagine the plight of the other fellows when they found themselves inside and discovered that their leader was nowhere to be seen! We were as happy and harmonious a family as you could come across anywhere. Pleasant associations we had, both in the pavilion at Tynecastle and out of it. You see we were all pals; even after we quitted the ground, it was quite the usual thing for us all to gather together.

McCrae might have called it *esprit de corps*: McCartney told *The Scotsman* he was 'proud' – the manager as mother-hen, perhaps. Another of his signings, Alfie Briggs, said 'it was the best bunch of lads you could imagine'. Briggs was 'kidnapped' from Clydebank Juniors in 1913. After starring in the international against Wales at Tynecastle, McCartney locked him in the dressing-room until he agreed to shake hands on a contract. The riveter from Partick was the bravest man in the team, a half-back who could tackle like a train. Together, he and Mercer were impossible to pass. Beside them, on the flanks, were Crossan and his partner Duncan Currie.

Currie was a hairdresser to trade. He was born in Kilwinning in 1892. When McCartney was manager of St Mirren, Duncan's elder brother, Sam, was making a name for himself in the Ayrshire Juniors. McCartney gave him a trial and offered to sign him at once. One of the St Mirren directors objected and the agreement was cancelled. McCartney persisted, however, and arranged that Sam would join St Mirren at the close of the season. Almost immediately the manager of Leicester Fosse stepped in and stole the lad away. There was an inconclusive SFA inquiry, and Sam's father, Robert (who was unaware of the transaction), apologised profusely to

McCartney, promising him first refusal on his *next* son, who was much the better prospect. Duncan joined Hearts as a left-winger: he was one of the quickest, strongest youngsters McCartney had ever seen and it was inconceivable that he should be omitted from the team. The manager therefore converted him to full-back. 'Another find out Gorgie way,' declared the *Evening News*.[11]

The goalkeeper (of course) couldn't make up his mind. Archibald Renwick Boyd had agreed to play for two clubs at once. Born in 1890, Archie was a shale miner from the tiny Midlothian village of Mossend. His performances in goal for Bo'ness United had attracted scouts from all over Britain, most of whom went home unimpressed. Early in 1914, however, Partick Thistle made him an offer. He accepted, but apparently forgot. A few weeks later, when McCartney came calling, he accepted his offer as well. An entertaining battle now ensued, but the Hearts boss prevailed. He also picked up Boyd's younger brother, Jimmy, who was working as a printer in West Calder. 'Young Boyd,' he told a journalist, 'puts me in mind of Bobby Walker. We will give him a chance and see if he makes the grade.'

At the close of season 1913–14 Hearts were third again: McCartney almost had the side he wanted. Elias Fürst, meanwhile, was striving to deliver a stadium to match it. The old pavilion (and its various additions) had once been described as looking like a 'country rail-halt': it was cramped, uncomfortable and dilapidated. The chairman persuaded his fellow board-members to take an almighty risk – £8,000 was set aside to fund the construction of what was hoped would be the finest grandstand in Great Britain. The famous sporting architect, Archibald Leitch, who had just completed a similar commission for Sheffield Wednesday, designed a handsome, streamlined structure, capable of seating 4,000 spectators, and incorporating a new boardroom and offices at the rear. A standing enclosure in front, sheltered by the grandstand's overhanging roof, would accommodate several thousand ticket-holders who preferred not to sit. At the same time, work was ongoing to transform the earthen embankments surrounding the pitch into properly (and safely) 'stepped' terraces. Leitch, an eternal optimist, promised that the building would be finished within budget by August. There was one important drawback. In order to raise funds for the project, McCartney would have to sacrifice a player. The supporters were terrified that Mercer might be tempted to move south. In the end, however, it was Percy Dawson, scorer of more than one hundred goals in only four seasons at the club. In February 1914 he was transferred to Blackburn Rovers for a world-record fee of £2,500. McCartney took this setback on the chin. It was Walker all over again: he had already found a replacement. In May 1914 he persuaded the directors to release £400 in order to purchase the Liverpool centre-forward, Tom Gracie.

Like most of the manager's signings, Gracie was an intelligent, good-humoured and modest young man. He was born in Yorkhill, Glasgow, in 1889, the son of a master butcher. Educated to Higher grade, he had trained for a commercial career, qualifying as a bookkeeper and working as a meat-salesman. His football career started with Shawfield Juniors; he moved on to Strathclyde FC, before joining Airdrieonians in 1907. In 1908 he was transferred to Hamilton; in 1909 he joined Morton. In 1911 he was named as a reserve for the Scotland team that faced England at Goodison Park, and signed for Everton immediately after the match. The following season he moved across the city to Liverpool, where (it was said) his clever style of play was too 'scientific' for his teammates. When he arrived in Edinburgh he told the press that he had felt 'unappreciated' in the south and that he was glad to be home. McCartney, meanwhile, was shaking hands with himself: Gracie was the last piece of his 'perfect combination'.

That summer the new centre was included in the party for Hearts' second visit to Denmark. They left Hull on the SS *Flora* on 3 June, defeated the Danish international side on 7 June and dispatched a Copenhagen 'Select' two days later, before attending a grand dinner in their honour, hosted by King Christian himself. McCartney told His Majesty that the club had received 'a pressing invitation' to play a series of exhibition matches in Brazil the following year, but that they hoped to return to Europe in 1916.[12] Some of the players remained on the Continent afterwards for a short tour; they reported back for training on 21 July. Tynecastle was a building site, so McCartney had secured the use of the ground at Logie Green to prepare for the new campaign. He was confident, he told the press, that the Hearts would win the League. In an early season competition, the Dunedin Cup, there was compelling evidence that he might be right. Hearts defeated Hibernian by six goals to nothing, running through the best defence in Scotland. It was an astonishing result. Then, on 5 August, the manager lost two men to the Army. Sinclair, in particular, was cruel, but the manager remained upbeat and promoted Jamie Low. When Hearts defeated reigning champions Celtic 2–0 at Tynecastle on the opening day of the League, it was no more than he expected. Wattie was outstanding, said the papers; Gracie led the line with skill and guile. Mercer left the field with a severely injured knee.

It was Saturday, 15 August: the war was ten days old. Before the game, and at half-time, some of Pat Crossan's female admirers had held a collection for the Prince of Wales's Relief Fund at the request of Sir George McCrae. Hearts were the first sporting organisation in Britain to sanction such a move.[13] The following Monday Harry Rawson, in his new capacity as chairman of the Edinburgh TFA, arrived at Tynecastle to ask McCartney if the club would use its influence to encourage recruiting. McCartney agreed to allow the authorities access to the ground on match days in order to canvass for volunteers. On 20 August he announced that the entire playing staff would engage in weekly drill sessions at Grindlay Street Hall to prepare them for the possibility of military service. In the meantime these would be conducted by the club's reserve half-back, Annan Ness, who was a former soldier; in due course he hoped that Captain Robertson might supply one of his assistants. He extended a cordial invitation to the players of Hibernian to join in. Several accepted.

Robert Mercer was unable to participate in these sessions. His doctor had diagnosed ligament damage and ordered six weeks rest. He returned to the side in October, only to break down once again. In his absence McCartney introduced a 25-year-old half-back from Easter Road, Walter McKenzie Scott. 'Wattie', as he was known, had been at Tynecastle since 1913, learning his trade as Mercer's understudy. He was unusually quick and a well-known figure on the local sprinting circuit, where he had run Pat Crossan close on a number of occasions. As the club advanced unbeaten throughout August and September, Scott was at the heart of the defence, confounding the doubters and starring in every game. He was a 'revelation', said the *Evening News*.

Mercer, however, remained Hearts captain – the most prominent player at the most prominent club in Scotland. The anti-football movement found its target, and he began to receive letters advising him to enlist. Some were friendly, some were cold. Some were downright sinister. Gracie was suffering too. On the morning of the match against Queen's Park at Hampden on 24 October, he opened an envelope to find a copy of the *Punch* cartoon that was inspired by Mr Charrington's campaign. There was no signature.[14] The centre scored a goal that afternoon, but was clearly out of sorts. Speedie got the other in a 2–2 draw: it was only the third point dropped that season.

The players were drilling twice weekly now: Hearts and Hibs together. Many of their unenlisted supporters, meanwhile, had joined the Edinburgh Military Training Association under solicitor Herbert Warden, who had severed his early connection with the Provost's Battalion over the contentious issue of 'enrolment'. Warden had already visited Tynecastle in order to secure the club's approval for his scheme.[15] 'EMTA' posters were now displayed liberally around the ground, along with those of Lord Kitchener and the Scottish regiments. The board had granted 'unrestricted access to the authorities before, during and after matches for the purpose of recruiting'. On Saturday, 14 November, Hearts, who remained comfortable leaders of the League, entertained Falkirk. In that morning's *Glasgow Herald* Tom Forsyth of Airdrie had cast grave doubt on War Office support for the game. Other papers carried speculation about the introduction of compulsory registration for military service. If it sounded like conscription, it was meant to. And of course there was black news about Ypres – the breakthrough of the Prussian Guard, the gallant stand, the dreadful losses. At half-time the Queen's Own Cameron Highlanders made an urgent appeal for volunteers: the initial response was disappointing, but come the end of the game several men stepped nervously forward. Among them was Jimmy Speedie.

'Three Hearts men with the Colours now!' announced the *Evening Dispatch*. McCartney was reported to be profoundly moved. He wrote a note to the boy's parents, explaining how much he admired him. The winger headed north to Fort George, near Inverness, where the 7th Battalion was training. On 16 November Mercer was admitted to hospital for surgery: he would not play again for some months. That same night the *Evening News* published a letter from 'Soldier's Daughter', who suggested 'that while Hearts continue to play football, enabled thus to pursue their peaceful play by the sacrifice of the lives of thousands of their countrymen, they might adopt, temporarily, a nom de plume, say "The White Feathers of Midlothian".'

White Feathers of Midlothian.

The players didn't like that one wee bit.

❋ ❋ ❋

On Thursday, 19 November a late edition of the *Evening Dispatch* briefly informed its readers that Sir George McCrae had volunteered for the Army. The following morning *The Scotsman* had more: the Colonel had, in fact, submitted an offer to the War Office to raise and command a battalion in the field. The offer being accepted, enlistment was expected to commence immediately.

McCrae on active service! George Street was besieged. At 4 p.m., to loud applause, he emerged in uniform from the door of 125. As the din died away he announced that recruiting for his battalion – the 2nd Edinburgh City – would begin on Friday, 27 November with a grand public meeting in the Usher Hall. The campaign would be short – seven days at the most – before a full complement was secured.

Seven days. The Provost had taken almost as many weeks. An incredulous murmur came up from the crowd.

'Seven days,' Sir George repeated, smiling broadly.

It was as if he knew something they didn't.

CHAPTER FOUR

'If it's football that you're wanting . . .'

Shortly after 2 p.m. on Wednesday, 25 November, eleven Hearts players enlisted in Sir George McCrae's battalion. They were Alfred Briggs, Duncan Currie, Tom Gracie, Jamie Low, Harry Wattie and Willie Wilson from the first team; and Ernie Ellis, Norman Findlay, Jimmy Frew, Annan Ness and Bob Preston from the second. Preston was a centre-half: McCartney had signed him in August as defensive cover after Mercer was injured. He worked as a coal miner in Bathgate; his cousin, Bob Malcolm, was already on Hearts' books. Ness came from Kirkcaldy. Still only 22, he was a trainee mining engineer who had spent three years in the ranks of the Royal Army Medical Corps. McCartney had spotted him in 1913, playing in the back line for Bonnyrigg Rose Athletic. Frew was another Fifer, a blacksmith from Kinghorn. He had also been at Tynecastle for a year and was Currie's main rival for the left-back position. Findlay and Ellis were close-season signings, the former a goalie from Blyth Spartans, the latter a half-back from Norwich City, one of a family of combative brothers who hailed from the Norfolk village of Sprowston.

They were gathered in the boardroom in the bowels of Mr Leitch's new grandstand, the cost of which was rising by the hour. Also present (among others) were McCrae, and the newly ennobled Sir James Leishman, chairman now of the National Health Insurance Commission for Scotland. The club was represented by Elias Fürst, John McCartney and vice-chairman, William Lorimer, one of the earliest subscribers to the 1905 share issue. There was a doctor standing by: he had examined the players and pronounced them in excellent condition, whereupon Sir James (in his capacity as a Justice of the Peace) had duly sworn them in. Soldiers they were. As Jamie Low rushed off to catch a 3 p.m. class at the University, his comrades were invited to change into their playing strips prior to meeting the press. After the obligatory photograph, it was left to McCartney to explain the astonishing events. At its last meeting, he announced, the board had decided that something should be done to 'remove the slur on the professional game'. They had approached the players and happily found them to be of the same opinion. The result was there for all to see. It was, he concluded, as simple as that. Only it wasn't – not by some considerable distance.

Sir George's letter to the War Office at the beginning of November was the product of long consideration. Not once in three months of hostilities had he spoken on the subject of recruitment. He knew that his standing was such that a single word on Lord Kitchener's behalf might deliver many thousands of men to the Colours. But how could he ask when he wasn't a soldier himself? His offer to raise a battalion, therefore, was contingent on his being allowed to lead it in the field, to share the risks of his men, to die (if fate decreed it) at their side. There would be no bargaining. Besides, he had read his history. The Jacobite, John Murray of Broughton, Charles Edward Stuart's secretary in Scotland, had once written that 'nothing has so great an effect upon brave and generous minds as when a person appears to despise their own private safety when in competition with the good of the country'.[1]

Harold Tennant's reply had been ten days in coming: the conditions were accepted, the battalion was approved. Now, of course, it only wanted raising. The Colonel, meanwhile, had received some intelligence from Inverness which indicated that Tynecastle Park (of all places) might be the perfect spot to start. His son, Kenneth, was a subaltern in the 7th Camerons: Private Speedie had been posted up to serve in his platoon.

We know roughly what was said: the pressure on his teammates was intense; Tom Gracie had almost come with him; others were considering their position.[2] Sir George was impressed. On the day before McCrae's formal announcement, John McCartney received a telephone call from Sir James Leishman, asking him if he would be prepared to meet at once in order to discuss certain pressing business. Leishman suggested his shop at 132 George Street as the venue, rather than the Insurance Commission offices in Princes Street. McCartney took a taxi into town, and was greeted with the bleakest possible description of the country's military prospects. At some point during this exchange, the door burst open.

> I am not sure [wrote the manager] whether it was accident or design that brought Sir George McCrae into the sanctum of Sir James. Be that as it may, I was asked if it were possible to get some of the Hearts players to join the battalion being raised by Sir George. It

was held that such a happening would ensure a mighty following and a quick formation of the unit. Of course I could not commit the club to anything, it being a matter primarily for the directors. The latter were called together and without hesitation left it to the players themselves to decide . . .[3]

But the players had already been approached. Harry Wattie bumped into a journalist from the *Saturday Post* in Leith Walk a day or two before he was officially consulted. He told the fellow to 'expect something shortly'.[4] Harry Lorimer, the vice-chairman's son, would later tell his daughter that Leishman had approached Gracie to find out if any of his colleagues might be willing to enlist.[5] The approach to the club, therefore, was made in the expectation of a positive outcome. The directors, however, remained unaware. By 21 November the *Evening News* was sensing something in the air. 'Thousands of men have a common bond of comradeship at Tynecastle,' declared the editorial. 'Under the auspices of Heart of Midlothian half a battalion of excellent soldiers could be raised with ease.' On 23 November McCartney met Leishman and McCrae again. This time he took his chairman with him. There was a board meeting at Tynecastle that night, and the minutes have survived:

> Chairman and Secretary reported meeting this day with Sir James Leishman and Sir George McCrae and discussing question [sic] of players joining the new Edinburgh Battalion for active service. After an exchange of views Mr Furst stated he would fetch the whole matter before his Board. The directors went fully into the state of affairs as affecting clubs, players, recruiting etc. It was ultimately the unanimous finding of the Board that no obstacle be placed in the way of any player desiring to join the colours. That should any of the players enlist, he be paid half wages when unable to play and full wages if he played during currency of [his existing] agreement. That should any or all of them return fit and well, they be re-engaged on old terms. To advise Sir James Leishman of this finding and ask him and Sir George McCrae to come out and meet the players, explain matters etc. Mr Furst also to be present and state the club's finding.[6]

Now McCartney takes it up again:

> Next morning I addressed the players in their dressing-room, informing them of the directors' decision, and asking those willing to join up to be upstanding. Practically all of them rose to their feet.

Sir George and Sir James were informed, and the same afternoon brought these gentlemen, with several other dignitaries and officials, to Tynecastle. The players were further addressed by Sir George and Sir James, Mr E.H. Furst, the chairman of directors, and others. The men adjourned to talk over the matter, and shortly afterwards returned, when, led by the modest and unassuming Tom Gracie, *sixteen* [author's italics] straightway signed the roll.[7]

Note that on this momentous day, there is no indication that the players asked any *questions*. McCartney was writing in 1921, seven years after the event, but he was almost right about the 'sixteen'.[8] In addition to the players who were accepted for service, five more were turned down on the basis of poor health. It will be recalled that Sir George had brought along a doctor. We don't know this gentleman's name, but it is greatly to his credit that he had taken the trouble to read the relevant War Office regulations. Under no circumstances were any volunteers to be accepted if they had a history of respiratory illness. These necessary instructions were often overlooked by recruiting staff: as late as March 1916, for example, the Army Council was still complaining about the enlistment of men who had suffered from tubercle of the lung.[9] Graham was excused for his asthma; Scott for rheumatic fever; Willie Aitken (reserve inside-forward from Gorebridge) for tuberculosis; and George Bryden (reserve winger from Walker in Northumberland) for a weak heart. Mercer, of course, was a cripple: there seems to have been an understanding that he would join the battalion as soon as he was fit.[10]

McCrae, however, had his men. He also had his campaign underway. Even as the players were enlisting, the local papers were publishing this appeal:

TO THE YOUNG MEN OF EDINBURGH

The present crisis is one of supreme gravity. World-wide issues are trembling in the balance. I appeal with confidence to the patriotism and generous enthusiasm of my fellow citizens. The noblest and highest duty finds expression in personal service. I say to the young men in this ancient capital of a free country: *You are Strong; Be Willing!* On you rests the awful responsibility of needlessly prolonging this devastating war. If you will only come forward in sufficient numbers you can stop the war. All cannot go, but if your home ties permit, and you shirk your obvious duty, you may escape a hero's death, but you will go through your life feeling mean. In the presence of the God of Battles, ask of your conscience this question: DARE I STAND ASIDE?[11]

Terms of Service were stated as follows:

> Age on enlistment 19 to 38. Ex-soldiers up to 45. Minimum height
> 5 foot 3 inches; chest 34 inches. Must be medically fit. General
> Service for the War. Men enlisting for the duration of the War will
> be able to claim their discharge, with all convenient speed, at the
> conclusion of hostilities.
>
> Pay at Army rates. Married men or widowers with children will
> be accepted, and if at the time of enlistment a recruit signs the
> necessary form, Separation Allowance under Army conditions is
> issuable *at once* to the wife and in certain circumstances to other
> dependents.

Interested parties were advised that recruiting would begin officially on the following Friday with a grand meeting in the Usher Hall. The battalion would comprise eight companies, in which volunteers could choose to serve according to their profession. The Colonel had secured backing from the Edinburgh & District Trades Council to raise four such companies from the ranks of builders, printers, engineers and brewers.[12] A further 'Students' company was already underway, while the local press was busy promoting the idea of a sportsman's company. McCrae also found time to address 500 veterans of the National Reserve in the Meadows to ask any unattached men if they would be prepared to add their military experience to the battalion. Miss Ethel Grant of Belgrave Crescent, meanwhile, was complaining to *The Scotsman* that newsboys were shouting 'Victory!' in connection with football matches. 'This word,' she insisted, 'should be kept sacred for favourable news from the front.' Some people, as they say, have little doing.

Next morning the papers were full of the Hearts. Messages of congratulations were pouring into Tynecastle from all over Scotland, while McCrae received telegrams from (among others) Tennant, Kitchener, Winston Churchill, Arthur Balfour, Bonar Law, H.G. Wells, John Buchan and Conan Doyle. Lloyd George wrote 'wishing you good luck in your plucky venture'. Asquith assured him that 'any help you need will be forthcoming'. By late afternoon news of the 'Edinburgh Sensation' had reached Westminster, where, following the alleged failure of the FA's special recruiting measures the previous Saturday, Sir John Lonsdale, Unionist MP for Mid Armagh, was about to confront the Prime Minister on behalf of the Charrington campaign. His timing couldn't have been worse. *Hansard* has recorded the exchange:

> Is the Prime Minister aware [opened the unfortunate Sir John] that

recruiting meetings held in connection with assemblies of men to watch football matches have produced disappointing results: and, in view of the gravity of the crisis and the need for recruits, will he introduce legislation taking powers to suppress all professional football matches during the continuance of the war?

Communications [replied Asquith] are taking place with those who are responsible for the organisation of football matches from which I hope for good results. I do not consider that a case exists for such legislation as the honourable Member suggests.

Is the right honourable Gentleman [continued Lonsdale] aware that on Saturday last, notwithstanding the most strenuous efforts at a number of football grounds attended by many thousands of people, only one recruit to the Colours was obtained?

Yes [replied Asquith], I saw that in the papers; but on the other hand, I am glad to say that in Scotland there was a very different response.

Put that in your pipe, Mr Fiend. Lonsdale blustered that legislation should be introduced to 'commandeer' all football grounds for military purposes, but Asquith now dismissed him with a smile: 'I would rather trust to the progress of the communications which have taken place,' he said calmly, 'and to the general good sense of all footballers.' That evening it was announced that Pat Crossan and Jim Boyd had joined their pals in what was already being called 'McCrae's Battalion'.

Crossan was an independent spirit. He had simply taken time to think the matter over. Boyd's position was more complicated. He and Archie had returned to Mossend to work out which brother was going to enlist. In the end it was Jim. Archie was engaged to be married; Jim was merely 'keeping company' with his girl, and while a marriage was expected, nothing official had yet been arranged. On 26 November, therefore, McCrae got two more men. By the end of the following night, he'd have 300.

❋ ❋ ❋

The Usher Hall was packed come Friday evening – 'filled in every part', *The Scotsman* noted. The doors were opened at 7.30 p.m., but a crowd of more than 4,000, advised by the press to come early, had been gathering since late afternoon. By 7.45 a line of patriotic ladies 'some hundreds strong' could be seen queuing down one side of the auditorium to leave the premises in order to make room for the many young men who were unable to get in. Those young men who had already gained entry, meanwhile, were presented with an enrolment form and a copy of the Colonel's appeal. They were also advised that the official recruiting station was already open for business. Hugh Mackay from Wick, proprietor of the Palace Hotel in Castle Street, had kindly provided rooms on the first floor of his establishment, while, downstairs, on the Princes Street corner, Melrose's tea merchants had installed a giant thermometer, primed to begin recording the battalion's numerical progress at 9 p.m. precisely.

Up on the stage Sir George was unveiling another of his innovations – a life-size cardboard cut-out of a soldier, his face entirely blank, save for a single scarlet question mark. Above it hung a banner: 'Young men, are you big enough to fill this picture? Then prove it now and uphold the reputation of Edinburgh and Scotland by joining Sir George McCrae's battalion for service in the field.' Several lads, already convinced, were heading off to Castle Street at pace. McCrae then stood back as the platform party, together with Hearts' players and officials, stepped up to take their seats. An *Evening News* reporter, arriving late, wrote afterwards that he had heard the cheer in Spittal Street.

As the noise subsided, Charles Price, Liberal MP for Central Edinburgh, rose to deliver the opening address. It was a passionate speech, echoing Winston Churchill's assertion that Belgium was merely the front line of the British mainland. The Kaiser, he insisted, would not stop at Calais or London, or Birmingham or Berwick. He would hold his Court at Holyrood unless he was prevented. And he *would* be prevented. There was one man in the hall who would face him single-handed if he had to . . . (for a fraction of a second, McCartney made to stand) . . . none other than our friend Sir George McCrae.

Alexander Ure, Lord Strathclyde, Lord President of the Court of Session, Lord Justice-General for Scotland, was quick to concur. 'In the light of Sir George's example,' he said, 'it would ill become the young, strong and fit if they stood back from the fray . . .'

Before Strathclyde could get himself into further trouble, the combined brass and pipe bands of the 4th, 6th and 9th Royal Scots struck up 'Rule, Britannia' as William Paterson, Professor of Divinity at Edinburgh University, prepared to move the first of the evening's twin resolutions: 'That this Meeting of Edinburgh Citizens, in view of the European War and the momentous issues therein involved, records its belief that it is the duty of all to assist in the National Crisis, and in particular to aid in securing recruits for the armed forces of the Crown.' This was seconded by Sir Ludovic Grant, the University's Regius Professor of Public Law, who in turn was supported by James Campbell, President of the Trades Council. 'I am a man of peace,' said Mr Campbell, 'but much as I know that war is evil, much as I know that it sets worker against worker, there is today a greater evil and it cannot be permitted to prevail.'

Amid solemn murmurs of agreement, Edinburgh advocate, Patrick Ford, secretary of the Scottish Unionist Association, rose to move the second resolution: 'That this Meeting of Edinburgh Citizens pledges itself to assist in obtaining recruits for the Active Service Battalion of the Royal Scots being raised by Sir George McCrae.' Ford then explained that he would be unable to help because he was travelling north within the hour to join his own battalion. James Hogge, seconding, said that every young man had a duty to go – his only son was already away; whereupon, with the resolutions carried to thunderous applause, chairman Price begged leave to interrupt. Sixty 'brave fellows', he announced, were anxious to enlist on the spot. Would any doctor present please come forward to conduct the necessary medical formalities? The meeting then resumed with the pipes, and the mournful, martial beat of Robert Burns's bloody call to arms, 'Scots Wha Hae', lately re-worded in the *Evening Dispatch* for the benefit of the new battalion:

> Who would bear a sword unsheathed
> While the guilty Kaiser breathed?
> Rise wi' vengeance steeled and teethed,
> Strike wi' George McCrae.

> Who for Britain's realm would stand,
> Fechtin' bravely man tae man?
> Freeman rise and in the van
> Gang wi' George McCrae.

For a moment Bruce's spirit seemed to hover in the air; then, as the final grace notes sounded, there came a cheer so sudden and so loud that John McCartney would later write: 'I was sitting quietly, surveying my knees and listening to the Bannockburn Address, when all at once there was a rousing ovation, the sheer power and volume of which nearly knocked me backwards off my chair. Of course you'll know it was the Colonel getting up to speak. I looked along at Mr Furst, who was seated on my left. He was trembling. I looked along at Currie on my right. He was exactly the colour of milk. Crossan, too. And poor old Harry Wattie looked quite ill. I don't believe that any of us realised until that moment what we had done.'[13]

As order was restored, a lone voice at the back of the hall shouted 'Well done, Sir George!' The Colonel set down his speech and stared into the darkness. 'This is not a night for titles,' he replied. 'I stand before you humbly as a fellow Scot. Nothing more and nothing less. You know I don't speak easily of crisis, but that is what confronts us. I have received permission from the War Office to raise a new battalion for active service.

It is my intention that this unit will reflect accurately all the many classes of this famous capital, and that it will be characterised by such a spirit of excellence that the rest of Lord Kitchener's Army will be judged by our standard. Furthermore, with the agreement of the authorities, I have undertaken to lead the battalion in the field. I would not – I could not – ask you to serve unless I share the danger at your side. In a moment I will walk down to Castle Street and set my name to the list of volunteers. Who will join me?'

And with that he was away, out the door and down the hill. The Usher Hall decanted in his wake. By midnight nearly 300 men had enlisted. The Palace Hotel was besieged. All through the weekend, the story was the same: Sir George obtained permission from the Moderator of the General Assembly, Reverend Tom Nicol, to recruit on the Sabbath. 'If our brave lads are fighting and dying on a Sunday,' said Professor Nicol, 'then we cannot refrain from strengthening their ranks on that same sacred day.'

On Saturday, sacred to some for entirely different reasons, Hearts maintained their excellent form with a 3–1 win at Hamilton. Wilson, Gracie and Graham were the scorers, but Harry Wattie was again the star. They returned to Edinburgh by train and found the Colonel at Waverley Station passing out recruiting cards and handbills. Gardiner Sinclair, proprietor of printers and stationers, Dobson, Molle & Co., had placed his St Clair Street workshops at Sir George's disposal to the tune of 500 guineas. David McBeth Sutherland, meanwhile, a lecturer at the Art College, had designed what *The Scotsman* described as 'several eye-catching posters', which were turning up in unexpected places. Sutherland – known as 'D.M.' to his many friends – had cheekily placed one outside William Robertson's office in Cockburn Street. 'Oh, it's not done,' complained the captain to the *Evening Dispatch*. 'It's not done at all.'

By Monday morning the battalion was half full: 520 men had come forward. McCrae had received 400 applications for only 30 commissions. The thermometer was broken (but not beyond repair); the Castle Street staff were exhausted; and Messrs Furst (who had dropped the *umlaut* in an attempt to look less German) and McCartney were busy composing a letter to the press:

> The Board of Directors of Heart of Midlothian Football Club hereby make a strong appeal to their supporters to join Sir George McCrae's Battalion. It is the earnest desire of the directors that an entire 'Hearts Company' be formed of players, ticket-holders and general followers. The players have shown the way and it is now up to the other sections named to complete the requisite number. For the information of intending recruits, be it noted that the

recruiting office is situated at 1 Castle Street. Heart of Midlothian applicants are requested to state when enlisting that they wish to be included in the Hearts Company.

Now then, young men, as you have followed the old club through adverse and pleasant times, through sunshine and rain, roll up in your hundreds for King and Country, for right and freedom. Don't let it be said that footballers are shirkers and cowards. As the club has borne an honoured name on the football field, let it go down in history that it also won its spurs on the field of battle.[14]

It appeared on Tuesday morning with predictable results. Sir George was among the first to respond, submitting his application to McCartney by letter. 'Being an old Hearts man myself,' the Colonel wrote, 'I could hardly stand aside.'

But Sir George's biggest problem lay in simply standing still. He was everywhere that week, often speaking at several meetings in quick succession. Early Monday evening, shortly after seeing son Kenneth off to Aldershot with the Camerons, he was at the Calton Hotel on the North Bridge, introducing his recruiting committee, including chairman, Sir James Leishman; secretary, Councillor Frank Robertson; and Fred Lumley, the former lightweight amateur boxing champion of Scotland.[15] Less than an hour later, he was up at the Old College in the South Bridge, persuading representatives of the University and Heriot-Watt Training College to refund the fees of any student who wished to enlist in his proposed 'University Company'. Lunch-time on Tuesday was split between Tanfield, where he addressed employees of printing firm, Morrison & Gibb; and Fountainbridge, where a similar mission to the North British Rubber works produced 14 volunteers on the spot. Less successful was his afternoon visit to Easter Road Stadium, where an appeal to the players of Hibernian was largely ignored. Only one man came forward – left-back Sandy Grosert, who had already applied to join the RASC as a driver. 'There is something lacking at Easter Road,' commented the *Evening News*, failing to add that Hibs had only 15 signed players, and most of them were married. Easter Road supporters, meanwhile, were flocking to Sir George's standard. One of them, Harry Swan, a young apprentice baker from Bonnington Road, would later serve as the club's most celebrated chairman. For the moment, he had trouble with his feet.[16]

Tuesday afternoon saw the arrival of seven Raith Rovers professionals – captain James Logan; backs George McLay, Willie Porter and Willie Lavery; and forwards Jimmy Scott, Jimmy Todd and Jock Rattray. Wednesday morning brought six players from Falkirk FC – John Morrison, Michael Gibbons, Frank Reilly, Bobby Wood, Alex Henderson and Andy Henderson, the former Hearts goalkeeper. These enlistments were the product of yet more McCrae diplomacy, a grand meeting of East of Scotland football clubs at Tynecastle Park on 26 November, which would continue to bear fruit for several days. On Wednesday afternoon the Hearts Company was further strengthened by eight members of Edinburgh Nomads, a mid-week Amateur League side made up mainly of young shop assistants. It was half-day closing and they had been playing down at Inverleith Park, when James Hogge, who was covering almost as many miles as McCrae, appeared on the touchline and persuaded them to accompany him to Castle Street. Without changing out of their strips, they marched up through Stockbridge and the New Town to be met at the Palace Hotel by a similar procession comprising 20 members of the Young Scots Society, all senior students from Broughton Higher Grade School, led by their bespectacled mathematics teacher (and fellow member), Peter Ross. Ross was a genius, the author of a standard work on algebra, and presently engaged in a definitive study of the Highland Clearances with a view to publishing in 1915. He expected presently to succeed to the headship of Broughton when the current incumbent retired. Born in Thurso in 1876, he had a strong Caithness accent, a wife called Alice, three children, and a reputation as a radical. 'Mr Ross's opinions on Land Reform are well established,' observed *The Scotsman* rather primly. Mr Ross – known familiarly as 'Wee Pe'er' on account of his native glottal stop – was 5 ft 3 in. tall.

That night McCrae attended a recruiting meeting at Tynecastle Parish Church Hall. Tom Gracie and Wattie Scott were on the platform with John McCartney. Next morning Scott quietly joined the queue at Castle Street in the hope of slipping past a different doctor. He was disappointed, however. 'It was the same man,' he later said. 'It was the same blinking man.' He would continue his efforts to join up, but he never spoke again on behalf of the battalion.[17]

On Thursday the Colonel addressed dinner-hour meetings at Younger's Brewery in Abbeyhill and Miller's Foundry in London Road. He was on the Mound that afternoon with Private Crossan. Several men stepped forward there: one of them was obviously married. 'Have you got *bairns*?' Pat enquired. The man nodded. 'Well then, dinnae be sae daft,' came the reply.[18] By the close of recruiting at 10 p.m. that night, 850 men had volunteered, including Gerald Crawford, 46-year-old Labour councillor for St Giles Ward. With no previous military experience of any kind, Crawford was seven years over the official age limit. He was a partner in a successful George Street engineering consultancy and lived with his three spinster sisters in a flat in Windsor Street. He had never married, possibly because he didn't have the time. Among his numerous commitments were membership of the National Executive of the Federation for Women's

Suffrage and chairmanship of the Edinburgh Federation of the Scottish Socialist Party. He was also conductor of the Edinburgh Symphony Orchestra, editor of the *Musical Star* and a member of the National Executive of the Amalgamated Musicians Union. A prolific composer, he was currently working on an untitled 'symphonic poem' which he hoped would portray 'the pomp and panoply of war'. He told the clerks at Castle Street that he would prefer, if possible, to serve in the ranks.

At this point *The Scotsman* noted the 'serious disposition of most of the enquirers'. Questions were being asked about length and terms of service, about the supply of uniforms and equipment, and (particularly) about dependents' allowances. Tommy Palmer, an apprentice boot-maker from Leith Street Terrace, was a fortnight short of his 17th birthday. He had lost his father two months earlier. Now his mother was dying and he was responsible for his eldest sister, Annie, and six younger siblings. The parish council was trying to have the children put into separate homes. Tommy calculated that Army pay (with allowances for the youngsters) would provide Annie with sufficient funds to keep the family together. He enlisted just a week before his mother passed away.

On Friday night McCrae was at the Oddfellows' Hall in Forrest Road with Lord Anderson and Tom Gracie. He announced that pressure on the Palace Hotel was so great that he was opening a second recruiting station. The Gladstone Liberal Club in Henderson Terrace was handily placed for Tynecastle Park, where (coincidentally) the first 'Derby' match of the season was scheduled for the following day. The Colonel had already circulated existing enlistments with a postcard:

> The Directors of the Heart of Midlothian Football Club have kindly offered to grant FREE ADMISSION to the match at Tynecastle to-morrow (Saturday), 5th inst., to those who have enrolled in the new Service Battalion being raised by Sir George McCrae. Sir George McCrae will be glad if you will 'fall in' at the foot of Ardmillan Terrace at 1.45 p.m.[19]

Eight hundred men took up the invitation. At two o'clock, preceded by the pipe band of the 9th Royal Scots, Sir George led them into Tynecastle, where they gathered in the enclosure underneath the new stand. Sir James Leishman was there, and *The Scotsman* spotted Harry Rawson in the crowd. Thunder, rain and hailstones greeted the teams, but Hearts were undeterred: their 'dainty, dazzling forward play' would tear the Hibs apart. At half-time McCrae marched his men round the touchline, where they were joined by several new volunteers, among them a diminutive 21-year-old gasfitter from Buchanan Street, James Stirling Brown. 'Wee Jimmy', who was barely 5 ft tall, had an unusually fine opinion of himself. He would turn up at Castle Street the following day and lie about his height. It is entirely likely that none of the assembled clerks, doctors and Justices of the Peace had the nerve to disagree with him.

During the second half, one of Crossan's clearances struck the skin of the band's base drum, leading (said the *Evening News*) to 'numerous comments of an ironical nature'. Wattie, Gracie and Low scored in a fine 3–1 victory. After the game Michael Kelly, a big easy-going Irishman, who tended the Meadows bowling greens on behalf of the Corporation, returned to his home at Boroughloch Square and informed his wife, Kitty, that he had enlisted in 'McCrae's' (as the battalion was now colloquially known). Kitty was preparing kippers at the time for the couple's three children: fish, frying-pan and expletives flew across the room, but the Colonel had another volunteer.[20] That same evening in Portobello, Councillor Crawford addressed a meeting at the Town Hall. Jimmy Hawthorn was there with some companions; they had been celebrating Hearts' win in the usual style. Hawthorn, 38, was a former Tynecastle player, a back-line partner of the great Charlie Thomson and a drinking pal of Bobby Walker's. He was currently employed as a contractor at the Prestongrange Brickworks, near Prestonpans. Moved to tears by Crawford's example, the lads repaired to Edinburgh, vowing to enlist together and never be parted like the good comrades that they were. Several hours then vanished in an alcoholic haze: when Jimmy woke up in the morning, he was the only one of the group who had gone through with his promise. There was no getting out of it now.[21]

That weekend brought in more than 200 men. Harry Lorimer, son of the Hearts vice-chairman, had joined up on Saturday morning. He was married (quite devotedly, to Isa) and worked as a lithographer at W. & A.K. Johnston's Edina Works in Easter Road. He was also one of the best-known referees in the East of Scotland Junior League. His daughter, Jane, was eight years old, and would later recall her mother's reaction: 'I'm not wanting you to go, but if you feel you have to, I will be with you all the way.'[22] Lorimer must have been at Castle Street when the Mossend boys arrived from Waverley Station. Jimmy Boyd's old team, Mossend Burnvale, had been newly promoted to the Junior level that very season. They were something of a Hearts 'nursery' side, and included Jimmy's cousin, Bob Boyd, whose father had starred for Everton and Scotland. They were known locally as the 'Cow-punchers' because they played their home games on an unkempt grazing field owned by the local doctor – which doctor, incidentally, was the father of Jimmy's sweetheart. Early Saturday morning ten of them travelled in to enlist, accompanied by some followers and committee member, William ('Wull') McArthur, 39-year-old secretary of the Scottish Oilworkers' Association. McArthur and most of his laddies (as he called them) were shale miners, employed in Crossan's home village of Addiewell by Young's Paraffin Light and Mineral Oil Company. Wull had a wife and five surviving children: the decision to join up did not come easily.

By Monday morning the thermometer indicated a battalion total of 1,120 volunteers, easily passing the original target of 1,008. The War Office, however, had now instructed Sir George to increase the number to 1,350 *plus* around 45 officers. The War Office also confirmed that the Provost's Battalion, which had been provisionally listed as a unit of the King's Own Scottish Borderers, would now be entitled the 15th Royal Scots. McCrae's, therefore, were taken on the strength of Lord Kitchener's Army as the 16th (Service) Battalion. The '16th Royal Scots' was official, but the lads knew which name they preferred. They were raised as McCrae's, they would fight as McCrae's. They would die, when the moment arrived, as McCrae's. During the following week, the men from the regions came in – the Bathgate and Armadale contingents (mostly coal miners), the boys from Kirknewton and Duns; an entire platoon from Penicuik, the paper-making town just south of Edinburgh. And finally the Dunfermline contribution – around 100 young lads from Sir George's old haunt, raised by local architect Stewart Kaye, who had already been promised a precious commission. They were mostly linen factory employees, but the group also included shop workers and railway servants, along with some miners from Buckhaven and Coaltown of Wemyss. And there were two representatives of Dunfermline Athletic FC: David Izatt, a half-back who made his living as a plumber, and Jimmy Morton, a cloth lapper at the Albany Linen Works, who sat on the management committee. On Friday, 12 December, as discussions opened in London to inaugurate an English 'Footballers' Battalion', Sir George declared recruiting closed.[23] That same day every volunteer received a letter in the post:

> The Battalion will fall in on TUESDAY *next*, 15th December, at twelve o' clock noon, opposite the Club, 111 George Street, or, if wet, in the Waverley Market, Edinburgh. You had better bring with you one pair good Boots, Topcoat, one Shirt, two pairs Socks, and Shaving Outfit.[24]

It was their mobilisation instructions.

❀ ❀ ❀

George Street was impassable. The crowds had started to gather shortly after 9 a.m.; two hours later one hundred constables (noted *The Scotsman*) were not enough to keep them off the carriageway and they had pressed forward on all sides to within touching distance of the battalion, which was drawn up opposite the Assembly Rooms in two long, overcoated columns. It was cold, but bright and very breezy. Sir George was mounted, uniformed, and *armed* – as if he expected the Prussian hordes to come marching up Hanover Street to threaten his boys before he'd got them ready for the fight.

Sandy Yule was shouting. He was a 34-year-old hose-maker at the Castle Mills factory of the North British Rubber Company, with a wife and daughter at home in West Fountain Place. Thirteen years earlier he had spent eight months in Caterham as a private in the Scots Guards before being discharged unfit. He was therefore one of the Colonel's prized ex-regulars, and had been allotted a platoon of around 30 men to shepherd through the day. Every time he got his charges settled, however, some relative or friend in the crowd would call out a name. Politeness demanded a reply; handshakes would follow, and within seconds his carefully dressed ranks would dissolve once again into sociable chaos. The Tynecastle lads were signing autographs: Sandy offered rather hoarsely to autograph some backsides with his boot, and order was eventually restored.[25]

On the stroke of 12, led by the combined pipe bands of the 5th and 9th Royal Scots, McCrae's moved off – slowly at first, picking up the beat of the drums, turning left into Charlotte Square, then left again into Princes Street, where every window, every balcony, every inch of pavement to the north and to the south was packed with cheering citizens. Just past the Palace Hotel the pipes struck up 'Sir George McCrae', a march commissioned by the recruiting committee and currently on sale at a penny a sheet for the benefit of battalion funds. The author, Tom Terrett, district manager of the Liverpool Victoria Friendly Society, was said to be particularly proud of his lyrics:

> Hark to the call! ye noble Scots,
> Hark to the call to-day;
> Our Country's need is what we plead,
> The 'Hearts' have led the way.
> And 'Paddy Crossan' took the bob,
> In the King's Own to play;
> A good round seven out of eleven,
> That's fine, Sir George McCrae.
> All hail, all hail, all hail, all hail,
> All hail! Sir George McCrae.[26]

There are another four (equally remarkable) verses, each ending in a chorus of 'All hails'. Up ahead on his horse, a pretty little chestnut mare, the eponymous hero was probably in pain. He much preferred Peter Ross's pawky version of 'Hey, Johnnie Cope', directed, by way of gentle warning, at the Kaiser:

> Hey, Billy boy, are ye waukin yet?
> Ye'll think the war's been won, I'll bet.
> But your soldier men will be beat, ye ken,
> When they meet wi McCrae's in the morning.[27]

One last turn — to the right at the Waverley Bridge — and the battalion disappeared for an inaugural steak-pie lunch in the vast, vaulted 'Market' next to the railway station. An hour later, full up with seconds, they emerged into daylight, retraced their steps along Princes Street (where most of the crowds had remained) and set off via Lothian Road, Tollcross and Lauriston Place for their new home at George Heriot's School.

McCrae had originally set his heart on the magnificent seventeenth-century Heriot's Hospital, which would have afforded ample shelter for all his men under one roof. Forbye it would be 'fitting', he had argued — an exceptional billet for an exceptional battalion. The governors of Heriot's Trust disagreed. They were willing, however, to let him have the adjoining Victorian Examination Hall and the modern Drawing-Class rooms, together with access after school hours to the swimming pool and gymnasium.[28]

Sir George was disappointed. Even at its fullest the Hall would sleep only 500 men. He had noticed, though, that the Trust owned the former Castle Brewery at Hunter's Close in the Grassmarket, and that the rugged four-storey building stood just below the back wall of the school playground. Impressing the governors with the sheer fortuitous logic of it all, he succeeded in getting the brewery as well and set to at once in order to render it habitable. The entire interior was lime-washed, electric lighting was installed, along with plumbed-in sinks and flushing latrines. The ground floor was fitted out with a kitchen and sufficient tables and chairs to accommodate 400 men at a sitting, while the upper levels were converted into dormitories with 300 straw-mattressed trestle beds each. Finally, to connect the two disparate halves of the new lodgings, a wooden footbridge was constructed between the brewery's top floor and the aforementioned playground, where a separate cookhouse and storage sheds had been built to service the Exam Hall. It was not, of course, the Hospital, but it was by anybody's standards an exceptional billet.

On 23 December the battalion attended a special performance of *Jack and the Beanstalk* at the King's Theatre. The usual pantomime script was heavily laced with military allusions. Halfway through the second act, when Jack struck his sword against the mighty portals of the Giant's castle, the gates swung open to reveal none other than the Colonel himself. Stepping to the front of the stage, he recited a short verse which had been presented to him by George Blaney, a 35-year-old Bristo housepainter and one of the first of the Castle Street volunteers.

> Do not ask where Hearts are playing and then look at me askance.
> If it's football that you're wanting, you must come with us to France!

That night in the Brewery the men slept sound and dreamed of wizards and maidens and magical deeds. In the morning when they woke, they had their uniforms. Merlin, it seemed, was a Tynecastle man. Well maybe not quite: Harry Lorimer unburdened himself to Isa:

> Well, Mrs L. What next? You'll be visiting your husband in the Calton Jail at this rate. Last evening we paid a visit to St Leonard's and came away with four good lorryloads of khaki cloth intended for a battalion in the south. Sir George McCrae had spoken, and his words revealed that our need was the greater and he knew the watchman. So there we were, twelve upstanding men of excellent repute (including an advocate, a schoolmaster and two writers) creeping about like footpads in the night. Not that we are common lock-pickers, mind, for the Colonel brought his crowbar. Yes, I'm in with the right crowd now, Edina's chosen sons. Anyway you will shortly be reading that McCrae's will have their uniforms by Christmas, and fine suits we're promised, for the cloth is just first class . . .[29]

St Leonard's was a goods yard, owned by the North British Railway Company. A few days later the *Evening Dispatch* helpfully pointed out that 'the battalion had been clothed to the last button thanks to the business capacity and skilful hustling of the Chairman of the Territorial Force Association, Harry Rawson. Without him and the intimate personal knowledge which enabled him to carry through the contract, they might have been waiting for weeks.' Note that no one was asking where the khaki had come from: khaki was like gold dust. There was a national scarcity. The Provost's Battalion was still parading round the city in its navy 'emergency serge', while some units south of the border had been wearing their civvies since August. The 'contract' in question was rushed through in record time using Territorial Army pattern-books and the services of various local penal institutions. The Trades Council was appalled, but still no one wondered whence the khaki had come. Or, indeed, 4,000 assorted pairs of ammunition boots, which appeared on Christmas morning at the Brewery. Mr Rawson is no longer available to comment.

At noon on Christmas Day the uniforms received their first official airing, when the battalion marched out in fours for a brisk tour of the city centre. *The Scotsman* remarked on their smartness, but Pte Andrew Smith later recalled that many of the tunics did not fit.[30] It was a detail, however, that would be sorted in time. Led now by their own kilted pipe band, which had been equipped by several generous local subscribers, they headed west along Lauriston Place towards Tollcross, turned down Lothian Road, then took in Princes Street, the Bridges, Nicolson Street, Hope Park Terrace, Buccleuch Street and Bristo before returning to Heriot's, where, divided between the Brewery, the Exam Hall and the Hospital dining room, they awaited their seasonal lunch.

Three venues and three courses. Sir George devised a plan. He would take his soup at the Brewery, his turkey at the Hall, his pudding at the Hospital – thereby doing his duty by the entire battalion and avoiding any charges of favouritism. The soup at the Brewery was fine; owing, however, to some confusion over timing, he was obliged to take it again at the Hall. Having disposed of his turkey, he assumed that the Hospital would by now have had its pudding; so he took a plateful where he was, then strolled across the playground to present his apologies. To his dismay the Hospital had only just finished its soup. Another turkey dinner later – and another pudding – he retired to a small room next to the Exam Hall which he had furnished as his office. There was a radiator, a desk, and a chair with a cushion. He closed the door behind him and sat down.

On the desk was a parcel, handed in that morning and as yet unopened. He untied the string and found a revolver with a note, which read: 'I am a minister in Leith. One of my parishioners has given me this to pass on to you. It served him well in the late campaign against the murderers of General Gordon, and he hopes earnestly that you will one day use it to account for one of the modern assassins as well.' Just then a car drew up outside. He opened the door. A small elderly woman was tugging at something – the Greatest Dane he had ever seen. 'This,' she said at length, 'is Jock.'

'Jock,' replied Sir George.

'Jock,' said the woman, handing him the chain. 'You'll be needing a mascot.'

With that she took her leave. She gave no name, no address, no advice on diet. She simply whispered to her driver and departed. Sir George closed the door, retook his seat and tied the chain around the chair-leg just in case. Jock surveyed his new surroundings, yawned, then curled up on the floor and went to sleep.[31]

The Colonel closed his eyes: a mascot wasn't quite what he was thinking. Now if only she had brought an RSM.

CHAPTER FIVE

'Marching wi Geordie'

❊Frederick Francis Andrew Muir was born in Machynlleth, Montgomeryshire, in December 1884, the son of Charles Muir, a peripatetic surveyor employed by the Ordnance Service. Raised and educated in Warrington, Lancashire, he began his working life at 15 as a foundry labourer. In April 1904 he walked into the local Army recruiting office and filled out Form B.217, committing himself to a 'Short Service' engagement of three years with the Colours. The regiment he chose was the Gordon Highlanders.[1]

In 1906 Fred extended his engagement to nine years; but in May 1908 he obtained an early discharge by paying the sum of £25 to the adjutant at Edinburgh Castle. He emerged with a pair of corporal's stripes, a good character and a wife called Rose, whom he had married twelve months earlier in the city of Cork. By 1914 he had three children and was living at Pinkie Road in Musselburgh, where he worked as a coal miner. He joined McCrae's at Castle Street on 28 November and (having declared his previous military service) was promoted to corporal on Christmas Day. One week passed, then on 3 January 1915 Sir George McCrae appointed him Regimental Sergeant-Major.

There were other candidates. The Colonel's appeal to the National Reserve had brought in about 30 old soldiers, several of whom had seen fighting on the North-West Frontier or the Veld. John Muirhead was discharged from the Royal Scots in December 1913 as a Colour Sergeant with 21 years' service. Cecil Neill left the Highland Light Infantry in February 1913 with 14 years' service. Tom McManus left the Royal Munster Fusiliers in February 1914 with 12 years' service. Dan Purcell left the Royal Scots in October 1913 with 12 years' service. These men were vastly more experienced than Muir, but they lacked what one officer would later describe as 'his commanding presence'.[2]

In the regular battalions of the Royal Scots, new recruits were welcomed into a regimental family that had existed for three centuries. They arrived periodically in manageable numbers and were inducted into an established structure in which rank was earned over many years of service. McCrae's Battalion had 1,400 new recruits and no established structure of any kind. Muir's unenviable task was to instil pride, discipline (and what the General Staff's 1914 *Infantry Training* manual called 'soldierly spirit') into a body of men with no previous communal history, who ranged in age from 15 to 54 and boasted every conceivable background from senior civil servant down to Corporation scavenger.[3] Donald Gunn was a journalist on the New York *Herald Tribune*. He came home to Edinburgh on vacation in July 1914 and decided to stay for the war. He joined McCrae's because he was a Hearts supporter; he was appointed a quartermaster-sergeant because he could type. 'I don't know how the RSM did it,' he later wrote. 'He drilled us and marched us and put us to bed. Then one morning we woke up as the finest regiment in the whole of Lord Kitchener's Army.'[4]

There was no help from the War Office. Early in January Sir George had received a letter instructing him that all battalions would now be formed on regular lines, with four companies instead of the expected eight. His recruiting campaign had been founded on the promise to volunteers that they would be allowed to serve with their pals or workmates in the company of their choice – sportsmen, printers, brewery and distillery workers, builders and joiners, public service employees, students, and men from the counties. In the fortnight since mobilisation these self-contained units had already started to develop their own peculiar *esprit de corps*, their own rivalries, their own informal leadership structures. All this would now be sacrificed in order to conform.

Four companies then – A, B, C and D – each comprising four platoons of 60 men apiece, numbered from 1 to 16. Each platoon was in turn divided into four *sections*, the basic unit of training and of fighting. A Company, composed almost exclusively of students, teachers, solicitors, bankers, civil servants and clerks, was billeted on the first floor of the Brewery. B Company, with its mix of Edinburgh artisans, dominated by employees of the city's great printing and publishing houses, was on the second. C Company, with its 30 professional footballers, more than 60 top-class Juniors, and 170 of the near-600 Hearts supporters who had responded to the directors' appeal, was on the third. The remaining 400 or so applicants for the proposed Hearts Company were now distributed throughout the battalion.

D Company, including the Dunfermline and Penicuik men, were in the

Exam Hall — along with around 200 of Sir George's unsuccessful commission applicants, who had agreed to form themselves into an 'Officer's Reserve' for the rest of the New Army. McCrae's own officers — some 45 in all — were quartered in two vacant houses on the north side of George Square, from where Herbert Warden, lately installed as the Colonel's second-in-command, wrote on 5 January:

> We are quite comfortable here, if a little crowded. Sir George has kindly arranged for us to have our own bugler to play reveille every morning sharp at six. We are usually up before the fellow arrives, so we see him shambling down the hill, doing up his tunic and tugging at his greatcoat. Round the front he stands on the pavement outside the main door, hands blue, face a frightful shade of pink, and blows so loud he is like to wake the dead. I can hardly look our neighbours in the eye.[5]

McCrae selected Warden because he knew him. There was no time for probation. His officers, therefore, were almost all known quantities. Third-in-command was Dick Lauder, who owned and managed A. & R. Scott Ltd, of Colinton and Dunblane, the famous porridge makers. Lauder had spent three years as a lieutenant in the 4th Volunteer Battalion of the Argylls. Warden had put in nine years with the Volunteers and the 4th Royal Scots before he resigned his captaincy in 1912 to concentrate on his legal practice.

As adjutant, with responsibility for day-to-day administration, Sir George chose 24-year-old William Berry Robertson, son of Sir William Robertson, chairman of the Scottish Liberal Association. Sir William, one of the Colonel's oldest friends, was proprietor of the St Margaret's linen works in Dunfermline; William junior had joined the company in 1907 and was now a director. As quartermaster, with responsibility for quartering, rations, equipment and supply, Sir George chose 30-year-old Andrew Whyte, chief clerk to the steward at the Royal Infirmary of Edinburgh. Whyte, another former Volunteer, had served as a sergeant in the Queen's Edinburgh Rifles.

For his four company commanders the Colonel picked a minister of the Kirk, an advocate, a rubber planter and a mechanical engineer. The minister was Alfred Warr, a 25-year-old assistant at Portland Park Church in Hamilton. He had served as a subaltern in the 4th Royal Scots while attending Edinburgh University. The advocate was another Edinburgh graduate, 34-year-old Napier Armit, who enlisted in the battalion as a private and had to be talked into leaving the ranks. The rubber planter was 25-year-old Lionel Coles, son of the Chief Surveyor to the Scottish Board of Agriculture. Coles had joined the Regular Army after leaving George

Watson's College, becoming a second lieutenant in the Border Regiment. He resigned within the year, however, and sought his fortune in the Malay States, where he had been working since 1910. He and around 100 other young Britons had shipped home on the outbreak of war at their own expense. The engineer was James Hendry, a 34-year-old Merchiston-educated Dundonian. Hendry had served his apprenticeship in Glasgow, then worked for some years in America; he returned home in 1908 to set up a consultancy in Rochdale before moving to Birkenhead, where he enlisted in August as a private in the 17th Battalion of the (King's) Liverpool Regiment. A keen sportsman, he had read about McCrae's in his local paper and wrote Sir George in person to apply for a commission.

Among the subalterns were several familiar names: Professor Lodge's giant son, Cuthbert; Peter Ross; and Harry Rawson's nephew, (also) Harry, a solicitor's clerk from Burnley in Lancashire. The rest were mainly young men who had served their time in the undergraduate Officer Training Corps or the Cadet Force of Edinburgh's various 'foundation' private schools. Most of the warrant officers and sergeants were drawn from Sir George's handful of former regulars. There were also around a hundred recruits with Territorial or Volunteering backgrounds; and numerous former members of the Boys' Brigade, whose spiritual training included some elements of military discipline. Donald Gunn, who was doing a little freelance work on the side, described life at Heriot's for the readers of the *Evening News*:

> During the first week or two the acting sergeants had a trying time getting the lazy ones to leave the comfort of their blankets. The command of 'show a leg' was looked on as a piece of humour and the funny men would push the blankets to one side to fulfil the command literally. The volunteer does not take long to learn, however, and nowadays the bugle call brings the Battalion from bed instantly.[6]

The bugle call was followed by a visit to the 'ablution benches'. D.M. Sutherland, the Colonel's poster artist, now a private in A Company, described the routine in a letter to a friend in Wick:

> Up at 6 a.m., run a hundred yards in the cold dark frosty mornings with towel around neck to a tap around which about 30 men are struggling to wash – dash back, make up blankets and mattress. Parade. Breakfast 9 a.m. – kipper and two ounces white bread plus coffee.[7]

Thick white bread with very little butter. There was unlimited porridge, bacon every second day and also the occasional egg. 'Some of the lads,' Cpl John Veitch later recalled, 'had never eaten so well.'[8] The trestle beds were squared away, the barracks swept, then it was out to the playground. 'Don't laugh now,' Harry Lorimer told his wife, 'but I have a stripe already. I am a probationary lance-corporal, for reason, I am sure, of being married. I am to instruct a dozen men in the art of drill, although quite who is to instruct me, I remain uncertain.'[9]

'Squad Drill' was the correct term. 'The instructor,' said the manual, 'must be clear, firm, concise and patient; he must make allowance for the different capacities of the men, and avoid discouraging nervous recruits . . .'[10] Veitch, a letterpress machineman in civilian life, remembered the complete exasperation of his sergeant. 'He was an old soldier and to begin with we were useless. The RSM, however, Mr Muir, was not a man for shouting, so the sergeant had to count to ten and start us off again.'

Dinner was at one – a choice of 'Irish Stew' or 'Stew, Irish' (D.M. Sutherland), with soup and tea or coffee. Then it was back to the playground for more drill, followed by what the RSM euphemistically described as 'a healthy march'. Muir's route marches (pronounced 'rout' in the old British Army) were about to get serious. 'At the outset,' said Veitch, 'he was running us in.' Donald Gunn sums up the rest of the day:

> After five o' clock tea, the men have some time to themselves before the evening lectures given by their company officers. Supper, consisting of biscuits and coffee, is served at nine and the preparations for bed begin. It is about that time that the funny men make themselves heard. Everyone is trying to outdo the other in the gratuitous disbursement of what might masquerade as humour and the billets are frequently convulsed in roars of laughter. A gentle warning from the sergeant that the lights will be turned off in a few minutes is the signal for a hurried undressing, and when the Last Post is sounded the men are all between the blankets. It depends how hard the day's work has been how long they remain awake, but the hilarious laughter and good-natured banter subside to a gentle hum of conversation, which gradually fades away as Morpheus takes command.[11]

One morning Pte Crossan awoke to discover that he had been stitched into his bed.

On Saturday, 9 January, while Celtic were winning 6–1 in Glasgow, Hearts defeated Greenock Morton 1–0 at home thanks to a goal from Tom Gracie, who had been unwell for most of the week. Several of his teammates had turned out in new boots, one size bigger than normal, in order to accommodate the dressings on their blisters. The *Evening News* described their performance as 'sluggish' and wondered whether military training was 'altogether agreeing' with them. Hearts' trainer, Jimmy Duckworth, was thinking the same. He announced that in future he would be accompanying his charges on their 'country outings' in order to treat any minor injuries as and when they arose. He was 63 years old. On the day of their enlistment he made a speech to the players, explaining that he had never married and he had no children, but they were all like sons to him and he couldn't have been prouder. At club nights he used to lead off the singing with 'Dainty Little Daisy, Standing at the Bar'. Wattie Scott recalled that on Monday mornings 'Duckie' could tell at a glance which of his players had over-indulged at the weekend. Defaulters were ordered to put on three sweaters and sprint three times round the Tynecastle perimeter. Those who had behaved were allowed to jog round once.

On the following Tuesday Muir marched the battalion to Balerno. It was a cold, dark afternoon; they arrived home at 10 p.m. and were up again at 6 for more drill and physical training. 'Influenza now took hold,' said McCartney, and on 16 January, while Celtic were winning at Falkirk, Hearts went two down at home to Dundee with only half an hour remaining. Gracie got a late pair and Bryden snatched the points, but it was a poor performance. Low was missing with a high temperature, Wattie with a badly injured ankle after a fall the previous night. Currie played on regardless: 'The lad is not at all well,' admitted the manager later. To compound matters the battalion was inoculated the following Thursday and many of the men suffered severe reactions.

A freezing mist descended on the Friday. Celtic's game was cancelled and Hearts could only draw 2–2 at Third Lanark. Their lead at the top of the table was four points. As the players waited at the station for the train to take them home, Herbert Warden was sitting in front of a blazing fire in the George Square common-room, composing a letter that in part explained their sudden loss of form:

> You will have heard of our nocturnal expeditions [he wrote to his wife Jessie]. It seems that battalions at the front often have to travel considerable distances under cover of darkness. We are therefore putting in some practice. It is a tiring business, but we have learned the art of sleeping on the march. You simply shut your eyes and hope that the fellow in front has his wits about him. After a pleasant hour or so you wake to find yourself in some forlorn village chosen by the fiend Muir for its treacherous approaches. I am sure that the natives in these places consider us mad. They may be right, but we

are also very fit and getting fitter by the day. None more so than the Colonel, who I learned tonight is 54. He is a most unusual man. Last night, well-on after 10, we took a breather outside Carlops. It was very dark and there was a sharp frost, but we had brought the lamps so we could warm our hands and see at the same time. Sir George had set himself down on a milestone, when a boy from No. 8 Platoon came up and gave him good evening. To our surprise he replied with his name, then asked after the lad's parents – not in polite ignorance, you understand, but with such knowledge of the family that you might have thought him related. 'Do you know those people?' I asked him when the boy had passed. 'No,' was the reply, and nothing more. Sir George is not the man for conversation. What the Army is going to make of us with our swagger and our football and our damned informal ways, I dread to think.[12]

Carlops is 13 miles south-west of Edinburgh – at least a five-hour march to get there and five more to get home. The battalion took their breather 'well after 10'; by the time they reached Heriot's, it must have been well-on after three in the morning. Tynecastle's 'soldier footballers' (as the papers were calling them) therefore faced Third Lanark with little or no sleep. Gracie was ill again after the game. Back at the Brewery he retired to his bed and remained there through the following week, struggling up on the Saturday to lead the line against Celtic at Parkhead, where Harry Graham scored a splendid opening goal before the home side equalised with the help (said the *Glasgow Herald*) of McAtee's hand. The lead remained at 4 points; both clubs had played 27 games.

For the home game against Kilmarnock on 6 February McCartney picked the team in the dressing-room before kick-off. Briggs was poorly but insisted on playing. Wattie had flu and was confined to his parents' home; Bob Malcolm, the Loanhead coal miner, deputised and inspired the team to a 3–1 victory. The manager later told the press that of the eleven lads who took the field, only three were fit. On the plus side, however, Gracie scored the second goal and (said *The Scotsman*) looked more like himself. Celtic, meanwhile were beating St Mirren at Parkhead. No change, therefore, at the top.

On Thursday, 11 February Muir took his men to the Pentlands Hills. Late in the afternoon it started to snow heavily, and at some point the battalion got thoroughly lost. It is clear that initially the officers tried to make light of the affair, passing it off as some sort of navigational exercise or 'test'. However, as the snow continued to fall and the biting wind increased in severity, the call went out to the ranks 'for any man with local knowledge'. Two members of the Penicuik platoon, Tom Webster and John Cleghorn, both gamekeepers, stepped forward and led their comrades down to the village of Straiton. Several members of the Penicuik contingent would later tell their families that 'many lives were saved that evening'. All ranks were excused duty the following day. The day after that – Saturday – Hearts travelled to Motherwell and won 1–0. Crossan, who had spent the week in bed in Addiewell, returned to play one of his best games of the season. Mercer broke down in his comeback with the reserves and on the Sunday Duckworth's assistant, Alex Lyon, died of influenza at his home in Westfield Road. He was twenty-five and married with two children. Duckworth was none too well himself but he attended the funeral at Dalry Cemetery on 17 February. Currie and Briggs helped to carry the coffin. That same evening the battalion suffered its first loss, when David Welch, a 32-year-old solicitor from Bruntsfield Place, died of stomach cancer at Craigleith Military Hospital. He had volunteered, it was said, to save another man from going.

The following morning C Company received its second inoculation. For typhoid, this time. Two days later, Hearts went four goals down to Rangers at Tynecastle before late scores from Gracie, Low and Willie Wilson almost stole a point. Wilson missed a penalty and struck the post with a terrific drive in the final minute. McCartney later revealed that Crossan, Wattie, Currie and Briggs had been sick during the interval and only came out for the second half because there was no one else available. Celtic, meanwhile, were beating Dumbarton at Parkhead. The lead had slipped to two points with eight games remaining.

On Friday, 26 February Jimmy Frew married his sweetheart, Jeanie Campbell from Dalry Road. Frew had left the battalion in January, transferring to the Colonel's son's battery of the Royal Garrison Artillery. His best man was Sergeant Annan Ness. Donald Gunn offered this insight to his readers:

> The majority of the First League men are in the same platoon, and they are bossed not by the recognised best player, but by a reserve team half-back. Imagine, a man whose footballing talent is practically unrecognised by the powers that be in the football world supervising the pipe-claying of a stairway and the scrubbing out of a room, with some internationalists and several candidates for 'caps' wielding the scrubbing brushes and the pipe-clay.[13]

Ness had already refused a commission in order to remain with his pals in the ranks. Alfie Briggs would later write: 'He was the sort of chap you'd want to follow for the sake of not letting him down.' It was still not enough to get him promoted at Tynecastle. On 27 February

McCartney took his usual exhausted eleven to Easter Road, where Hibs held them to a 2–2 draw. The entire battalion was present to see Crossan score a fine own goal. Celtic won 2–0 at Partick: the lead was down to a single point.

On 6 March Hearts entertained Dumbarton without Harry Wattie, whose father had died mid-week. Bob Malcolm deputised again, and Tom Gracie scored three in a 4–1 win. Celtic went one better, hitting five against Hibs. The following week Hearts drew at Airdrie while Celtic's game was cancelled. The lead was two points again, but the champions now had a vital game in hand. On 20 March Hearts beat Partick 3–1 at home and Celtic were idle again. Four points, but *two* games in hand. Gracie, meanwhile, was reported to be 'extremely unwell'. He rose from his sickbed on 27 March to score Hearts' second goal in a 2–0 win over Clyde at Tynecastle and felt so poorly after the game that he was immediately admitted to the Royal Infirmary for tests and observation. Celtic defeated Raith 3–1 at Parkhead but Hearts were still in front.

On 3 April Gracie missed his first game of the season, the long trip to Aberdeen. Bob Malcolm played at centre in his place – a 'mistake', the *Evening News* decided. Wilson was missing, Wattie was ill. Neither team could score. Celtic put three past Airdrie at Parkhead and moved to within three points of the leaders. Two days later they beat Queen's Park 3–0 at Hampden in the first of their outstanding fixtures. One point behind and the remaining game in hand.

On 10 April Hearts lost 2–0 at Greenock Morton. The battalion had arrived back from night manœuvres just in time for the players to catch their train. Gracie returned, but missed a penalty, driving the ball straight at the keeper. Nellies took another and sent it wide. Celtic defeated Aberdeen to climb to the top of the League. Hearts' last game was at St Mirren on 17 April. Love Street was their 'unlucky' ground; they hadn't won a point there in a decade. They duly went down 1–0 while Celtic put four past Third Lanark without reply. On 24 April Celtic drew with Motherwell in their final match to take the title by four clear points. In the absence of any complaints from Tynecastle, it was left to the press to voice the opinion held by many in the game that a grave injustice had occurred. 'Hearts,' declared the *Evening News*, 'have laboured these past weeks under a dreadful handicap, the like of which our friends in the west cannot imagine. Between them the two leading Glasgow clubs have sent not a single prominent player to the Army. There is only one football champion in Scotland, and its colours are maroon and khaki.'

While Celtic deserve credit for their fine unbeaten run in the season's closing weeks, there is no doubt that military training played the biggest part in depriving Hearts of the championship. A comparison of the club's record before and after mobilisation tells the story well enough:

15 August to 26 December

Played	Won	Lost	Drawn	Goals Scored	Goals Conceded	Points
21	19	1	1	52	13	39

2 January to 17 April

Played	Won	Lost	Drawn	Goals Scored	Goals Conceded	Points
17	8	3	6	31	20	22

In the final nine games fifteen goals were conceded, compared with thirteen in the previous twenty-four. 'Only the team's great fighting spirit saw them through the programme after Christmas,' McCartney told the *Evening News* on 20 April. 'They played at times so tired and sore that they could hardly stand; yet they took Celtic to the last day of the season and left Rangers foundering 11 points behind. They gave their best throughout and that is all that anyone could ask. Edinburgh is proud of them.' Two days later he received a touching letter from the parents of Pte John Williamson Campbell of A Company, the battalion's second casualty, who had died a fortnight earlier, aged 21, of double pneumonia contracted during the course of his training. 'Our son,' they wrote from their home in Royal Park Terrace, 'had hoped to see his comrades win the League. He was just so pleased to be serving with the Hearts boys. It is all so very sad . . .'[14]

Annan Ness sent a note on behalf of the players. He was now the sergeant-major of C Company, a position he inherited from one of Sir George's old campaigners. Archie Ewing had spent 15 years in the Argylls, serving conscientiously in India and South Africa, before his discharge in 1910. In 1914 he was working as a pit labourer near Dunfermline, where he re-enlisted in his former regiment on 20 August. At this point his career took a turn for the worse. Following a series of misadventures with the 10th Battalion at Bordon Camp near Aldershot, he was dismissed by his commanding officer on the grounds that he was 'a man addicted to continual drinking'. That was on 11 November. On 7 December he re-enlisted yet again, providing the Castle Street staff with details of his first engagement but omitting to disclose his return to the regiment and his subsequent fall from grace. Sir George made him a sergeant at once, and he must have been a strong candidate for RSM. In February 1915 he was appointed company sergeant-major and began to take his responsibilities as father and protector of his charges a little too seriously. There was a 'treating' problem in Edinburgh: civilians were standing drinks for young soldiers. A bye-law had been introduced, partly at the behest of Sir Richard Lodge, to prevent what the *Evening Dispatch* had called 'this hindrance to sobriety and discipline'. CSM Ewing favoured a public house at the foot of the Vennel, five minutes' walk from his billet. On any given evening he might be found there, on the look-out (so he said) for anyone breaking the rules. So assiduous were his efforts in this direction that he frequently remained in the same corner seat far beyond the nightly curfew, returning to the Brewery in the small hours to argue with the sentries and serenade the door. He was, however, a good soldier and it says much for him that he was permitted to retain his stripes when Ness was promoted above him.[15]

Archie took the shameless route, but the curfew could be broken much more quietly. There was a guard on the close that led up to the Brewery, there was a guard on the Heriot's gates; there was no guard, however, on the high stone wall that divided the school from Greyfriars Churchyard. That wall could be crossed, and the cemetery gates were (in the words of Cpl Veitch) 'eminently scaleable'. The married, the thirsty, the lonely and the brave: this was their way out and (inevitably) their way back in. Messages were dropped during route marches to be picked up by small daughters who just happened to be waiting close by: 'I will try to get home on Thursday evening and I'll maybe bring a pal. Look for me the back of 8 and put the kettle on.' Murdoch McLeod of D Company, a maltman with McEwan's, was one of the battalion policemen. At 37 he was also 'Scotland's Strongest Man', a veteran of countless challenges at athletics meetings and summer fairs across the country. In mid-March he had apprehended Pte Robert MacMillan attempting to follow a stray cat out of the Heriot's grounds after hours. MacMillan, 41, was a dock labourer from Smith's Land in Leith, a serial defaulter, whose previous military service consisted of three years as a Volunteer in the Duke of Edinburgh's Own Artillery Regiment. His feline fixation had first become apparent in January, when he followed a kitten to Home Street and back. There were further expeditions, as well as other unexplained absences. He was brought before the battalion doctor, who observed 'a slight peculiarity of manner' but otherwise concluded he was fit. On 23 April McLeod spotted him again – on the roof, this time, of the Examination Hall, conversing with a stranded tabby. Like the prince on the battlements, he would be known forevermore simply as 'Hamlet'.[16]

That same afternoon Edinburgh was shocked to read the first accounts from Flanders of the latest German outrage – the release from prepared cylinders on 22 April of a cloud of chlorine gas against the northern flank of the Ypres salient. Two divisions of French and Algerian troops had been overwhelmed: many were asphyxiated where they stood; survivors fled in panic to the rear. The resulting breach in the line was quickly filled by British and Canadian reserves, but as darkness fell that evening, the Germans had advanced two full miles. On the morning of 24 April a second gas offensive was beaten off by the Canadian Division, which included in its ranks former Hearts back, Robert 'Scrappy' Gray. Gray, a Boer War veteran, wrote McCartney on 26 April. 'We have had a time of it, all right. But we have come through well enough and now the Fritzes know not to disturb us . . .'

The Fritzes, of course, knew nothing of the sort. Over the next few weeks they kept the salient under constant pressure, forcing a British withdrawal and fuelling speculation that McCrae's would soon be called upon to step into the fight. Fraser MacLean, a sergeant in A Company, was principal Science master of the Edinburgh Ladies' College in Queen Street. On 30 April he wrote a former colleague:

> The question on everyone's lips seems to be, 'When are you going?' The answer, I'm afraid, is that we simply do not know. A battalion is like a public wash-house – rumour is our currency. For myself, I do not think it will be long, for they seem to be very short of men at the front. This gas has got the fellows very angry . . .[17]

MacLean was an uncaught defaulter. On mobilisation day he was dismantling his steak pie at the Waverley Market when he suddenly remembered that he hadn't informed his employers, the Edinburgh Merchant Company, that he had enlisted. Orders had been posted that no one was allowed to leave the premises, so he tore a page out of his diary and wrote himself a pass. The sentry let him out. Next day he returned to the college and resumed teaching. A fortnight later, fearing arrest, he made discreet enquiries and discovered that his comrades were living in a brewery. He nipped down to join them and found out he'd never been missed. In March, when the battalion was first issued with its old Mark I Lee-Enfield magazine rifles, he had secured a good one for himself by 'swapping with a sleeping comrade'. Such initiative did not go unrewarded: on 7 May he was commissioned and placed in command of his old platoon.[18]

On 10 May McCrae's finally received their embarkation warning – not for the front, but for Ripon in Yorkshire, where they would join the other units of their designated brigade. No specific date was given, so a series of Farewell Concerts was hurriedly arranged, starting at the Usher Hall, moving on to Bristo Congregational Church (where the battalion had its Reading Room and club) and finishing at the Gaiety Theatre in Leith. The War Office had also informed the Colonel that a reserve company would have to be maintained in Edinburgh for reinforcement. Since around 200 men had already departed Heriot's for reasons of health or age, Sir George obtained permission to resume recruiting. December's whirlwind effort was repeated, and in five days the 16ᵗʰ Royal Scots were back to full strength. 'Echoes of the winter are resounding still,' declared the *Evening News*. 'An entire company in less than a week is a splendid reflection on the city's manhood.' Also on the board of the Edinburgh & District Tramways Co., which promised its employees half-pay for the duration and their jobs back when they returned *if* they enlisted in McCrae's. More than 30 men stepped forward, including David Philip, a 34-year-old office clerk, who had played for Hearts at full-back in the 1906 Scottish Cup win over Third Lanark. Philip applied for the players' platoon and was quickly promoted to corporal.[19]

Then on 18 May Lord Kitchener asked for a further 300,000 volunteers. Sir George was quick to respond, offering to muster a second battalion along the same lines as the first. Pte Blaney chewed his pencil and came up with the inspiring epic, 'McCrae's Own Farewell to Auld Reekie':

> So, Come lads and Join our Battalions
> He's trying another to raise;
> Just be like the gallant Italians,
> And stand by our Colonel, McCrae's.
> Just think of our lads in the Trenches,
> They're fighting like hell for your hame;
> And if they've left their wives and their wenches,
> Why the hell can't we all play the game?[20]

The Colonel, meanwhile, increased his evening march-outs in the town, reasoning that the 16ᵗʰ in full flow was a powerful recruiting instrument in itself. At the head of the column came 16 pipers and 8 drummers, led by their portly pipe-major, Sgt William Duguid. 'Duggie' had spent 12 years in the Gordon Highlanders (overlapping Muir by 18 months). He took part in the storming of the Dargai Heights during the Tirah Expedition of 1897 on the North-West Frontier. In South Africa he saw fighting at Paardeberg and in the Transvaal. He was discharged in 1905 with a sheaf of friendly testimonials and joined the Corps of Commissionaires, working for various employers in Glasgow and Edinburgh. In May 1914 he secured the position of head porter at the capital's Chalmers Hospital at a salary of £52 per annum, plus coal, gas, uniform and free accommodation in the adjacent 'lodge', a cosy little cottage in Lauriston Place. For a man of 40 with a wife and family it was a splendid bit of luck, but he surrendered it all for the Colonel. The hospital governors immediately appointed a replacement; his wife was removed from the lodge and there was no promise of re-employment after the war.[21]

On 24 May Duguid's band led the funeral cortège for 214 members of the 7ᵗʰ Royal Scots who had died in the railway disaster at Quintinshill, near

Gretna. The following day – 'in the interests of enlargement', said *The Scotsman* – they took to the streets again. Blaney had adapted a familiar anthem:

> Come and bring your whistle, boys,
> We'll have another song,
> Singing down old Princes Street
> To help the War along;
> Sing it as we roll it out
> A solid thousand strong,
> When we are marching wi' Geordie!
>
> Hurrah! Hurrah! we bring the Dandy Corps!
> Hurrah! Hurrah! we've all been there before!
> The Kaiser knows we're coming, boys!
> He'll not want any more,
> When we are marching wi' Geordie![22]

Around 300 men had already come forward by the time McCrae received word from the War Office that his efforts were unwanted. The Army Council conveyed its thanks but suggested that for the moment Edinburgh's Territorial units should have first call on local volunteers. The new intake was billeted in a large marquee pitched on the lawns fronting Lauriston Place, the very spot where Sir George was wont to practise his golf. There was a tradition among battalion survivors that a tenement-dweller at the back of Forrest Road had received a visit one evening from a certain red-faced colonel who insisted on paying to have her broken window replaced.[23]

On 28 May McCrae's paraded 1,600 strong at Inverleith Park for their last Edinburgh inspection. The salute was taken by Sir John Spencer Ewart, General Officer Commanding in Scotland, who complimented the battalion on its progress and presented Alfred Warr with a handsome silver shield that Sir James Leishman had commissioned back in December 'as an incentive to excellence in company drill'. Then, on the stroke of 12, preceded by pipe-band and mascot, Sir George mounted up and led the 16th out into Fettes Avenue through a cheering crowd of spectators. Back at Heriot's there was a special lunch to celebrate the end of the beginning. On the morning of 18 June, after a hectic fortnight of final preparations, 1,100 officers and men marched down the Mound and Market Street to the southbound platform of Waverley Station. The town came out to see them off and Princes Street was blocked. The pipers, complete with active service aprons on their kilts, were playing a Duguid favourite, 'Miss Drummond of Perth', while over in a corner Sir George was saying goodbye to Leishman, Hogge and Harry Rawson senior. Although access to the train-side was restricted, several hundred relatives and friends had pushed past the constables and barriers to bid their farewells. Provost Inches had been jostled as he tried to make a speech.

Messrs McCartney, Furst and Duckworth were attending their players. Currie was a sergeant now; Low, Gracie, Findlay and Briggs were corporals. Boyd, Ellis, Wattie and Crossan remained privates. Robert Preston was in hospital with flu and Willie Wilson's shoulder was troubling him again, so they would both remain at Heriot's with the reserve company, as would Hamlet, Harry Lorimer, Archie Ewing and nearly 600 others. Alice Wattie was there for her brother and her sweetheart. Paddy would not let go of her hand. Ernie Ellis's fiancée, 17-year-old Belle Armstrong, had come with her parents. Ernie was lodging with the family at their home in Gorgie Road and love took its course. She didn't want him to leave: there were tears and he started to blush.[24] Eleven years divided them in age. Currie's parents had come up from Kilwinning and the Boyds had arrived from Mossend. Alfie Briggs's wife, Alice, had brought her two-month-old baby in to see his dad. Robert Mercer was there too, having lately discarded his sticks. His knee, however, remained so damaged that even walking was painful. His surgeon, Alexis Thomson of the Royal Infirmary, had been quoted in the press, confirming his condition, but still the letters trickled in from England. As he shook hands with his teammates and watched them board the train, he heard the crowd give three cheers for the Colonel.

And when all the kit was stowed away and safety catches fastened, when all the packs were loaded up and counted, when the last hapless stragglers had escaped from their mothers' embraces, the carriages began to move – first back with a lurch, then slowly forward. McCartney later recalled: 'There was a moment, a long moment, of unexpected silence – of disbelief, I think, that it had come to this. I could not move. I stood quite still with my hand on Rawson's shoulder, and then I heard the cheering start again. The finest men I ever knew had gone . . .'[25]

✳ ✳ ✳

Six hours later they were pulling into Ripon. 'It was oppressively hot,' wrote Gerald Crawford, now a sergeant in B Company.

> We worked up quite a sweat just sorting out our gear and disentraining. Oddly the place seemed deserted. We found a ticket collector dozing in his office. He woke up with a start in the shadow of the Colonel and took a little turn. Mr Warden obliged with some brandy and I am told that the fellow bucked up considerably

thereafter. It transpired that the station was some distance from the camp, so there was nothing for it but to form up in the main street and do what we do best. Sir George set the pipes to their task and away went Edinburgh's finest. I believe we must have tramped for three miles or more through narrow, dusty country lanes until at last we reached our destination. The natives call it 'Stoodley' . . .[26]

A sprawling canvas camp near Fountains Abbey, Studley Royal was already occupied by two of the remaining three battalions of the 101st Infantry Brigade – the 10th Lincolns, raised in Grimsby and district in October 1914, and the 15th Royal Scots, lately arrived from Troon in Ayrshire, where they had been brigaded since February with the Glasgow City units of the HLI. The 11th Suffolks, raised in the city and county of Cambridge in September 1914 by the local TFA, turned up the following day. Jimmy Crawford, a 17-year-old apprentice compositor from Meadowbank Terrace, sent a 'Souvenir of Ripon' to his mother:

> There are 12 of us in a tent [he wrote] but our section will only have nine so we are all right. The people here are very funny speakers, you can hardly make out what they are saying. They all call you 'Scotty'. I don't think they ever heard bag-pipes before. The Lincolns were all waiting to hear them when we reached camp . . .[27]

Tommy King, an 18-year-old house-factor from Crown Street in Leith, had 13 in his tent. 'It is uncomfortably cramped,' he told his family, 'but our Brigade commander walked up with the Colonel last night and promised us plenty of exercise.' [28]

Brigadier-General Hugh Fitton was 61, a veteran of the Sudan and South Africa. Until recently he had been serving as Director of Recruiting at the War Office. He was as good as his word. Pte King wrote again within the week:

> We have scarcely time to breathe. Reveille is at six. We are allowed one hour to wash, breakfast and dress before parade and inspection at seven. Yesterday was our first time out with the other battalions. I believe we would do better on our own but I suppose we will get along in time. It is still very hot. I spent the morning digging trenches, then in the afternoon we were attacked by the English boys. We beat them off all right, then marched back home for tea. We are supposed to get the evenings to ourselves but there is always some little job to do, so we are never quite at rest . . .[29]

Tommy was describing 'Brigade manœuvres', special exercises designed to prepare the battalions for what the manuals called 'engaging with the enemy'. Their weapons, for the moment, were the rifle, the bayonet and the spade. Musketry training placed a high priority on 'rate of fire', the ultimate goal being 15 aimed rounds per minute. Fire support was essential for the movement of troops against any defended position. Section would cover section, platoon would cover platoon, advancing up an entrenched hillside with the bayonet fixed and ready. 'It is believed,' said *Bayonet Fighting* in 1915, 'that it will be only by a series of bayonet assaults carried out by men skilled in the use of that weapon and confident in their superiority that positions held by a determined enemy can be captured.' L/Cpl David Philip, an 18-year-old insurance clerk, from Upper Gilmore Place, recalled:

> Our bayonet was twelve and one quarter inches long. 'Sword bayonet' was the correct military term. Now we were mostly intelligent lads. My own imagination was no more and no less vivid than the average. Shooting a man several hundred yards away, or tossing a bomb in his direction, were remote acts. Thrusting a bayonet into his body necessarily took a bit of contemplation. Especially if, as expected, he was trying to do the same to you.
>
> I surveyed my companions and saw only a small handful of men who were comfortable in the drill, a smaller number still, moreover, who I thought would be likely to carry their skill and enthusiasm into the real fight. Reckoning that any enemy force with which we came into contact would boast much the same thin sprinkling of potential 'killers', I drew much consolation. Unless I was dreadfully unlucky, I consoled myself, I was quite likely to find myself facing an adversary every bit as squeamish as myself. If I could only keep my nerve, therefore, I felt I would prevail. I imparted these thoughts to my friends only to be roundly mocked for my foolishness. Privately, however, in days to come, a number of them asked me did I really believe I was right. Oh yes, the bayonet got us thinking, I must say . . .[30]

L/Cpl John McParlane, a 35-year-old electrician from Henry Street, wrote to his wife:

> We started with our bayonet work today and the boys are liking it fine. There is much talk of seeing a German on the other end rather than the sandbags we are using. Some of the lads are very keen to get to grips with the enemy. For myself it would suit me

fine if the war ended about a week after we arrive in France. I am all for a taste of adventure, but I'm not wanting an entire feast. I am content to be one of the brave lads who comes home to his loved ones.[31]

A journalist from the *Evening News* had travelled down to watch them. 'It looks just like a glorious picnic,' he wrote. 'The camp has a lovely site among the woods and dales of Yorkshire.' Woods and dales, however, have limited appeal and Ripon itself was disappointing. 'A great many of us came back disgusted with the place,' wrote Pte Thomson Bonar, an 18-year-old medical student. 'I thought it rather decent but then I am not keen on amusements and girls etc., also the town is a good way from the camp which will help in saving my pay. There is great disgust among most of the chaps because most of the womenkind here have formed a sort of League against speaking with soldiers . . .'[32]

Harry Sutherland, a 19-year-old grocer from Fowler Terrace, agreed. 'The place is all right,' he scribbled on a postcard, 'but the girls are the opposite. We never get a good laugh.'[33] In a novel attempt to overcome the problem, Jimmy Brown took to telling any passing beauty that he was Paddy Crossan. One afternoon he was strolling out with two pals, Jock Ward and Jimmy McEvoy, when a group of lads from the Lincolns and Suffolks – the 'Cats and the Cabbages' because of their badges – started making fun of his glengarry. Brown was incensed and immediately went on the offensive. 'I think there were 15 of them,' McEvoy later recalled, 'and Jock and me had to back the wee bugger up. They kicked the crap out of us.'[34]

D.M. Sutherland, a second lieutenant since March, sought refuge in nearby Harrogate. 'It is a relief,' he wrote his mother in Currie, 'to get into town after a week of drill amid trees and grass.'[35] Sutherland had just been appointed the battalion Sniping Officer with responsibility for the training of around 40 marksmen and observers, who would be used in the trenches to gather intelligence and harass the enemy. At thirty-two – two months senior to Fraser MacLean – he was the oldest subaltern in McCrae's. Born and educated in Wick, he spent two years training with a local firm of solicitors, then moved to Edinburgh to complete his apprenticeship before abandoning the law for a career as a lithographic artist. In 1906 he became a full-time student at the Royal Institution on the Mound and subsequently transferred to the Royal Scottish Academy. In 1911 he was awarded a travelling scholarship and spent the next two years studying in Spain. In 1913 he toured the galleries of Holland and Belgium, and secured a lecturing position at the Edinburgh College of Art. He was on holiday in Caithness when the war broke out and volunteered as a deck-hand on a trawler servicing the fleet at Scapa Flow.

Four months later he returned to Edinburgh and enlisted. On 1 July he wrote to his mother again:

> We had a tremendous thunderstorm here yesterday. It poured heavily for about four hours and the thunder and lightning was very violent. The lightning struck a tent in the 15th Royal Scots lines quite within forty yards of where we are and killed one man and injured seven others. Altogether I hear there are five people killed among the different battalions around . . .[36]

William Turnbull, a 29-year-old asylum attendant from Morningside, was the 16th's only casualty. He was carried off to hospital in shock and awoke to find Tom Gracie in the next bed. Gracie, who had been ill since leaving Scotland, was awaiting transfer to Leeds Infirmary for further treatment. The pair therefore missed the following night's entrenching practice, which was conducted in pitch darkness and pouring rain. Pte Bonar complained to his parents in Colinton:

> I jolly well do feel ratty. We were out from 10 p.m. to 3 a.m. and it was a miserable night. Just after we reached the trenches it started to rain and we got soaked to the skin. We dug away at the ground but had a very faint idea of what we were doing. One chap in B Coy got a pick driven into his back. By the time we got back to camp we looked like a crowd of drowned rats. Almost the worst part was getting off our wet things and getting our beds down without touching the tent. We piled our rifles outside, threw our greatcoats over them, threw our equipment out in the rain and got to sleep somehow . . .[37]

To his surprise, shortly afterwards, Bonar was told he would be leaving the battalion. On 1 July Sir George had received a request from the War Office for 'qualified scientists' to be transferred to the newly formed 'Special Companies' of the Royal Engineers. Britain was preparing its 'gas reprisals', and needed the men to discharge them. McCrae protested, only to receive a peremptory letter pointing out that the Special Brigade (as it was called) was to have priority. Accordingly 25 of the best and brightest other ranks in A Company, including several NCOs, were removed without the option of refusal, breaking another of the Colonel's solemn promises. They would find themselves in France before the autumn. The Specials tried for Jamie Low as well; he avoided them by applying for a commission in the Seaforths. It was another good man lost.

On 3 July McCrae received a further message from Whitehall. His second son had been killed five days earlier during an assault on the Turkish defences at Gully Ravine on the Gallipoli peninsula. He had been there a fortnight, having transferred to the 4th Royal Scots to bring the battalion up to fighting strength. A letter from a comrade gave more details: 'His company got word to get over the parapet and charge the trench in front of them. George got out and shouted them on. They followed him splendidly, but he had made himself too conspicuous . . .'[38] There were 16 officers and 204 other ranks dead; 6 officers and 141 other ranks had been wounded. The two short companies of the 7th which had avoided the Gretna disaster lost 11 officers and 230 men in the same engagement. Neil Moreland, on attachment from the HLI, came through unscathed. 'The camp,' wrote D.M. Sutherland, 'is now subdued. Many of us have relatives or friends in these battalions. It is the uncertainty of waiting until a name appears in the papers that is the worst. We do not know who has survived.'[39]

As the marching and skirmishing continued, Sir George returned briefly to Edinburgh. On 8 July Jimmy Speedie embarked for France, landing at Boulogne the following morning. He wrote to McCartney, who wrote in turn to Briggs. The Hearts men clubbed together to send him some comforts. He replied, enclosing a piece of shrapnel. McCartney was assembling his squad for the coming season and had recruited two local Juniors, Jimmy Hazeldean and Teddy McGuire, both privates in the Heriot's reserve company. Hazeldean was 20, a bottle-blower from Portobello; McGuire was an Armadale coal miner. The new lads attended Ernie Ellis's wedding in Edinburgh on 29 July. Willie Wilson was best man; he had planned to accompany the bridegroom back to Ripon but once again his shoulder let him down. Their footballing comrades, meanwhile, opened the Brigade Championship with an 8–0 drubbing of the Lincolns. In Gracie's absence Duncan Currie played at centre and scored three goals. Harry Wattie got two. Falkirk's Andy Henderson, preferred in goal to Norman Findlay, was one of the battalion comics. 'We had our hardest challenge yet the other night,' he wrote his family in Penicuik.[40]

The players' strip consisted of emerald green jerseys with a broad scarlet band running across the shoulders. Cuthbert Lodge, who was running the team, had picked them up in a Ripon sports outfitters at a knock-down price. 'No one else was daft enough to want them,' wrote Jimmy Boyd to his sister. In the next match (against the Suffolks) they were worn by the reserves, which must have seemed the decent thing to do. They duly triumphed 7–2 and the first team returned for their next match, against a 15th Royal Scots eleven led by the former Hearts back Roddy Walker. Currie, Wattie and Falkirk's inside-forward Bobby Wood scored two apiece in a 6–1 victory. Three so-called 'return' fixtures proved equally one-sided and on 3 August they defeated a Brigade select 5–0. Jimmy Speedie wrote again two days later. He had been sniped at and shelled. 'We look forward to you coming,' he concluded. 'Hearts are all the talk out here.'[41]

On 10 August the battalion marched to Ripon and entrained for Strensall Camp, five miles north of York, where 101st Brigade was officially taken over by the War Office. Two weeks of intensive musketry training followed before they moved again. Their destination this time was Ludgershall, near Andover in Hampshire. The journey was long and hot. John Veitch recalled that Red Cross ladies were waiting at every halt to distribute tea and buns. They 'detrained' in the late afternoon and marched a mile to Perham Down Camp, near Tidworth. 'Canvas again!' wrote Jimmy Boyd. The tents were unsanitary and full of holes, noted D.M. Sutherland – it was not a pleasant spot.

Next morning a bedraggled, shirt-sleeved figure wandered into the lines of the 15th Royal Scots. He had travelled alone all the way from Edinburgh. The Reverend James MacDougall Black of Broughton Place Church was 36 years old, prematurely grey and the most charismatic preacher of his generation. Born in Rothesay, he was educated at the local academy before moving on to Glasgow University in 1898. Two years later he joined the Young Scots Society. In April 1901 he was arrested in Glasgow during a student demonstration against the civilian internment *laagers* which had been set up in the Transvaal and Orange River colonies of South Africa. Conditions in these so-called 'concentration camps' were appalling and inspired a popular campaign for their abolition. Black spent a night in the cells before his father came down to bail him out. His arrival in Hampshire was the result of much quiet reflection: the decision to apply for active service had not been taken lightly. Odd, then, that the Provost's Battalion should turn him away. Captain Alfred Harrison, a woollen merchant from Davidson's Mains, later explained:

> I happened to be orderly officer and searched out the C.O. to ask where I should put him. Colonel Urmston looked up over the paper he was reading and said, 'Anywhere you like so long as you don't bring him here. I'm not going to have any so-and-so parson in my Mess.' I handed him on to the 16th, but in the months to come we all, including the C.O. himself, regretted our inhospitality.[42]

Archie Urmston had been in command of the 15th since Troon, succeeding Sir Robert Cranston, whom the War Office considered too elderly. Born in Barnstaple in 1860, he had risen to the rank of colonel during the war in

South Africa, where he commanded the Royal Marines contingent under Lord Roberts. He saw fighting at Kimberley, Magersfontein, Paardeberg and Driefontein and was mentioned in despatches. He had retired in 1903 and volunteered for his old regiment in August 1914, hoping for 'service afloat'. He was disappointed, therefore, to be sent to an infantry battalion and was considered by his men to be somewhat 'detached'. Black had served before the war as padre to the 6th Royal Scots: he picked up his bags and sought out Sir George, who welcomed him with open arms. 'When I arrived in the lines of the 16th,' he later wrote, 'it was as if I had come home.' He was billeted in a tent beside Captain John Crotty, a dissolute Catholic priest from County Waterford, who had recently been posted to the 16th by mistake. Crotty had no intention of leaving (no matter how many War Office letters he received) and the two became good friends. Black, a Hearts supporter, immediately set about getting to know the men, engaging in their banter, offering advice, playing football with them and holding impromptu services in tents and on the training field. 'There was no side to him,' John Veitch recalled. 'He just mucked in like one of the boys. He was the perfect chaplain for McCrae's and he found us by accident.'[43]

On 28 September the 101st received orders to entrain for Sutton Veny, near Warminster, on Salisbury Plain. Here they would link up with the two remaining brigades of the 34th Division before embarking for some still unidentified theatre of war. They arrived the following morning and were billeted in the wooden huts of No. 2 Camp at Green Hill. There were 'Geordies' everywhere: the 102nd Brigade ('Tyneside Scots') consisted of four battalions of Northumberland Fusiliers with Scottish connections from Newcastle and district; the 103rd Brigade ('Tyneside Irish') consisted of four battalions of Northumberland Fusiliers with Irish connections from the same area. The Divisional pioneers, moreover, were yet another NF battalion. The Edinburgh lads were so outnumbered that they dubbed these new comrades with their strange habits and impenetrable dialect the 'Tyneside Chinamen'.[44]

Divisional training now proceeded apace: mock assaults, field days and 'tactical route marches' to precise timetables. The battalions lost their two heavy Vickers machine-guns (which were now grouped together by brigade) but gained four Lewis automatic rifles, which would lend close, flexible support to the hoped-for advance. A 'Transport' section was formed to carry the battalion's equipment – five limbered 'G.S.' wagons for small-arms-ammunition alone, two for tools, and more besides for water, rations and other impedimenta. A 'Maltese' cart for medical supplies. Four field kitchens. More than 50 horses and pack cobs. Lt Robert Husband, a 22-year-old stockbroker from Dunfermline, drew the job of Transport Officer because he could ride. His father was the provost of the town and an old friend of the Colonel's.

The 34th Division's commanding officer was 53-year-old Major-General Edward Charles Ingouville-Williams, known to all ranks as 'Inky Bill'. The dug-outs of 16th Brigade, which he had lately commanded in France, still echoed to tales of his narrow escapes in no man's land, where he insisted on conducting his own reconnaissance patrols. He was absolutely fearless, gathering eight mentions in despatches in a career dating back to 1878, when he enlisted as a private in the old Militia. His commission in 1881 was followed by service in the Sudan, on the Nile, and in South Africa, where, as a lieutenant-colonel on Warren's staff, he witnessed the awful carnage of Spion Kop. He could turn his hand to anything. An exhausted company of his old regiment, the East Kents, came down from the line one morning to find him doling out dry socks and mugs of self-brewed tea. Since returning to Britain to take over the 34th, much of his time had been spent visiting the various battalions to get to know the officers and men. Shortly after the 16th's arrival at Green Hill, he turned up to make an informal tour. Willie Duguid broke out two bottles of Younger's ale and invited him to loosen his collar. Side by side in deck-chairs, the two old soldiers watched the sun go down.[45] Five days later the General crashed his car into a traction engine. He was unconscious for a week with a suspected fractured skull. Within a fortnight, desperate not to lose his new command, he rose from his bed and returned to duty.

The men, meanwhile, were becoming impatient – 'over-trained', thought Herbert Warden. They had been fully equipped for several weeks and expected orders to embark at any time. On 5 October it was announced that three-day leaves would begin. This was insufficient for a decent stay in Scotland and the allotment was deeply resented. That same day Annan Ness picked up a message from Tynecastle. It was terrible news: during the British offensive at Loos on 25 September, Jimmy Speedie had been killed. Ken McCrae, wounded two weeks earlier, had confirmed the information from his hospital in London. When they were withdrawn that night, the 7th Camerons mustered fewer than 80 effectives out of nearly 900 men committed in the morning. On 15 October McCartney received a month-old censored letter from the front, enquiring after the Hearts lads and asking him to pass on the author's best wishes. It was signed simply 'James', with the 'Speedie' added later as an afterthought in brackets.

Sir George had just returned from France, where he and other senior officers of the Division spent an 'instruction' week in the trenches. On 23 October he watched the battalion football team defeating the 18th Northumberland Fusiliers in the final of the Divisional Championship. After the match, in which Currie scored four of his side's six goals, he visited the players to make an announcement. That morning, at two minutes past eight, Tom Gracie had died of leukaemia at Stobhill Hospital in Glasgow. The illness, it transpired, had been diagnosed in March; Scotland's leading scorer had told no one but his manager. Towards the end Sir James Leishman visited him at the family home in Glasgow's Duke Street. On 25 October he wrote to McCartney:

> He [Gracie] admitted to me that he played when he ought to have been in bed; and stuck to his training for football and the Army when he should have given in. He was ever a sound trier, and he had all the quiet resolution and courage which makes men like him hang on until they drop. Although he was not a man who wore his heart on his sleeve, I could easily discern that he was a good son and a loyal comrade; and I feel convinced that he would have proved a first-class fighting man . . .[46]

On 26 October Tom was laid to rest at Glasgow's Craigton Cemetery, within sight of Ibrox Park, where only the year before he had starred in a famous victory. His brother, John, was killed at Loos; his sister's husband, Tommy Reid, had fallen in June at Gallipoli. The Gracie family had no cause to smile. Tom's mother, Harriet, wrote McCartney, thanking him for bringing her son to Edinburgh. He found his home with Hearts, she said, and never was so happy.

At the end of November all leave was cancelled. Initially the men thought that embarkation was imminent; it transpired, however, that they were being punished. Several hundred members of the Tyneside brigades had over-stayed their passes, so the privilege was withdrawn. Only 16 members of the 101st – and only *one* man in McCrae's – had transgressed. 'It was not fair,' Jimmy McEvoy remembered. 'We did nothing wrong. The married men had promised their kiddies they would be getting home. Some of those lads would never see Edinburgh again. We were bloody angry.'[47]

On 5 December the men exchanged their old Lee-Enfield rifles for the improved 'Short' version, converted to fire the new Mark VII high-velocity bullet. It was a formidable weapon. Jim Steuart, a 20-year-old bank clerk from Broxburn:

> We have got our new rifles now, and were shooting with them to-day in the pouring rain. It was pretty miserable slopping about in muddy trenches, and the rain in our eyes blurred the targets. Most of us just blazed away and never bothered aiming. It was just a farce shooting on a day like this. I never worry now, just slop along and don't care when things are rotten. It is really the best way to keep going.[48]

Steuart was a big friendly lad, who had declined a commission largely because he didn't fancy the responsibility. A week later he wrote to his sister:

> On Thursday we were out in the pouring rain all day. Every time we started after a halt we could feel the water sloshing about our bodies. All down the battalion you could hear the groans and cries of discomfort. The latest rumour is that we go to Egypt in a week. I am certain from things going on around that we will be away soon. I don't expect I will feel much leaving England, as I would if I left Scotland, for really this is a foreign country to us, not in the nasty sense, but customs are quite different. But I expect I will miss even England when we get to the Land of the Pyramids – good luck to it.[49]

Land of the Pyramids. McCrae's had been preparing for France. On 18 December sun helmets were issued along with tropical uniforms. Next day the Division assembled at Codford St Mary for a grand inspection. The King had been expected to attend, but His Majesty suffered a fall while visiting the troops in Flanders and was forced to call off at the last minute. Inky Bill stepped into the breach, assisted by a party of Japanese officers. 'The rain fell continuously throughout,' wrote Fraser MacLean, 'but we didn't put a foot wrong.' As the columns marched past, the General was asked if he would single any of them out. 'McCrae's,' he replied. 'I like that battalion. It has a dash about it.'[50]

Dash was the word. On 26 December the tropical equipment was hurriedly recalled, their old kit reissued, and France reinstated as their destination. There was no festive break. The officers gathered ankle-deep in mud for Hogmanay at 'Rotten Veny'. Napier Armit, editor of the battalion's journal, the *Weakly Rumour*, described the scene:

> Then came the hand-shaking, and the hearty good wishes of all were extended with a will. In the midst of this the worthy Duguid struck up the pipes and we marched down to first-foot the men, headed by the C.O. Here, and in the Sergeant's Mess, conviviality reigned. We were a' Jock Tamson's bairns. It would be unfair to say who excelled in gaiety, for everyone did his best and hospitality was rampant. Lights out at 12.15 and a good New Year to all.[51]

Five days later, orders were received to mobilise. On Friday, 7 January all beds and tables were removed from the huts. The battalion had to sleep on wooden boards. Next morning they left camp at 6 a.m., tramped to Warminster and entrained in three separate parties for Southampton.

There, with the vastness of the Channel stretching out beyond the docks, some wag came round and warned them for a night march.

Embarkation Dinner, December 1915. Duggie gives the toast: 'Good health today and always!' (D.M. Sutherland)

CHAPTER SIX

'An awful biz'

His Majesty's paddle steamer *Empress Queen* was the jewel in the crown of the Isle of Man Steam Packet Company. Built in 1897, she was designed as a pleasure craft with a passenger capacity of 2,000 and held the speed record for the journey between Douglas and Liverpool. In February 1915 she was chartered by the Admiralty, painted military grey and converted into a troopship. The moonless evening of 8 January 1916 found her sailing at 6 p.m. from Southampton bound for Havre with 1,100 members of McCrae's and 300 members of the Provost's Battalion all peering out to sea in search of periscopes. 'We were told,' wrote Sgt Crawford, 'that crossing the Channel is to be treated as a night march. Have you ever heard the like? The Colonel has us walking on water. No noise or lights are permitted for fear of submarines.'[1]

Shortly before embarking, each man was issued with a confidential letter from Lord Kitchener to be kept in their Pay Book at all times:

> You are ordered abroad as a soldier of the King to help our French comrades against the invasion of a common enemy. Remember that the honour of the British Army depends upon your individual conduct. It is your duty not only to set an example of discipline and perfect steadiness under fire but also to maintain the most friendly relations with those whom you are helping in this struggle. Be invariably courteous, considerate and kind. Never do anything likely to injure or destroy property, and always look upon looting as a disgraceful act. Your duty cannot be done unless your health is sound. So keep constantly on your guard against excess. In this new experience you may find temptations in wine and women. You must

117

resist these, and, while treating all women with perfect courtesy,
you should avoid any intimacy.[2]

John Veitch recalled the response of one of his more seasoned comrades.
'It's only wine and women that keeps me sound,' he said. 'I owe it to the
Country to indulge.' Veitch also remembered that the crossing was
particularly choppy. Herbert Warden passed the evening on the bridge,
drinking the Captain's whisky and watching his fellow officers being sick
over the side. Sir George had bagged a stateroom and slept for several hours.

They docked at midnight, disembarked at dawn and marched four miles
to a rest camp outside town. The following afternoon – 10 January – they
marched back into Havre and made for the station, where a train
comprising three ancient engines, one second-class carriage and no fewer
than forty strawless cattle-trucks waited to carry them on the next stage of
their journey. The carriage had just five compartments – a tight squeeze for
32 officers and their baggage, but the last word in Continental luxury
compared with the lot of the other ranks. Once the horses, wagons, carts
and the rest of the battalion's extensive paraphernalia had been loaded,
only 28 'coaches' were left for the men – now 1,200 strong, following the
arrival of 100 stragglers who had departed Southampton on a separate ship.
They entrained 43 to a car. The door was bolted on the inside and the only
air thereafter came from 16 small, barred windows set in rows towards the
ceiling. 'It was anything but comfortable,' wrote Tom Young, a 25-year-old
cashier from Penicuik.[3]

They moved off at 6 p.m. Morning broke well beyond Amiens; there was
no breakfast, no lunch, no food at all since the previous day. The train
rattled on with the men taking turns at the windows and shouting down
the names of stations as they passed: Abbeville, Etaples, Boulogne, Calais
and finally – at 1 p.m. – St Omer. To the east, 20-odd miles away, lay the
front line. They detrained, recalled Gerald Crawford, 'to the sound of the
guns'. It was raining hard and at first the distant rumble was mistaken for
thunder.

The sign above the platform read 'Blendecques'. There was no one there
to meet them. At 2 p.m. a red-tabbed major drew up in a car, presented the
Colonel with a sealed envelope and informed him that the battalion would
find billets 'not far off' at the village of Wallon Cappel. Major Warden
consulted his map. Wallon Cappel was 15 miles away. Undeterred, they
assembled in the station yard and tramped back through St Omer along the
worst roads any of them had ever seen. In the centre was the *pavé*, a rough
causeway of broken setts, reserved in the main for wheeled traffic; on either
side, for those on foot, was deep, adhesive mud. 'I will never forget that
march,' wrote Cpl Young. 'Fifteen miles in full pack.' At 4 p.m. they struck

the village of Renescure and had to beg for water from the padlocked civic well. An hour later they passed through Ebblinghem, the column lengthening in darkness as the older lads broke down. Finally, soon after 6 p.m., they reached their destination. They were not expected and it was several hours before sufficient houses were secured to accommodate the men, 300 of whom had to pick up their kit and stagger off to Hazebrouck, some three miles further on.

Early next morning the Lincolns arrived. The 34th Division was now scattered over a wide area in the immediate rear of the Armentières sector of French Flanders. This was generally regarded as a quiet part of the line, a suitable spot for inexperienced troops to serve their apprenticeship. In 1914 many of the local towns and villages were briefly occupied by the Germans and they therefore bore the scars of liberation. Ruined farms were all around. With their ancient network of drainage ditches disrupted by bombardment, the flat, clay wetlands had reverted to quagmire in the winter rains. It was just the place, decreed Brigade on 14 January, for an invigorating route march.

'Route march!' wrote Herbert Warden the following night. 'It was a glorious moment for the C.O. The very words conjured up our Edinburgh nightmares of Princes Street and the Bridges. And so, if you had been here yesterday morning, you would have beheld this wonderful battalion assemble in battle array, with horses champing, and afterwards march off, led by the pipes and drums of the noble army of Duguids, with the Colonel behind the band as of yore and the men in fours, heavily laden . . .'[4]

The next few days were taken up with lectures – how to keep your feet dry, your rifle clean and yourself alive. They were warned that German snipers were particularly keen, a point reinforced on 19 January when Brigadier-General Fitton was shot during an instruction visit to the line in front of Ypres. He died the following day. Dick Lauder, who was engaged to his niece, wrote home: 'Now we know, if we didn't before, that we are all fair game. I must learn to keep my head down.' Fitton's final order, signed the morning he left HQ, took McCrae's three miles further east on 23 January to the small town of Morbecque. They spent two nights there, scattered between a dozen barns and cottages, before marching off across country to the village of Vieux Berquin, where a telegram was waiting for the Colonel. The battalion, it advised, would proceed to Fort Rompu the following day. The day after that – 27 January – they would go up to the line.

27 January was the Kaiser's birthday.

✵ ✵ ✵

In the early hours of 26 January, from his farmhouse billet near Vieux Berquin, Gerald Crawford wrote home to thank his sister for a comforts parcel. He had distributed the contents among the lads in his platoon and they were all extremely grateful. 'I spent a sleepless night,' he then continued by way of killing time before the move up to the front, 'for we have arrived on a salient in the British sector and the noise of guns is now continuous on all sides. Brother Boche occupies much of the ground to the north and south, as well as to the east, so we are perfectly besieged . . .'[5]

Astride the River Lys, in the centre of the salient's perimeter, stood the old Flanders textile town of Armentières, defiantly going about its business in spite of constant shelling. Just beyond the suburbs, a little to the south on the Estaires road, lay a small cluster of ruined buildings known locally as Fort Rompu. The billets here were dreadful – rusting heaps of corrugated tin, draped in canvas and soaked by a thin, misty drizzle. Rompu was subject to occasional bombardment, so every shelter had its own 'funkhole', a shallow trench awash with scummy water. The flashing guns were louder now, but they quietened down a bit as darkness fell.

Morning came in cold but somewhat clearer. A mile or so to the south, they could see the village of Fleurbaix with its chipped and broken church-spire. Beyond that lay the British reserve and support lines, beyond these the front. It was dusk before they were allowed to move up, counted into small groups to reduce the risk of casualties if the Germans shelled the road. They kept to the crown, but now and then a lorry would appear, forcing them into the mud. The German gunners were apparently asleep, so it was 'pitch black and quiet' when the battalion came at 8 p.m. to the village of Bois Grenier, from where a long communication trench, Shaftesbury Avenue, led up to the firing line. They were met by guides from the units to which they would be attached during their four-day stay. The 11th West Yorkshires and 10th West Ridings would show them the ropes; next time, assuming all went well, they would garrison the sector on their own.

The 'avenue' proved to be no more than a shallow ditch, protected on both sides by sandbagged earthworks; a duckboard track, all but submerged in a river of foul-smelling slime, ran the length of its foot. The ditch was 'traversed' – divided into crude zigzag bays in order to minimise the effect of shellbursts. Sgt Crawford told his sister:

> The trench is not wide but the boards are frequently loose so that if your pack makes you top heavy, or your boots are slippery with mud, you run a fair chance of a dip in the muddy depths below. Sometimes the enemy may know of your movements, but if they do not they just keep up an intermittent fire on the off-chance of

catching someone. When you hear the crack of a rifle or the ping of
a bullet, you cannot help ducking your head instinctively at first,
but in a few minutes you get over it. When you finally emerge into
the first-line trenches you are again in another world . . .[6]

In fact the front line fire positions were not 'trenches' at all. The water
table was so high that it was impossible to dig down more than a foot or so.
The parapet, therefore, consisted of a continuous series of traversed
breastworks, five or six feet high and four to five feet thick. The passageway
was marginally broader than the avenue but with the same repulsive sludge
along its bottom; on either side were narrow, low-roofed alcoves, known as
dug-outs. 'I'd seen bigger coal-sheds,' recalled Jimmy McEvoy.

It took more than an hour to bring all the men up and distribute them
along the line, one section to a bay. By 10 p.m. McCrae's and their hosts
occupied an uninterrupted front of roughly one and a half miles. A short
distance across the fields – no more than 50 yards at one point – lay the
German trenches. One man in each section was told off to a periscope; the
others were allowed a couple of hours to settle in. Charlie Goodall, a 28-
year-old librarian from Broughton Road, had only just arrived when he was
sniped in the shoulder. The battalion's first casualty on active service was
reportedly embarrassed and argued with his sergeant as they put him in the
stretcher. He didn't want to leave. D.M. Sutherland was visiting his sentries
shortly afterwards, when there was a sudden whoosh and a deafening
explosion away towards the rear. It was quickly followed by another. The
birthday celebrations had begun.

It was the heaviest bombardment ever seen in the sector. More than 2,000
shells crashed down, while the British replied with twice that number. 'We
had a very trying time,' wrote Napier Armit, 'and we were all overcome
with a peculiar heavy, drowsy feeling, which we are informed is the usual
thing after artillery fire at close range.' The shelling petered out into an
exchange of rifle and machine-gun fire as each side tried to exploit the
damage to their respective parapets. By midnight all was quiet. At 3.45 a.m.
the sentries were relieved and repaired to their dug-outs. Robert Russell, a
19-year-old power-loom mechanic from Dunfermline, had just climbed into
bed, when the bombardment resumed. A high explosive shell landed in the
doorway of his shelter, killing him instantly. Armit again:

> I got up and toddled out into the darkness to see the flashes of
> bursting shells over our fire trenches, one here and there coming
> uncomfortably close to our quarters and landing about our support
> trenches, and then a few behind us. They were sending them over so
> thick at times that we got to the stage of thinking that a shell could

121

hardly help dropping in our midst. Fortunately, however, after two hours, it stopped, just as suddenly as it started.[7]

There was a further machine-gun exchange at dawn, which turned out to be the regular morning 'hate'. This was followed by breakfast at 9.30 a.m., when the shelling started again. Fraser MacLean:

> Our dug-out got the first two quite close, and all our butter was spoilt with flying earth. This shelling went on at intervals until 3 p.m., when it became intense. It was really a most entrancing sight to see the shrapnel bursting and the Jack Johnsons smashing into the earth behind. It was an awful biz. You sit in the mud and hope that the next won't be near you. The show went on till dusk, when it died out again . . . [8]

Russell, meanwhile, was buried that evening in the tiny cemetery at Bois Grenier. Three of his pals went along. Their platoon commander, Lt Bob Martin, 27-year-old manager of the Bothwell Linen Works in Dunfermline, helped to carry the stretcher. Martin was a big, friendly giant of a man, endearingly clumsy and close to his 'lads'. He had a fine, bass baritone and often joined his sections for a song around the brazier. He wrote to Russell's mother, describing the service, which took place under intermittent shell-fire. Some of Padre Black's words have survived:

> Lord, here is a young man who came to this land of his own will to free it from an uninvited evil. He has done his small bit cheerfully and without complaint. Here are his friends, who have shared the best days of his short life, and who face this worst day bravely like the soldiers that they are. Nothing can be said against Robert. He was a good scholar, a hard worker, a good son, a good brother and a good companion. We bury him far from his family and home, but in future when we sit of an evening to contemplate the past, he will be near and we will feel the better for his presence. We commit him to your care . . .'[9]

As the little party filed back to the trenches, Willie Duguid stayed behind, playing a gentle, haunting pibroch in the darkness. The Colonel composed a note to Mrs Russell the following morning: 'If you have lost a son, we have lost a gallant comrade.' In a strange twist, Sir George's first fatality was a nephew of his late, lamented wife.

The next few days were mercifully quiet. 'We "stand to" an hour before dawn and an hour before dusk,' wrote Gerald Crawford. 'In between we keep our heads down and go about our duties, which mainly consist of drying socks and rubbing anti-frostbite on our feet.' On the evening of 31 January the battalion was relieved. They spent the night at Fort Rompu, marched ten miles to Vieux Berquin the following morning and eight miles to Morbecque the morning after that. It was bitterly cold and several men fell out along the way, including Jimmy Muir, a 29-year-old insurance clerk from Buccleuch Place. Muir had been unwell for a week. He'd gone up to the line with his pals because he didn't want to let them down. He was driven to a convent in the town of Aire, near St Omer, where he died of pneumonia on 8 February. The Colonel contacted his father, who quoted Jimmy's final letter in his reply: 'Do not worry about me,' he had written, 'for I am in the best of company and the boys will see I come to no great harm. Only one thing, though, I do not like the chill . . .'[10]

For Alfie Briggs the worst part was the fierce typewriter rattle of machine-guns. 'It comes right along the line,' he wrote McCartney, 'every bullet just skipping the parapet.'[11] Crossan, it transpired, was more afraid of rats than of the enemy. On 10 February he wrote the manager to thank him for a comforts parcel. Since his first night under fire he had been giving the war much consideration and had come up with a novel solution to the stalemate on the Western Front. 'I think that instead of fighting we should take the Fritzes on at football. I am certain we would do it on them.'[12]

The next morning Archie Ewing turned up in charge of a small party of reinforcements. He was still a sergeant and he promised the Colonel that he would behave. Two days later, Ernie Ellis received a telegram informing him that Belle had given birth to a daughter named Kitty. Compassionate leave was denied. On 17 February Jimmy Crawford took the chance to write his mother:

> We all were sent for a bath on Tuesday morning. It was some bath. There were six big tubs and about three inches of water in each. That had to do six men, one after the other. (I didn't bathe that day.)[13]

He had recently been issued with a waterproof cape and 'big gum-boots' to keep out the wet. On 19 February he was fitted for a sheepskin 'furry' and a steel shrapnel-helmet. Adding the rest of his kit, he humped around 60 lb of clothing and equipment back up the road to Vieux Berquin. He was 5 ft 6 in. tall. Napier Armit thought some of his men looked 'like Christmas trees, stumping along with things hooked on to every available hook or button, and carrying [besides] sandbags full of wood and coal which they had "borrowed" for the brazier fire'.[14]

On 20 February they returned to the line. They were on their own now.

'This is winter in the trenches with a vengeance,' wrote Herbert Warden. 'The coldest I have experienced,' added Fraser MacLean. 'My platoon,' he continued, 'is occupying a salient only 80 yards from the Boche, so there is little chance of sleep. The enemy, however, is very quiet and has not disturbed us much. The excitement of watching their movements through a loophole by day and over the parapet by night is delightful, and night-patrolling in front of our wire is a thrilling occupation.'[15] There is a full measure of Scottish irony in the last sentence, and more in Donald Gunn's dispatch for readers of the *Evening News*:

> The first night two corporals and half a dozen men passed through our own wire and obtained valuable information regarding the location of German patrols, so that our machine-guns might have a likely target later. Trench warfare is a very stale business and after a day of staring through periscopes it lends a deal of interest to the game to have the opportunity of going out in search of adventure.[16]

On the night of 22 February a hostile machine-gun caught three members of A Company in the open about 30 yards from the German line. Frank Taylor, one of Peter Ross's Broughton boys, was wounded in the hip. Cpl David McIvor stayed with him while John McAra nipped back for help. The duty officer, 2/Lt John Stewart, a 30-year-old solicitor from Corstorphine, crawled out to supervise the rescue, and the three of them managed to carry Taylor home. Stewart was awarded the Military Cross; McIvor, who was the same age and worked as a clerk with the Ormiston Coal Company, got the Military Medal. Pte McAra had to make do with a handshake from the Colonel. Taylor was stretchered off up Queer Street. Two nights later, Stewart made the same journey after being shot through both ankles on his first independent patrol.

On 25 February McCrae's were relieved by the 15th Royal Scots and moved back to billets at Streaky Bacon Farm on the Rue Deletrée between Fleurbaix and Armentières. Just behind Bois Grenier and still well within range of the enemy guns, the area was designated 'Brigade Reserve'. Since only two of the 101st Brigade's four battalions were required to man the front line, a short spell by rotation in 'stand-by' or reserve was supposed to provide the remaining two with some respite from the breastworks. In practice, troops in these billets were seen as a convenient source of labour for repairs to the forward defences, so there was no rest at all. On the afternoon of 28 February John Brodie, the battalion's canteen sergeant, was cooking for a working party in the support line, when one of the men tried to bring down an enemy Taube with his rifle. The bullet hit Brodie in the left thigh and the air turned blue. The sergeant, a 40-year-old veteran of

South Africa, was proprietor of the Cross Keys Hotel in Dalkeith. Famous in McCrae's for his thirst and his ability to secure scarce commodities, he would be greatly missed. That evening, 2/Lt Russell Tod, a 21-year-old bank clerk from Stockbridge, was hit by a stray bullet while supervising a work detail in the front line. The projectile passed through his left buttock and had to be extracted per anum. 'It caused me considerable inconvenience,' he wrote later from hospital at Le Touquet.

There were no further casualties that night. The following evening the battalion moved up in heavy rain to relieve the 10th Lincolns. James Jollie, a 19-year-old steel pattern-maker from Bathgate, was caught in the stomach by a round from an enemy machine-gun as he climbed down into a communication trench. He died eight hours later in a dressing station near Sailly. The previous day, he had written his mother to describe the great care he was taking to come home in one piece. By the time the letter reached Scotland, he was three weeks in his grave. The rest of the relief had gone off quietly – as did the ensuing five-day sojourn in the line. There was a bit of shelling and the usual vicious sniping but they were becoming hardened now – 'more resigned', said Tommy King. Ernie Becker was a hairdresser from West Claremont Street. The 28-year-old signaller recorded his thoughts in verse:

> I sit in my dug-out now sad and forlorn,
> My nerves and my temper are both badly worn.
> Since I joined the army I have led a fine dance,
> I am tired of existing 'Somewhere in France',
> This dug-out holds two, but there's six in it now.
> There's a fire in the centre and sweat on my brow.
> My comrades are sleeping all tied up in knots,
> The sentries and Boches are exchanging shots.
> The snow it is falling, the wild wind does moan.
> Do you wonder at all I am dreaming of home?
> Conditions are bad and the rations are few,
> The trenches are muddy, the outlook is blue.
> I am strafed by the weather and the enemy's shots.
> I rue the day that I joined the Royal Scots . . .'[7]

Herbert Warden observed that some of the men were becoming demoralised, blaming the constant need for nocturnal repairs. 'Any new work on the trenches,' he wrote, 'is spotted at once and usually shelled.' MacLean blamed the weather. Sgt Crawford wondered at 'the awful randomness of injury and death'. Harry Harley, a 34-year-old warehouseman from Braid Place, was angered by the absence of leave. He was corresponding with daughter Chrissie, his 'wee darling', and ached to get back to Edinburgh for even a short visit. 'I will give you a good box of chocolates when I come home,' he wrote. 'I remain your loving Daddy.' John Thomson, a 27-year-old compositor from Heriothill Terrace, was unhappy with his billet:

> The place we sleep in is very cold, having walls only on three sides, and these only half way up to the roof. There is a canvas screen on the other side. The roof is full of holes and the melting snow drips down on top of us. For a bed we have the hard ground and a waterproof sheet . . .[18]

Some of the officers went to unusual lengths to maximise the comfort of their men. Peter Ross was a captain now, having succeeded to command of A Company shortly before embarkation. One night he had an unexpected visit. Walter Vignoles, second-in-command of the 10th Lincolns, recalled the details:

> *Scene.* − A fire-trench with a sheet of corrugated iron over it. 'Inky Bill' storming and pointing out that this directly contravenes Divisional Orders. The little Scots captain with the strong Scottish accent, as soon as Inky Bill pauses, says, 'It's like this, Sir. My boys are University boys, and if they got wet they would soon be ready for hospital. But if the Boche come over, we will have the roof off in a second, and if we cannot get at them with a bayonet, we will bite them with our teeth.' Bill looks at the little fellow with astonishment, taps him on the chest and says, 'I like you, you little ------. In future you do just as you damn well please, and if anyone says anything to you, say that Major-General Ingouville-Williams told you to do it.'[19]

Lionel Coles permitted a certain amount of latitude with regard to uniform regulations, allowing C Company to shred precious sandbags in order to 'lag' their legs against the cold. 'It was much appreciated,' remembered Jimmy McEvoy, 'and absolutely forbidden by the QM.' McEvoy was in the line on 12 March, when the Germans opened a hurricane bombardment. It was short, sharp and violent: 'shrapnel bursting everywhere', he said. The footballers' platoon was on duty at the parapet. Six privates were wounded, including Jimmy Todd, a 20-year-old railway clerk from Easter Road, who played on the wing for Raith Rovers. Todd took a large shell-fragment full in the chest; he was carried to a dug-out and died before the guns had finished firing. Alfie Briggs, who attended the funeral at Erquinghem, wrote to McCartney: 'Jimmy was in everything, a constant source of solace to us all with his good humour and cheerfulness. He is a sore loss.'[20]

The battalion suffered a further casualty the next night. 2/Lt Norman Walker, a 26-year-old law apprentice from Glasgow, was leading a patrol in no man's land. The Germans put up a flare and opened fire with two machine-guns. Miraculously Walker was the only one injured, a single bullet passing through his right hand and left forearm. He was led back to the British line cursing liberally and waving his bloody fist in the direction of the enemy. Shock, John Veitch recalled, took different people different ways. Next evening, amid another fierce bombardment, McCrae's were relieved by the 27th Northumberland Fusiliers of 103rd Brigade and moved back for a well-earned break in Divisional reserve at Erquinghem. The battalion was joined here by a replacement draft from Ripon, led by Harry Rawson, who was now a full lieutenant. He had brought two 'subs' with him, both former A Company privates, lately commissioned. George Russell was a 20-year-old banking apprentice from Howe Street; Bill McMichael, a 20-year-old dental student from Inverleith. Among the 43 other ranks in the party were Jimmy Hazeldean, Teddy McGuire and Hamlet MacMillan. All three were sent to C Company. On 19 March Annan Ness wrote to McCartney to inform him of their safe arrival and to reply to a recent letter about a proposed 'bumper comforts parcel' for the footballers:

> Briggs and myself put it to the boys. The result was a merry meeting in our hut last night. We were all present, being out of the line for a few days. Before going into the matter of comforts, the boys would like to thank you and the directors for your kindness. I am sure you have plenty of work on hand and we appreciate your efforts. The position with ourselves is very quiet. Nevertheless we are looking forward to a lively time soon. After talking the matter over carefully, we came to the conclusion that the articles mentioned here are the most desired: a melodeon (for Crossan); a few mouth-organs (to keep Fritz happy); socks (always); no underwear (please); chocolate, sweets, dried fruit; toilet soap; candles, matches, cigarettes, tobacco; old magazines; writing paper and envelopes. As the authorities are desirous that the men smoke pipes, could you send us some. The list need not be strictly adhered to. Anything will be appreciated.[21]

On 23 March the battalion returned to Brigade reserve at Fleurbaix. Florance Kelly, a 44-year-old grocer from Springvalley Terrace, wrote home to his 'bairns':

Our platoon is billeted in what was once a very fine house. There are eight apartments and a large attic. You have a choice of four entrances. It would be a fine place for playing in. There is also a large garden, which has been a good one before the war. This town must have been very prosperous. The 'Germhuns' occupied it for six days in 1914 and it has had a terrible battering. The streets are in ruins and the church has also had its share. The clock in the spire on one side has stopped at eight minutes past eight, and on the other side at seven forty. There are very few people about. The town is well fortified. One side of the main street is protected by barbed wire and a few of the houses are mined. When I look at the state of this place and picture dear Auld Reekie, I acknowledge we have to thank God for a lot . . .[22]

'Flo' was a member of B Company, which had yet to suffer a single casualty. On 27 March, as they prepared to relieve the 15th Royal Scots in the front line, one of his pals was killed by shell-fire. George Peters, a 35-year-old letterpress printer from Buccleuch Place, left a wife and two sons. Two nights later, the battalion's Lewis gun officer, James Moir, a 24-year-old spirit merchant from Blackford, led a small party into no man's land to lay a listening wire. The Germans heard them working and sent up a flare. A machine-gun opened fire and Moir was shot in the right shoulder. The bullet smashed through the bone and punctured his lung. John McParlane carried him to safety. Moir protested that the injury was less serious than it looked. The doctor told him that if he didn't keep still he would die. He was strapped into a stretcher, placed in an ambulance, and driven very slowly to St Omer. Before he left, he promised he'd be back.

The following afternoon the Germans resumed their bombardment of the front line: 'Jack Johnsons, whizz-bangs, woolly bears and all sorts,' wrote Sgt Crawford. The A Company officers' dug-out received a direct hit. Walter Winning, one of the servants, was cooking in the adjoining 'kitchen'. A shell fragment struck him in the back. He died within a quarter of an hour. Walter had travelled all the way from Catrine in Ayrshire to enlist in McCrae's. He was a 21-year-old coal miner with a Pitman's certificate for shorthand. His officer, 2/Lt Joseph Bell, wrote that he was 'straightforward, willing and faithful'. Bell's fellow sub, Matthew Warren, sustained multiple shrapnel wounds in the blast and was badly concussed. He had been drinking tea when the shell landed; now he was coughing blood. Bell and Warren, both Ulstermen, were recent arrivals. Bell, 21, was an Arts undergraduate at Belfast University and a follower of Sir Edward Carson; Warren, two years older, was a Redmondite librarian from the Ormeau Road. At home, they might have tried to kill each other; in France, young Joe was weeping for his friend. Two privates, Andrew Kay and John Koerber, had to be dug out of the ruins. Kay was a bank clerk from Gilmore Place; his father and uncles had been founder members of the Hearts. Koerber was a wages clerk from Kirk Street in Leith, who had enlisted after a young woman handed him a white feather near the foot of the Walk.

On the evening of 31 March the battalion moved back to Fleurbaix reserve, where a parcel from McCartney was awaiting Annan Ness. The inventory is remarkable: 240 pairs of socks; 141 lb of black tobacco; 12 dozen pipes; 5,000 cigarettes; 200 boxes of matches; 25 harmonicas; 2 fiddles; 100 boxes of Edinburgh Rock; 400 bars of Fry's milk chocolate; 300 candles; 20 cases of toilet soap; 12 dozen writing pads; 3,000 envelopes; 14 pairs of football boots; 3 balls; 2 pumps; 1 melodeon; assorted magazines and books. 'I hope this will suffice,' wrote the manager. 'Should you require anything else, please do not hesitate to ask.' Crossan's melodeon was stamped 'Made in Germany'. There was also a tin of Jean McCartney's special tablet for Cuthbert Lodge, who was having a harder time than most. It was said that picture postcards of his head showing above the parapet were circulating in Berlin. Ness replied that some playing cards and board games might help to relieve the monotony. He added:

> Most of our time is spent digging holes in bits of France to fill other holes in other bits of France. Much of the country is now contained in sandbags. The rest is in our boots, our pockets, our rifles and clarted thick all over our uniforms. We are not at all the smart battalion you remember. Yesterday we built a road up to a trench on our front line, nothing very rugged, just a wooden planked affair. To-day the Germans shelled it, so this evening we must start again. Still we can smile through the grime. One of the boys has just sent a parcel of dried mud home to his folks, together with instructions on how much water they must add in order to achieve the correct 'trench consistency'. Oh we have all the wags out here, all right . . .[23]

McCrae's returned to the line on 4 April, worried over rumours of a Zeppelin raid on Edinburgh, in which several people were said to have died. Sir George spent much of the following day on the telephone trying to establish the facts. The airship passed over Heriot's and the Castle. Bristo was bombed: six people were killed in Marshall Street alone, and four more elsewhere. Tom Penman, a 36-year-old fish salesman from Abbeyhill, was furious. He opened a loophole and chambered a cartridge. It was broad daylight and he had been warned that such an action could prove fatal. A waiting sniper put a single bullet straight through his eye. He left a wife and four children. Next morning Sgt John Duncan from Buccleuch Street was fusing a box of Mills grenades in the bomb-room of the battalion's headquarters at Foray House, when he mistakenly released a pin. Realising the danger to his pals, the 21-year-old librarian rushed outside and (in Veitch's words) 'took the blast to himself'. He was killed instantly. Sir George immediately asked Brigade to consider him for a gallantry award. The request was refused on the grounds that the incident had arisen through his own carelessness.

Foray House stood in a little hollow about one and a half miles south of Fleurbaix on the Rue David. A red-brick farmhouse with a thatched roof, it remained virtually intact in spite of the Germans' best efforts to blow it apart. There was a shell-hole in the kitchen and the walls were marked by bullets, but otherwise it was warm and well-appointed. 'Successive units,' wrote Sir George, 'had added to the comfort of the Mess.' On 8 April he was visited there by Lieutenant-Colonel G.H. Knox of the 23rd Australian Infantry Battalion, lately arrived from Gallipoli via Alexandria and Marseilles. In a few days these 'colonials' (as Herbert Warden insisted on calling them) would be taking over the sector; in the meantime McCrae's — seasoned veterans by now — were showing them the ropes. Knox was particularly taken by the farm and told the Colonel he was looking forward to a quiet tenancy. He rode off with a bottle of whisky and a contented smile.[24]

By 10 April preparations for the hand-over were well-advanced. The Australians were expected that evening. At 1.15 p.m. Sir George was sitting down to lunch with Warden and Bill Gilmour, the battalion's Canadian doctor. Jock Miller, the Signalling Officer, was about to join them. There were about a hundred other ranks on the premises, mainly HQ men and orderlies. Five minutes later, a whizz-bang exploded in the field to the front of the building. Immediately afterwards another exploded to the rear. Warden jumped out of his chair:

> While the officers sought refuge in the C.O.'s dug-out, I ran round the farm, shouting to everyone to go to the orderly room shelter, which they did in double quick time. Just as I was pushing the men in, a coal box landed right in front of the building. The noise and smoke were dreadful. The next shot was a miss, and so was the next; but after that the Boche put an incendiary shell right through the front building and set the thatch on fire. Then commenced a regular shelling, composed of whizz-bangs, coal boxes and heavy 5.9 shrapnel. It lasted an hour. Altogether the Germans fired 90 shells into our poor old farm. Soon the whole buildings were in flames. Our dug-outs were filled with smoke and the smell of brimstone and lyddite, and we had rather a lean time. Realising that the Boche

meant us in earnest, I pushed the men out, three or four at a time –
to rush round the back of the farm, across an open piece of ground
for about 20 yards, into the comparative safety of the trenches. My
last view of our Mess showed the whole room ablaze.[25]

Sir George, meanwhile, was still in his dug-out, which was attached to the
rear wall of the main building. He takes up the story:

It was an elephant-fluted, tuppeny tube arrangement, consisting of
a half-circular iron covering. A 4.2 inch shell quickly chipped the
end of it. Had there been a direct hit from a 5.9, we would all have
been killed. The orderlies slept in an adjoining room. They had
hurriedly taken cover, leaving their packs, with 120 rounds of
ammunition each, lying on the floor. When the fire reached the
room, the bullets went 'pop pop' against the dug-out wall and the
iron covering became almost red-hot. It looked as if we would be
roasted alive.[26]

Warden again:

After the men were all clear, I advised the C.O. and the officers to
make a bolt. Sir George and I made our dash and gained the trench
in safety. I looked back at the farm. It was a blazing congeries of
beams, lath and furniture, and was practically level with the
ground. The bursting shells gave a blinding flash and screech of
shrapnel, or else a cloud of black smoke, mixed with bricks, pieces
of furniture and debris. We finished lunch in the first line, courtesy
of Captain Hendry and the officers of D Company.[27]

There were no serious casualties. Jock Miller had a burn on his hand. He
was a mathematics teacher at George Watson's College and had been with
the battalion since Ripon. His nickname was 'Smiler'. He was 33 but
seemed older, like a father figure to the younger officers. Bob Martin
remembered his 'kindly cynicism, putting out a few staccato remarks
between long silences filled with the aroma of Three Nuns from the bent
pipe'. Miller's signallers were trained initially in the use of semaphore, but
he was increasingly running courses in telegraphy and telephones, teaching
linemen and operators to work quickly under fire. Doc Gilmour patched
him up and he wandered off to replace the kit lost in the bombardment.
Charlie Robertson went with him. D Company's CQMS was a provision
merchant from North Berwick and the Quartermaster's most reliable
scrounger. Cpl Veitch recalled a simple maxim: 'If it wasn't nailed down, it

belonged to McCrae's. Come to think of it, if it *was* nailed down, it still belonged to McCrae's and we'd have the nails as well.' James Moir had once written: 'If you want to take the city of Berlin from the Kaiser, send out the Army of McCrae. They take every blessed thing they come across, and if Bill gets off even with his trousers, he will be lucky.'[28] By evening Miller had everything he needed. Lieutenant-Colonel Knox, meanwhile, arrived to find that he didn't even have a roof.

The battalion was relieved at 8 p.m. and marched back to reserve billets near Sailly. The men, noted D.M. Sutherland, were grumbling about overdue and cancelled leave. Over the next three days, they retraced the twenty-five miles to Blendecques. On 14 April they marched finally to Houlle, six miles north of St Omer, for a fortnight's training. The rest of the Division was already in the area. Herbert Warden wrote his wife: 'We are to have a rest tomorrow, but start our strenuous work the following day. Officers and men all round are being recalled from leave, and leave is absolutely stopped.'[29] Sgt Crawford observed that 'the country here is very different from the place we have left. There are lots of low, undulating hills and pretty little woods breaking into leaf.' On 16 April Divisional manœuvres began – three weeks of 'rifle, bomb and bayonet'. At the end, they were out on their feet. 'I think,' wrote Harry Rawson to his uncle, 'that we are getting ready for a show. I don't know where (and I couldn't tell you if I did), but I know that when it comes we will be ready. After that Zeppelin business the boys are spoiling for a scrap, and I think they'll prove a handful for the Hun.'[30]

Harry must have been clairvoyant.

CHAPTER SEVEN

'My little all to Mother, with best love'

Twelve weeks earlier, on a dark, wet, afternoon at Wallon Cappel, the 34th Division stood for three hours on the Hazebrouck road until a small, black unmarked car was driven past. The passenger rolled down his window to inspect them. He looked like an elderly inmate of some private institution. General Joseph Joffre, commander-in-chief of the French Army, was the author of an ambitious plan for a grand Allied offensive that coming summer. Forty of his own divisions and twenty-five British would attack side-by-side on a thirty-nine-mile front astride the River Somme in France. The war, in theory, would be over within months. It was a strange choice of ground: there was nothing much to aim for, no great strategic prize to spur the breakthrough. Worse, despite his assertion that the sector offered many advantages to the attacking force, there was ample evidence to suggest that the long, wooded ridge on which the Germans were entrenched was quite the strongest defensive position in the entire western theatre.

Joffre's newly appointed British counterpart remained uncertain. General Sir Douglas Haig favoured mounting his offensive in Flanders, but he had been instructed by Kitchener and the War Committee of the Cabinet to 'cooperate' with the French. Such cooperation would of course be tempered by his desire to maintain a substantial measure of independence. Haig was concerned that the BEF was far from ready for the task. Poorly trained and quite untried, his new battalions needed time to settle in. He therefore declined to give Joffre a firm date for the British to take over the French line at Arras, arguing that the move would involve monstrous logistical effort when his men should be preparing for the decisive attack of the war. For the same reason he also resisted Joffre's suggestion that the British armies be used for a long series of preliminary assaults designed to 'wear down' the enemy reserves prior to the main offensive. He foresaw in that process the wearing down of his own divisions, and they were much too precious. They must be preserved for the most propitious moment. Then, like Loos without the blunders over planning and supply, they would strike, cutting a great hole in the German defences and sweeping all before them. Preferably in Flanders.

But Joffre was insisting on the Somme – the southernmost point on the British front, the point at which the Allied armies met. Here he could be certain of having *les Anglais* under his control, certain of their full commitment to what was, after all, a predominantly Gallic effort. On 14 February the two men met at Chantilly and a bargain was struck. Joffre withdrew his demand for prolonged wearing down operations, agreeing instead to Haig's suggestion of limited actions confined to the fortnight before the main attack. He also conceded that for the moment, at least, the Arras sector would remain in French hands. In return, despite his reservations, Haig accepted the Somme as the site for the offensive and instructed General Sir Henry Rawlinson, commander of the embryonic Fourth Army, to prepare a plan for British participation. Within a week, however, the Germans moved on the French stronghold at Verdun. As French divisions hurried south to hold the line, Haig was forced to relieve the Arras front immediately. His First Army spread out to take over the northern half; his Third, which had been dug in on the Somme, stepped up to cover the rest, leaving a gap for Rawlinson's command – now three corps strong – to fill down to the river. As he proceeded with his reconnaissance of the ridge, beset by tales of horror from Verdun, 'Rawly' consoled himself with thoughts of reinforcement. In stages from late March to early May a fourth corps would arrive. By then the rest of his Army would already be in place and he would know exactly what he had to fight with – even if he wasn't entirely sure what he was being asked to fight *for*.

❋ ❋ ❋

It was Princes Street in Picardy, a thick cloud of dust on the Amiens road. You could hear them long before they came in view – the skirl of the pipes playing 'Bonnie Dundee', the beat of the drums, a battalion in step and a thousand Scottish voices through the haze:

> Kaiser Bill he came marching o'er Belgium and France
> To challenge the Empire with warlike advance.
> But the bravest of Hearts volunteered for the fray
> And threw in their lot with old Geordie McCrae!

> Come pack up your footballs and scarves of maroon.
> Leave all your sweethearts in Auld Reekie toon.
> Fall in wi' the lads for they're off and away
> To take on the bold Hun with old Geordie McCrae![1]

They were half a mile from Raineville, Willie Duguid out in front, blowing red-faced in the heat. Two hours behind, to the south of the Somme, lay the railway halt at Longueau, where they had detrained at noon, a further nine hours on from Houlle. They marched at ease in columns four, rifles balanced on their shoulders, muzzle forward, in the manner they had learned from the old hands at Ripon.

> Just a twelve-month ago Private Wattie was said
> To be sure of a national cap for his head.
> Now he wears the Glengarry, right proud of the day
> That he marched to the standard of Geordie McCrae!

As Blaney's rousing chorus was repeated, word was passed to shoulder arms and straighten. The village deserved a proper entrance in good military order. In an effort to impress the locals, the band struck up a shaky 'Marseillaise'. But the people here on 5 May were mostly British soldiers – Suffolks and Lincolns and 15th Royal Scots – while the Tyneside brigades were already billeted close by. 34th Division was the last unit to join Rawlinson's reinforcing corps, numbered III and commanded by Lieutenant-General Sir William Pulteney. The remaining two divisions in III Corps were the Regular 8th, which contained a substantial contingent of Yorkshiremen, and the New Army 19th, which had been recruited in the main from Lancashire, Wales and the English Midlands. Each of the 36 infantry battalions – like the 16th at Houlle – had spent much of the preceding month polishing their bayonet skills and practising assaults. On 7 May, from his tent outside the village, Harry Wattie wrote home with the latest censored news:

> We have shifted again, a long way from the last place. We travelled all night in the train, forty to a cattle-truck, and then had a ten-mile march, so we were pretty fed-up when we landed. I enjoyed the journey, though, as we came through some lovely country, quite a change from the other parts. The weather has been warm with the occasional thunderplump. We had a pretty strenuous time at the last billet, as we were up Sunday and Saturday and all week at half past four and out all day. The heat when we were marching was terrific and we sometimes went without our shirts. I believe it will

135

be even warmer here. I don't know how long it will be before we go back to the trenches, but it won't be so bad if this weather holds good. For the past fortnight I have slept out in the open, as it is not a bit cold. Every one of us is as brown as a berry and we are all in the best of health . . . [2]

He was right about the lovely country. It reminded the Midlothian lads of the rich, rolling farmland around Ratho or Kirknewton – only more open, for there were few trees, except in scattered woods, no hedges, and scarcely any isolated houses. The natives seemed to huddle in their ancient red-tiled hamlets, surrounded by cider orchards and linked across the cornfields by a profusion of narrow, winding lanes. 'This place,' wrote Harry Rawson on 8 May, 'is both so pretty and so peaceful that it is hard to believe there is a war just up the road.'

But there was, and the following evening McCrae's marched ten miles closer, arriving after dark at the village of Franvillers. They stayed the night and all next day before marching on to Bresle, where the 101st Brigade was billeted in Divisional reserve on the Albert sector of the Somme front. The 102nd was nearby, but a further four miles distant, where the Very lights were hanging in the moonless eastern sky, 103rd Brigade had already gone into the line. Two days later the battalion was invited to visit a large hut on the outskirts of town. The rooms were filled with poison gas. Herbert Warden:

> It was fizzing out of a cylinder. Just to see that the gas helmet works, the doc and I sat down and remained there while the men passed through. It is uncomfortable to breathe through the helmet for any length of time, but it is absolute protection, as neither Doc nor I were in the least gassed. Afterwards we had to walk through a trench filled with lachrymatory gas, which the Boche sends over in shells, and we wore only the special goggles given to us. I don't think mine were properly fitted, because my eyes were very sore when I came out and I wept copious tears into my handkerchief. The Germans are using both chlorine and phosgene gas hereabouts . . .[3]

Training continued through a week of blazing sunshine. Then at 7.30 p.m. on 22 May they surrendered their billets to some incoming troops, assembled in the main street and set off for Brigade reserve. The distant guns grew louder as they marched – north-east at first for half a mile, then south until they landed on the main road to Bapaume, an ancient Roman highway, lined along its length by a single row of tall, undamaged elms. It had rained for three hours before they left, so the air was cool, the dust, for once, subdued. A dispatch rider buzzed past on the rearward run to Amiens and Tommy King was recording every detail for a letter to his family in Leith:

> Heaven help old Fritz! We saw hutments and canvas and mountains of crates, pioneers working like beavers, signallers burying great drums of cable. We passed a 60-pounder with a Glasgow crew. They were digging out a gun-pit and asked for cigarettes. Some of the lads obliged, so at least they would get a smoke break. Their bombardier was watering his Clydesdales. Paddy Crossan got talking with the chap. Did you know that Paddy used to work the pit-horses out at Addiewell? You won't get that in the *News*. He is a grand fellow, not a bit of side to him. All the Hearts men are the same, even Sjt.-Major Ness who could be excused acting up his rank. But no – he, too, is 'one of the boys.'
>
> It was pretty dark by 9 and we had another half hour's tramp before we reached the little town from which I write. I will call it 'A', although 'R' for rubble would serve just as well, for it has been badly knocked about. Even the kirk has not escaped the Fritzes' wrath. The drumfire is much louder here, for we are not far from the front.[4]

'A' was for Albert, menaced by the Germans from the high ground two miles east, where they had dug themselves in after being chased out of town by the French in September 1914. The civilian population – some 7,000 strong before the war – had mostly fled, though a few brave souls remained to serve the troops. There was an excellent pâtisserie and a little shop which 'specialised in everything but socks'. Albert was dominated by the battered shell of the church of Nôtre-Dame-de-Brebière, whose 200-foot belfry was topped by a copper dome, on which stood a gilt figure of the Virgin holding the infant Jesus. The dome had received a direct hit, but the statue did not fall. It remained, groaning sometimes in the wind, suspended by a thread of twisted girder. They said that when it struck the ground, the war would surely end. But nobody believed them. D.M. Sutherland wrote to his mother:

> A very interesting place, once a thriving small town, now absolutely deserted save for a few haunted looking natives who resort to their caves during bombardments. The principal part is a mass of crumbled ruins, in which bits of bedsteads and other metal goods project here and there. Rose bushes and honeysuckle bloom in the gardens. You can hear the distant rumble of artillery and the chatter of machine-guns in the night.[5]

Albert lay in the shallow, marshy valley of the narrow Ancre river, sheltered from enemy observation by two low hills, named Usna and Tara. McCrae's spent four days here, and four sleepless nights. On the evening of 27 May they marched up to relieve the Provost's Battalion in the front line. A mile or so beyond the town, the road began to level, and passed thereafter through a slight depression in the Usna-Tara ridge, coming quickly within sight of the enemy machine-guns. It was unsafe to proceed above ground, so the highway was curtailed 500 yards short of the brow by a large corrugated pile known as the 'Barrier'. From here, two long communication trenches, Perth and St Andrews Avenues, paralleled the road on either side, leading eventually into the British front-line system on the ridge's forward slopes. Perth was crowded with members of the 15th coming out. They had had a bad tour – one man dead and ten more left with fearful wounds after their introduction to the German 'oilcan', a two-foot metal drum, packed with high explosives, nails and scraps of sharpened iron, then fused to burst above the trench bay. McCrae's were therefore directed to St Andrews, which, like all the other trenches in the sector, had been signposted by battalions of the Black Watch and Gordons when they assumed control from the French back in November.

Narrow, dark and fully ten feet deep, St Andrews burrowed straight for half a mile before the first unlikely junction – Dunfermline Street – then wandered down into a traversed maze of familiar Scottish names. By first light the battalion was installed on a 1,200-yard front directly astride the forbidden road. C Company was on the left, with D tucked in beside them. Then came A and finally B, next to the Suffolks, who had relieved the Lincolns on the right. The Suffolks took the line south-east a further 875 yards, so that the Divisional front totalled 2,075 yards along its awkward, twisting length – overlooked by the enemy at every turn, for in truth the Usna-Tara ridge was no more than a low *spur*, a neglected offshoot of a much larger feature, which rose up on the opposite side of a narrow valley to completely dominate the British position.

Sir George was in Pitlochry Street, a broken, battered ruin that passed for more than half of his support line. Keeping low along the parapet, he found a loophole, drew aside the shutter and peered out. About 400 yards down the slope he could see the sandbagged British fire-trench, then beyond it in the valley, no man's land – on the map a quarter inch before you hit the fortified village of la Boisselle; on the ground a mass of craters, shell-holes and long-abandoned saps, where the two opposing armies almost met. This was the 'Glory Hole', a 300-yard stretch of front so treacherous that you could stumble into the enemy positions and out again without knowing. The craters were a legacy from the French. During the bitter fighting of early 1915 they had tried to dislodge the opposition by tunnelling under their trenches and blowing them up. The Boche had responded in kind, so that the once-pretty little hollow was now utterly corrupt – a dark, unsettled wasteland, garrisoned on either side by isolated sentries. Breastworks constructed across the divide were effectively *shared*.

Sir George's glasses shifted to the village, which rose from the valley to another, higher, spur so that the first German line sat well above its British counterpart, as did each successive trench going up the slope. La Boisselle itself was a smoking heap of red-brick rubble, crossed and covered by the chalk-mound parapets of a defensive system so intricate that it resembled a monstrous spider's web, wired thick and bristling with machine-guns. North of the Glory Hole, the two front lines drew sharply apart, the German cutting back at right angles to follow the Bapaume road for 500 yards before moving roughly parallel to the British again, at a distance of 800 yards. South of the Glory Hole, the two lines remained fairly close for 400 yards, but then no man's land widened as the ground fell away into a second valley, 'Sausage', a near relation of the first, which of course was christened 'Mash'. On the German side this shallow depression was guarded by Bloater Trench, which climbed out to join the northern flank of Sausage Redoubt, or 'Heligoland', some 600 yards from the British line. From the rear of this strongpoint, which was 250 yards wide, Kipper Trench emerged to curve south, then west, then south again into the sector occupied by XV Corps.

A second line, protected by its own deep belts of wire, ran approximately 200 yards behind the first. A third, about 400 yards further back, passed through the cellars of la Boisselle, then followed the crest of the hill before descending into Sausage Valley and climbing out into Scot's Redoubt and Wood Alley. Behind this, also wired, was a fourth line; behind that, wired again, was a fifth. The system was formidable: there was no random element in its design. The placing of trenches and barbed-wire entanglements had been carried out only after much consideration. Every curve, every straight, every sudden corner had its predetermined purpose in drawing maximum advantage of enfilade and cross-fire from the undulating ground. Moreover, la Boisselle was not isolated: the ridge was 12 miles long and consisted of an uninterrupted *series* of similarly fortified killing zones. To the north lay Ovillers and Thiepval; while, to the south, the Fricourt salient was the cornerstone of the entire German position on the Somme, the point at which the line swung east past Mametz and Montauban then down into the French sector.

There were no apparent weak spots. All along the British front you could see the rising shelves and terraces of the German first-line defences – the chalk-spoil of the trenches, the brick-dust village ruins, the rank grass snarled with endless belts of wire. This was not the end of it, however, for the Germans had dug a second position two miles behind the first, across the ridge-top from Grandcourt in the north, past Pozières, Bazentin, Longueval and Delville Wood to Guillemont – six more lines of trenches, seven belts of wire, and a fine view over Albert to the Amiens approaches. But even this was not the end, for, sure enough, two miles behind the second, a *third* position was being constructed from Pys, past Le Sars and Flers to Combles – three more lines, and still four miles before you reached Bapaume.

Daunting was hardly the word. But the British had only themselves to blame. When they first moved down to the Somme in autumn 1915 they found the trenches curiously quiet. The departing French had arrived at an understanding with the Germans: an atmosphere of amity prevailed. There had been no serious fighting in the sector for months; sniping was unheard of; shelling was restricted to the daylight 'working' hours. Fresh from the hostile wetlands of Ypres and Armentières, the British generals were appalled and took immediate steps to rectify matters, introducing trench-raids, telescopic sights and round-the-clock strafing – partly to accustom their untried battalions to the dangerous realities of war, but principally to foster the grim offensive spirit deemed essential to the success of the forthcoming 'Push'.

This sudden and sustained display of belligerence shook the Germans out of their complacency. They reckoned anyway that the Tommies' arrival indicated that an attack was imminent – a suspicion confirmed from February onwards by greatly increased activity behind the British lines. Clearly visible from the Pozières heights were the 'hutments and canvas and mountains of crates' which had impressed Pte King during the march up from Bresle. The Amiens road was black with transport. All along the ridge, intelligence reports noted an unprecedented concentration of troops and *matériel*; and this knowledge, coupled with more immediate problems caused by localised aggression, forced the Germans to strengthen and extend their defences. Now, not only would the attackers have to cross as many as 15 lines of trenches before they reached open country, but *underneath* those trenches, unsuspected for the moment, was a complex network of subterranean passages, incorporating barrack-rooms and shelters, hospitals and stores, cut straight into the chalk sub-soil, up to 40 feet deep. Secure against the heaviest bombardment, they were steel-doored, plumbed and timbered, with driven air and generated light. By the time McCrae's descended on the Somme, the relatively weak enemy position of late 1915 had been transformed into a veritable fortress.

Sir George disliked the strafing from the first. 'I do not know why we must provoke the opposition,' he wrote. 'They hold both the high ground and a considerable artillery advantage, so that any exchange of fire inevitably leaves us the worse off. Our trenches are a shambles, quite untenable in places. Our little slope is so exposed, the Hun machine-gunners and snipers so 'hot' that our working-parties cannot set themselves properly to the task of repairing the damage.'[6] Herbert Warden found the battalion's HQ dug-out, lately vacated by the 15th Royal Scots, 'so knocked about as to be uninhabitable. The officers' Mess has been smashed up too, so we are using a kind of cellar, 10 by 12, which enters from the foot of the trench. The only air comes from the staircase shaft, and there is practically no light.'[7]

D.M. Sutherland assured his mother that he felt quite safe from 'the biffs and bangs that at times disturb the ground level', but still left her wondering why, if that was the case, his dug-out walls were reinforced with chicken-wire to prevent them bursting when the earth shook.[8] The Fritzes' walls were shored with iron and lined with wooden panels; the British had their chicken-wire and a small official manual, which advised them to retire beneath a table when the shelling got too close.

A table or a bunk. Sgt Crawford had neither. On arriving at B Company's portion of the support line, he discovered that the little row of dug-outs assigned to his platoon had been flattened in the night. Since there was no way they could effect the necessary reconstruction in four or five days, he resigned himself to spending his tour in the open and settled down to write his sister:

> We are back in the trenches at last. And what trenches they are! It is 6.30 a.m. by your watch and we have had two quiet hours while the Boche prepare their breakfast. Other than this welcome spell each morning, I gather that the shelling will be constant. I can hear the picks and shovels all around, both sides are getting on with some urgent repairs. The larks are singing sweetly, the cook-fires smoke away and there is much loud shouting. The Germans like to greet us in the morning. There is at least one fellow with excellent English. He keeps calling out 'Newcastle!' for some reason. I may shout back 'Berlin' in a moment, just to keep him happy . . .'

No sooner had he pocketed his pencil than the day's bombardment started. Around noon a shower of rifle grenades descended on C Company. This weapon was only effective at close range, so the Germans would burrow into no man's land and dig manholes through which the muzzle of the rifle could be pushed before firing. The effects were random and terrifying. John Anderson, a 20-year-old shop assistant from Grove Street, was killed instantly; Wattie Deans, a 29-year-old lithographer from Henderson Row, was wounded in the neck. He wrote home from hospital that he was sorry to be leaving his pals.

At dawn on 28 May Fraser MacLean was resting in the fire-trench, having spent his night investigating an old cart on the enemy wire near la Boisselle. The Germans opened a sudden bombardment: as he ran for cover, a lump of casing caught him in the back. His men were placing him in a stretcher when a rifle grenade exploded on the parapet just above his head. His eardrums were ruptured and he didn't hear the shell which injured two more men. On 29 May another rifle grenade killed Sgt Robert Miller, one of the battalion's oldest members. He was hours short of his 49th birthday, and his platoon had bought him a cake. Miller was a former regular; he had served with the regiment in South Africa and worked for a spell as a waiter at the Liberal Club in Princes Street. Around 1906 (with a reference from Sir George) he secured the position of commissionaire at the Conservative Club in Selkirk, where he had ample time to practise his bowling. Like Willie Duguid, he gave up everything in order to enlist. As they were carrying his body from the line, an oilcan exploded in a neighbouring bay. It turned out to be the first of five. Alfie Briggs was there. 'It was like a violent shower of fizzing, red-hot rivets,' he wrote McCartney. Nobody was injured.

And so the strafe continued through the hazy morning heat – grenades and oilcans, oilcans and grenades, a slow, remittent rhythm of destruction. You could hear the German fire-commands, harsh and guttural; the sing-song taunts that followed each explosion; the barking of the strays in la Boisselle. Now and then a single shot would ring out across the valley, to be answered by the usual droll defiance. The Fritzes had a gramophone and favoured Schubert's 'Eighth' – *unfinished*, like the British trenches. The picks fell, the chalk flew, the sandbags rose and tumbled as the working parties toiled amid the ruins. Deep below ground the 'resting' sections – named by some comedian at staff – shivered in their dug-outs, marking off the hours until the ten o'clock relief. At noon the British heavies started strafing the enemy trenches around Heligoland. The response was swift and overwhelming. Herbert Warden:

> We got the lot: the lightning-like whizzbang, the black-smoked Jack Johnson, the green-smoked 5.9. Some of the shells burst on graze, ploughing up tremendous holes; those are usually high-explosive. Others (shrapnel) burst overhead. There is also a combination of H.E. and shrapnel, which is particularly annoying. You hear them all (except the whizzbang) some seconds before they land or burst, and the bigger ones make a noise like an express train. Couple that with the noise of the firing and then multiply the result by two or fifty

for the number of guns, and you will get an idea of the din. And think of the great clouds of smoke that arise from every explosion and you will get an idea of the thickness of the atmosphere . . .'[10]

It was the same story for the next two days. On 30 May, Sandy Brown, an apprentice grocer from Henderson Street, was killed by a rifle grenade. On the morning of 31 May six men were seriously wounded. During a lull in the bombardment Jimmy Crighton, one of A Company's snipers, abandoned his observation post to take shelter in a dug-out. The shelling resumed and he was killed by a direct hit. He was 21, a medical student from Tranent. He had enlisted with his best pal and classmate, Tommy Millar, who was now a subaltern in C Company; Crighton didn't fancy a commission but their friendship had survived. Millar wrote: 'We had an agreement that he would only salute me if there was another officer present. Apart from that we kept to first names. I am so dreadfully sad . . .' That evening, when McCrae's were relieved, he escorted Jimmy's body back to Albert, where it was buried in the communal cemetery. He spent the night on his own at the graveside.[11]

On 1 June the battalion marched back into reserve at Bresle. Warden thought they were in for some 'strenuous training', but he still didn't know *why*. Then at 6.30 a.m. on 6 June they marched four miles west to the village of Lahoussoye to find several thousand yards of red ribbon pegged across the adjacent fields. Drawing closer, they saw several dozen signposts: 'Bloater', 'Kipper', 'Sausage Redoubt' and all the rest. It was a full-scale model of the front at la Boisselle. Since the entire brigade was present, only one conclusion was possible. 'We had been sent to the Somme to take part in the Push,' said Cpl Veitch. 'And this was our objective. The General had given us the short straw.'

❋ ❋ ❋

On 3 April Rawlinson and his chief-of-staff Archie Montgomery had submitted the results of their reconnaissance to GHQ. They were sufficiently impressed by the depth of the opposing defences to divide their operations into two phases – one to capture the German first position between Serre and Maricourt, the other (following an indefinite period of 'consolidation') to assault the third position on the line from Serre to Combles. 'An attack to rush the whole of the enemy's defences in one will involve serious risks and be in the nature of a gamble,' they wrote. Better to seize points of tactical importance and then kill as many Germans as possible during the inevitable counter-attacks. They also recommended that the initial assault be preceded by a prolonged bombardment aimed at cutting wire, destroying trench-works and limiting the movement of supplies.[12] Haig was unimpressed. He considered the plan too cautious and offered his own optimistic alternative: a short, intensive bombardment followed by the immediate capture of the enemy's entire first-line system along with a substantial portion of the second. His letter, dated 12 April, made no mention of wire and seemed to consider the objectives as places to be occupied by right rather than taken after heavy (and unpredictable) fighting. 'It is usually wiser to act boldly,' observed the commander-in-chief.[13]

It took Rawlinson seven days to respond. 'After further consideration,' he wrote, 'it still seems to me that an attempt to gain more distant objectives involves considerable risks. I, however, fully realise that it may be necessary to incur these risks in view of the importance of the object to be attained.' Haig's scheme was reluctantly accepted. Rawlinson held his ground on the bombardment though, reasoning that the vast belts of German wire could not be destroyed in a few hours. He added:

> Bearing in mind the existence of numerous dug-outs and cellars in the enemy's lines, I do not think that the moral effect of a short bombardment will be so great as that of one extended over several days. The effect of a long bombardment which will pulverise strong-points one-by-one, gradually knock in communication trenches, prevent reliefs being carried out and systematically beat down the enemy's defences, will be much greater. A long bombardment gives the enemy no chance of sleep; food and ammunition are difficult to bring up, and the enemy is kept in a constant state of doubt as to when the infantry assault will take place . . .[14]

GHQ replied on 16 May, apparently conceding the point. 'As regards artillery bombardment,' said the letter, 'it should be of a methodical nature and continue until the officers commanding the attacking units are satisfied that the obstacles to their advance have been adequately destroyed.'[15] This was nonsense. Since the date of the assault would have to be set well in advance and coordinated with the French, it followed that the advancing troops would still have to tackle the obstacles even if they remained substantially intact. Moreover, with a sweep of his pencil, Haig had doubled the area that required to be suppressed: since no extra howitzers were available, it followed also that the vital concentration of bombardment had effectively been *halved*.

On 17 May Rawlinson's commanders were given their objectives. The high ground beyond Pozières and Contalmaison went to III Corps: it was indeed the shortest straw. Red ribbons didn't do it justice. Lahoussoye sat astride the Bapaume road and was dressed to play the role of la Boisselle. According to GHQ's instructional paper, 'Training of Divisions for Offensive Action':

> A complete system of hostile trenches and at least the first line of a second system together with the defended localities between these two should be marked out on the ground to full scale from trench maps and aerial photographs. The assault over the area should be practised several times by the division as a whole.
>
> Every attacking unit must be given a clearly defined objective, to be captured and consolidated at all costs; the assaulting columns must go right through above ground in successive waves or lines, each line adding fresh impetus to the preceding line when it is checked and carrying the whole forward to the objective. From the moment the first line of assaulting troops leaves our trenches, a continuous forward flow must be maintained from the rear throughout the division. Divisions must be practised in passing of a fresh body of troops through the troops which have reached their objective. The second attack will then be carried out on the same principles.[16]

Rawlinson had little confidence in the ability of New Army volunteers to demonstrate initiative under fire. These manœuvres recall nothing so much as the attack of the Old Guard at Waterloo. They also represented an unattainable ideal. Since 34th Division was still occupying the front line and the reserve positions behind it, at no point did all 12 infantry battalions get the chance to rehearse together. Divisional training was effectively *Brigade* training. Ernie Becker described it as a series of 'sham attacks on German trenches. We came home each day in motor transport.'[17] Bob Armour, a 25-year-old grocer from Loanhead, noted that it rained constantly.[18] John Veitch compared Inky Bill to the Grand Old Duke of York – 'he marched us up to the top of the hill, then he marched us down again'. It lasted only six days: by 10 June they had apparently been 'trained'. Fourth Army's 'Red Book' was the principal tactical authority for the operation, but it was a far from satisfactory document. Here, for example, it speculates on the suppression of enemy strongpoints which have 'escaped the bombardment':

> The Lewis gun, owing to its lightness and invisibility, may provide the solution to this problem. It is suggested that Lewis gunners, either under cover of darkness, smoke or artillery bombardment, may be able to creep out into no man's land and establish themselves in advance of our assaulting troops in saps, shell-holes or long grass.

> From these positions, where it will be difficult for them to be
> detected, they will be able to fire on enemy emplacements and so
> assist the infantry to advance.[19]

The Lewis automatic rifle weighed 27 pounds and employed a 'team' of 6
men – a firer, a loader/observer and 4 magazine carriers. It was neither light
nor remotely invisible. It suffered also from a limited effective range –
hardly the weapon to engage and destroy well-entrenched machine-guns. It
was itself extremely vulnerable and the attacking battalions would have (at
best) only two per company. The compound of uncertainty in the above
passage is breathtaking: the author was fighting his battle on Salisbury
Plain. 'Training of Divisions' and the Red Book indicate that the generals
were struggling at the foot of a learning curve every bit as steep as that
faced by the humblest private. Few of them, however, had the brains to
realise it. When the infantry attacked, the manuals and the ill-considered
theories would be superseded (once again) by the rifle, the bayonet and by
loyalty to your pals. It was really all they had.

On 6 June it was announced that Lord Kitchener had drowned en route
to Russia, when the cruiser *Hampshire* struck a mine off Orkney. Ten days
later, Haig and Joffre finally agreed a date for the offensive. Following a
preliminary bombardment of five days, the assault would go in on the
morning of Thursday the 29th – not under the protection of dawn, but
three hours later, at 7.30 a.m., to assist artillery observation. French
involvement had been drastically reduced, so it was now primarily a British
operation – on a 14-mile front from Serre in the north to Maricourt in the
south. Five divisions of the French Sixth Army would attack in support on
the banks of the Somme itself. If the British were successful in breaking the
German second line, the way would be open for the cavalry from Hubert
Gough's Reserve Army to move on Bapaume. What they would do after that
remained uncertain.

34th Division's task was simple: an advance of 3,500 yards on a front of more
than a mile, capturing two fortified villages and six lines of trenches. Inky Bill
planned to move his command in four columns, each three battalions deep.
101st Brigade would take the right, opposite Heligoland; 102nd Brigade the left,
either side of la Boisselle. The village itself would not be directly assaulted;
instead a special force of bombers from 102nd Brigade would infiltrate the ruins
and neutralise any opposition. 103rd Brigade, meanwhile, spread out along the
divisional front, would follow in reserve. The leading battalions were to
capture the German defences up to and including the first reserve line, an
advance of 2,000 yards. They were given until 8.18 a.m. to achieve this. The
support battalions would then pass through this line to assault the
'intermediate' position in front of Contalmaison village, which would fall by

8.58 a.m. Finally, 103rd Brigade, having come all the way from the forward slopes of Usna-Tara, would carry the attack on to a line east of Contalmaison. By 10.10 a.m. they would be brewing up.

These timings were crucial: Major-General Pulteney and his staff had taken the Red Book at its word. 'The assaulting troops must push forward at a steady pace in successive lines,' was the official instruction. III Corps would adhere precisely. This was the essence of the Lahoussoye manœuvres – a slow advance to strict schedule, protected by the divisional artillery, which would 'keep its fire immediately in front of the infantry as the latter advances, battering down all opposition with a hurricane of projectiles'. Once more it was cuckoos on Salisbury Plain: there was no allowance for the possibility that the opposition might have plans of their own. On the night of 4–5 June Robert Kirchstetter, a private in the 1st Battalion of the German 110th Reserve Infantry Regiment, had been captured during a raid on the enemy trenches around Heligoland. He informed his interrogators that the front-line dug-outs at la Boisselle were buried at least six metres deep and that they were all connected up below ground. The morale in his unit was excellent and he believed that Germany would be victorious in 1917.[20] The message was passed on, but it seems that no one chose to read it.

❋ ❋ ❋

On 15 June McCrae's marched up to the village of Dernancourt, three miles south of Albert, and were billeted in reserve on the right-hand sector of the divisional front. When they went into the line this time, they would occupy the trenches to the south of the road – directly opposite their scheduled objectives. That night the men opened their Pay Books at page 12, the 'Short Form of Will':

> In the event of my death I give the whole of my property and effects to my mother, Mrs Mary Atkins, 999, High Street, Aldershot.
>
> (*Signature*) *THOMAS ATKINS*
> *Private, No. 1793,*
> Date, *5th August, 1914* *Gloucester Fusiliers*[21]

Most of them copied it verbatim, altering the names to suit their chosen beneficiary. David McIvor, MM, produced a novel variation: 'My little all to Mother, with best love.' Andrew McNulty, a 27-year-old grocer from Penicuik, was a pacifist and a member of the Independent Labour Party. He had joined up to fight a 'greater evil'. He made several bequests to his family, then added the following:

I don't think there is anything more. But you will ask all my friends
to think of me at my best, to remember the good in me and forget
the bad. To sometimes remember to say a little prayer for me. I wish
also to thank you all for all you have done for me, and trust that the
McNultys may long live in Peace and Harmony with each other.
May God bless you all.[22]

Harry Wattie left everything to his mother and advised her that Hearts
might be prepared to help her out if the worst happened. Currie wrote his
father, stating flatly that he wouldn't make a will because it wasn't needed.
And so the scribbling continued: young men who had nothing much to give;
older men with property; anxious husbands, passing on some last precious
piece of advice to the mothers of their children. Padre Black told his wife
that the men were 'so terribly selfless in this dreadful hour. It is humbling
to read their little letters. Many bring a tear and a smile in the same instant.
Please God that they come safely through.'[23] On 18 June William Thomson,
a 42-year-old plumber from Dalgety Avenue, died of a heart attack in his
sleep.

Next evening McCrae's relieved the Provost's Battalion in the right
sector of the front line. The trenches here were even poorer than the
last. The dug-outs, wrote D.M. Sutherland, were overcrowded and the
atmosphere stifling. They were greeted by a heavy shelling which lasted
until dawn and continued through the following day. Donald McLean, a
37-year-old scientific-instrument maker from High School Yards, was
killed by a rifle grenade as he settled down to lunch. John Miller, a 25-
year-old glass-blower from Portobello, also died in the bombardment.
He was with his brother, Tommy, at the time. They had volunteered
together at Tynecastle during the victory over Hibs and both claimed a
place in the Hearts Company. Two other men were seriously wounded
and died during the night. Willie Turnbull, a 21-year-old labourer from
Riego Street, had enlisted under the pseudonym 'John McLeod' and
took his reasons to the grave. John McKeen, a 40-year-old iron-moulder
from Wellington Street, left a wife and five children. The following
morning Willie Brydie, an apprentice heating engineer from Merchiston,
was sniped during 'stand to'. George Blaney recorded his death and
burial:

A laddie grown, no more, no less, he rose up wi' his rifle,
Then keeked abune the parapet and caught a bluidy eyeful.
We sewed him in his blanket-plaid wi' stitches coorse and clarty,
Then laid him doon beneath the glaur wi' sundry ither parties.

But whaur's the point, ye noble lairds?
Ye red-tabbed, titled worthies?
Ye'll no come oot an' fecht yersels.
Ye're just a flock o' scurvies!

So keep ye a' yir fancy schemes tae tak an' hold thae ditches.
We'll just awa' an' leave ye here tae tremble in yir britches.

A man can dream,
A man can hope,
A man can hae his notions.
But ye're the boys who hae the power
Tae end this vile commotion.

So tak tent a' ye noble lairds, as sit ye on yir benches.
When every common sodger's deid, *ye'll* hae tae man the trenches![24]

Blaney had been posted out from the reserve companies in May. He was sent initially to the 15th Royal Scots, but (along with several other McCrae originals) agitated for a transfer. Archie Urmston had already been blown up twice and was close to a nervous breakdown; he raised no objection to the move.

On the afternoon of Brydie's death, 2/Lt Willie Gavin (pronounced 'Gaveen'), a 22-year-old law student from Trinity, was also caught by a sniper – shot through the right forearm as he lifted up his field glasses. It was the first of five wounds for this remarkable young man, all serious and all sustained with McCrae's. Jimmy McEvoy said he refused to be sent to any other unit. The following night the battalion was preparing for relief, when a bombardment opened on the support line. Most of A Company were sheltering in deep dug-outs. Fred Bland, a chromo-lithographer from Montgomery Street was sitting beside his best pal, Campbell Munro, when a blast of shrapnel came down from the entrance. Fred, who had just celebrated his 24th birthday, was killed at once; Munro was untouched. 'It was decreed,' he wrote, 'that we should be together at the last.' He was nineteen and had eight more days to live. The same explosion injured one of the best NCOs in the battalion. Jock Ainslie had been at school with Bland; he was an ironmonger's clerk from Rosemount Buildings and another Tynecastle volunteer. He died of his wounds the following morning; as did John Dougan, a 23-year-old coal miner from Motherwell. Archie Ewing got a 'Blighty' that night: a piece of shrapnel took the sight from his left eye. He had kept his promise to the Colonel though: it was another good sergeant gone.

The relief proceeded quietly. By the afternoon of 23 June the battalion was billeted in Brigade reserve at Bécourt Wood, just behind the front line. Albert was being evacuated in anticipation of German retaliation during the forthcoming barrage. Primrose Fairweather, a 27-year-old schoolteacher from Leith, wrote to his sister: 'We are entrenched in the grounds of what was once a rather handsome country house. A château, I believe. Comprinny? We will be here for about a week and I hope to get some rest.'[25] Before the war, 'Prim' played football for Leith Amateurs. He was always short of money. The château remained largely intact; Sir George had claimed one of the better rooms for himself. HQ was in the kitchen. At six o'clock the next morning the house was shaken to its foundations by what John Veitch remembered as 'the most tremendous din I ever heard'. The great bombardment was finally underway.

Wire-cutting was the first task. This was carried out mainly by the 18-pounder field guns of the divisional artillery, firing case-shrapnel fused to explode directly above the entanglements in an effort to break them up. Done correctly, it tended to work. The technique, however, required skill and practice – two commodities as yet in short supply among the gunners of the New Army. As darkness fell, the systematic shelling of communications began. The process was repeated the following day. As the smoke of the shell-bursts rose above the enemy trenches, Jim Steuart and his pals dug grave-pits behind Bécourt. 'Cheerful job!' he wrote. Dick Lauder walked up to Panmuir Street for a look across the valley. A whizzbang exploded on the parapet, wounding him in the leg. He had been acting second-in-command of the battalion for the previous fortnight; next to Warden he was Sir George's most experienced officer. As events unfolded over the following month, his loss would prove more critical than anyone imagined.

During the night the wood was heavily shelled. A scouting party from the 26th Northumberland Fusiliers entered the enemy line about 500 yards south of la Boisselle and found 'the trenches and dug-outs full of Germans'. The captain in charge 'soon discovered that to get out was the only thing to do'. The wire entanglements were 30 yards wide, at least 5 feet high, and substantially undamaged. They had to use ladders to cross them. It was not good news.[26]

At dawn McCrae's moved back to a canvas camp near Dernancourt. After lunch Sir George was officially informed about 'Zero Day'; he told the men before they had their tea. Steuart wrote his father: 'Don't be alarmed if you don't get a letter from me. I will try and manage a field postcard now and then.'[27] D.M. Sutherland reported that (with few exceptions) the lads were bright and hopeful. 'The Colonel is in great form,' he added. Cecil Nisbet told his mother that he was ankle-deep in mud, but otherwise fit. Cecil celebrated his 17th birthday at Foray House on 8 April; he and his elder brother, Herbert, had enlisted together, claiming to be twins.[28]

That afternoon aerial reconnaissance indicated that the howitzers and heavies were not making satisfactory progress; field guns were diverted to supplement their fire. The following day – 27 June – was damp and overcast; in the evening McCrae's trudged back to the wood in order to complete their final preparations for the assault. The noise and concussion had now been continuous for more than 100 hours and the men were getting rattled. 'We couldn't sleep,' recalled Jimmy McEvoy, 'and the ground would not keep still.'[29] The rain was now incessant, and on 28 June the attack was postponed for 48 hours, with the artillery programme stretched out accordingly. That night Tommy Millar took a patrol out to check the wire in front of Bloater and Heligoland. He found it 'knocked about' but worryingly intact. The divisional artillery was directed to address the problem and the next evening Millar was ordered out again to assess the results. He divided his command into five parties and made good progress until he reached the German entanglement:

> It consisted of a good row of long-pronged wire, erected on what seemed to be iron stakes about 3 feet long, crossed near the end to form a support. We cut our way through this. After a space without wire of about 10 to 13 yards, a second heavier row of wire was found. This row consisted of heavy knife-rests, wired up with several heavy kinds of barbed and plain wire. The patrol, with difficulty, cut a way through. Some French wire was next encountered, and after that there was between us and the enemy parapet another row . . .[30]

At this point – midnight – they were discovered. The Germans put up Very lights and opened fire with rifles and machine-guns. Four men were killed where they stood. A further two were wounded. The patrol withdrew. Millar's report to Division concluded: 'The wire showed very little signs of shelling and was not destroyed to any considerable degree whatever. It formed a very effective obstacle.'

Uncut wire and angry machine-guns. The message was again passed to the commander of the divisional artillery, but this was not in Rawly's script. Most of the casualties came from A Company. Edward Watt was 17, an apprentice engineer from Easter Road; Frank Wood, a 32-year-old Musselburgh miner with a wife and two sons. Willie Spence was twenty but looked six years younger. His parents lived in Leith, where he worked as a clerk at the local flour mill. L/Cpl David Jack was the same age, a medical student from Dalkeith. He had a weak and irregular heartbeat and had tried

151

three times to enlist in the battalion. He was finally accepted as a medical orderly and was the first man to volunteer for the patrol. He died trying to help his pal, Magnus Foster, a miner from Coaltown of Wemyss. Foster had been shot in the chest and was caught on the wire. David wouldn't leave him; Magnus was carried away to die later.

Peter Ross took on the task of writing to the families. Each house got a letter in his neat and careful hand. All are dated 30 June. 'The General,' he told Wood's widow, 'informed our Colonel that the information obtained during the raid has saved the lives of many men. Your husband did not die in vain.' Eddie Watt was one of his former pupils: he therefore knew the parents. Their version is rather more intimate:

> Sir George is greatly grieved over your son's death, and I feel it as a personal loss, as I have learned to love him as a son. I assure you that you have my sincere and heartfelt sympathy. I only wish I could have brought him back with me, but I know not what awaits myself to-morrow. I put my trust in God and go to do my duty with one of the finest Companies in the British Army . . .[31]

That night Jim Steuart wrote in his diary: 'Had a great concert in our dug-out for our farewell. Going over the top in the morning.' John Buchan, a 30-year-old plumber from Livingstone Place, sent a last letter to his mother: 'The boys are not in the best of spirits. There is terrible artillery work going on and Fritz must be in a dreadful plight. I do not think it will be long ere we get home for good.' James Jamieson, 31, a bottle-merchant from Leith, set out a codicil to his will:

> I expect the Government to give at least 20 shillings per week. That along with 20 shillings from my money will come to 40 shillings. Out of that total, I want my wife to give my father 5 shillings a week for a period of five years and then 4 shillings a week as long as my money lasts. Over and above her weekly money, I want the rent and taxes paid of the house.
>
> To my dear son, at 21, my gold chain, silver watch, engraved match-box and gold wedding ring. To my dear daughter, Georgina, my half-loop lady's ring. To my other dear daughter, Charlotte, my diamond cluster scarf pin. I would also like if her mother would give her the pick of the rings I gave her before we married . . .[32]

Just above 'gold wedding ring', Jamieson marked the manuscript with a little cross, adding below: 'If it is recovered from my body.'

Work continued, meanwhile, to prepare for the attack. Covered by the bombardment, pioneers were digging 'jumping-off' trenches in advance of the front line. Accessed by shallow saps, these (it was hoped) would allow the assaulting companies to cross no man's land with sufficient speed to catch the defenders huddled in their dug-outs. Simultaneously, 200 yards further out, a special trench-mortar emplacement was constructed opposite Heligoland. It was manned by McCrae's mortar section − 2/Lt Leslie Kitton and 12 other ranks. Their orders were to 'engage and suppress' the strongpoint in the morning. They had two three-inch Stokes guns and would be drawing a great deal of attention to themselves. Kitton was a 21-year-old civil servant from Trinity, another of A Company's commissioned privates.

At 1.05 a.m. a message was received from Brigade, withdrawing all battalion HQs from the attack. Brigadier-General Robert Gore, the Argyll & Sutherland Highlander who had taken over the 101ˢᵗ after Hugh Fitton's death, gave no explanation for the order. The rest of the division was unaffected: he was acting on his own initiative. Nothing has survived to tell us why; but it's likely that this able and insightful officer simply didn't like the way that things were going. Sir George was sufficiently taken aback to request confirmation on the telephone.[33]

Some reorganisation was therefore required. Ross's company would now lead the assault. B Company, acting as 'carriers', would bring up the rear with all the equipment needed to consolidate the captured positions. An officers' meeting took place at 2 a.m. in the château. Half an hour later, hot bacon and eggs were served to all ranks, courtesy of Lt Donald Munro, who had taken over as Quartermaster from Andrew Whyte while the battalion was at Warminster. Munro was an accountant in the office of Edinburgh's City Chamberlain. He had recently mounted a foraging expedition into Amiens; the bacon and eggs, and two bars of chocolate for every man, were the result. Elsewhere in the division, cold biscuits and water would suffice. Whyte, incidentally, would lead D Company in the morning; James Hendry had been sent on an instruction course.

While the men were eating, a message was relayed from German headquarters at Contalmaison through the honeycomb of shelters underground. At 10.17 p.m. a listening post near the southern edge of la Boisselle had picked up part of a telegraph message from Fourth Army HQ to the attacking battalions:

> In wishing all ranks good luck, the Army commander desires to impress on all infantry units the supreme importance of helping one another and holding on tight to every yard of ground gained. The accurate and sustained fire of the artillery during the bombardment should greatly assist the task of the infantry [34]

Rawly no doubt meant well, but the carelessness was criminal. The enemy now knew that they were coming.

At 5 a.m. the leading platoons left Bécourt Wood for their assembly positions. All ranks were dressed in 'fighting order'. The load carried was reported to be around 66 lb, but this included the weight of their shirts, tunics, breeches, braces, boots, web equipment and underwear. They did not take their large packs, or their greatcoats; their haversacks contained a mess tin, eating utensils, shaving kit, gas helmets, iron ration and socks. In fact they would 'carry' about 40 lb in total. Their rifle and bayonet weighed 11 lb; 220 rounds of small-arm ammunition weighed around 13 lb; two Mills hand grenades (to be passed to trained bombers) weighed around 3 lb. A full water bottle weighed about the same as the grenades. The distribution, however, was awkward, most of the burden being borne towards the front. John Veitch said that on top of all the rest, the 70 extra rounds (in bandoliers) and the two bombs were enough to pull you over if you stumbled. 'It took a bit of getting used to,' he recalled.[35]

At 6.15 a.m. the battalion was reported in position. As Sir George moved up behind them with HQ Company, coincidence once more reared its strange, disturbing head. The death of Robert Russell had been odd. But on this, the most momentous morning of his life, he was walking down a road that held a secret from the past. The trench in which he stopped was 'Bon Accord Street'.

CHAPTER EIGHT

'A tall, grey-haired soldier'

The morning was breathless and shimmering blue. A cool mist lingered in the valley, but the sun was already burning through. You could tell it was going to be hot. At 6.30, according to schedule, shelling of the German fire-trenches intensified. All along the line, enemy batteries continued to reply. There was even some ominous sniping. Jimmy Black had spent much of the night with the Provost's Battalion, who were due to go over in front of McCrae's. Shortly after seven, he led them in Charles Wesley's famous hymn, 'Jesus, Lover of my Soul':

> All my trust on thee is stayed;
> All my help from Thee I bring;
> Cover my defenceless head
> With the shadow of Thy wing.

The singing was uncertain and restrained. About 200 yards further back, Lionel Coles had removed his tunic: he was wearing the standard 'other ranks' equipment and carrying a rifle. His shirt-sleeves were rolled to the elbow. He moved from section to section, shaking hands with every man. 'I think he had us all by name,' wrote Cpl Robert Stewart, a shipbroker's clerk from Broughton. John McParlane later recalled:

> Some of my particular pals looked very pale. These were older men, you understand, like me, with wives and bairns. Then we looked along the line a bit and heard four or five youngsters from our platoon cracking a joke. I remember one was Artie Bell, one of our young characters, another was young Ward, who was killed later on.

155

The others were Bob Moyes and wee Jimmy Brown. Anyway, Bob says to Jim: 'Jim, I've forgotten my rifle!' And Jim replies, quick-like: 'Never mind, pal. Take mine, and I'll bide here until you get back.' Quite dead-pan, it was.[1]

Sandy Yule, the rubber-hose maker, was a platoon sergeant now. His eight short months in the Scots Guards had left him with the reassuring manner of a very old campaigner. Jimmy McEvoy remembered:

He was a grand figure to us younger men. We were about to go over the top and I was shaking so much I could barely speak, when I saw Sandy coming down the trench. I can still hear his very words. 'Steady, lads,' he said. 'And mind you're Royal Scots. Mind your pals and they'll mind you.' Well he stopped right by me and I remember thinking how lucky I was, for I knew that nothing could touch him.[2]

Pte Murdie McKay, a 24-year-old lithographer from Logan Street, was with Duncan Currie. He said that most of the Hearts men were together at the last. Crossan was quiet; he and Wattie had palled up with Jimmy Hazeldean, and the three of them were now inseparable. Alfie Briggs and Teddy McGuire were writing home: they gave their letters to Donald Gunn for safe-keeping. Ernie Ellis was waiting with Sam Brindley. Annan Ness and Jimmy Boyd were up at Company HQ. Boyd was now Coles's personal runner.

Sir George had worked his way down into Monymusk Street, where he found the trenches too crowded to continue. The stretcher-bearers were waiting there with B Company. Willie Duguid came up and asked permission to pipe the battalion over the top. Sir George refused. Duguid countered that the band of the 15th would be going. Firmly, but kindly, Sir George refused again. Archie Urmston's decision to allow three of his pipers to lead the attack was consistent with tradition but otherwise senseless. Urmston was now terribly unwell: although he remained at HQ, command of the 15th had effectively passed to Major Arthur Rose, director of an Edinburgh paint manufactory. Rose was in the front line with the padre and was reportedly taken aback when his pipe-sergeant appeared with written orders. David Anderson, a 26-year-old police constable from Dalgety Street, was clutching the piece of paper as if it were first prize in a raffle. He would not be dissuaded.

Peter Ross, meanwhile, was concerned that the German wire still appeared to be substantially unbroken. Tom Hunter of the 15th later recalled that the shelling had simply moved it about. Ross was looking for a likely entrance. Sgt Charlie Anderson, a law clerk from Merchiston:

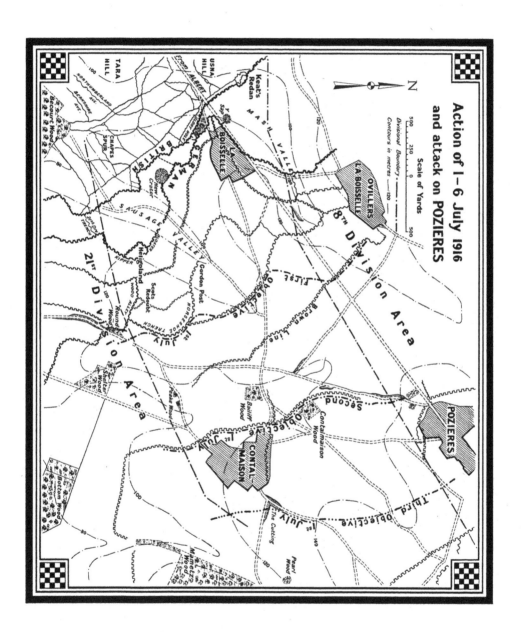

I dare say the other officers were in much the same predicament, for we had three runners from the 15th, all tearing down our trench as if their breeches were on fire. Anyway Peter hands the periscope to Willie Scott and Willie hands it on to me, and, right enough, I could see great bands of the foul stuff about 400 yards in front of our line. There were certainly gaps, but the wire had not been destroyed.[3]

CSM Scott was from Springburn. Before the war, he'd worked as a railway engineer in India. At Bécourt Wood, he told Donald Gunn he doubted he would see the evening. David Smart, a bookseller's traveller from Jeffrey Street, offered to lead a few men out with wire-cutters, but Ross turned him down. Smart was Prim Fairweather's best pal; they would go over the top side-by-side. At 7.25 the guns quickened their fire in one last desperate assault on the enemy front line. The order was given to fix bayonets. At 7.28 there was a quiet *sooch* as the ground was shaken by the explosion of two deep mines on either flank of la Boisselle. 'Stones and rocks and all sorts rained down on us,' said Murdie McKay.[4] 'The very sky turned black.' A crater, over 100 yards across, had opened in the centre. It fell just short of its target: the German trench behind it had survived. Over on the left, the trench-mortar sections of 102nd Brigade began bombarding the village with smoke. Simultaneously an RE detachment threw four red phosphorous bombs down into the valley from Pitlochry Street, forming a secondary screen on the right.[5] At 7.30 the whistles blew. 'From front to back,' wrote Herbert Warden, 'the entire infantry of the division rose as one man and set off down the hill.'

The artillery now lifted to the German second line. David Anderson climbed from his trench and started up 'Dumbarton's Drums'. Two members of the band, Privates Stubbs and Flynn, joined in beside him. Over on the left the pipes of the Tyneside Scots could just be heard above the guns. Someone was playing 'Blue Bonnets o'er the Border'. Almost at once a machine-gun opened up from Bloater Trench, cutting viciously into the leading ranks of the 15th and the Lincolns. Stubbs was hit, then Flynn as well. Both battalions were advancing with three companies deployed in line, each platoon about 150 paces behind the one in front. As they searched the wire for crossing points, the German gunner cut them down like corn before the scythe. Most of their officers fell here: killed at once, or seriously wounded. When Jimmy Black saw what was happening, he tried to join them. Only the threat of arrest from Major Rose stopped him.[6]

It was four minutes after zero before McCrae's got properly underway. Sir George had planned the advance by company, each platoon in line abreast. Ross's men were first. They were starting from the front line proper, and therefore had further to go. The leading sections mounted their ladders and climbed out almost unopposed, making good progress down the hill. As they approached the enemy wire, however, they were caught in flank by machine-gun fire from the lip of the new crater. A second gun then opened up in Heligoland, directly to their front. Prim Fairweather, David Smart and several others were closest: they died immediately. Cpl Bill Thomson, a solicitor from Leith, was shot through the forearm. Tom Halliburton, a commercial clerk from Gilmore Place, was caught on the wire and shot behind the right ear. The bullet passed through his face and lodged in his jaw. Bob Johnston, a colour etcher from East London Street, was shot in the hip. Harry Downie, a post office parcels clerk from Orwell Place, was hit in the chest. One bullet struck a metal mirror in his pocket; a second pierced his lungs. John Crichton, a trainee publisher from Easter Road, broke his leg when the ground gave way beneath him. CSM Scott got through the wire and was shot dead moments later. 2/Lt Willie Crombie, who had taken over Fraser MacLean's platoon, took a full burst in the stomach. Frank Scott, a trainee chemist from Lerwick, was in the middle of it. Five shots passed through different pieces of his kit:

> It was pure Hell, crossing that ground, owing to their machine-guns and shell-fire. It was awful seeing all your chums go under and not being able to do anything for them. Some of us managed to get over all right and found their front line absolutely battered to bits, practically just chalk heaps and hardly anybody in it. Those left were so demoralised that they hadn't a fight left in them but surrendered right away.[7]

Much of this damage had been caused by Leslie Kitton's trench-mortars. Kitton and his detachment had worked furiously to keep the fire from the strongpoint down, drawing a disproportionate reply from the German field batteries. Trapped in their forward emplacement, the young officer and seven of his men lay seriously wounded. The remaining five were dead. Both their guns had been destroyed.

Next up was C Company. Coles went over smoking his pipe, the Hearts lads close behind him. The German bombardment was heavier now. Several men fell back from the ladders. Murdie McKay remembered one man's anger: 'Ye dirty bastards,' he cried. 'I'm comin for ye!' He took off down the hill at a run and was never seen again. Sandy Yule had barely got started when two of his twenty-year-olds, Jock Wylie and Peter McColl, were hit by shrapnel in the legs. He was well beyond the new assembly 'cuts' and you weren't supposed to stop, but he couldn't leave them lying in the open. He slung his rifle and took hold of each boy simultaneously by the belt, lifting and dragging them back to the ditch before setting off again. Jimmy

McEvoy was just behind him. 'They flung everything at us but half-crowns,' he recalled. 'I saw one lad putting his hands in front of his face as if to shield himself from the hail.'

D Company now followed, with Whyte in the lead. D.M. Sutherland had been withdrawn from the attack during the night, seconded to Brigade as Intelligence Officer. Command of his platoon had passed to 2/Lt Robert Pringle, a 41-year-old warehouse manager from Barnton, who had been with the battalion for 12 days. He was relying on his sergeant to keep him right. George Jones was a 42-year-old stoker from the Pleasance. His men thought he was English but he was born in Currie. He had picked up his Portsmouth accent during a spell in the Royal Navy.

By now the Provost's men were over the first line and heading for the second. Their ranks were dreadfully thin; flanking fire had pushed them too far south and the Lincolns on their left had almost vanished. Tom Hunter was a bomber. 'There were some bloody exchanges in the second trench,' he recalled. 'Me and a pal were working our way along towards the village and I was in the lead. I stopped for some reason, and he passed me, poking his head round the bay to see what lay beyond. They shot him dead. I threw my bomb round the corner and the lads followed up with the bayonet. It did not last long.'[8] Davie Anderson was still in the lead. He crossed the second line and was heading for the third, when a bullet struck him in the side. 'I was not flustered at all,' he later said. 'In fact the coolness of everyone was one of the most surprising things. I had to stop playing at that minute, and I sat down to ease the wound. I had to lean forward in my sitting posture, and although I made another attempt to play, I could not manage it, and I was right sorry.'[9] At this point the 15th had only two officers standing. Major Harris Stocks, a 45-year-old ship-owner from Kirkcaldy, was out in front with the remains of his platoon. He had been wounded in the arm. Lt Leonard Robson, an undergraduate from Manchester, was in command of what was left. The fighting in the second line was grim. A German gun-team had continued firing until the last possible moment, then threw up their hands in surrender. They were shot where they stood. Men cowering in dug-outs were bombed without mercy. As each piece of ground was secured, the defenders withdrew along the maze of switch lines and communication trenches. By the time that the Provost's men were assaulting the third line, substantial numbers of the enemy had filtered back behind them to oppose the oncoming platoons of McCrae's and the Tyneside Irish. The 15th were effectively cut off.

At 8 a.m. Sir George received a message that the battalion had attacked.[10] There was nothing further. In fact the leading companies had fought their way through the tangle of wire, flanked Heligoland and crossed Kipper Trench only to get bunched up on the second German line, trying to

Mackay's Palace Hotel, Princes Street, 1914.
(Edinburgh City Libraries)

Jimmy Speedie.

Sir George McCrae.

Harry Rawson senior.

Tynecastle Park,
25 November 1914 –
The Hearts players
shortly after enlisting.

Back: John McCartney,
Ernie Ellis, Tom Gracie,
Duncan Currie,
Jimmy Duckworth,
Middle: Willie Wilson,
Norman Findlay, Bob
Preston, Harry Wattie,
Front: Alfie Briggs, Jimmy
Frew, Annan Ness.

Mobilisation of McCrae's Own, George Street, 15 December 1914.

Tom Gracie.

Sir George McCrae
outside Palace Hotel,
3 December 1914.

Murdo McLeod
(killed) – 'Scotland's
Strongest Man'

Group of professional footballers at Heriot's, May 1915.

Back: Duncan Currie, Jimmy Scott, Ernie Ellis,
Alex Henderson, Jimmy Low,
Seated: Norman Findlay, Alfie Briggs, Pat Crossan,
Andy Henderson

Sandy Yule's section at Heriot's, January 1915.

Standing: unknown, unknown, Harry Harley (killed), unknown, John Taylor (killed), Alfie Don (killed). Seated: Peter Cockburn (wounded), Willie Mackie (died of wounds), Bob Burnett (killed), Sandy Yule (severely wounded), Norman Campbell (wounded), Peter McColl (died of wounds), unknown.

The 'Cow-Punchers' at Heriot's, January 1915.

Back: Willie Cowan (wounded), Bob Boyd (wounded), Alex Prentice (severely wounded), Willie Ellis (died of wounds), David Farquhar (wounded), Fred Lewis (killed). Middle: James Lafferty (wounded), Alex Crombie (wounded), Murdie Mackay (wounded), Jake McKenna (killed). Front: Bob Bird, Tom Bird, unknown.

16th Royal Scots – Battalion Football Team, October 1915.

Back: Cecil Neill (killed), Jimmy Todd (died of wounds), Alfie Briggs (severely wounded), Pat Crossan (severely wounded, gassed), Andy Henderson (wounded, gassed), Alex Henderson (wounded), Annan Ness (wounded), George McLay (killed), Fred Muir. Middle: Jimmy Boyd (Killed), Harry Wattie (killed), John Fowler, Sir George McCrae (invalided), Cuthbert Lodge (killed), Bobby Wood (wounded), Jimmy Scott (killed). Front: Duncan Currie (killed).

C Company group at Strensall.

Back: Andy Henderson (wounded), George McLay (killed), John Scott (killed), Jimmy Todd (died of wounds), Alfie Briggs (severely wounded), Pat Crossan (wounded, gassed), George Cowan (wounded, MC). Middle: unknown, Tommy King (died of wounds), Norman Findlay, unknown, Jimmy Hazeldean (wounded), Robert Gibb (wounded), Alex Henderson. Front: Annan Ness (wounded).

Jimmy Black.

D.M. Sutherland.

Bob Martin.

Harry Rawson.

Jim Davie.

George Cowan.

Peter Ross.

George Russell.

Lionel Coles.

Percy Bayliss.

Arthur Stephenson.

Fraser MacLean.

Donald Gunn.

Willie McGrouther
(killed).

Thomson Bonar.

James Crawford
(died of wounds).

Billy Sloan, left, (killed)
and Tom Halliburton
(wounded).

Jimmy Hawthorn
(killed).

Mick Kelly with his
wife Kitty.

Willie Duguid and Jock.

John Veitch with his
wife Isabella.

Gerald Crawford.

Frank Weston (left) and
Andy Ramage.

Fred Bland (killed).

Finlay MacRae, MM
(killed).

Cecil Nisbet (killed).

Tommy Palmer (killed).

C Company section at Ripon.

Standing: Peter Yorston (killed), David Gray (severely wounded), George Gillespie (wounded), Jimmy McEvoy (wounded), Tom Teviotdale (wounded), Jimmy Brown (wounded). Seated: unknown, John Ward (killed), unknown.

La Boisselle and Sausage Valley, 1 July 1926.

Bobby Hogg, MM (killed).

Jim Steuart (died of wounds).

recapture positions already abandoned by Robson and Stocks. The battered Tyneside battalions, coming up quickly behind, were just adding to the confusion. 'German dead were everywhere,' said Murdie McKay. 'And a terrible number of our lads as well.' John Pevey, a coppersmith from the Dumbiedykes, stumbled over the body of his brother-in-law, Tommy Burt, a private in the 15th. Gerald Crawford saw one man kneeling, as if in prayer. 'He was quite dead,' he later wrote. George Cockburn, a draper from Duns, found his brother, Peter, lying wounded in the chest. He removed one of his puttees to use as a dressing, then continued on his way, turning round just once to shout, 'We've got them on the run!' He was never seen again. Willie Ellis, one of the Mossend Cow-punchers, was blown into a collapsed dug-out. His pal, Fred Lewis, pulled him out and put him in a shell-hole. 'You'll be all right now,' he said. As he stood, a German shot him in the throat. Sandy Yule was hit in the left arm. He tried to go on, but a machine-gun burst caught him through both legs and he fell to the ground. Jimmy McEvoy took his spare ammunition. He thought the sergeant was done for.

It was probably the same gun that 'chased' Jim Steuart. 'Imagine me fleeing for dear life with a whole machine-gun to myself,' he later wrote.[11] Alfie Briggs was not so lucky. He seemed to get caught in its sights. One bullet broke his right leg, another his left foot, another passed directly through his right arm. Another entered his right ankle, travelled all the way up his calf and came out above his knee. The last one glanced across his forehead, knocking him unconscious. Jimmy Brown was hit shortly after. A bullet creased the inside of his forearm and buried itself in his elbow. 'The pain was just cruel,' he later said. 'I went down quickly and tried to find a bit of cover. I could see the boys going forward, and one or two would check me as they passed, but I kept my head down and tried to stop the blood.'[12] Harry Harley was shot through the chest. His pals saw him fall into a shell-hole. Jimmy Scott of Raith Rovers was hit in the stomach. As he dropped to the ground, he was shot through the neck. Drummer Bill Smith from Bathgate had the narrowest of escapes. A bullet struck his rifle stock, bounced off his pick and grazed his thigh. He turned to see his pal, Fred Innes from Leith, shot in both feet. He picked him up and carried him back down the hill before resuming the advance.

Briggs and Brown fell just in front of the entrance to Wood Alley, a communication trench which led back to the German third line. Peter Ross arrived here around 8.15: he was the last remaining officer in A Company. Crombie was dead; Bill McMichael and Joe Bell had been wounded in no man's land. He gathered the remnants of his command in order to rush a second machine-gun further down the trench. As he moved forward, the gunner shot him in the stomach, almost cutting him in two. Sgt John Jolly, a librarian from Dalkeith Road, now took the lead. He was shot through the head within seconds. Ross, meanwhile, was still alive and in unimaginable pain. He begged someone to finish him off. In the end it came down to an order. Two of his own men reluctantly obliged. One of the witnesses would kill himself 20 years later.

By 8.30 B Company had reached the first line, having dropped most of the supplies they were carrying. Nap Armit seems to have done this on his own initiative, reasoning that the forward companies were more in need of reinforcement than of shovels. They had suffered dreadfully in the crossing of no man's land, coming under a hail of shrapnel. CSM John Muirhead, the 45-year-old veteran from Temple Park Crescent, was among the first to fall. L/Sgt Jerry Mowatt, a Newington blacksmith:

> To see a man I had looked up to and thought a much better soldier than myself go under made me think I could not be far behind him. It shook my faith in every certainty. Your officers, your pals, maybe even men you didn't care for much, all falling in front of you. Not a day goes by that I don't think of that bloody morning, and I always seem to settle on the awful moment when I saw [the CSM] go down. Right up to the last, there was a grave effort to maintain his dignity. Even on his knees, he looked to the direction of his men. 'Be brave, my boys,' he cried before he fell. I looked back as I passed over him, and he did not stir.[13]

Flo Kelly was hit in the hand; another bullet cracked past his ear. John Thomson was shot in the chest. The bullet passed through his New Testament and killed him instantly. Ernie Becker was shot through the cheek. His pal, Colin Campbell, a postman from Atholl Terrace, tried to help. 'He never spoke,' he later wrote. 'He simply looked, and then I had to continue on my way.'[14] Willie Duguid and the band were following with stretchers. They found L/Sgt Billy Sloan from Blackhall dying in front of the German wire. 'Don't bother about me,' he told them. 'I'm done. Bring in somebody else.'[15] His pal, John Tait, a law apprentice from Pilrig, lay dead beside him. Murdo Bethune, one of the pipers, was shot in the head as he tended the wounded.

On the left, the Tyneside Scots had been wiped out. The special measures designed to neutralise la Boisselle had failed; machine-gun fire from the trenches south of the village was tearing into the 101st Brigade's right flank. The Lincolns and Suffolks (who were closest) no longer existed. The Tyneside Irish had the furthest to travel. As they stumbled down the Usna-Tara ridge, they were easy targets. Machine-guns swept the hillside; shrapnel showered from the sky. By the time the 24th and 27th NF arrived at Heligoland, they had lost more than half their strength and most of their officers. By 9 a.m. the remnants of the two brigades were trying to consolidate their limited gains in the German second line around Wood Alley.

Beyond this position several small parties were attempting to continue the advance. Lionel Coles and around 60 other ranks had reached the far end of Birch Tree trench, less than 1,000 yards from Contalmaison. Harry Rawson appeared with some D Company lads and asked where Captain Whyte was. Coles had no idea. In fact Whyte was just a short distance ahead, moving through the sunken road that led into the village. He had Robert Pringle with him and a further 30 men. At 9.05 they emerged from the hollow and advanced on Quadrangle trench in the German fourth line. A machine-gun opened up directly to their front. Whyte was caught in the face, George Jones below the left ear. Pringle was hit in the leg but managed to withdraw the survivors to the shelter of the road. He sent two of his men back for help and formed the remainder into a thin, defensive screen beside Peake Wood. Around 9.15 he fell out to dress his wound, telling the lads to push on if they got the chance. Ten minutes later, as he tried to rejoin them, he was shot in the neck. Stumbling forward from shell-hole to shell-hole, he found himself being prodded by a bayonet. He looked up. 'It was not,' he later wrote, 'a friendly face.' The Germans carried him to a dressing station in Contalmaison, where he found Whyte and Jones already under guard. Whyte had lost a good part of his nose.

Harry Rawson, meanwhile, having heard the firing, was moving up in support. At the very moment that Pringle was captured, he came out of the hollow to be shot through both legs. He was carried back to Wood Alley by Sgt Willie McFarlane, a 32-year-old sheep-farmer from Wyoming. McFarlane, whose family lived in Tom Purdie's home village of Ashestiel, was one of the ablest soldiers in the battalion. Shortly after bringing Rawson in, he returned to the line and was shot in the left thigh. A and D Companies no longer had a single officer between them. One CSM was dead, the other wounded; most of the sergeants had gone. Command now passed to other ranks. For about an hour David McIvor was in charge of his platoon. He was killed just after 10 a.m. Not long before that, Harris Stocks had turned up with the remains of his party. They had drifted to the south and found themselves trapped for a while in Birch Tree Wood. He had been wounded again (in the side) and was very poorly. His servant, Alfie Bishop, was propping him up.

By some miracle, C Company remained largely intact. Coles still had all his officers and just over half his men. There were also some lost souls from other units. He decided to make another try for the village. They came out of the sunken road to find at least three machine-guns trained on them. Tommy Millar was shot in the chest. The same burst caught Cpl Tom

Teviotdale, a shop assistant from Sciennes, in the head. Willie Redden, a joiner's labourer from Stewart Terrace, was hit in the arm. The three contrived to help each other crawl into a shell-hole. By now the German field guns had joined in. Teddy McGuire was struck in the arm by flying shrapnel. As he fell, a machine-gun round grazed his head. Ernie Ellis and Jimmy Hawthorn went down in front of the wire. Jimmy Hazeldean took a bullet in the thigh. Murdie McKay was caught in the side. Annan Ness saw Duncan Currie hit in the right shoulder. He also noticed Harry Wattie fall. Crossan was racing forward beside two Suffolks, when a shell exploded in front of them. There was nothing left but a crater and some khaki. Jim Miller from Kirkcaldy:

> It was just cruel. We had no chance. You remember Jimmy Dods that we used to pal about with? I saw him fall beside me. We were going over together when he was hit in the chest. I do not think he knew anything. That was when I got mine, only I was lucky for it was just my leg. I crawled into a shell-hole with poor Jimmy just behind me, where I could see the bullets still tearing into him. It was just awful to see. I think it was deliberate on the part of the Hun, for they were potting at the wounded all day long. Thank God he was dead by then. Others were not so lucky, and I cannot rid myself of the sound of their cries. I saw Jock Marshall go down, just cut in two by machine-gun bullets. He is dead for certain. And Willie Hadden. Stevie, the drummer, was hit while trying to help the wounded, him and Willie Robb, who was already hit when he got another in the chest. The bullets were like hailstones . . .[16]

George Johnston, a baker from Duns, was shot in the side. The bullet lifted him up and spun him round. Another bullet caught him in the hip as he fell to the ground. John Laing, a Penicuik baker, was killed as he tried to bring his Lewis gun to bear. His brother, Sandy, a police constable in Leith, died beside him. L/Sgt Wilbert Steele, a linen-factory clerk from Dunfermline, was shot twice in the knee. Robert Stewart passed through the storm with his head bowed:

> I was so unspeakably terrified by the sights I had seen and by the true carnage and the thick hail of metal that the Germans were flinging at us, that I was quite praying to be wounded to get out of it. It was then that I looked at my arm and saw that it was bleeding. And I thought, 'I am hit!', and of course you know that I went down double-quick, both guilty and glad in equal measures. And then the oddest thing happened. I saw one of our boys, a lance-corporal from another

platoon, moving forward in the open and rallying his men. 'Come on, lads!' was his cry, and I'm dashed if I didn't rise up and follow, along with several other wounded men. Anyway, I was spared any further trouble in this direction by a second bullet, which knocked me such a blow upon the thigh that I crumpled up and fell away behind.[17]

Andy Ramage, a printer's clerk from Brunswick Street, was advancing with his pal, Frank Weston, a student at Heriot-Watt. Ramage was hit in the throat by flying shrapnel; Weston pulled him into a shell-hole and was shot in the groin as he climbed out.

Meanwhile, 2/Lt George Russell had eluded the guns, found a gap in the wire and crossed Quadrangle just south of the main road. He had around 30 men with him, including Michael Kelly and L/Cpl George Cowan, a 21-year-old colliery clerk from Larkhall. They worked their way into the village and were joined by a dozen other ranks from the Tyneside Irish, who had broken through further north. At 10.35 he sent a runner to request assistance. He was 200 yards from the ruined church, he said. The Germans were counter-attacking in force and he needed immediate support if he was to hold his position. Elements of 103rd Brigade, he added, were present in Bailiff Wood.[18] Shortly after this they were almost overrun. Russell was shot in the head and died immediately. Cpl Kelly took command and decided on a tactical withdrawal. He had nine men left and all but two were wounded. Cowan stayed behind to cover them: he was an excellent shot. Kelly took off down the road, hoping to find some friendly troops coming up to help. They were approaching Quadrangle again, when their way was blocked by a party of German signallers. Kelly was quickest to react: he charged them with bullet and bayonet, dispatching five before he was shot in the chest. He pressed home his attack, killing two more, and struggling with a third until he choked him. He then led the remains of his section back through the German line into the relative safety of the cratered fields in front of the village. Shortly before he passed out, he discovered that he had a souvenir: one of the signallers' flags was still clutched tightly in his hand.[19]

At 11 a.m. Lionel Coles made a last attempt to cross Quadrangle. He was running up the left side of the road when a machine-gun caught him in the chest. His servant, John Bird, a hotel waiter from Springwell Place, was shot as he hurried to help him. Both men died before they hit the ground. It was the end of any thoughts of Contalmaison.

❊ ❊ ❊

By noon the sun was blazing. The wounded had been lying since early morning and their cries for help could not be answered. All along the line, enemy machine-guns and snipers continued to pick off anything that moved. Stretcher-parties were recalled for their own protection: they would resume their work at nightfall. The Germans had re-occupied much of Heligoland and Bloater, trapping Nap Armit and his men in a small portion of the second line, near the junction with Wood Alley. The first 300 yards of that trench remained hostile; further on, beyond the dog-leg, Lt Robson's little party continued to hold their ground. Robson had been joined by two captains, Osbert Brown of the Suffolks and James Bibby of the 27ᵗʰ NF. From the north they were being pressed by the German reserves who had counter-attacked Russell and Coles. The survivors of C Company had withdrawn along the sunken road and fought their way back down Birch Tree trench. Makeshift barricades were erected behind them and the oncoming Germans were stopped in their tracks. Around lunchtime Robson was working his way slowly along the alley in an effort to establish the precise location of his western flank. He edged around a traverse and found Cuthbert Lodge sitting on a sandbag, tucking into a tin of bully beef. Robson asked him how far his left went. 'Two bays down,' said Lodge. 'And who's next door?' 'Oh, just the Boche.'[20] Lodge had come up with B Company. Finding himself a little way ahead, he and part of 6 Platoon had moved into the German line before the door was slammed behind them. They had been fighting their own little war for several hours.

Shortly after this, Fred Buchanan turned up. McCrae's Lewis gun officer was an apprentice engineer from Kirkintilloch. In August 1914 he enlisted as a private in the Scots Guards and spent a year on active service in the ranks. Commissioned in March 1916, he was posted to the battalion as a replacement for Jimmy Moir. When the attack was launched, he had remained with HQ; at 11.45, however, Sir George sent him down to find out what was happening. He slipped across the German line, missed Armit completely, and stumbled across Robson and Lodge by accident. They described the situation, but he was anxious to see for himself. He set off along Wood Alley and took a wrong turn into Horseshoe trench, which was still held by the enemy. He got about 30 yards before he realised his mistake, then nipped back and carried on as far as Birch Tree Wood, where someone sent a bullet past his shoulder. He retraced his steps, saw Lodge as he passed, and told him he was off to see the Colonel.[21]

During the afternoon and evening the enemy maintained a steady bombing pressure on the barricades. Above ground, machine-guns played along the parapet while snipers shot at anyone who dared to show his head. Wounded men were crawling in from the surrounding fields and the trench was full of dead from either side. About 150 yards to the north, they could hear the sound of shovels. Sentries reported that a new sap was being dug, almost exactly parallel to the alley. When it was finished, the Germans would use it to launch an attack. At sunset, 9 p.m., two further officers appeared – both 27ᵗʰ NF. They had fought their way back from Bailiff Wood with a handful of men. Major Dick Temple had served in South Africa with the 60ᵗʰ Rifles; 2/Lt Robin Neeves, commissioned in January, had been with his unit since June. No one knew if Stocks was still alive: he had not been seen for several hours. The last sighting had Bishop badly wounded and the Major trying to help him. Around 10 p.m. an attempt was made to link up with Armit, but it failed for want of bombs. The position was as bleak as it could be: they were cut off and surrounded, short of water, food and ammunition. At midnight a runner arrived from HQ. He'd got through the German lines without his rifle.

Sir George McCrae was coming up to join them.

❈ ❈ ❈

Inky Bill had watched the attack from Usna-Tara ridge. By mid-morning it was plain that the 102ⁿᵈ and 103ʳᵈ Brigades had effectively been wiped out. The commanding officers and adjutants of all four Tyneside Scottish battalions lay dead in no man's land. Reports from wounded Lincolns and Suffolks, moreover, indicated that the 101ˢᵗ Brigade had also suffered gravely in the crossing. The Germans had already re-occupied the entire front line. Beyond it, there were reports of heavy fighting, but nothing very concrete. It was quarter to noon before the first runner arrived at 101ˢᵗ Brigade HQ. He had left Major Stocks in Birch Tree trench two hours earlier. At noon a message was received from Sir George McCrae, indicating that 2/Lt Russell had entered Contalmaison. On his own initiative, McCrae had sent an officer forward to find out more. The attack of the 8ᵗʰ Division on the left had failed to make any progress; while the 21ˢᵗ Division on the right was getting forward, but only very slowly. Inky concluded that if he still had any advanced units, they were in a pickle.[22]

During the afternoon an attempt was made to bomb the Germans out of Bloater: the composite party assembled for the task was wiped out by machine-guns.[23] Efforts by units of the 21ˢᵗ Division to bomb their way along Kipper were repulsed with heavy casualties. There seemed to be no way through. Engineers from the 21ˢᵗ were digging a sap across no man's land along the divisional boundary, but this, at best, would shelter carrying-parties from hostile fire. It would not be the means of a major assault.

At 6 p.m. Fred Buchanan finally arrived back at Battalion HQ, which had been pushed back to Carnoustie Street by heavy enemy shelling. His report was relayed to Brigade and an artillery order was given to bombard the upper end of Horseshoe in the hope of relieving some of the pressure on Robson and Brown's garrison. Sir George, meanwhile, offered to mobilise the brigade's small 'battlefield reserve' to move on the enemy line as soon as it was dark. At 6.45 his suggestion was politely declined. For the moment Brigade concentrated on trying to get supplies through. The sap was completed by 8.30 but all efforts to make contact with any forward elements of the division failed. At 9 p.m. an order was finally dispatched to the HQ companies of 101ˢᵗ Brigade to advance and assume command of any friendly troops they encountered. Owing to casualties among the runners, only McCrae's received it. It arrived at 9.20 precisely.[24]

HQ moved out within five minutes. The Colonel sent a runner ahead to warn the defenders they were coming. Bobby Hogg, a 22-year-old butcher from Nicolson Street, was a nephew of the Ross brothers who used to carry Hearts' goalposts. He swapped his rifle for the RSM's revolver and promised he'd return it later on. They proceeded in two parties: one would take the new sap, the other would go directly across no man's land, south of Kipper. They were armed to the teeth, draped in extra bandoliers, and loaded down with small-packs full of bombs. McCrae, Warden, Buchanan, Muir and Black went first, with an artillery liaison officer, observers and guides. The second group consisted of Bill Robertson, Jock Miller, signallers, runners and two battalion policemen. It was, Black later recalled, a solemn parting.

❋ ❋ ❋

At 3.15 a.m. the Wood Alley garrison noticed a sudden, heavy bombardment of the fields around Willow Patch, around 600 yards to the south. The guns were German and the shells were drawing closer. At 3.30 sentries reported a hostile presence approaching from the same direction. 'Stand to' was ordered, and they were on the very point of firing, when Fred Muir shouted, 'Dinna shoot now, boys! We're comin in.' As McCrae climbed down from the parapet, he was met by Cuthbert Lodge, who nearly shook his arm off. Lodge explained that he was holding the divisional right, a front of around 120 yards. He had 140 men from the 16ᵗʰ, and a single officer – George Hamilton, a 23-year-old warehouseman from Milngavie, who had been in command of 8 Platoon until Armit sent him forward after dark. A barricade and breastwork had been erected at the junction with Horseshoe. The Germans were bombing across it. On one flank, the enemy was pressing from Birch Tree trench; on the other, they retained most of the alley and the strongpoint known as 'Scots Redoubt'. There was no evidence of friendly troops anywhere else on the front. For 120 yards to the left, the line was held by Robson, Bibby, Neeves and Temple. Osbert Brown remained on duty, but he had been wounded. They had around 150 men, mainly 15th Royal Scots and 27th NF. Only 14 Suffolks remained; the 10th Lincolns had been reduced to four other ranks. There were two Lewis guns, but few magazines; rifle ammunition was short, as were rations and water. Sir George sent a runner back to Brigade, requesting stores and stating that the garrison would hold until relieved.

The Colonel established his forward HQ in a dug-out opposite the Horseshoe junction. The entrance faced directly towards the enemy. His servant, Joseph Jardine, was a footman from Morningside. While McCrae was unfolding his maps and emptying cartridges from his pockets, Joe started making the tea over the flame from a borrowed candle. For the rest of the night they were continuously harassed by rifle grenades and artillery. Around dawn, a trench-mortar opened fire from somewhere in front of Horseshoe. Scavengers were sent out to collect ammunition and water-flasks from the dead; they returned with yet more casualties from the previous day. Working parties tried to repair the parapet, but as the sun came up, it became too dangerous to continue. At 5.30 Bill Robertson finally arrived with his party. They had fought their way through Kipper and found B Company at 4.15. Unable to progress any further, they had doubled back and come up by Willow Patch, creeping from crater to crater. Robertson reported that Armit still had about 100 men and that they remained remarkably cheerful. Lt Jim Davie, the battalion's bombing officer, was celebrating his 22nd birthday and the lads had given him a song. Davie, a Scottish international sprinter, was born in Natal of Orcadian parents. He was a boarder at Daniel Stewart's College in 1914.[25]

At 6.30, under cover of a low mist, bombers launched a frontal attack on Robson's position. At the same time, a further bombing party tried to force the left barricade in Wood Alley. They were repulsed but returned ten minutes later, reinforced from Scots Redoubt. Shelling, meanwhile, intensified on the right rear: the Germans were testing their strength. At 7.45 bombers attacked the right barricade, supported by a machine-gun in Horseshoe. Simultaneously the artillery shifted to their left. Rifle grenades fell all along the front. At 7.50 bombing parties broke into Wood Alley at the minor barricade on Horseshoe sap. They were followed by a rifle platoon, pouring out of the back of the redoubt. Robson and a small group of 15th Royal Scots bombers met them head on. It was a desperate exchange. At the last moment, Annan Ness brought a bayonet section up in support. His charge was enough to dislodge the intruders. Sir George was on the parapet with Jardine. Jimmy McEvoy later recalled: 'We had to stop the German bombers getting within throwing range. The Colonel was a marksman; he took his rifle, and with his servant spotting for him, dropped a Fritz with every shot.'

By 8.15 the worst of it had passed.[26] At 10 a.m. a runner arrived from

Inky Bill. His message placed McCrae in command of all forward troops in the division. Dick Temple was appointed his staff officer. Robin Neeves joined the major at HQ and met Sir George for the first time:

> He left a vivid impression on me. I had been in France only a short time, only three weeks, a raw officer who had started the day with forty men and now could not find more than six. I was uncertain whether I was more in fear of shells than of a Court Martial for heavy casualties; and then a tall, grey-haired soldier appeared out of a dug-out, minus helmet, quite unperturbed by the war and the general mix up of troops and apparent chaos. He wandered about in a nasty bombardment as if taking a stroll round his garden miles away. After that one lit a pipe and mentally assured oneself that everything was going according to programme.[27]

The most immediate of the numerous problems facing the new commander was Scots Redoubt: the enemy presence here was much too close for comfort. It had to be assaulted and cleared. At noon McCrae gathered his officers to discuss the operation.[28] It was decided to mount a bombing attack in two simultaneous movements. Robson would lead a party directly into the redoubt, capture it and attempt to bomb his way up the connecting saps into Horseshoe. George Hamilton would enter Horseshoe at the main barricade with Wood Alley and bomb his way north to join the others. The attack went in at 1 p.m.; by 2 p.m. the strongpoint had been taken, along with nearly 40 prisoners. Robson made no progress with the saps. On the right, Hamilton succeeded in clearing 150 yards of Horseshoe, but stubborn resistance prevented any further advance. Both sides threw up barricades and waited. During the afternoon sentries reported heavy fighting to the west. Brigadier-General Gore had borrowed two companies of the 7th East Lancashire Regiment from 19th Division and sent them in to clear Heligoland. By 5.30 the Germans had apparently withdrawn.[29] They remained in Bloater and Kipper, however, and continued to sweep no man's land with rifle and machine-gun fire. Inky Bill, meanwhile, was riding through the valley on his horse, spotting wounded for the stretcher-parties. His aide-de-camp, Captain E.J. Needham, later wrote:

> The General was out on the 2nd and 3rd, continually being sniped at. He found several men and had them brought in. Often I saw the tears come into his eyes as he told us of some poor devil that he had found lying badly wounded. He was deeply affected by our terrible losses. I do not think he was ever the same man; the heart had gone out of him. He had made the Division, nursed it, trained

it, coddled it and cursed it, and now it was smashed and disintegrated through no fault of his own.[30]

Heligoland had fallen, but Bill still had no clear idea of what was happening beyond. At 6.20 p.m. the Germans shifted their attention to McCrae's vulnerable rear. Under cover of machine-guns, a small party succeeded in entering Wood Alley, close to the junction with Horseshoe. They were ejected with heavy casualties, but not before HQ dug-out was destroyed by a grenade. The small reserve of rifle ammunition was inside. Shortly afterwards a similar approach was repulsed on the parapet. Intensive covering fire from the hostile portion of the alley was allowing the enemy to do pretty much as they pleased. Sir George decided that it would have to be suppressed. His plan was simple: Robson's bombers would bomb back along the trench, while Armit's bombed their way forward. If all went well, the Germans would be squeezed out somewhere in between. Armit was notified by runner and at 8 p.m. a flare was fired to start the attack. It was surgical and quick: by 8.45 the position had been cleared. Barricades were erected, but as Armit and Davie moved up, the enemy crowded in behind them along a myriad of communication trenches, ditches and shell-holes. Once again, the garrison was surrounded: they had used up all their bombs and were down to only 30 rounds per man.

At 9.15 a detachment of the 207th Field Company arrived. They had come up by 21st Division's sap and sustained heavy casualties en route. They brought picks and shovels and several coils of wire, but no substantial stores of ammunition. Sir George set them to work consolidating the defences and mobilised his scavenging parties to bring in anything they could find – single bullets, charger clips, bandoliers or panniers. A wireless party also turned up and was able to establish immediate contact with Division, who asked the Colonel to clear Wood Alley. McCrae was able to reply that it had already been done.[31] At 10.45 sentries reported increased activity in the adjoining trenches. Machine-gun fire intensified all along the parapet. Ten minutes later, a shower of rifle grenades came down in the redoubt. A heavy artillery bombardment opened all across the rear, cutting off retreat and reinforcement. Scavengers raced back, shouting that the Germans were coming on every side. At 11.10 bombers attacked the new barricade in Horseshoe. There were no bombs to reply. Simultaneously, above ground, bombers and riflemen emerged from the hostile portion of the trench and charged down on the defenders. Lodge withdrew his command to the Wood Alley junction and held the intruders at bayonet point until Sir George came to his assistance with a scratch company of HQ men and walking wounded. Jimmy McEvoy later recalled picking up a German grenade and flinging it back at the thrower: it was 'bloody, hand-to-hand stuff at the death', he said. 'We had nothing but our rifle-butts and bayonets.' Fred Muir took on two big Bavarians, giving one his last round and sticking the second. He couldn't get his bayonet out. As he struggled with the blade, a third German got him round the throat. He shot him with his revolver. The Colonel was in the thick of it. John Veitch spotted him with Lodge and Annan Ness, 'directing the defence and picking off the bombers with his rifle'.

As the crisis came at Horseshoe, another German unit was assaulting the redoubt. Herbert Warden had been given command of the strongpoint with the remains of Armit's Company as a garrison. He had one Lewis gun, which kept the enemy off until it stopped firing. Bombers poured into the left-hand trench and were engaged at close quarters. Simultaneously, a further attack was mounted on the right by a full company. This was repulsed with difficulty, just as a second wave came up in support. They withdrew in the face of withering fire, but Warden had now used all his bullets. Robson and Temple, meanwhile, were under similar pressure on the left, while Hamilton was slightly wounded when his makeshift platoon was attacked in force from Round Wood on the right. At 11.45 the position might have fallen, but the Germans lost their nerve and went to ground. As artillery activity slackened off, carrying parties finally arrived. They had struggled through a terrible bombardment. The first man in, with water and a crate of ammunition, was James Porteous from Dalmeny, acting RSM of the 15th Royal Scots. He was followed by Donald Munro and Charlie Robertson of the 16th. Munro had somehow contrived to supply a cooked meal for every man in the garrison.

About midnight an order was received from Brigade to occupy a considerable portion of Fetlock trench, nearly 800 yards to the north. 19th Division had attacked la Boisselle that afternoon and was scheduled to continue the operation during the small hours. Brigade asked Sir George to 'cooperate'. Clearly Robert Gore had yet to grasp the extent of McCrae's predicament. We have no record of the Colonel's reply.[32]

At 12.15 a.m. Captain Reginald Dumaresq of the 101st Machine-Gun Company appeared with two Vickers guns, which were immediately placed in Scots Redoubt, facing north towards the village. At 12.30 sentries reported that the enemy were feverishly digging saps from the north end of Horseshoe towards Wood Alley. An hour later, the redoubt was bombarded with rifle grenades. Machine-guns swept the parapet. Two sections were diverted from the alley to meet a possible attack. At 2.15 a.m. bombing parties assaulted the redoubt's right front. Warden's men managed to keep them beyond throwing distance. Ten minutes later, a full company emerged from the saps to attack the alley centre. They succeeded in entering the trench, threw up a barricade on the right and bombed their way along towards the left, where they were met by a rifle section led by Annan Ness. Again it was bloody and brief. Robin Neeves came up to help and by 2.45 the intruders had been ejected.

Alfred Warr turned up at 3 a.m. with the combined reserve of 101st and 103rd Brigades – 7 officers and 390 other ranks. They arrived just in time: by 3.15 enemy artillery fire had intensified all along the right rear while infantry was reported massing in Horseshoe. Bombers attacked the left front at 3.20, supported by mortars in Bloater reserve. Simultaneously, a further bombing force attacked the redoubt's weak north corner, where a barrier had been constructed across the entrance to a communication trench leading back to la Boisselle. Shelling increased on the centre and engineers were reported to be laying explosive charges behind the Horseshoe barricade. McCrae ordered an immediate withdrawal and a makeshift 'block' was raised across the gangway. Bill Robertson was almost left on the wrong side. At 3.25 the charges exploded. Bombers followed up in force, supported above ground by several waves of riflemen, who were held on the parapet by Warr's reinforcements. 'Our block was no more than a shallow pile of sandbags,' John Veitch recalled. 'I think there was a crate or two. Certainly, it was nothing like a breastwork. The Fritzes were very brave: they kept coming at us until we bombed them all to hell. When it was over, we made the prisoners bury their pals.'

The attack petered out around 4 a.m. and the remainder of the scavengers returned. George Aitchison, a grocer from Duns, had stumbled into Jimmy Brown. It wasn't exactly the warmest of reunions, as the wee man later explained:

> I stayed put until nightfall, which was awful long in coming. I had used up all my water and rations and was quite exhausted through the heat and the pain. The only thing to be done was to try to get back under cover of darkness, for I knew I wouldn't last another day in the open. I think I had made about 20 yards, when who should I come upon but Dod Aitchison of my own platoon. Dod was smiling like we'd met in Gorgie Road on our way to see the Maroons, and it was all I could do to keep his voice low. Well I got him down beside me and it turned out I had lost a whole day, for it was the small hours of the third. Of course I'd been unconscious on and off and just lost track. Anyway, Dod says can I move at all, and I say I think I could with a bit of help. So we decided to try it, but, as I say, I was for going back, and fairly set on that course. Dod, though, was for pulling me up towards the German side! Well naturally I thought he was daft. I was wanting off in the other direction, and pulled myself away, giving him the sharp edge of my tongue. He pulled back and so did I as best I

could, so there we were, as quiet as mice, having our own tug of war in the middle of no man's land. I kept whispering leave me be, for I'm wanting back to our lines, and poor Dod kept trying to tell me that the Germans were behind us. Our only hope, he said, was to go up and join the Colonel. Well that was it for me! I thought wherever the Colonel was, I wanted to be by him. So Dod led the way. It wasn't easy going, though, for he had been sent out on his honour to gather rifle ammunition and magazines for the Lewis guns, and of course he would have me collect all I could. And you'll guess we couldn't spot the gun-teams in the darkness, although the Germans kindly put up flares to help us. After about half an hour we had packed our pockets and packs with as much S.A.A. [Small Arms Ammunition] as we could manage. I had ten water bottles rattling round my neck as I crawled along among the dead. I said to Dod I was about fully loaded and by that time we'd been joined by a lad from the 15th, so we were a ripe party indeed for the Fritz gunners if we were heard. It was getting lighter now, so I said let's get home lads. By the time 15 minutes had passed I was sure we were headed into German hands, but, sure enough, Dod saw us safely home, for no sooner had I decided to haul off on my own, than I heard a whispered voice and found myself being pulled down into a captured trench by an English lad, who I cursed loudly until I saw he was an officer of the Suffolks . . .'[33]

Osbert Brown's introduction to his namesake was followed by the arrival of several more casualties from the first day. Some of them had struggled back from Contalmaison. Murdie McKay turned up around the same time. Jim Steuart had thrown in with a unit of 21st Division. He didn't care for them and eventually sloped off to look for 'the old 16th'. Kelly and Hazeldean arrived together – 'one good man between the two of us', Michael later said. Briggs was found in a shell-hole just behind the alley: enemy bombers had crawled over him during the abortive attacks before midnight. The wounded were lodged in a German 'hospital', 30 feet below the redoubt. It remained untouched by the shelling and had its own electricity supply.

At 6 a.m. a party of East Lancs reported, having fought their way up from Heligoland. For the first time since 1 July, the garrison had friendly troops behind them. At 7.45 Sir George and his officers felt secure enough to attempt a limited forward movement of their own. The objective, once again, was Horseshoe trench. At 8.15 Jim Davie led a bombing section over the parapet of Wood Alley, rushing forward and dropping grenades into Horseshoe from above. Leonard Robson, meanwhile, took a platoon over the main barricade and bombed his way north from below. A machine-gun followed Davie as he ran. 'He was a fine rugby player,' recalled John Veitch, 'and the gun was determined to get him. He sprinted this way and that, but simply couldn't shake it off. In the end he sold the gunner the most outrageous dummy and managed to get himself safely installed in a shell-hole.' By 8.45 the attack had gained 100 yards of trench, which was blocked and garrisoned immediately. Saps were thrown out at right angles in order to discourage any further frontal attacks over ground.

Shortly before 9 a.m. troops from 21st Division were reported to have entered enemy positions around Shelter Wood, only 500 yards to the right and well within shouting distance of Hamilton's platoon. On the left, 19th Division had taken most of la Boisselle and were extending south and east along the trenches leading to Horseshoe and Fetlock. Towards the rear, small parties of Lincolns and Tynesiders, trapped in the mine crater since the first day, were clearing out the old German front line. At 10.35 sentries reported that the enemy had withdrawn from a substantial length of the communication trench adjoining the redoubt. There was a short and somewhat hollow cheer. Moments later the newly captured portion of Horseshoe was subjected to a fierce bombardment, which forced the garrison to withdraw. A party of enemy bombers immediately re-occupied half the captured section, set up a block and (in the words of Jimmy McEvoy) 'made a right bloody nuisance of themselves'. Minor raids continued through the morning, supported by mortars and machine-guns. Around lunchtime signs of heavy fighting were observed in the rear. At 2.45 p.m. a further group of East Lancs appeared and pronounced Bloater, Heligoland and Kipper finally clear of the enemy. Minutes later, bombers attacked the redoubt in force, but were beaten off before they could enter the trench. While the men were reloading, Inky Bill dropped in for a visit.

Ignoring the continuing threat from German snipers, the general had walked up from Kipper trench with an aide and two bodyguards. He was carrying a rifle and a small field telescope. He asked for HQ and was directed to a battered sandbag breastwork surrounded by empty ammunition crates. Sir George was sucking on a pan-drop: he had grown a stubbly white beard and resembled nothing so much as a poorly dressed scarecrow. There was blood on his tunic and his face was streaked with dirt. Bill marched up and seized him by the hand. Tears were welling in his eyes. 'Well done, Colonel,' he said. 'Oh, well done.' And turning to the men, he added: 'Well done lads, well done. You've all done damned well.' McCrae then took him off on a tour of the defences, at which point the enemy opened a heavy bombardment on the newly captured portions of their front line. 'I think the poor old fellow must have shaken hands with every blessed one of us,' Gerald Crawford later wrote. 'And he never even twitched while the shells were coming down.'[34]

Bill left around 5 p.m. McCrae, meanwhile, sent out fighting patrols to establish the extent of enemy presence in the surrounding trenches. They returned with more wounded from the first day. At 8 p.m. all stretcher cases were finally evacuated; shortly afterwards, a telephone message announced that the garrison was about to be relieved.[35] The necessary preparations were made, and just before midnight the first units of 23rd Division arrived to take over the line. By 2 a.m. the transfer was complete. D.M. Sutherland was waiting anxiously at Bécourt Wood:

> I found Lt Munro, who told me he had been up at the redoubt. He made it sound like a stroll in the country, but his shrapnel helmet and tunic told a different tale. He said that our losses had been severe and named some of those known or believed to be dead. I had heard something of this over the weekend, but his words still came like blows none the less. By this time the first ragged ghosts were beginning to show themselves. These were Lincolns and Suffolks for the most part, though with Tynesiders and all sorts among them. They moved quietly, without speaking. Our men went up to shake their hands, but with little response. I saw a young sniper from the Lincolns, whom I knew quite well. His face was a brown chalk mask, caked with blood, mud and sweat. His eyes were rubbed sore, and I doubt if he could blink. He was dragging his rifle along behind him. He didn't seem to hear me and passed on regardless. Major Rose was with me by then and told me that the 16th had remained behind until everyone else had got out.
>
> It must have been 4 a.m. when the first of the battalion appeared, an A Company lad, Heb Nisbet, whom I had known from my own spell in the ranks. I called him by name, but he didn't seem to know me. The next man was one of our Q sergeants, Charlie Robertson, who had no business being anywhere near the front. Like Nisbet, he looked exhausted and was in no state to stop and exchange pleasantries. Behind him came some stretcher-parties and to my immense relief I found our pipe-major, who was, as ever, a credit to the battalion, as cool as only an old soldier like him could be under the circumstances. He had a heavy load to bear and was no youngster, but he was getting on with it. He gave me his best smile as he went past, as much as to say, just another day's work, sir.
>
> This early trickle slowly increased until I was becoming quite hopeful. Then, just as I was thinking that at least one company was safely back, the trickle stopped. I realised that it wasn't one company, but all that was left of the entire battalion. And still there was no sign of the Colonel. I felt that since I was supposed to be an

intelligence officer, I should find out what had happened. It was quite light at that point, but the atmosphere was 'thick' enough to afford me as much cover as I needed. I set off down the trench. Almost at once I bumped into a familiar figure, who cursed me for a silly ass and then apologised when he recognised my rather shaken features. This veritable tramp was our immaculate RSM, Mr Muir. Major Warden's servant came up next with a German rifle in place of his regulation issue. Warden was behind him, as filthy as Muir; then came Buchanan, and Miller, who was nearly 'all in'. I found Robertson and Ness, and, finally, the Colonel, his tall figure only slightly bent. 'Ah, Sutherland,' he said, smiling. 'It does me good to see you!' I took his arm, and at the end I believe he was helping me to get along. Sir George was the last member of the garrison to quit Scots Redoubt.[36]

The men were ordered to 'fall out'. Most of them just sat down where they were. As the sun rose, birds started singing in the stumps of shattered trees. It was impossible to sleep. John Veitch recalled:

I tried to rest, but I wasn't able. In the morning we marched off again. I must have been exhausted, for I remember not knowing that it was morning. Someone said that it was only seven, and I said will we be getting our tea then, and he replied that it was seven in the morning and I felt such a fool. Sir George himself came down the line while we were on the go and asked me how I was getting along. I said I was fine and how was he doing himself. He rubbed his beard and said he would tell me better once he had got his nap. He looked very tired.[37]

The march took them to Long Valley, near Millencourt, about four miles behind Albert. They arrived at 9.45 and were told they could rest until 1 p.m. It rained heavily during the forenoon and there was no shelter. Munro supplied a hot lunch. At 2 p.m. Fred Muir walked up with his roll-books. The men assembled by company and platoon for the names to be called. The RSM's blue pencil never stopped: at the end, he did his sums:

A Company:	0 officers/18 other ranks
B Company:	4 officers/88 other ranks
C Company:	0 officers/25 other ranks
D Company:	0 officers/29 other ranks
HQ Company:	5 officers/9 other ranks[38]

Including HQ, 21 officers and 793 other ranks had taken part in the assault;

12 officers and 624 other ranks were missing from their companies.[39] John Veitch again:

> I don't think our losses registered with me until the roll was called. We were still in our platoons when we came out of the line, and, though there were gaps, we assumed that the rest of the boys were just elsewhere in the confusion. I couldn't bring myself to believe they had gone. I convinced myself that some of them – maybe even most of them – were alive and would turn up in time. It was only when the RSM got us lined up in the old ranks that it hit me. My section was away. Two men left out of fifteen. But A Company was the worst. They had fewer than 20 men present and no officers. I mind there was only Alf Green of the sergeants left and Mr Lodge was sent over to take command. Green cries out, 'A Company, 16th Bn. The Royal Scots, all present and correct, Sir!' It nearly had me greeting, to think of that fine company, the best in our fine battalion, lying out there in no man's land.[40]

In the evening Charlie Robertson appeared with a bag full of personal effects that had been collected from the battalion's jumping-off trenches. Other bits and pieces had been picked up by some English lads around the German first line. There were letters and keepsakes, photos of sweethearts, children, parents, groups of pals. At the bottom was a book: James Hogg's *Private Memoirs and Confessions of a Justified Sinner*. The spine was broken, the pages stained with dirt and blood. Inside was a postcard, a shirt-sleeved section smiling in the Ripon sunshine. There were 11 names on the reverse and most of them were dead.

❊ ❊ ❊

Four miles to the south, in a tent near the village of Dernancourt, Arthur Stephenson was pondering his future. He was a 35-year-old major in the 9th King's Own Yorkshire Light Infantry. A tin helmet, pierced by shrapnel, lay beside his pack. His head was bandaged. He had been wounded on the morning of 1 July during 21st Division's assault on the German position south of Round Wood. In the afternoon he was driven back to Rawlinson's headquarters at Querrieu, just north of the Amiens road, in order to be interrogated about his experiences. The commander-in-chief was there: Haig had motored down from Beauquesne after lunch. The discussion turned to the extent of the casualties and the progress of the attack. Sir Douglas informed the gathering that offensive operations would continue. Stephenson was moved to interrupt. 'Sir,' he said, 'anyone going into a further attack will be slaughtered. The Germans have overwhelming machine-gun power and are well dug in. These are human beings you are asking to attack again. They are exhausted and frightened and they do not want to die. I beg you to reconsider.' Haig no doubt noticed that the officer was bleeding. Also that he wore the ribbon of the Military Cross. He flushed a little, then repeated his insistence that the offensive would proceed as planned. 'Well then, sir,' said Stephenson, 'you are no more than a bloody butcher!'[41]

At 9 a.m. on 5 July McCrae's marched one mile east, to a canvas camp at Henencourt Wood. The rest of the divisional remnant was already nearby. At noon Sir William Pulteney, commander of III Corps, drove up to inspect the troops. He complimented them on their bravery and tenacity, drawing particular attention to their stout defence of 21ˢᵗ Division's vulnerable flank. Had that been turned, he said, the whole attack to the south might have failed. He then invited McCrae to join him, singling out the 16ᵗʰ for its efforts. Their colonel, he added, had raised a fine battalion and they had fought like regulars, maintaining their discipline and structure when almost every officer was gone. It was the highest praise he could think of. After Pulteney departed, it was announced that several gallantry awards had been approved with immediate effect. There was a Distinguished Service Order and a Mention for Sir George; Military Crosses for Armit and Davie; Military Medals for Willie McFarlane, Willie McDougall, a coal miner from the Dumbiedykes, Bill Mark, an ironmonger's assistant from Banff, and Finlay MacRae, an asylum attendant from Inverness. MacRae was goalie of the Scottish hockey team and travelled to Edinburgh specifically to join the 'Sportsmen's Battalion'. He was severely wounded during the defence of the Redoubt.

Wull McArthur, of the Cow-punchers, got the Distinguished Conduct Medal for bombing a dug-out and capturing 43 prisoners on his own. He was called from the ranks to receive a piece of paper bearing the notification. As he walked back, he screwed it up and threw it to the ground.[42] Muir was also mentioned in despatches, but there was nothing for Kelly or Lodge. Cuthbert's brother wrote home to their father that he was 'one of *the* heroes of the hour'.[43] There were, however, no commissioned witnesses to his conduct, so he (and Michael) had to settle for the recognition of their comrades. That night Jock, the Great Dane, died of a heart attack, caused (they said) by sadness at the loss of so many of his friends. He was buried in the wood with full military honours.

On the morning of 6 July Herbert Warden was poached by staff and appointed 'town major' for the divisional billeting area. With Dick Lauder still recovering from his wounds in a hospital near Edinburgh, there was a temporary vacancy at second-in-command. The new man turned up shortly after lunch.

It was Arthur Stephenson.

CHAPTER NINE

'Such a wall of steel and shell'

✳ Almost from the start they called him 'Steve'. He was born in the district of Stoke Damerel, near Devonport, on 9 August 1881, son of a bank manager from Beverley in Yorkshire. On leaving school, he joined the Post Office, working as a clerk and graduating later to telegraphist. In 1900, following a disagreement in the family, he gave up his job and signed on as a stoker on a ship bound for South Africa. In Cape Town he secured a position with the postal services, but when war broke out in October he left to enlist in the Imperial Light Horse. For the next two years he rode many hundreds of miles around the Free State and the northern Cape, chasing elusive Boer commandos with the Orange River Scouts. He was demobilised in May 1902, a penniless sergeant with no special skills. Unable to find employment locally, he spent his last few shillings on a ticket to Rhodesia, where he managed to get a job with the office of Posts and Telegraphy in Bulawayo. Six months later, he was transferred to Salisbury, where (in addition to his professional duties) he became a Squadron Sergeant-Major in the Southern Rhodesian Volunteers. In 1904 he was offered the chance to extend the postal service into north-west Rhodesia, which was then in the early stages of white settlement. At that time, the railway to Victoria Falls was still under construction, so he travelled on a flat-bed waggon stacked with sleepers and camped each night in the bush. He walked the last 100 miles to the Falls and crossed the Zambezi by canoe to the small town of Livingstone, where he established the first post office in the country.

In 1906 he was moved to Kalomo and (shortly afterwards) to the lawless mining community of Mwombashi, near Broken Hill, where he discovered he was the only government official in the area – a sort of Sheriff and

Commissioner combined. It was a little bit like Tombstone. In 1909 he returned to Livingstone to resume control of the expanding postal service. He resigned in 1912 to become an inspector in the Native Labour Bureau, with responsibility for the whole of Northern Rhodesia. For the next two years he covered most of the country on foot, walking 3,000 miles a year and living entirely under canvas. When war broke out in August 1914, the local militia mobilised to meet the threat from German East Africa. He volunteered at once. In May 1915 he sailed for England and secured a commission in the 10th Devonshires. While training with this unit at Bath, he learned that an old friend, Colmer Lynch, was commanding the 9th King's Own Yorkshire Light Infantry at Witley, near Godalming. He was granted a transfer and joined them in time to embark for France in September. A fortnight later, at the Battle of Loos, he was awarded the Military Cross for rescuing a wounded soldier under heavy artillery fire. He was promoted to major in April 1916, and was serving as second-in-command when he was hit by flying shrapnel on the first morning of the Somme. Lynch was killed that day, and Stephenson had every reason to believe he would get the battalion. Following his outburst at Querrieu, however, he was instead moved sideways – five miles sideways, to be precise.[1]

Henencourt was a depressing spot. Veitch recalled an endless wait for the Red Cross prisoner-of-war lists, as the men clung to the hope that their missing pals had been captured. Sir George described Jimmy Black walking about the camp, clenching and unclenching his fists as he wrestled with the enormity of the tragedy. The men, apparently, were asking him *Why*? Doc Gilmour was on the verge of a nervous breakdown. Spirits were lifted somewhat on 8 July, when Crossan reappeared. He had been buried by the explosion and came round the following morning to find that the Suffolks beside him were dead. It took him three days to crawl back to safety: some English lads had directed him to a dressing station, where he was pronounced fit to return to his unit. He remained so concussed, however, that he couldn't see straight for a week, and didn't regain full hearing for several months.

On 10 July Contalmaison fell. John Smith, a 24-year-old draper from Loanhead, was sitting in a dug-out, awaiting transfer to hospital. He had been hit in the shoulder by shrapnel on 1 July and lay in a shell-hole for 36 hours until the Germans picked him up. He could hear British soldiers outside and called for help. They replied with a grenade, which exploded on the floor and broke his leg. He couldn't work out how he hadn't been killed. 'You can guess,' he told his parents, 'that I have been shaking hands with myself ever since.' As the fields around the village finally became safe to walk, Andy Ramage and Frank Weston were also found: they had lain out for nine days and nights, scavenging water and rations from the dead.

181

Wilbert Steele was discovered on 11 July in a shell-hole just beyond Quadrangle. He told his family:

> Owing to the wound in my leg, I was unable to crawl toward our trenches. There were quite a number who had been killed lying within a few yards, and it was with difficulty that I was able to drag myself alongside of them and so get to their biscuits and water-bottles to keep me alive. Also their field-dressings to dress my wounds.[2]

Among the bodies were Currie and Coles. They were buried with Peter Ross in a battlefield plot beside the la Boisselle–Contalmaison road. The remains of 80 men were identified during the first 2 weeks, leaving 534 unaccounted for. The Colonel and the Padre were inundated with requests from next-of-kin, but it wasn't until the 'wounded' lists began to come in from the regimental depots at Rouen and Boulogne that they were able to make an accurate statement of the number of 'missing' – 149 in total. Letters to the dead, meanwhile, continued to accumulate at HQ. On 8 July Barbara Buchan wrote to her son, John, enclosing a postal order and the usual family gossip. There was no reply, so six days later she wrote again:

> We are anxious about you. We hear you were missing when the roll was called after the advance. I hope, dear son, you have been spared. We are hoping you have been wounded or taken a prisoner. This is a terrible war. What a sad home this is and what a suffering. I am praying to God to end these terrible times. Hoping and trusting you are spared to receive this . . .[3]

It would be another four weeks before Army Form B.104–82 arrived from the Infantry Record Office in Hamilton to inform her that John had been killed, and a further fortnight before the War Office in Whitehall replied to her early enquiries. In the meantime hope was all she had.

In hindsight Mrs Buchan was lucky. John's body had been found. Harry Harley's hadn't. Like Ellis and Hawthorn and Wattie, he was typical of those who had simply disappeared. His wife, Susan, received an official letter informing her that 'the above-named soldier has been reported missing since the 1st of July 1916' and referring her to Hamilton for all future correspondence. Hamilton, it transpired, was overwhelmed with enquiries and unable to assist. Her only recourse was the battalion. She began to canvass Harry's comrades, some still in France, others now in hospitals at home. The results were a strange mixture of encouragement and sympathy, and amounted in the end to less than nothing. In despair, she began to take his photo round the convalescent wards.[4]

182

The 'old 16ᵗʰ' was now scattered to the winds. Alfie Briggs was in Epsom. He had been stretchered from the redoubt to an advanced dressing station near Bécourt, where he was placed in a tent with the 'hopeless' cases. Too weak to protest, he fell asleep. Some hours passed before an orderly noticed he was breathing. The doctors decided to move him back to a field hospital, where the process was repeated. Eventually, he was able to communicate his intention not to die, and had since been making a remarkable recovery. Teddy McGuire was in Glasgow, mending 'nicely'. Jimmy Hazeldean was in Middlesex: an 'explosive' round had been removed from his leg. Sandy Yule was in Edinburgh: he had lost his arm. Michael Kelly was in Leicester, where he was visited by his wife. He had kept the bullet that the doctors found in his lung. Tommy Millar was in Woolwich; Tom Teviotdale was in Bradford (with John Smith); Willie Redden was in Kent. Willie McFarlane was in York and had lost his leg; Harry Rawson was recovering slowly in Manchester. The list changed constantly as men were shifted around. Progress was imperilled by infection; further amputations were required. Bad news trailed the good by several days. Come the end of the month, 19 of the wounded would be dead.

The battalion, meanwhile, was 'refitting'. On 10 July the first reinforcements appeared – 64 Glasgow lads, originally intended for the 16ᵗʰ Highland Light Infantry. They were joined next day by 54 members of the 5ᵗʰ Scottish Rifles and 200 members of the 6ᵗʰ Scottish Rifles, seasoned Territorials from the steel towns of Lanarkshire, most of whom had been in France since the spring of 1915. Three contingents of Royal Scots also arrived – 30 members of the 5ᵗʰ who had seen service at Gallipoli, 60 pioneers from the 8ᵗʰ and a handful of men from the 6ᵗʰ who had just returned from Egypt. Five new subalterns showed up – green youngsters, straight out of officer training. Several of A Company's surviving 'originals' now chose to apply for commissions themselves. With their pals gone, they no longer saw the point in remaining. Jim Steuart decided to stay but on 16 July he wrote that it seemed 'awfully funny to be among so many strangers'. The losses incurred by the Tyneside brigades were so great that they had been temporarily posted away to recover. Two brigades from 37ᵗʰ Division arrived to replace them, increasing the old hands' growing sense of isolation and unease. When training and drill resumed on 12 July, it was (said Sgt Crawford) 'introductions all round'. On 20 July Ness wrote to McCartney:

> We had a match the other evening, but oh, Mr McC., we did miss the boys. Talk about football. It made the tears come to our eyes. But have a good heart, guv'nor, we shall soon be in Berlin. My best regards to the directors and yourself . . .[5]

They spent the next two days practising wood fighting. On the evening of 22 July word came through that Inky Bill had been killed on one of his infamous reconnaissance patrols. It happened near Montauban. He was walking back to his car with an aide, 2/Lt Tom Grainger Stewart of the 16th, when the Germans started shelling the road. He tried to take cover, but was caught in the blast and died immediately.[6] Stewart, a student at Edinburgh University, was unhurt. He wrote home to his parents in Moray Place that the General had been like a friend to him. Bill's funeral took place at Warloy the following day. McCrae's provided the guard of honour, and Duggie played the old man to his grave. On 25 July Major-General Cecil Lothian Nicholson arrived from 16th Brigade to take over the Division. Nicholson, a product of Marlborough and Sandhurst, had been wounded at Neuve Chapelle in March 1915 as colonel of the 2nd East Lancs. He did not visit the battalions of the 101st and may therefore have failed to realise their continuing state of unreadiness. The Suffolks and the Lincolns consisted almost entirely of new drafts, while the 15th Royal Scots still had insufficient officers. McCrae's were scarcely any better off. Sir George gave A Company to his senior surviving lieutenant, James Mackenzie, a 30-year-old solicitor from Blantyre. Mackenzie had been struck on the forehead by a lump of flying shrapnel during D Company's advance on Contalmaison; he insisted on remaining with the battalion, however, and was the best available candidate. Armit, of course, still had B; the prodigious Davie was given temporary charge of C. James Hendry, meanwhile, had returned from his course to resume command of D. McCrae could have done with Herbert Warden and two experienced captains. Instead, he got a convalescent major and some nervous but enthusiastic boys. There was a storm coming, and his umbrella was full of holes.

❋ ❋ ❋

The first day of the Somme offensive was a disaster. Almost 20,000 men were dead; almost 40,000 had been wounded. In the north, the attack was repulsed; in the centre it had stalled in the trenches around Scots Redoubt. Sir William Pulteney, though, was correct: 34th Division's stand had anchored the modest advance in the south. Mametz and Montauban had fallen; Fricourt was outflanked and almost encircled. On 2 July the Germans withdrew from the village to their support line in front of Contalmaison and Mametz Wood. In an effort to exploit this success, Haig now shifted his attention to the right: the next two weeks were taken up with a series of minor operations, designed to secure the starting point for a major attack on the enemy's second position between Bazentin-le-Petit and Longueval. The so-called 'Bazentin Ridge' was finally assaulted shortly before dawn on 14 July.

This time the preliminary bombardment lasted just five violent minutes and the defenders were utterly surprised. Within hours, Bazentin-le-Petit and Bazentin-le-Grand had fallen, while Longueval was in the process of being cleared, although Delville Wood on its immediate right proved impossible to enter. As resistance folded in the centre, the ultimate prize seemed there for the taking. About a mile to the north, across a shallow valley planted with ripening corn, High Wood was the most commanding feature on the entire plateau. Largely untouched by shell-fire, it was linked to the defences around Martinpuich and to the fortified village of Flers in the enemy's third position by a thickly wired trench known as the Switch Line. Rawlinson might have committed his small reserve of infantry and captured it before breakfast; instead, with his mind still firmly fixed on a breakthrough towards Bapaume, he ordered up the 2nd Indian Cavalry Division. It was evening before they arrived. The delay was fatal: as the horses galloped up the slope and plunged into the trees, they were cut down in their hundreds by massed machine-guns. In something close to panic, 33rd Division was sent up to occupy the cornfields and establish a defensive position inside the wood itself. The following morning they were ordered to move on Martinpuich; simultaneously a brigade from 7th Division was supposed to clear the wood to prevent any hostile fire falling on the flank of the advance. It might have looked fine on paper, but both attacks perished on the Switch Line wire. That evening Rawlinson evacuated the wood completely, content for the moment to flatten it with shells. On 20 July 33rd Division was ordered back in. Despite heavy losses they reached the northern edge, only to be driven out at dusk by intense bombardment. On 23 July it was the turn of the 51st (Highland) Division. Two hours after zero the battalions were back in their starting positions. Six nights later, they assaulted a strongpoint on the wood's eastern corner – with similar results. On 30 July they tried again, and managed to advance 200 yards. Over on their left, meanwhile, the 10th Royal Warwicks and 7th Shropshires of 19th Division had attacked a key position about 500 yards south of Switch. The results were mixed: one half of the objective remained in German hands; the other was now resolutely British.

It was the 'Intermediate Trench'.

❀ ❀ ❀

July 30 was a Sunday and (according to Jim Steuart) 'fearfully hot'. In the morning McCrae's moved up from Henencourt to Bécourt Wood. The following afternoon they marched five miles through the cratered fields south of Quadrangle and Mametz Wood to relieve the Warwicks and the Shropshires. Shells were falling all along the way.

185

Positioned directly in front of Bazentin-le-Petit, the Intermediate had started out as a sap leading south from Switch Line; following the attack of 14 July, however, the Germans started shovelling eastwards in an effort to link up with the defensive system in High Wood. Within days they had dug more than 1,000 yards and worked it into a substantial fire-trench protected by a narrow entanglement of fresh barbed wire. Machine-guns in Switch made any approach from the left particularly hazardous, as 19th Division had discovered to its cost. Their attack was repulsed here, but succeeded on the right, supported by enfilade fire from the 51st Division on the edge of the wood. The Warwicks and Shropshires bombed their way along as far as the centre, where a hasty block – christened the 'Barrier' – was erected, leaving the Germans with about 600 yards of the trench to themselves. John Veitch later said: 'If they wanted it that bad, we should have let them keep it.'

McCrae's went into the line about 6 p.m. and were heavily shelled during the night. The next day was spent improving the defences; after dark, however, they mounted a series of assaults on the Barrier from above and below ground. James Hendry led them himself. Five times he took his bombers over the parapet; five times they were repulsed. Almost 40 men were wounded and 12 were killed. At 9.20 the following evening, they were ordered in again. As Hendry dashed along, tossing out grenades, a machine-gun in Switch Line caught him in the left elbow. A second bullet struck him in the leg. 2/Lt Alastair MacLachlan, a 21-year-old student from Craigmillar Park, assumed command and continued the attack. The fighting was bloody, hand-to-hand. It continued until daylight: 5 more men were dead, another 30 wounded, but 150 yards of Intermediate had been gained. Just after dawn, the Germans counter-attacked and took back 30 yards, but MacLachlan's bombers threw up a barricade and held them there.

'The Fritzes responded with shell-fire,' wrote Sgt Crawford, 'intermittent through the morning, heavy and persistent after lunch.' Ness got some shrapnel in his right arm but chose to remain with the company. Shortly afterwards Jimmy Boyd was hit in the side by a piece of casing. It was a serious wound. A stretcher-party was brought up and they set off for the dressing station south of Bazentin-le-Petit. By this time the shelling was intense. At 5 p.m. Sgt Sandy Lindsay climbed out of B Company's NCO dug-out to check on his sentries. Thirty seconds later, the shelter was struck by an explosive incendiary. Four men were killed outright: CSM Angus Cameron, a 35-year-old letterpress printer from East London Street; Sgt Archie West, a 30-year-old upholsterer from Watson Crescent; Sgt Tom Hill, a 41-year-old miner from Musselburgh; and L/Sgt Tom Cawley, a 33-year-old miner from St Mary Street. Cpl 'Dod' Simons, a 39-year-old bookbinder from Moncrieff Terrace, was trapped 10 feet underground by a fallen beam. The remains of the interior were alight and flames were licking round his face. He managed to reach his rifle and had chambered a cartridge with the intention of shooting himself, when he heard Lindsay's voice coming down from the surface. The rescuers worked like demons and pulled him out within minutes. He was badly burned but otherwise unhurt.[7] His last remaining pal was not so lucky: Sgt James Martin, a 27-year-old stereotyper from Stewart Terrace, had sustained appalling injuries. He was carried unconscious to a dressing station and would not see the end of the week.

Up to this point, B Company had suffered fewer casualties than the rest of the battalion. Cameron had only just succeeded John Muirhead, who fell on 1 July. Most of the other NCOs had held their rank since Heriot's. Now, quite suddenly, Lindsay was the only sergeant left, promoted on the spot to CSM. The apprentice draughtsman from Spottiswoode Street was still four months short of his twentieth birthday.

At 5.15 p.m., as the shelling continued, Sir George summoned his officers to HQ. It took well over an hour for everyone to report. He announced that Brigade had ordered a frontal assault on the hostile portion of Intermediate – to be carried out that night by two companies of the 16th and two companies of the Suffolks. Zero hour had not yet been decided, but the operation would proceed in conjunction with a major attack on the left flank, where 23rd Division would move on the trenches south of Martinpuich while the Anzac Corps attacked the enemy line north-east of Pozières. The assault would be delivered from an old German fire-trench about 250 yards to the south. It ran roughly parallel to the objective, and Brigade considered it the ideal jumping-off position. The fact that 19th Division had failed from this very point on 30 July was ignored: this time the artillery support would be overwhelming. It all sounded worryingly familiar.

The decision to commit 101st Brigade to this assault can be traced back to a meeting between Nicholson and Gore at Divisional HQ on Tuesday, 1 August. Initially the operation was dated for the small hours of Friday; later in the evening, however, Gore received a memo from Nicholson's chief staff officer, Lt-Col. R.H. Mangles, which postponed it until Saturday.[8] The General, he added, was anxious to employ 'as many Stokes Mortars as possible' for a hurricane bombardment immediately prior to zero, and wanted to see Gore's offensive plan before the end of Thursday. While Gore and his staff were poring over their maps, however, the attack was returned to early Friday morning. In the ensuing rush, it would appear that clarity of thought went out the window.

Mangles's memo had wisely stressed the lessons learned from 19th

Division's failure – particularly the German artillery response, which was prompt, accurate and devastating. From a line immediately behind the assembly positions, the enemy fire had crept south to smother Bazentin-le-Petit and its adjoining wood with shrapnel and high explosive. All telephone cables had been broken. When the Suffolks came up on 31 July, they had established their HQ at the top end of the village, in the middle (unwittingly) of the danger zone. Sir George had chosen a dug-out in the ruined cemetery 300 yards to the east. For some unfathomable reason, Brigade now ordered McCrae to move into the village and share the Suffolks' quarters.[9]

On 2 August, the Colonel attended a Brigade conference, where he was informed that they would probably be required to carry out an operation similar to that attempted by 19th Division. A plan of attack was outlined, but nothing very specific. He returned to the battalion and told his company commanders. During the afternoon of 3 August he made two separate telephone calls to Brigade, asking for detailed instructions. Gore's operation order was finally delivered to the joint HQ at precisely 5 p.m. Zero hour remained uncertain beyond 'tonight'.[10]

A thousand yards to the north, even as Sir George was busy reading, Dod Simons was being dragged out of the collapsed dug-out. McCrae could not have known of the tragedy that had befallen Armit's tight little family of printers and tradesmen. It would have made no difference if he had. Gore's plan specified the employment of two companies and involved bombing the Germans out of Intermediate by the manual. B Company remained largely intact and was the only part of the battalion that still had a substantial number of trained bombers. D was exhausted from two nights of continuous fighting; C had been holding the line during the same period. The burden must therefore pass to B. They would be joined by A Company, which James Mackenzie had been rebuilding from the Scottish Rifles drafts since mid-July.

The objective was simple – to clear the enemy out of their remaining portion of Intermediate. Brigade's chosen method was frontal assault. The Suffolks would attack on the left, entering the German line and blocking the sap that led back to Switch; McCrae's, meanwhile, would attack on the right and bomb their way along to meet the Suffolks bombing east. An intense artillery bombardment would continue to batter the enemy position for 30 seconds after zero, allowing the infantry time to break in before the defenders could get organized. Bearing in mind that McCrae's had drawn no man's land at its broadest – 250 yards – this was cutting it a little fine in full 'fighting order'. On the left, the distances were shorter: at one point the Suffolks would have to cover only about 70 yards. The enemy defences included a substantial machine-gun presence in Intermediate itself, supported by covering fire from strongpoints in High Wood and Switch. There were also an unknown number of emplacements in the cratered fields behind the trench – only two of which had been identified by the time that preparations were getting underway. It was 'hoped' that the artillery shoot would take care of these.

Around 7 p.m. the battalions received written notice of the time for the attack. Zero would be 1.10 a.m. This was odd: 101st Brigade had not trained for assembling in the dark. It further transpired that the right marker for the advance would be a flashing lamp raised above the Intermediate barricade. Since the supporting bombardment would presumably obscure most of the objective, this sounded a bit too much like one of Mr Heath Robinson's cartoons. There was worse to come. Around 8 p.m. it was announced that the attack on the left by 23rd Division and the Anzacs had been cancelled. McCrae's and the Suffolks would be going in alone. Astonishingly, it seems that someone at Division even suggested that the four companies should attempt to move *beyond* Intermediate and assault part of Switch as well. A memo survives from Gore to Nicholson, in which the notion is politely opposed:

> As these operations are now not in conjunction with troops on either flank, I would prefer not to push on beyond the intermediate line but to make one job of this and have it properly consolidated. The battalions are more than one half quite raw drafts and this one operation in the dark is all I think it is safe to ask them to do.[11]

You get the feeling that the man who withdrew his commanding officers from the first day of the offensive was having misgivings again.

Since A and B Companies were still occupying the British portion of Intermediate, they had to be relieved before they could move to their jumping-off positions for the attack. This was a complicated business in itself. There was only one way in or out: a shallow ditch (under observation from enemy machine-guns in High Wood), which led back into a narrow, winding fire-trench in the old German support line. Bear north-west and you would end up in the new front line, directly below Intermediate; bear south-west and you would find yourself in the open fields that led to Bazentin-le-Petit. Either route involved a trek of at least 1,200 yards. If anyone happened to be coming in the opposite direction, progress could be achingly slow. Relief should have taken place at 4 p.m. One company of the King's Royal Rifle Corps was expected. They were supposed to take over the support line from C Company, who would move well back out of the way. Then the companies in Intermediate would come out, while the KRRC tried to squeeze past them. Keep in mind that at no point could the British portion of the trench be left unattended. As it turned out, C Company was not relieved until 8 p.m. and it took a further hour for the Intermediate garrison to be replaced. At all points, movement was severely hindered by carrying parties for Major-General Nicholson's Stokes gun ammunition. Again we find senior officers issuing orders and timetables without familiarizing themselves with conditions on the ground. A trench-mortar bombardment was indeed desirable; and it would have been good to have the relief carried out on schedule. The two, however, were incompatible in the allotted time. Ingouville-Williams would have been up to see the trenches for himself, spotted the bottlenecks and planned accordingly. His insistence on personal reconnaissance, however, may have discouraged the development of a conventional intelligence function within the Division. When he died, the 34th was left with *two* huge voids: Nicholson filled the obvious one; the other, as yet, had clearly not been noticed.

By 9.30 Armit and Mackenzie were leading their men up to the assembly positions, hampered by hostile shell-fire and yet more Stokes ammunition. As they struggled through the narrow trenches, the platoons became badly broken up. George Philp, a 25-year-old chauffeur from Kirknewton, was one of Duggie's pipers. Detailed as a stretcher-bearer, he waited in a dug-out as the sections plodded by. His younger brother, Tommy, looked in and smiled as he passed. Tommy was with Alfie Anderson, who had just celebrated his 37th birthday. Alfie was a tall lad with a thick moustache and a permanent grin. He worked as a surfaceman for the North British Railway Company. His second wife, Agnes, was looking after their nine surviving children in a rented flat in Arthur Street. He wrote her long, dreamy letters in a fine, copperplate hand.

The Suffolks' right company, meanwhile, was halfway to Pozières: their guides couldn't find the turn-off for the front line.[12] Armit reached the jumping-off point at midnight to discover that there were no troops on his left, and that most of his own company was missing. Over on the right, Mackenzie was having similar problems. At 1.09 – zero minus one – the shelling of no man's land began, and the Suffolks still hadn't appeared. At 1.10 the artillery lifted on to Intermediate: two platoons of B Company and one of A were still stuck in the communication trench. Up at assembly, D.M. Sutherland blew his whistle and crossed the parapet, followed by a handful of men. Almost immediately (as Mangles predicted) the German artillery opened a heavy counter-bombardment. Sutherland withdrew to cover. Over on the extreme left, the remaining Suffolks company, led by Osbert Brown, had dashed forward behind the guns and broken into the German line. With no support on their right, however, they were meeting stiff resistance. Of Armit and Mackenzie, there was no sign.

Gore's plan of attack ordered the laying of a telephone cable between the

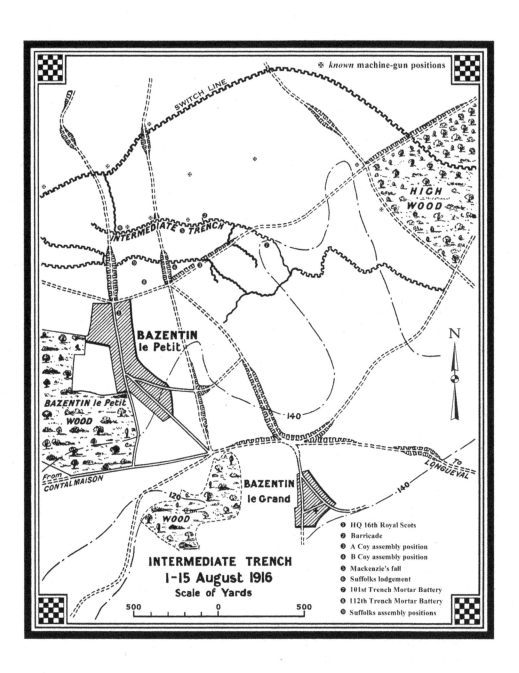

⚹ *known* machine-gun positions

SWITCH LINE

HIGH WOOD

INTERMEDIATE ❷ TRENCH

N

BAZENTIN
le Petit

BAZENTIN le Petit
WOOD

140

BAZENTIN
le Grand

TO
LONGUEVAL

140

From
CONTALMAISON

120

WOOD

INTERMEDIATE TRENCH
1-15 August 1916
Scale of Yards

500   0   500

❶ HQ 16th Royal Scots
❷ Barricade
❸ A Coy assembly position
❹ B Coy assembly position
❺ Mackenzie's fall
❻ Suffolks lodgement
❼ 101st Trench Mortar Battery
❽ 112th Trench Mortar Battery
❾ Suffolks assembly positions

front line and battalion headquarters. Sir George had gone for *two* and both of them were cut. The little HQ dug-out now found itself in the eye of a veritable storm of shells. Hearing no word from Armit by 2.30, the Colonel dispatched a runner with instructions to find 'any officer, 16th Royal Scots'. Half an hour later, a second man was sent. At 3.30 he ordered Stephenson forward to 'investigate'. At 3.45 a runner arrived from Armit, explaining that the attack had not taken place. McCrae phoned Brigade; Gore informed Division and was instructed to continue the assault 'on the front originally ordered'. This was conveyed to Sir George at 4.10 a.m. Nicholson's decision is inexplicable: since the supporting artillery shoot was now long finished and no effort was made to improvise a new one, he was condemning the attacking platoons to death. Stephenson was informed by runner and ordered to launch the attack without further delay. It was now quite light.

At 4.51 the whistles blew. Both companies climbed over the parapet and advanced 30 paces. At that point the machine-guns opened fire. Armit was on the left, leading his bombers. He got as far as the German wire, where he was shot through the head. John Veitch was behind him, rushing forward with his pal, Bob Johnstone, a housepainter from Orwell Place. A shell exploded between them, catching them both in the legs. Wull McArthur got a bullet in the shoulder. George Blaney was shot in the thigh. Alfie Anderson got through the wire before he was hit in the chest. Tommy Philp went past him and reached the German trench. He was the only one.[13]

The right fared even worse. Alex Sutherland, a trainee teacher from the village of Latheronwheel in Caithness, was killed on the parapet by a shrapnel burst that took out most of his section.[14] Chris Gill, a 20-year-old student book-keeper from Livingstone Place, had only just returned to the battalion after being wounded at Scots Redoubt. He was shot in the stomach. Charlie Goodall, briefly famous as 'McCrae's first casualty', was hit in the legs. Fred Buchanan almost lost his left hand. Dan Purcell, A Company's CSM, was peppered with shrapnel. 'We were met,' he later recalled, 'by such a wall of steel and shell that it took the breath from our bodies and hurled us back across the field.' Somehow James Mackenzie got through it. There was a machine-gun directly in front of him. He charged forward with his rifle, fell into the trench and was never seen again.

Stephenson sent a runner to HQ, advising that casualties were likely to be heavy. The phone line to Brigade was broken, so Robertson passed it along by runner. About 30 men were dead; more than 100 had been wounded. Brown's beleaguered party of Suffolks was withdrawn from its lodgement and both battalions marched back into reserve around Mametz Wood. Nicholson, meanwhile, was fuming at the failure of his first operation as Divisional commander. He immediately launched an enquiry 'into the state of the 16th Royal Scots', insisting that the blame for everything lay squarely with McCrae. The report was sent to III Corps, typed over his own signature:

> I have no doubt in my mind that the failure of the operations was due to an almost entire absence of detailed arrangements by the commanding officer; to a complete misconception of his duties in the matter of such arrangements; and failure to understand the orders issued to him, especially with regard to the necessity for adhering exactly to timetable.
>
> Two companies were engaged, each under a separate commander, one of whom was very young. No senior officer or member of the battalion staff was sent to supervise either the assembly of the companies in the forming up trench, nor the conduct of the attack. No forward report centre was established, and the only alternative means of communication to the telegraph was an order to send runners to Battalion Headquarters.
>
> Sir George McCrae's personal gallantry is well known and unquestioned, as is also his unfailing cheerfulness under all circumstances, and the devotion to him of his men, but he does not appear able to grasp the fact that it is necessary in this War to think out every detail and make every possible arrangement to secure success, that it is necessary not only to issue orders, but also to ensure their being carried out, and that an order issued to him must be carried out, no matter what loss may be incurred.
>
> For these reasons, I do not consider that he is qualified to command a battalion in the field, and I concur in the opinion of the G.O.C. 101st Brigade that he be given command of a reserve battalion. I am forwarding a separate application for the removal of the adjutant of the battalion from his appointment.[15]

Stephenson later wrote that he believed the attack on Intermediate failed because the Germans were expecting it – hence the constant heavy shelling throughout the day.[16] He was there and the General wasn't. By 1921 Nicholson himself appeared to agree, citing 'enfilade observation from High Wood'.[17] It's a pity he didn't consider that at the time. Sir George, certainly, was guiltless. Since the operation was handed to him at extremely short notice, with his battalion still in the line, it is hard to see what measures he could have taken to address the problems of overcrowding in the trenches. It was a narrow, congested system with far too many men in it. They had all been sent there by Division and Brigade. Moreover, it made no sense at all to blame McCrae for the failure of the Suffolks; indeed the very fact that a second battalion suffered identical difficulties indicates a flaw in the plan at a level far beyond the Colonel's involvement. There is clearly a substantial deflective element in the report: the most pressing question to emerge from the whole sorry mess remained entirely unaddressed. How, since no concurrent operations were dependent on the immediate capture of Intermediate that morning, did an elaborate assault originally thought to require the participation of the Anzac Corps and two British divisions, finally end up in two exhausted *companies* being ordered to attack in daylight with open flanks and no artillery support? Why, once the problems had become apparent, wasn't the assault simply cancelled? The General might have done well to direct some of his comments to Rawlinson and Pulteney.

Nicholson was about to become a very good divisional commander. By 3 August, however, he had been in the job for only a week. Fresh from a regular brigade, the step up to a New Army division which had suffered so severely on the opening day of the offensive, must have been something of a shock. The consistent flaw in his condemnation of Sir George is a remarkable degree of ignorance – suggesting that he simply hadn't had the time to acquaint himself with the units under his command. Nowhere is this more evident than in his critical comments about personnel. One of the commanders (he observed) was 'very young'. James Mackenzie was in fact thirty, only six years younger than Armit. A month after the battalion was almost wiped out, he was Sir George's senior surviving lieutenant and the only man *left* to take the company. Nicholson was also unhappy that no 'member of the battalion staff' was sent forward in a supervisory role. The 16th Royal Scots had no 'staff' other than McCrae, Stephenson and Robertson. Division itself was holding Warden captive. Nap Armit was the only remaining rifle captain and he was leading the assault. Beyond that, there was only Black and Doc Gilmour. The General plainly failed to appreciate just how short his battalions were of officers. Moreover, Brigade's operation order made no mention of a 'forward report centre', while Nicholson's comments about 'telegraph and runners' require an explanation of their own. Flares were notoriously unreliable, and flag semaphore was useless in the dark, so what alternative did he have in mind? McCrae exceeded the required number of telephone cables and it was Brigade who instructed him to move into the village, where they would surely be cut.[18]

Since 19th Division's July attack had failed under similar circumstances, Nicholson should not have discounted the possibility that the Intermediate Trench itself was to blame. Maybe it couldn't be taken by frontal assault; maybe they shouldn't have tried. Further attempts were destined to collapse in much the same chaotic manner. It finally fell to 15th (Scottish)

Division at the end of the month. The method was clever – ingenuity borne of exasperation. The 13th Royal Scots dug a sap directly north from the back of the British section. They then turned left and dug their way along behind the Germans, cutting off reinforcement and supply. The garrison surrendered at once.[19]

Robert Gore chose to keep his head down. Had he taken McCrae's side, his own position would have become untenable. The Colonel replied to the document, refuting every one of Nicholson's criticisms, and concluded with a pointed little barb. 'I regret,' he wrote, 'that an unfavourable report has been considered necessary on my battalion, especially as it has been frequently complimented on its efficiency by the late Divisional General and higher commands.'

Inky Bill must have been birling in his grave.

❋ ❋ ❋

While Nicholson was busy passing judgement on the 16th Royal Scots, his own command was coming under scrutiny from higher levels. It was plain that the 34th Division needed time to rebuild. On 15 August the 101st Brigade was finally removed from the line; four days later it entrained for its old haunts around Armentières to reunite with the 102nd and 103rd. The promised period of 'rest' would last until the following April.

Sir George did not accompany his battalion on the journey: on 19 August he was admitted to hospital at Abbeville, suffering from the effects of ptomaine poisoning. The doctor noted diarrhoea, headache and a feeble pulse. Bill Robertson was in the same ward, diagnosed with pyrexia, the medical term for what was commonly called 'trench fever'. This may or may not have been significant, but it should be pointed out that D.M. Sutherland and Alastair MacLachlan were also unfit: there had been some bad water in Bazentin and everyone at HQ drank from the same source.[20] George Hamilton, who had been wounded in the thigh two days before they left the trenches, also turned up on his way home for further treatment.

McCrae's arrived at Bailleul on 20 August and marched to billets at Erquinghem. Ness informed McCartney that Jimmy Boyd had almost certainly been killed. Neither he nor his stretcher-bearers had been heard of since they set off for the dressing station. It was assumed that they died in the shelling. James Hendry wrote from hospital in Rouen: his arm was infected but he thought that the doctors would be able to save it. He and MacLachlan had been awarded the Military Cross for their gallantry; D.M. Sutherland and Jock Miller were both mentioned in despatches. Miller spent most of the night of the attack, crawling round the village trying to find breaks in his phone cables. Jennie Armit, meanwhile, was insisting that her husband wasn't dead. In spite of confirmation from several survivors, she believed there was still hope, citing 'secret Belgian internment camps' in which the Germans were supposed to be holding captured British officers. She had been married for just over a year and couldn't bring herself to accept the truth.[21]

The battalion went back into the line at Bois Grenier on 21 August. Three days later, Arthur Stephenson formally assumed temporary command. His first task was to welcome three replacement captains. None of them was older than the men already there. Michael Claude Hamilton Bowes Lyon was 22, the fourth surviving son of the Earl of Strathmore. He had been concussed by shell-fire while serving with the 2nd Royal Scots in 1915. On his return to England, he was diagnosed with neurasthenia and had not been back on active service since. Comrie Cowan was 20 but looked 10 years older. Before the war, he was employed as a trainee manager in his father's Penicuik papermill. Commissioned in August 1914, he had served briefly in France on attachment to the South Lancashire Regiment. John Macdonald was a 25-year-old solicitor from Portobello and a founder member of the Provost's Battalion. This was his first overseas posting.

For the surviving 'originals', life now settled into a familiar rhythm, reminiscent of their first spell in the sector. Jim Steuart described the routine to his sister:

> We go into the same old trenches, receive the same old shells from Krupps and return the compliment with interest, come out to billets and go into trenches again on working-parties. At night we drink French beer if we have any money, which isn't often. Sometimes we are lucky enough to be billeted in a village a few kilometres behind the line, and there life is a bit more brisk. We can have a feed of chips and eggs for a franc, or go to the divisional theatre to see the 'Chequers', a very fine concert party, for the large sum of two francs. Also, there is a YMCA, where we can read and write in peace, and get tea and cakes of a kind – quite a nice wee place . . .[22]

Casualties were few and far between. In the early hours of 25 August Tommy King was on sentry duty at Moat Farm. He had come through the fighting on the Somme and promised his mother that he would be home before the end of the year. An oilcan exploded directly above his post, showering him with shrapnel. He died that evening in a field hospital near Steenwerck. At Rouen on 6 September James Hendry succumbed to gas gangrene. Only the previous day, he had written to Bob Martin, speculating that he might be in hospital for at least another fortnight. A pretty Red Cross nurse had wiped his face. 'Life is very pleasant,' he concluded.

Sir George finally caught up with the Division on 14 September. Arriving at Bailleul, he was appointed to temporary command of 101st Brigade. Five days later, Robert Gore returned from leave and the Colonel resumed his duties with the 16th.[23] He did not look fit. Over the following weeks several more casualties of the Somme fighting reappeared. For the most part (officers included), this was a matter of luck. Recovered wounded were seldom posted back to their parent battalion: the regimental depot simply sent you wherever you were needed. Harry Rawson turned up in October, just in time to say farewell to Pte Crossan. Pat was in the front line on the 9th, when a shell exploded on the parapet. Several pieces of shrapnel struck him on the left leg. A shard of casing pierced his boot and almost took his toes off. Doc Gilmour could do nothing but send him back to the same field hospital where Tommy King had died. Here, he lost consciousness and came round to find a label pinned to his tunic. He was listed for amputation. One of the orderlies happened to be a captured German surgeon, who persuaded his British colleagues to allow him to try and save the foot. The operation was successful, and the middle of November found Crossan recovering in Stourbridge, where he was visited by Alice.[24] He wrote McCartney that he expected to be kicking a ball again 'quite soon'; McCartney replied that Jimmy Boyd's body had been found and buried near Bazentin. The family was anxious to visit his grave.

On the night of 23 November Comrie Cowan and Harry Rawson led a party of 42 men in a raid on the enemy line opposite Grande Flamengrie Farm. McCrae was unwell, but remained at HQ in order to monitor events. The raiders were discovered by the Germans, who opened a heavy bombardment on no man's land. Cowan got his men home without losing anyone. Sir George's report, written next morning, commended the Captain for his leadership and gallantry. Shortly after sending it to Brigade, he was visited by John Shakespear, Lieutenant-Colonel of the Divisional pioneers, who later recalled:

> He was sitting out in the garden of his billet, the 16th Royal Scots being out of the line. I found him very sad, for he had just been told that he was not thought medically fit for further service in France. He was quite broken hearted.[25]

The Colonel was suffering from exhaustion. His August illness had resulted in substantial loss of weight. He was pale, gaunt and almost entirely grey. Jimmy McEvoy thought that he suddenly looked very old. On the morning of 25 November the battalion assembled near la Rolanderie to see him off to England. Arthur Stephenson:

At that moment I was very conscious of being an outsider. The survivors of the original battalion were immensely attached to Sir George. He was like a father to them, and they, in turn, were fiercely protective of the old chap. Heaven help anyone from beyond their ranks who tried to make fun of him. I remember speaking to a member of the Divisional staff, who admitted that in the early days many of his colleagues wondered what on earth he was doing on active service. Well he certainly gave them cause to change their opinion. I was privileged to hear many stories of his conduct during the opening days of the Battle of the Somme, and from all accounts he stood shoulder to shoulder with his men in the thick of the bloodiest fighting. I fear it is a tale that will never be told. Do you know that if you brought the subject up, he was embarrassed. I came across many a fellow who did much less and bored you stupid. Sir George created a fine battalion, one of the very best, I believe. He took them to France, fought at their side and would have done almost anything to have been able to stay with them until the end. But it was not within his power . . .[26]

A staff car arrived to take him to the station at Bailleul. He walked along the ranks, shaking hands with the Heriot's men. Some of them proffered small gifts – sweeties for the journey, good luck tokens. Fred Muir gave him a German book, which he'd found in a dug-out in Wood Alley. The Pipey played a song by Robert Burns:

> When wild War's deadly blast was blawn,
> And gentle Peace returning,
> Wi' mony a sweet babe fatherless,
> And mony a widow mourning:
> I left the lines and tented field,
> Where lang I'd been a lodger;
> My humble knap-sack a' my wealth,
> A poor and honest sodger.[27]

Sir George left the lines and tented field as a brevet brigadier-general with a DSO and two Mentions for gallantry. It was the end of 38 years' military service. Arthur Stephenson was confirmed as his successor. When the Major returned to his billet, he found a note waiting for him. 'It is with regret,' it said, 'that I take my leave of the battalion. I am confident, however, that it has passed into an able pair of hands. Do not think ill of the men should they continue to use the old name. It is an ancient Scottish tradition for a regiment to be called after its colonel. It will always be "McCrae's Own", but that implies no possession on my part. It is a common title, proudly held. You are one of us now, and I wish you every bit of luck.'

It was signed plain 'George McCrae'.

Sir George McCrae
(D.M. Sutherland)

CHAPTER TEN

'The Offensive Spirit'

Robert Burns had a verse for most occasions. In November 1785 he composed one of his greatest poems, a work of simple genius, directed at a 'tim'rous beastie' he had disturbed with his plough. 'The best-laid schemes o mice an men,' he observed, 'gang aft agley.' It might have been written for Sir Douglas Haig.

In November 1916 representatives of the Allied powers met at Joffre's Chantilly headquarters to plan their strategy for the coming 'season' of campaigning. In essence, they settled for more of the same. The Western Front would continue to be the main theatre of operations and the offensive on the Somme would be resumed as soon as weather permitted. This would press home the advantage gained during recent fighting and wear down the enemy reserves in the lead up to the decisive attack of the year. The timing and location of this final offensive would be settled 'later', but Haig remained intent on Flanders. On 10 December Joffre finally came round to his view. A major operation was proposed to break the German line north of Ypres, clear the Channel coast, and capture the important railway centre of Roulers. Carried to a successful conclusion, it would render the German position in Belgium untenable.

Haig was delighted and relieved. Four days earlier, however, events had begun to turn against him: Asquith's government was replaced by a Conservative-dominated coalition headed by David Lloyd George, who made no effort to conceal his contempt for the military leadership and its preoccupation with the 'Western' approach. The new prime minister immediately began to promote his favoured option of an offensive in the Balkans. When the French government sent Joffre into retirement on 13 December, all bets were off. The General's replacement, Robert Nivelle, had impressed the politicians with an ambitious scheme for a decisive initiative of his own. Nivelle was the author of two stunningly successful counter-attacks at Verdun, which had recaptured almost all the ground gained by the Germans since the summer. Applying the same principles on a broader front, he believed that he could 'rupture' the enemy line in two days and bring hostilities to a satisfactory conclusion shortly thereafter.

Haig met Nivelle for the first time on 20 December and thought him 'straightforward and soldierly'. Nivelle stated bluntly that none of Joffre's commitments remained in force. As an alternative, he proposed to avoid the broken ground in front of the German salient on the Somme, and to attack instead on its vulnerable 'shoulders'. The French would assault the southern sector between Soissons and Rheims in an effort to seize the Chemin des Dames ridge, north of the River Aisne. The resulting breach would be rapidly enlarged; 'armies of manœuvre' would pour through and exploit the inevitable panic. In the north, around Arras, the British would mount a 'preparatory' attack, aimed at drawing the enemy reserves out of position. Acknowledging Haig's preference for Flanders, Nivelle left open the possibility of an offensive there 'if the need arises' but was sufficiently sure of himself to add that 'as a consequence of the retreat of the German Armies' the Belgian coast would fall into Allied hands without being directly assaulted.

Nivelle's proposals implied nothing less than the complete abandonment of all Haig's plans for 1917. In order to release sufficient divisions for the main attack, he was also being asked to assume control of Nivelle's line from the Somme down to the Amiens–Roye road. It was like the start of 1916 all over again. Forced by Lloyd George to conform to French command, Haig retreated to his fallback position, offering only a conditional agreement – British participation on the understanding that operations remained of short duration; that (in effect) they would be broken off if they did not prove immediately decisive. Meanwhile preparations for a major offensive in the north would continue. The Belgian coast, he insisted, must be cleared during the summer.

On 27 December Haig was appointed Field-Marshal as a New Year gift from a grateful King and Country. It was the coldest winter for 40 years: in a draughty billet at Rolanderie Farm, Gerald Crawford was tinkering with his symphonic poem, now provisionally entitled 'Europa'. He had a painful, hacking cough and there was blood on the cuff of his tunic.

✲ ✲ ✲

The first anniversary of McCrae's arrival in France passed quietly. For the surviving originals, it was a time to think of absent friends. Jim Steuart wrote that he had a great deal to be thankful for. He was the last man standing: the rest of his Heriot's section were dead or gone. On 9 January Jimmy Black returned to Scotland; the following day Crawford was carried off to hospital and Bill Robertson left the division for a job on the staff of the Second Anzac Corps. None of them would be back. Jimmy McEvoy recalled that familiar faces disappeared, never to be seen again. Some of the tradesmen sought transfers to technical arms; potential officers resisted the lure of a commission only as long as their pals remained. Sickness and disease continued to take their inevitable toll. Among the new drafts were the first of the conscripts – bewildered young men who had never fired their rifles. Steve leaned heavily on his 'old hands' during this period and made few changes. He was, however, noticeably strict. Bob Martin (who had peered beneath the crust and liked what he found) wondered if it was a deliberate attempt to distance himself from Sir George's more relaxed style.[1] Sgt James Baigrie, a 25-year-old shop assistant from Gifford Park, thought him 'hard but fair'. Baigrie, captain of the Edinburgh Nomads football team, had returned to the battalion after recovering from a leg wound sustained in Contalmaison with George Russell's platoon.

On 15 February a familiar name appeared in the discipline book. Shortly after arriving in France, Pte MacMillan had fallen out with Lionel Coles. The charge was 'insolence'. Coles ordered extra drill; Hamlet decided to go home. He was apprehended in St Omer, attempting to board a train for Boulogne. The matter was brought before the Colonel, who sentenced him to seven days Field Punishment No. 2 – in essence heavy labour, his civilian occupation. He went over the top on 1 July and took part in the fighting at Intermediate Trench; his behaviour for a while was plainly good. On 14 October, however, McCrae had to fine him seven days pay for failing to comply with an order to bathe. It was the start of a troublesome spell, and over the next few weeks he disappeared several times. On 19 January the temperature suddenly dropped. The flooded ground around Boesinghe, which protected the northern approaches to Ypres, froze so hard that it was feared the Germans might try to improvise an attack. 34th Division was bussed north to the town of Meteren in order to cover the line. Hamlet must have objected to his new surroundings: on 31 January he was awarded seven days Field Punishment No. 1 for lateness. This involved being tethered to a fixed object for two hours every day. While he was serving his sentence, the battalion moved up to Berthen, near the Belgian border. It was miserably cold – 'an absolute dump', Jimmy McEvoy recalled. On 13 February MacMillan was awarded 14 days forfeiture of pay for 'absence from the ranks'; two days later, having failed to turn up for defaulter's parade, he was arrested pending Court Martial for disobedience.[2]

While Hamlet was fighting his own private war against authority,

Stephenson was busy preparing his battalion for the real thing. With one eye fixed on Flanders and the other turned to Arras, Field-Marshal Haig was concerned about the training of his men. Late in December the General Staff had issued a confidential manual, *Instructions for the Training of Divisions for Offensive Action* (SS 135), which drew upon the lessons of Verdun and the Somme. Of particular importance was close cooperation between artillery and infantry:

> Success in recent operations [it stated] has been due, more than anything else, to the infantry keeping close up to the artillery barrage and entering the enemy trenches immediately the barrage lifts from these trenches, and before the hostile garrison have time to man their defences. The greatest attention, therefore, must be devoted to this point during training, and the vital importance of following the barrage closely, even at the risk of a few casualties from short bursts, must be impressed on all ranks.

In theory the so-called 'creeping barrage' would act like a protective curtain.

SS 135 was augmented in the middle of February by SS 143, *Instructions for the Training of Platoons*, by some distance the more radical document. Assuming one Lewis gun per platoon (a target not yet fully met), Rawlinson's rigid lines were replaced by four self-sufficient specialist sections: bombers, Lewis gunners, riflemen and rifle grenadiers. The attack would proceed in two 'waves': riflemen and bombers in the lead, Lewis gunners supporting their advance with suppressing fire. The rifle grenade (quaintly described as the 'howitzer of the Infantry') would 'dislodge the enemy from behind cover and drive him underground'. Training in these methods would infuse the men with 'Offensive Spirit', give them confidence in their weapons, and instil discipline and *esprit de corps*; more importantly, it was acknowledged that the process would take several weeks and require to be reinforced at regular intervals. There was one other important innovation: heavy casualties among senior officers on 1 July 1916 had led to Robert Gore's independent directive being adopted as official policy. Battalion headquarters would no longer be permitted to take part in the initial advance. They would wait behind 'until the objective had been gained'.

The battalions of 34th Division began working under SS 135 while they were in the frozen north. On the Somme, the gunners had remained in the line: the Lahoussoye manoeuvres were conducted in isolation. Now the divisional artillery worked with them: live rounds were employed, distances measured, speed of advance calculated for different kinds of ground. In the absence of direct radio contact with advancing troops, however, there remained one unavoidable danger. The artillery 'lifts' would be *predetermined*. As the infantry followed close behind, there was a possibility that they could be caught under the fire of their own guns. It happened during field days; it would happen at the front.

On 19 February McCrae's moved back to Morbecque. It was the start of a slow march south in stages towards Arras; training continued at Diéval and Chelers on the way. The new tactics demanded a greater degree of teamwork and coordination than anything they had encountered before. Each man was expected to become proficient in his own specialty, and since all ranks would still carry a rifle and (at least) two grenades, musketry and bombing practice could not be neglected. Hamlet, meanwhile, was practising being tied up: following his trial at Chelers on 27 February, Stephenson sentenced him to 42 days Field Punishment No. 1. The weather was unremittingly awful and the prospect of yet another 'decisive' offensive to win the war by Christmas no longer carried the same uplifting promise that it had in 1916. Jim Steuart, newly returned from his first leave in a year, wrote to his father:

> France is looking bleaker than ever. I am sure Fritz is sorry that he ever tried to take it. If it wasn't for the principle of the thing, I am sure we would make him welcome to the stinky, muddy old mouldy midden, or, to make it a proper alliteration, malodorous mouldy midden. Bon, eh? I'm afraid I need a dictionary. The platoon helped me to spell these words, but I am doubtful of them yet.[3]

On 9 March the battalion arrived at the town of Anzin St Aubin, just north of Arras, and officially joined XVII Corps in General Edmund Allenby's Third Army. They were immediately detailed for working parties in preparation for the offensive, which was scheduled to start at the beginning of April. Six days later, the Germans began an unexpected withdrawal from the entire front between Arras and the Aisne, surrendering the old Somme battlefield in the process. In one bold move, they divested themselves of an awkward salient, reduced their trench-front by 25 miles, and released 14 divisions to bolster the line elsewhere. Their new defensive position – the Hindenburg Line – was twenty-five miles further east and had been under construction for seven months. It was a sophisticated network of killing zones, protected by concrete gun-emplacements and formidable belts of fresh barbed wire. The withdrawal – codenamed *Alberich* – involved laying waste to everything en route. When it dawned on the Allied generals that the ground in front of them was no longer occupied, they sent their troops forward into a devastated wilderness of shattered villages and poisoned wells.

The Hindenburg Line effectively 'snipped off' the Somme salient at its roots. In the south, it stopped just short of the Chemin des Dames; in the north, it joined up neatly with the existing defences around Arras. The withdrawal would have scuppered Haig and Joffre's intentions; Nivelle's plan was largely unaffected. The British element of the operation covered a front of 14 miles. In the centre, Allenby's Army would attack directly east of the town. Their job was to break the line, then turn south-east to threaten Cambrai and take the Hindenburg in rear. Their northern flank would be protected by the Canadian Corps, which was expected to seize the commanding heights of Vimy Ridge. The original objective to the south had been the Bapaume salient; however, with its sudden disappearance, the plan was adjusted to include a limited assault by Hubert Gough's Fifth Army on the Hindenburg Line around Bullecourt. Elaborate artillery preparations, incorporating lessons learned from the Somme, would minimise casualties among the advancing troops. Compared with 1 July 1916, more than twice as many guns had been assembled and long practice in wire-cutting was slowly beginning to make perfect. The preliminary bombardment would last for three weeks, much of it aimed at specifically selected targets. Four days before zero, the shelling would intensify to terrifying levels and maintain that pitch for 96 hours.

On 20 March, McCrae's returned to the line. It was raining and the mud was ankle-deep. Their trench-front – 'K Section' – ran due north from the Bailleul road for 1,500 yards and was named after a series of mine craters in no man's land: 'King', 'Kite', 'Kick', 'Kent', 'Kate' and 'Claude'. On the other side of the wire, the enemy position climbed up a high, grassy ridge. At the summit were some haystacks and the ruins of a farm called Point du Jour. Enemy artillery observation was excellent: during the four-day tour, three men were killed and five wounded by shell-fire. On the 24th the battalion moved back to billets at the small town of St Nicholas. One night, when it was getting dark, Steuart ventured out to see the sights:

> Arras was so near the German lines that movement during daylight was dangerous. Fritz took a delight in plunking huge shells into the main Square. The town is built of pure white chalk and must have been a beautiful place in peacetime. We came to the Cathedral at last and walked up the steps, the only undamaged things to be seen. A good bit of the walls remained standing, but the inside has been horribly smashed. While admiring the old place, I heard one of Fritz's heavies humming over. Knowing how fond old Fritz was of cathedrals, I got the wind up, so we hopped it. We made for the main street. It was getting near 8 p.m. and the shops were not allowed to open till then. I saw some pretty souvenirs in silver or mother-of-

pearl, but beyond my humble purse unfortunately. Nearly everyone was buying these silk-worked cards to send to their families.

The streets were getting thicker with people, so we made for 'home', dropping in on an estaminet on the way to see what it was like. The beer is a terrible price. It is a weird sight to see the ruined houses suddenly showing up in the bluish flare of Very lights from the trenches. It gives one a sinking feeling of despair and hopelessness of life in general. It is uncanny going through these dead streets in that flickering glare and imagining all the happy people who must have lived there only two years ago. You expect to meet their ghosts at every corner.

We Tommies and Jocks haven't much sympathy for the French, but oh, if the war had been in England or Scotland, we would understand then. Imagine Edinburgh ruined and lit up by the occasional flash of big guns and the blue lights, with all the streets dead quiet except for the squeaking and scurrying of rats.[4]

They had 12 days out of the line. There was no respite, however, from the carrying and digging. Jimmy McEvoy was baffled. 'We were supposed to be getting ready for a big push,' he later recalled, 'but they were working us like slaves.' Stephenson convened a meeting of his officers to discuss the attack. Zero hour was scheduled for 5.30 a.m. on Easter Sunday, 8 April. The battalion would form up in no man's land, as close as possible to the enemy wire. At that moment the barrage would concentrate on the German front line for four minutes, giving the assaulting waves time to move in behind the curtain. When the barrage lifted, they would enter the enemy position before the defenders had a chance to organise. There were three main systems to be crossed – Black, Blue and Brown – and this process would be repeated at each of them. If the timings were adhered to, the assault would be irresistible. The ridge would fall by lunchtime.

The staff work leading up to this operation was meticulous. One factor, however, remained beyond anyone's control. By 5 April the weather was so bad that the attack had to be postponed for a day. Stephenson briefed his officers; they, in turn, explained the details to their men. That evening the battalion marched back to the trenches. They were passing an ammunition dump at Chalk Farm, when a shell came down on one of the platoons in A Company. Alfred Norrie, a 21-year-old hotel-boots from Glen Street, had only just returned to the battalion after recovering from wounds sustained on 1 July. He was blown to pieces. Two more men were killed and three wounded. The rest of the relief passed off quietly. That night, patrols were sent out to ascertain whether the enemy line was still occupied. Unnerved by the audacity of the March withdrawal, Haig was concerned that the

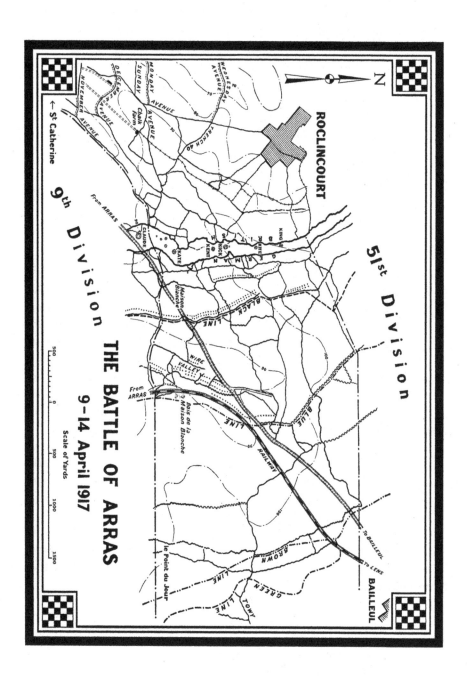

THE BATTLE OF ARRAS

9–14 April 1917

Germans might try to pull it off again.[5] On the evening of 7 April Comrie Cowan was ordered to lead a raiding party of 3 officers and 100 men into the trenches south of Roclincourt. Jim Steuart went along:

> Our artillery was bombarding the Boche third line, leaving his first and second for our kindly attention. Then over we went. It was a weird experience. Our fire lit up no man's land with a red glow and the air was thick with lyddite. I kept cursing and falling into mine-craters and shell-holes and getting entangled in the remains of Fritz's barbed wire. We crossed over his first line, which was badly smashed up and scarcely recognizable as a trench at all. A Boche potato masher bomb dropped near me and gave me a shock. Then a lot of bombing started on my left. I didn't throw mine as we were a bit mixed up and I was afraid of hitting our chaps. However, we got a prisoner and popped back at the toute-de-suite for our own lines.[6]

Cowan and six others were reported missing. Tommy Palmer was dead. 2/Lt John Watson, headmaster of St James Episcopal School in Edinburgh, had been killed in the initial rush. John Wright, a 25-year-old boot-maker from East Adam Street, was shot through the thigh trying to help him. In spite of his injury, he succeeded in fighting off two German bombers, a deed for which he would later be mentioned in despatches. Doc Gilmour was hit in the shoulder when he went out to rescue a wounded man. The raid, however, had yielded more than just a prisoner. They now knew that the enemy wire had been destroyed and (more importantly) that Fritz had no intention of withdrawing.[7]

At 4.30 a.m. on 9 April the battalion struggled from its dug-outs in a cold, persistent drizzle. The trenches were knee-deep in mud. It was dark and they had some difficulty forming up for the attack. At zero the barrage settled on the enemy front line; Steuart thought that 'it beat the July bombardment hollow'. They went over on the dot.

The first trench was crossed as if it wasn't there. Black Line, the *fourth* trench and first objective, was 500 yards further on. They took it at 6.03, two minutes ahead of schedule. The leading waves got caught in the barrage. Steuart again:

> We had advanced rather too fast and so got among our own shells. I took cover in a trench. While crouching there, I got a fearful bang on the head and felt warm blood running down my face and body. I thought my head had been blown off but a corporal who was with me said it was my ear. I looked round for my helmet, which had been blown off my head and found a huge slice out of it. My box

respirator had two large pieces of shrapnel embedded in it and my right breast pocket containing my cigarette case had gone. I must have had a whizzbang practically to myself.[8]

Blue Line, more than twice as far away, was expected to be tougher. At 6.30 the survivors formed up 40 yards behind the curtain and moved off. To their immediate front, the ground dipped into a shallow valley, thickly wired, then climbed out towards a railway-cutting which skirted Maison Blanche Wood. As they emerged from the hollow, machine-guns opened up along the line. One, in particular, proved difficult to pass. Lt Arthur Flett, an Edinburgh accountant, and 2/Lt Erik Thurburn, a bank clerk from West Kensington, led a bayonet charge. Both men were killed as they entered the cutting, but the gun was silenced. Blue Line fell at 7.15. The battalion halted to consolidate, leaving 15th Royal Scots to come through and assault Brown at 12.10. Alfred Harrison (who had turned Jimmy Black away at Perham Down) could find only 100 men. It was 2,000 yards to the top of the ridge and they were allowed 46 minutes to make it. At the last moment, a battery of German field guns, concealed on the reverse slope, opened fire and cut them to shreds. When they hit the line at Point du Jour, there were fewer than 50 of them left.[9]

The leading battalions were supposed to halt at Green Line, a few hundred yards beyond the crest, overlooking the towns of Bailleul and Gavrelle. Here they would consolidate again, mop up any remaining opposition and prepare for further advances the following day. But the ground directly in front of them was now undefended. The next German line was just 2,500 yards away – a reserve position, poorly wired and thinly garrisoned. Break that, and they were through to the last substantial system in the sector, the so-called Drocourt–Quéant 'switch' spur of the Hindenburg defences. The attacking units, however, were utterly spent and since this was intended to be no more than a 'subsidiary' operation, Haig had made no provision for reserve units to exploit any success. It was another opportunity lost.

Across the front, the attack had taken most of its objectives. Demoralised by the accuracy of the bombardment, the Germans had surrendered in their thousands. In the north, the Canadians were established on the crest of Vimy Ridge. In the centre, 4th Division had advanced more than three miles towards Fampoux, the furthest penetration in a single day since trench deadlock took hold in 1914. On the right, south of the River Scarpe, units of VI Corps captured the fortified village of Neuville-Vitasse and broke into the Hindenburg at its northernmost point.

Late in the afternoon McCrae's were ordered up to Brown in order to help the 15th form a defensive front. They arrived around dusk in a snowstorm.

There was no shelter, and (as instructed by Brigade) the men had left their greatcoats back in Arras. The expected counter-attacks failed to develop and they spent the next five days shivering on the hillside in half-dug trenches and shallow depressions scraped out of the mud. Periodic reconnaissance patrols reported at least half a mile of unoccupied ground to the front. German field guns and heavies had been abandoned by their crews. On the morning of 10 April, Willie Gavin (who had returned to the battalion in November) led a small raiding party deep into the Gavrelle approaches and captured a battery of three 5.9-inch howitzers.[10] The following night he passed out with the cold. Brigade's War Diary recorded the conditions: 'heavy snow alternating with blinding rain and wind, blowing almost with the force of a gale'. On the 12th, two men died of exposure.[11]

The battalion was withdrawn from the line on the evening of 14 April and marched back to the Arras–St Pol road, where Donald Munro met them with tea, rum and hot soup. A total of 610 other ranks had taken part in the assault; 310 were now unaccounted for. Most of them were thought to have been wounded; at least 60 were certainly dead.[12] In addition to Flett and Thurburn, Stephenson had lost six more officers. John Macdonald died of wounds on the 11th; the rest were on their way to Blighty. On the plus side, Comrie Cowan had been found in a dug-out behind the railway cutting. During the raid, his right leg was broken above the knee by a grenade blast. The Germans were unable to evacuate him because of the bombardment. On 10 April an operation was performed at number 20 Field General Hospital and the leg was removed. Three days later, he wrote a cheery letter to his father. 'I'll soon get used to it,' he said. Steve sent his name in for a gallantry award: within the month he would have his second Military Cross.[13]

Shortly before lunch on 15 April, the battalion was carried back to billets at Averdoingt in several converted London omnibuses. Haig had ordered a pause in the offensive – ostensibly to prepare a plan for the next phase. In fact his divisions were exhausted, in dire need of rest and reinforcement. The following day a draft of 105 men arrived: some of them had been in the Army for only 3 months. Stephenson had to train them up as 'specialists' in a matter of days. Bob Martin:

> We were standing at a crossroads late one afternoon. Steve's batman and runner were, as always, within hailing distance. As we talked, three small figures appeared, staggering along in full marching order – pack, haversack, rifle, etc. Stephenson stopped them. They were a draft for the Lincolns and they were small – very unlike the type that could stand up to the rough Hell that is war. The Colonel was at once strangely gentle; he ordered his batman and runner to

help them to their billet. After they had gone, Stephenson said to me: 'What a bloody shame, sending these poor little buggers out here. Only swelling the bloody base camps.' But I could see that he was merely covering a feeling of compassion that he probably was ashamed of. I shall never forget that incident. It was not the Steve we knew, but it *was* Steve.[14]

On 16 April Nivelle's offensive opened in Champagne and foundered on ferocious opposition. There was no sudden rupture, unless it was to the General's reputation. Haig was now at liberty to concentrate on Flanders. Since he had insufficient resources to fight two great battles at once, the Arras sector would be starved of men and guns. Maintaining pressure in the south was important: he could be seen to be supporting the ailing French, and, at the same time, distract German attention from his preparations elsewhere. Operations, however, would take on a hollow and improvised air.

McCrae's moved back to the line on 24 April. They had only ten Lewis guns, six having been lost in the recent fighting. The new drafts had never seen a rifle grenade, and had only the vaguest notion of how to fuse and throw a bomb. Listen carefully and you can still hear the sound of the SS manuals being torn up and tossed out the window at HQ. That night Willie Gavin was wounded by shell-fire: Stephenson had 17 officers and only 459 other ranks, including his Transport and 'Q' men. Late on the afternoon of 25 April, Lieutenant-General Sir Charles Fergusson, commander of XVII Corps, visited Lothian Nicholson to inform him that the 34th Division had been ordered to undertake a major assault on the morning of the 28th.

Haig had decided to renew his offensive by concentrating on a 12-mile front astride the River Scarpe from Gavrelle in the north to Croisilles in the south. The principal obstacle in the northern sector was a low promontory called Greenland Hill. In the immediate aftermath of 9 April, the Germans had quickly fortified the western slopes with a network of shallow trenches and isolated outposts. Down to the river, its southern approaches were protected by a railway-cutting and a scattering of buildings on either side of the Gavrelle road. There was the railway station, a chemical factory, and a château with its own walled grounds. The position was screened by machine-gun emplacements in Mount Pleasant Wood, and, further south, in dense plantation of mature trees and bushes, which curled around the river-bank to enfilade every possible line of attack. Finally, huddled close to the Scarpe, was a ragged cluster of houses with an almost unpronounceable name. It was the village of Rœux.

✹ ✹ ✹

Rœux and its adjacent 'Chemical Works' had been captured on the 23rd by units of 51st Division only to be lost the following day to a fierce counter-attack. Nicholson was ordered to rectify the situation by retaking both strongpoints simultaneously and pressing on to establish a defensive line 100 yards beyond. His battalions were down to fewer than 500 officers and men, about a third of whom were entirely new. A worrying feature of 51st Division's attack had been the failure of the infantry to keep sufficiently close to the creeping barrage. Such tactics, he concluded, were designed for open ground, not for fighting slowly through a village. In any case, there was no time to practise, no time to register the guns. He decided on a risky alternative, a throwback to the Somme. Instead of 'lifting' smoothly, the barrage would advance in three successive 100-yard 'bounds', pausing for several minutes at each stage to allow the infantry to deal with opposition on the ground. A further alternative – pounding Rœux and its surroundings into dust – was attractive but impossible. Time, again, was simply far too short.

Two brigades would attack in line – 103rd to the north of the railway, 101st to the south. The Suffolks drew the Chemical Works; the Lincolns, in the centre, drew the cemetery and its adjoining buildings. 15th Royal Scots got the short straw – the lower wood and the main part of the village. McCrae's were detailed to follow the lead battalions and 'mop up' any lingering resistance. The German position was deeply unfamiliar, consisting mainly of a series of shell-hole outposts and cleverly concealed machine-gun nests. There were few trenches. Inadequate artillery preparation was compounded by the elusiveness of the defenders.

Zero hour was 4.25 a.m. It was so dark that some units were unable to determine the direction of advance. In the north, 103rd Brigade was halted by unexpectedly strong opposition, which had somehow survived the bombardment; south of the railway, the barrage missed the front line altogether. When the Suffolks moved forward, they were appalled to discover thick barbed wire along the entire length of the château's boundary hedges.[15] As they struggled through the entanglement, machine-guns picked them off in little groups. 2/Lt Bernard Armstrong, a 22-year-old bank clerk from Carlisle, was following with the C Company 'moppers'. He led his section up to some houses in front of the factory and bombed one gun out of action. He then attacked another, but was forced to withdraw by the weight of hostile fire. Willie Rhind, a 32-year-old plumber from Eyre Terrace, was pursued by a sniper as he tried to assist a wounded comrade. He was the captain of Penicuik Juniors and it was no way to treat him.

With the Chemical Works still occupied, any advance further south was doomed. The Lincolns were followed by D Company. They got as far as the cemetery but found themselves enfiladed on both flanks. To their front, the

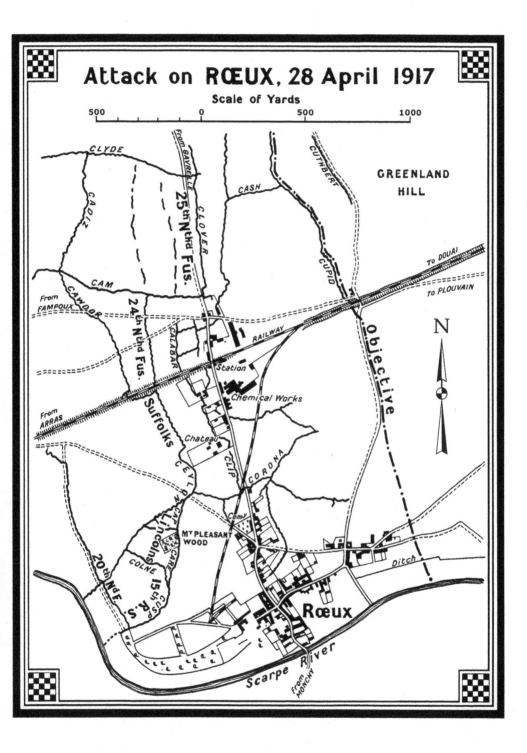

Attack on RŒUX, 28 April 1917

Rœux–Gavrelle road was crawling with snipers.[16] The barrage had 'bounded' over them. Machine-guns started firing on the leading platoons and they, too, were forced to withdraw. The Germans responded by mounting a charge into Mount Pleasant Wood, where they ran into four 16th bombers led by Finlay MacRae, not long returned after recovering from his wounds of 1 July. Sgt MacRae, a stocky little man with a thick moustache, was by repute the best soldier in the battalion. Geordie Watson, a 20-year-old oilworker from Oakbank in Midlothian, saw him in action that morning. 'He was cool as anything,' he recalled. 'There was no way the Fritzes were getting get past him. He wouldn't allow it.'[17]

On the right, the leading waves of the 15th Royal Scots entered the wood to find all the paths and adjacent undergrowth thickly wired. Routes around these obstacles were covered by machine-guns. Taking advantage of the darkness, however, they managed to fight their way into the village and advance to their objective in the open fields to the east, where they dug a defensive line and waited for the Lincolns to come up on their flank. In command was Captain Gavin Lang Pagan, 44-year-old minister of St George's Parish Church in Edinburgh, who had joined the battalion as a private in November 1914. He had about 175 men, some of whom were wounded. He gave Leonard Robson one of two remaining Lewis guns and sent him off to hold the left.

Meanwhile, back in the village, around 70 members of the 16th were trying to mop up the unmoppable. A Company, commanded by Mike Lyon, and B Company, commanded by Alfred Warr, had moved up with the 15th. They entered the wood ten paces behind and sustained heavy casualties as they battled their way through. Warr's platoon, bringing up the rear, had the door slammed in its face and was forced to take cover in a series of shell-holes on the western edge of the tree-line. The remaining platoons and Pagan's command were now cut off. Unaware of his predicament, Lyon proceeded to clear the buildings in accordance with the prearranged plan:

> The company was rather disorganised but they went looking for cellars etc. We took a few prisoners and I found myself with about a dozen men. We came across a lot of sniping from the top of the village, which B Coy were mopping up. We started a little way up but word came of some Germans down the main street, so we went for them, leaving B Coy to see to their bit. We got into the main street in driblets and had to take refuge from sniping behind some debris on each side of the road.[18]

Lyon and his party attempted to reply but the enemy fire was so intense that they could barely raise their heads. 2/Lt George Henderson, a 27-year-old clerk with the Local Government Board for Scotland, had moved up in the other direction to try to make contact with B Company:

> I mopped up the houses and cellars in my area, taking a few prisoners. I arrived at the extreme end of the village and met 2/Lt Howat. Between us we had only a handful of men. Here we encountered what appeared to be a preliminary counter-attack by the enemy. For some time we maintained our position by rifle fire and bombing in the hope of reinforcements arriving.[19]

Howat, a railway station foreman from Salisbury, Rhodesia, continues:

> From the end of the village, we could see the 15th digging in about 200 yards away. Our next duty was to report to Captain Warr at the church, so we started off slowly to look for him. About halfway up, we were hailed by a party of 8 or 10 men who were standing in the street about 200 yards distant. The light was bad, so for a time we could not tell whether they were friend or foe, till fired on by them. We returned the fire and cleared the street, however the Germans continued sniping at us. At this time Lt Henderson was shot in the hip and the Germans bombed us. We returned the bombs but had to cross the street for shelter. We succeeded in doing so, and in killing the majority of an M.G. team and causing the remainder to disappear. We then tried to get along the river bank to the mill, whence we intended getting to the church. However, the firing was exceedingly heavy and it was only by running from shell-hole to shell-hole that we ultimately reached the mill. Most of my men had been wounded by that time. We tried to reach the church but found it impossible due to M.G. fire, so we settled down to sniping. Just then, the Germans came on to us. I and one unwounded man ran to a shell-hole to try and get to the wood, but the enemy played an M.G. on us, killing my companion and keeping me down. I was immediately surrounded and obliged to surrender my arms.[20]

The Germans were pouring into the village from the direction of the Chemical Works. Within a matter of minutes, the moppers had been mopped up themselves. Lyon retired to the river-bank and tried to make a stand, but he was overrun and captured. Willie Sponder, a 33-year-old grocer from Temple Park Crescent, was the battalion's machine-gun sergeant. His right arm was fractured by the same bullet that killed one of his pals. He, too, went into the bag. Years later, he would compare the assault on Rœux to poking a wasps' nest with a pointed stick. 'We should have left it well alone,' was his opinion.

With the village secure, the Germans turned their attention to the rest of their intruders. Pagan was shot in the throat and took ten minutes to die. Robson held out until 9 a.m., then, despairing of relief, led a few unwounded men into the river. He was shot in the leg and taken prisoner. At 9.30 Stephenson ordered Alfred Warr to withdraw his survivors. When the rolls were called that evening the battalion mustered 8 officers and 201 other ranks. Another 6 officers and 170 men were missing; a few were already known to be dead. Among them was Hamlet MacMillan.[21]

By late afternoon the remains of the division were back in their original trenches. Blame for the disaster was placed on the bounding barrage, which survivors agreed had 'lifted over all the worst bits' and left the defenders essentially untroubled. Inexperience on the part of the drafts was also mentioned, as well as the short notice given for the operation. In the end, however, it may have come down to bad luck. A German prisoner told Alfred Warr that at the very moment the assault began, he and his comrades had been marching to the village under cover of darkness in order to mount an attack of their own. 'This fact,' Warr later wrote, 'accounted for the large number of enemy encountered and for the extreme tenacity with which they held their ground.'[22]

McCrae's were relieved on 1 May and bussed back to billets at the village of Sus-St Leger, 15 miles south-west of Arras on the Doullens road. Two days later, George Hamilton turned up with a draft of 47 men: it wasn't much to work with, but all they would be getting for a while. On 6 and 7 May they marched 18 miles further south to the village of Berneuil, deep in the back area of the old Somme front. It was a pretty spot and the weather was fine. The battalion was temporarily reorganised on a three-company basis and resumed training, paying particular attention to the replacement of Lewis gunners and rifle grenadiers. Village and wood fighting were practised as well, but the greatest attention was devoted to musketry. 'Every effort,' wrote John Shakespear, 'was made to break down the cult of the bomb and to re-establish the rifle as the infantry soldier's chief weapon.'[23]

On 11 May a familiar face appeared. Jimmy Moir, wounded many months ago at Bois Grenier, marched into HQ and promptly collapsed. Initially he claimed to have been passed fit from hospital and posted; on closer questioning, however, it emerged that he had been detailed to join the staff of an instructional school in the rear. He preferred McCrae's and decided to 'post' himself. He remained unable to lift his arm, but insisted he was ready to rejoin. Steve made him orderly officer pending further enquiries. Several days later, Jimmy was sent on his way.

The battalion stayed at Berneuil for three weeks. On 28 May, however, they were bussed back up the Arras road. Bob Martin did not go with them. He was 'done in' and had secured a transfer to the Indian Army. As he left, Tommy Millar returned. Two days later, they were back in the line. It had barely moved while they were away. Their trenches were on the forward slopes of Greenland Hill and they endured a grim fortnight of sniping and shelling which claimed the lives of 21 men, including George Hamilton, who was killed during a bombardment on 9 June. Hamilton had been depressed: leaving Glasgow after recovering from his wounds, he told his family that they would never see him again. He shook hands with everyone and bid them an earnest farewell. Two days before he died, he wrote to his cousin, apologising for worrying him and saying that he felt much better. His replacement in D Company was a 22-year-old civil servant from Gilmore Place, 2/Lt Robert William Fairfield Johnston.

❈ ❈ ❈

Bobby Johnston was born on 1 May 1895 at Glencorse Barracks, near Penicuik, where his father was a sergeant in the Pay Corps. In 1914 he was working as a clerk at the War Office in London; on the outbreak of hostilities he returned to Edinburgh to enlist in the 9th Royal Scots. He served for over a year with them in France before putting in for a commission. He was transferred to an Officer Cadet Battalion at Gailes in Ayrshire and discharged three months later as a second lieutenant. His background had given him broad experience of both the Regular Army and the Territorial Force. The 16th was something altogether different. 'McCrae's,' he later said, 'enjoyed a legendary reputation among the fighting soldiers on the Western Front. This was partly for their football, of course, but mainly for their show at la Boisselle. I don't think anyone today realises what they did. The old 34th was highly respected and the standard for the division had been set by Sir George's battalion. When I joined them, there were only a few of the old hands left, but the *esprit de corps* was very strong – very like a regular unit, I would say. They had a regimental pride that was unusual for a Kitchener outfit.'[24]

On 19 June, Johnston took his new platoon out of the line. The battalion was bussed back to billets near the rearward village of Magnicourt to refit in preparation for a move. Further drafts arrived, bringing the strength up to 20 officers and just over 500 men. At midnight on 5 July they marched six miles to the station at Ligny-St Flochel and entrained for Péronne.

Before 1914 Péronne was perhaps the prettiest town in the entire *département* of the Somme. The Germans arrived that September and stayed until the Hindenburg withdrawal. Before leaving, they fired a charge in every building and reduced the place to rubble. The countryside around had been laid waste: wells fouled, farms wrecked, villages destroyed. It was the embodiment of *Kultur*. McCrae's marched nine miles east and pitched their tents in a valley south of Poeuilly. On 9 July they went into the line near the village of Pontru on the banks of the Omignon river. To the south were the French; the battalion, therefore, had the honour of holding the extreme right flank of the British Army. Their defensive front consisted of a series of isolated outposts, positioned to support each other in the event of an attack. No man's land was treacherous and broad; on the far side, beyond a similar system of detached posts, the German trenches climbed up the forward slopes of Cologne Ridge, which squatted like an enormous sentry 2,000 yards in front of the Hindenburg Line. Every night, patrols went out to gather information. It was a dangerous job, but Johnston preferred it to sitting around in a hole:

> One bright, moonlit night I was detailed to verify if a particular post was held by night as well as day. I went forward with three men, moving quietly in an arrowhead formation. This took a long time as we had to check our positions with each other and listen for enemy movement. We must have been about 100 yards from our target, when fire was opened on us from a flank. I threw a Mills bomb towards the enemy, heard it explode, raised my head and saw what I believed was the face of a German some 20 feet from me. I fired at it with my revolver. I then heard Cpl Fox, who was behind me, jump up with a shout and turned to see him clubbing a Boche on the head with a knobkerry while another Boche rushed away. We all stood up and threw grenades and saw about ten Boche retiring. Fox tore off the shoulder strap of the Boche at our feet, took his paybook and letters from his pocket, and we got back as quickly as we could. Fox was cursing and swearing as he had cut his hand on some barbed wire and wanted to stop to have it bandaged![25]

Dick Fox was a 33-year-old labourer from Bonnybridge, near Falkirk, a Boer War veteran who could start a fight with his own reflection. He embarked for France with the 2nd Royal Scots in September 1914 and had been busted twice from sergeant for general indiscipline. He was posted to McCrae's shortly before they moved down to the Somme in 1916. The idea was to add a little regular seasoning to the NCOs.

The battalion remained in the line for a fortnight, then moved back to billets near Hancourt, where A Company was finally reconstituted and a period of intense training in musketry and bayonet work began. Stephenson had been given two weeks to bring his drafts up to standard. They returned

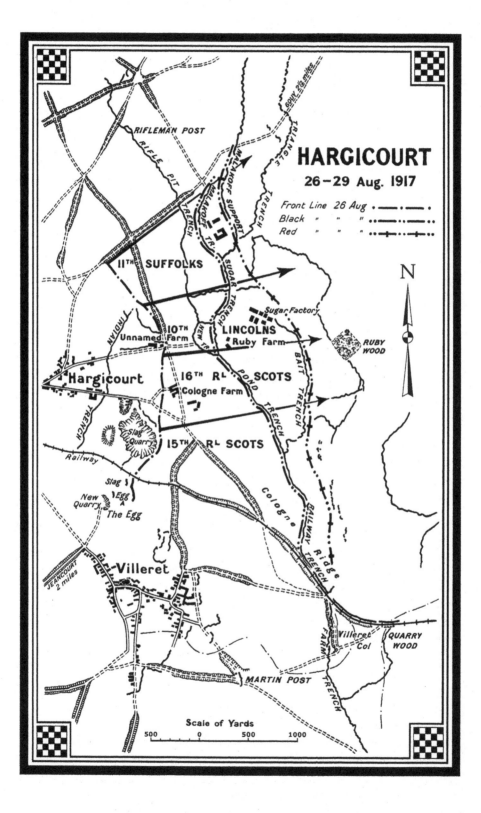

to the line on 3 August, a little further north this time, in front of the ruined villages of Villeret and Hargicourt. The Colonel told his officers that an operation was being planned for the end of the month. It was proposed that the 101st Brigade, alone and unsupported, should mount a surprise attack on Cologne Ridge, seize the high ground, and thus open the way for some future assault on the Hindenburg itself. All ranks, therefore, must be encouraged to familiarise themselves with the ground. A further fortnight later, after a tiring but largely uneventful tour, the battalion was withdrawn to Divisional reserve at Hervilly, where a full-scale model of their objective had been scraped out in the turf. For the old hands, it was Lahoussoye again – although red ribbon was no longer in fashion. Bobby Johnston recalled:

> Replicas of the enemy trenches were spitlocked in the deserted fields and we practised hard at timing the distances and directions. The 'barrage' was made up of a line of signallers waving flags with drummers beating their drums and advancing 100 yards every three minutes. We had to learn to 'lean' into the barrage, i.e. to get as close to the bursting shells as we could with safety. Experience is the only way to acquire this art. There are gaps in any barrage and if you stationed yourself near such a gap, it was possible to get closer to the enemy trenches and get into them before he popped up with his machine-guns.[26]

These manœuvres lasted for a week. The attack, meanwhile, was fixed for 26 August. Four lines of trenches would be assaulted; the first was screened by six broad bands of wire. On the night of the 24th, the battalion left its billets and marched up to Roisel, just behind the front line. At 5.20 the following morning, a 'Chinese' barrage was opened on the enemy position in the hope of provoking a response to establish where any counter fire would fall.[27] For the rest of the day, the artillery worked on cutting channels through the entanglements. At 9 p.m. the assault units moved silently forward to their jumping-off positions. By 2 a.m. McCrae's had reached a sunken road on the western side of Cologne Farm. They huddled in their companies and waited while patrols went out with tapes to mark the gaps in the wire. Willie McDougall, who had won the MM at Wood Alley, went up to Johnston and asked him to write to his wife. 'I'll no be seein Auld Reekie any more,' he explained. At 4.15 a.m., under cover of a short preliminary bombardment, they crept out into no-man's land and lay down.

At 4.30 the barrage proper opened. It smothered the front line for three murderous minutes while the infantry dashed in behind. McCrae's went over in two waves with the Lincolns on their left and the 15th Royal Scots on their right. Johnston again:

I got through one of the gaps and jumped into a communication trench that led back into the Boche second line. There were no Germans there and we reached the second trench without anyone being hit. I could hear Mills bombs and rifle fire on my left, and, going to the top, saw my Lewis gun section firing at some Germans. Some stick grenades went off among the gunners, then I heard Mills bombs bursting in the German support line. Hurrying along, I heard Scottish voices calling out and found we were in touch. We then hurried on after the barrage and got to the third trench, from which the Germans were retiring. We could see them running back. On we pressed until we reached our objective, the fourth line of trenches, just over the crest of the ridge. Below us we could see numerous Germans bolting down the slope towards the village of Bellicourt, a mile distant.[28]

Red 'Bengal lights' were set off in the captured trenches as a signal to the Flying Corps. A squadron of S.E.5s was covering the assault. Any trench without a flare was mercilessly 'strafed'. 2/Lt Jimmy Baird from Blackhall forgot to bring his matches and was shot through the jaw. By 8 a.m. the position was secure.

Consolidation now began: trenches were deepened, and a continuous belt of barbed wire was thrown out along the slope. The work took all day and was interrupted periodically by shell-fire. The following morning, it rained heavily and the trenches filled waist-deep with mud. Fire-steps collapsed and ration boxes floated. The enemy bombardment intensified during the evening. Cuthbert Lodge retired to a dug-out. He had his CSM with him. James Martin, a 26-year-old housepainter from Springvalley Terrace, was a Heriot's veteran and the two of them had become pals. About midnight their shelter received a direct hit. Both men died instantly: they were buried where they lay.

McCrae's came out of the line late on 28 August. Any satisfaction they might have felt for a job well done was countered by thoughts of the cost. Quite apart from Lodge and Martin, the ridge had claimed a number of old friends. Fin MacRae and Willie McDougall had been killed by snipers. Jimmy Bryson and Jerry Milligan, who lived in the same stair at 6 Freer Street and had enlisted together at Tynecastle, were last seen alive in the third German trench. They were two of C Company's 'characters' and had eleven children between them. Dolphy Farrow, a law clerk from Smithfield Street, had four. He was killed as he tried to help an injured comrade. Jim Davie was caught in a shell blast on the night of the relief and was so badly injured that Harry Rawson didn't recognise him. 'There was no part of him that was not hurt,' Harry wrote to his uncle. Nobody thought he would make it. There were 2 officers and almost 60 men dead; 9 officers and at least 130 men had been wounded.[29]

They trudged back to Hervilly, hoping for a rest. As usual, they were disappointed. Andy Henderson complained to his family:

> We are in 'reserve' just now, but do not think we are getting it soft. I think someone is playing a joke on us and pretty soon we will hear him laughing. We are up at six to get a good day in at the training, then out all night on what we call 'working parties'. I can tell you that cakes and lemonade are strictly 'off the menu', for all we do is dig. I haven't slept right in a month.[30]

On 11 September McCrae's returned to the ridge. Annan Ness went looking for Cuthbert's dug-out to ensure that it was properly marked. He could find no trace.[31] Ness had recently been promoted RSM following Fred Muir's departure to England for officer training. On 16 September he received a note from McCartney. The remains of Ernie Ellis had been found near Contalmaison, and his widow was anxious to visit the grave. This was a repeat of the Boyd letter and reflected a deep and growing ignorance at home about conditions on the Western Front. The manager wanted to know if Ness could help. His reply was polite but disappointing.[32]

Willie Gavin, meanwhile, had turned up 'bound and bandaged' after recovering from his April injuries. On the night of 23 September he was wounded again. Pte James Meechan, a 19-year-old apprentice fitter from Glasgow, had only just been drafted to the battalion from a reserve unit of the HLI. It was his first time in France and he had yet to fire a single round. He was cold, wet and scared. Years later, he would recall the 'tall laddie' being carried from the line on a stretcher:

> Someone said it was the third or fourth time he'd been hit. Third or fourth! I wasn't wanting to be hit even once if I could help it. I remember the shells coming down and thinking we were getting it bad, then a boy who had been out for a while told me that it was no more than a few squibs and I would see much worse if I was lucky.[33]

Meechan was a Partick Thistle supporter. When he learned that his new unit was the famous Edinburgh Footballers' Battalion, he wrote home to tell his family. 'It was a feather in my cap,' he explained. 'I was in *McCrae's*.'

On 25 September they were bussed back to Péronne and entrained for Boisleux-au-Mont, about six miles south of Arras. There followed a seven-mile march across country to billets at Berles-au-Bois, where they underwent a week of intensive training in night operations. Gas helmets were worn at all times. On 6 October they marched to the village of Saulty and moved by rail to Peselhoek, near Poperinghe, in Belgium.

※ ※ ※

Haig had opened his Flanders offensive on 7 June. Nineteen deep mines, containing one million tons of high explosive, were detonated beneath the Messines-Wytschaete Ridge on the southern flank of the Ypres salient. The shock was felt in London. Under cover of the ensuing barrage, nine divisions of Herbert Plumer's Second Army captured the entire German position – or what was left of it – within a matter of hours. Staggered by the magnitude of his achievement, Haig convinced himself that it was possible to repeat the coup further north. Impatient with Plumer's meticulous planning, he handed responsibility for the main thrust to Hubert Gough. Gough was like a racehorse. Shown the objective – Roulers and the Flemish coast – he adjusted his blinkers and chose the most direct route. The Passchendaele-Staden Ridge was in his way.

The enemy commander was General Sixt von Arnim. His 'Flanders Position' was formidable. From the heights of Pilckem and Passchendaele in the north, Broodseinde in the centre, and Gheluvelt in the south, it dominated every inch of the barren plain that the British called the 'Salient'. His artillery observation was so complete that in large parts of the Salient, movement by day was impossible. Not that movement at any time was easy: three years of bombardment had so corrupted the ancient network of drainage channels that the ground was no more than a shallow swamp, disfigured by countless thousands of foetid craters. Secure on their ridges, the Germans had constructed a defensive system of awesome strength. The front line (or 'forward zone') consisted of an unconnected screen of outposts, which were only periodically occupied. Since entrenchment was prohibited by flooding, these would most likely be sandbag redoubts. Their purpose was to check and blunt the initial assault: they were not expected to hold out for long. The main line of resistance was constructed further back. This so-called 'battle zone' was thickly wired and comprised at least three lines of breastworks, concrete blockhouses and fortified farm buildings, all bristling with machine-guns and protected by field artillery. Finally, some distance to the rear, a line of stout, shell-proof bunkers sheltered the reserve (or 'counter-attack') battalions, ready to fall upon the intruders when they were at their most vulnerable. Assaulting troops would effectively pass through a filter: those who reached the furthest would be lucky to survive.

It took six weeks after Messines for Gough's Fifth Army to move into line. He was hoping for rapid movement, but a month-long preliminary bombardment directly in the path of his assault only added to the enemy's advantage. Along with the wire and the occasional strongpoint, the very ground itself was stricken: churned into porridge and pitted with shell-holes. Finally on 31 July the attack was launched. Initially progress was good and the forward zone fell quickly. On the left, the French took Bixschoote while the British seized the minor ridge at Pilckem. In the centre, the approaches to St Julien were reached. On the crucial right, however, the advance stalled on the western edge of the Gheluvelt Plateau, whose shattered woods concealed a multitude of unexpected dangers. During the afternoon it started to rain; by nightfall it was pouring. Three days later, the offensive was suspended while Haig peered hopefully at his barometer. It turned out to be the wettest August in 80 years.

Gheluvelt was Gough's undoing. On 24 August Haig went back to Plumer, who proposed a series of 'bite and hold' operations aimed first at seizing the troublesome plateau, then (with his right secure) moving on to capture the ridges at Broodseinde and Passchendaele. The objectives were conservative, the tactics cautious. Above all, the infantry would not be permitted to advance beyond the range of their artillery support. Preparations would use up another three weeks. The ghost of the Menin road ran right across the high ground, and Plumer's opening phase was named after it. The assault was preceded by a devastating barrage. The enemy fell back. Bite two was delivered on 26 September and seized control of Polygon Wood. There was a brief digestive pause before bite three on 4 October. The German counter-attack divisions were caught directly under a storm of shrapnel and high explosive. By the end of the day, as the rain came down again, Gheluvelt and Broodseinde were in British hands.

This might have been a good point at which to stop; Haig, however, smelt blood. 'The enemy is faltering,' he said. The Flemish coast might be beyond his reach but the remaining ridge and the railway hub at Roulers most certainly were not. He ordered the offensive to continue: the Battle of Passchendaele was about to begin.

❋ ❋ ❋

The arrival of 34th Division in the Salient was sudden – prompted by an unexpected order on 2 October. Absorption and instruction of the new drafts under SS 135 was rudely interrupted and the battalions moved north unprepared. From Peselhoek, McCrae's marched back to Porchester Camp, near the village of Proven, about ten miles behind Ypres. It was raining heavily and the tents leaked. Next evening – 8 October – they entrained for Elverdinghe in the immediate rear of the Passchendaele front.

That night the rain became torrential: GHQ's meteorological experts held out little prospect of improvement. Haig, however, still harboured hopes of a late breakthrough. His initial move would be made around the fortified village of Poelcappelle on the ridge's northern approaches. The attack went in on 9 October and foundered in the mud. During the fighting, McCrae's were employed as labourers to repair the Langemarck–Poelcappelle road. They worked under constant shell-fire and continual rain. Eleven men were killed and thirty wounded. Each morning they retired to a foul encampment at Saragossa Farm, where rats the size of dogs nipped at their toes. On 12 October Haig renewed his assault, aiming this time for the village of Passchendaele itself. There is no evidence to suggest that he had the slightest appreciation of conditions on the ground. D.M. Sutherland:

> The landscapes around here are unfamiliar. We were never quite in this region before. I think the word landscape can hardly be applied. Such a tortured, twisted torn mass of shell-holes large and small, with stumps of willow trees protruding here and there. Villages have been completely wiped off the surface and nothing remains above but the chipped concrete pill-boxes which the Boche have been forced to evacuate. I remember a drawing of Doré's, illustrating Dante's Inferno, which approached the look of the land here.[34]

Several men drowned after straying off the corduroy and stumbling into slime-filled craters at the roadside. Rifles became clogged, Web equipment saturated, ammunition useless. Alfred Warr was out of it – ordered back to England for a course. On 14 October his temporary replacement arrived. Major Thomas Bussell was a 38-year-old Boer War veteran, a Royal Scots regular from Caterham in Surrey. He had retired from the Army in 1913 after complaining of gout in both feet. It was incurable, painful and aggravated by cold and damp conditions. Mobilised in 1914, he served briefly in France with the Royal Scots Fusiliers before being wounded. His arrival at HQ was unexpected and bizarre: he was wearing a tightly tailored tunic (complete with South African medals), a pair of tartan riding breeches and what appeared at first glance to be slippers.[35]

That same afternoon McCrae's trudged two miles west to Bridge Camp, south of Elverdinghe, for a week's training. Two days later, thoroughly confused, they were ordered back to Saragossa Farm, where Steve informed his officers that the battalion was scheduled to participate in an attack on the morning of the 22nd. All ranks prepared to move at five minutes' notice. The following evening a German aeroplane flew over and bombed the tents occupied by D Company. Eight men were killed.[36] Pte Meechan recalled one of the Lewis gunners climbing up on the bed of a lorry to fire into the air. 'The spent cartridge cases were flying everywhere,' he said, 'I had never seen that happening before.'

They passed the night of 19–20 October at Stray Farm, just behind Pilckem Ridge, shivering in the open under waterproof sheets. At first light their position was shelled: Stephenson was gassed and evacuated; Tom Bussell assumed command. That evening they marched up the narrow track to Tranquille House near Poelcappelle Station. The shelling continued en route and 50 men were wounded. Bobby Johnston was Signals Officer now. In addition to his kit, he carried a heavy roll of telephone cable:

> It took us four hours to cover the two miles to the Ypres–Staden railway line, which was only identifiable by the fact that it was slightly above the level of the countryside and chunks of broken sleepers and rails obstructed our passage. HQ was a few yards from the station, of which only a few bricks remained, but there was a road crossing which helped us establish ourselves.[37]

About 1,000 yards beyond HQ was a thin screen of fortified shell-holes. They were full of water. An abandoned German blockhouse was the main strongpoint. It had been captured only ten days previously and evidence of bloody fighting was everywhere. Bloated corpses floated in the craters. The smell was unbearable. During the night the shelling intensified. In the morning several aeroplanes appeared and the pilots took a fiendish pleasure in chasing carrying-parties along the duckboards. You could see them grinning. Five more men were wounded. At lunchtime a message came through from Division: the attack would be delivered before dawn.

In theory the operation was intended to strengthen the left flank of the assault on Passchendaele Ridge. Taking their line from the railway, they were instructed to advance 1,200 yards and seize the Six Roads junction south of Houthulst Forest. Johnston pored over his maps but couldn't see the point. There was nothing *there*. Bussell, he recalled, was equally baffled and a major from Brigade apologised profusely. It was not a gesture designed to inspire confidence. D.M. Sutherland wrote to his mother:

> In the event of my not coming back, I wish you to know that I leave you everything I possess in money and in kind. It is not very much but with it goes all my love and affection and the hope that you will be brave and strong to bear the sorrows that come to you in these extraordinary times. I would like you to think of me as having said 'Goodbye' with a smile, and to know that there was a feeling of content within me and a feeling of courage.[38]

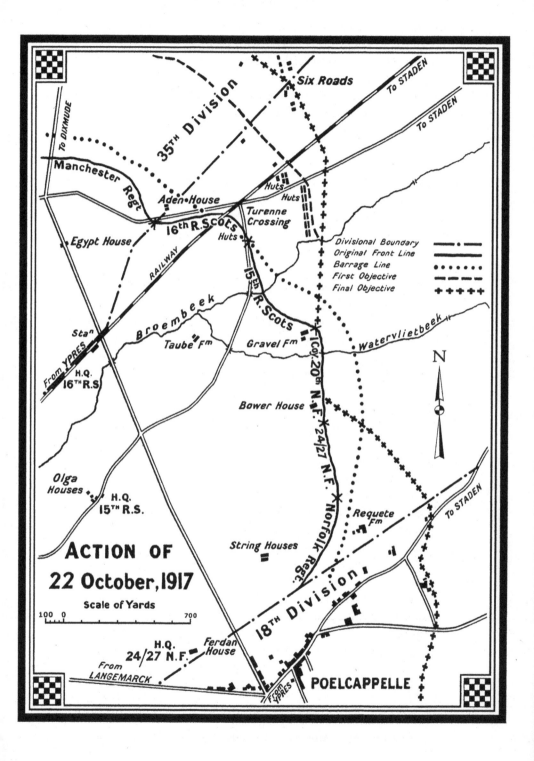

Action of 22 October, 1917

Scale of Yards
100 0 — — — 700

Divisional Boundary — · — ·
Original Front Line ————
Barrage Line · · · · · ·
First Objective — — —
Final Objective +++++

To STADEN

Six Roads

35TH Division

To DIXMUDE

Manchester Regt

Aden House

Huts

Huts

Turenne Crossing

16th R.Scots

Egypt House

Huts

RAILWAY

15th R.Scots

Stan

From YPRES

H.Q. 16TH R.S

Broembeek

Taube Fm

Gravel Fm

Watervlietbeek

1 Coy. 20th N.F.

24/27 N.F.

Bower House

Norfolk Regt.

Olga Houses

H.Q. 15TH R.S.

Requete Fm

To STADEN

String Houses

18TH Division

H.Q. 24/27 N.F.

Ferdan House

From LANGEMARCK

From YPRES

POELCAPPELLE

N

Sutherland was in command of C Company: at his disposal were three officers and ninety-four other ranks. With each platoon reduced to fewer than twenty-five men, his 'specialist' sections were dangerously weak. One of the Lewis guns was misbehaving and there were no discharger cups for the rifle grenades. Altogether, Bussell had only 405 other ranks, about a third of whom were raw drafts. After the long march up from Pilckem, they were cold, scared and utterly exhausted.

The attack frontage was no more than 500 yards. Two waves were deployed in the plan. A and D Companies would lead to the first objective, which included a group of concrete 'huts' near Turenne Crossing on the remains of the Staden road; B and C would pass through behind the barrage and complete the advance. The 23rd Manchester Regiment of 35th Division were on the left; on the right, south of the railway, were the 15th Royal Scots. Shortly after midnight, starting tapes would be laid in no man's land. Zero hour was set for 5.35 a.m. Neatly typed, it all looked fine on paper. When the guides went out to hammer in their markers, however, they were heavily shelled. No tapes were laid. Five minutes later, the German gunners raised their sights and found the assembling platoons. B Company was commanded by Randle Evans, a 23-year-old Post Office storeman from Wolverhampton:

> Before reaching the 'jumping-off' place, at least 30 per cent of my company became casualties. On arrival I found two platoons of D Company under a junior officer and part of A Company under Lt Gavin, the company commander. While arranging details with him and 2/Lt Farquharson, we were all wounded by one shell. The other two were so bad that I had to evacuate them. I could just walk and stayed to organise the battalion. I got into touch with the 15th Royal Scots on my right but could not find Captain Sutherland with C Company on my left. Enemy shell-fire and local conditions made it impossible to keep all the troops under control. I estimate that not more than 200 men moved to the attack at zero.[39]

Willie Gavin had only just returned from hospital. He had multiple shrapnel wounds. Archie Farquharson's left arm was nearly blown off. D.M. Sutherland, meanwhile, had lost two of his platoons in the dark and was attempting to form up with only forty men. At 5.35 precisely, the offensive barrage was begun. With synchronisation impossible, friendly shells now added to the danger. The two waves merged and crept towards the guns. Evans limped off after them:

> I could see the men were bunching badly and went to them to aid in attacking the huts. After about 300 yards the enemy machine-gun

fire was very heavy and the men not hit took cover. I organised about 30 and with 2/Lts Linn and Hope led a rush to a gap in the huts. I saw Linn and many men killed and I was wounded again myself. The survivors were scattered around in the mud. Many wounded undoubtedly drowned. We were taken in by the Germans. I was unconscious most of the time.[40]

In fact Evans was pulled into the safety of a flooded shell-hole by his servant, George Fotheringham, a miner from Coalburn in Lanarkshire. George's elbow had been shattered by a machine-gun bullet and Evans sent him back to get it dressed. His pal, Jack Gourlay from Govanhill, a printer with the *Glasgow Herald*, was forced into a ditch by the same burst that brought down Peter Linn. Every man in his section was killed or captured.

So much for the right. Over on the left, meanwhile, Sutherland's little party made better progress. Within an hour they had reached a row of pillboxes north of Six Roads, slightly in advance of their objective. Immediately beside them, the Manchesters had entered the edges of the forest. One of C Company's Lewis sections was covering their advance from a concrete blockhouse. D.M. was in the open, trying to work his way through a double apron of screw pickets to get at the pillboxes with his bombers. Suddenly the Manchesters bolted: both his flanks were now in the air. Machine-guns started firing from all directions. Sutherland hit the ground and was shot in the elbow. 2/Lt Andrew Baxter was struck on the wrist. A second bullet pierced his heart. Big George McLay, the Raith Rovers centre-half, was hit several times inside the German entanglement. His pal, Willie McGrouther, got up to go and help him. He was shot through the forehead. Robert Gibb, the old Hearts trainer, was sniped in the leg. Willie Rhind and Jerry Mowatt were captured on the wrong side of the wire; Geordie Watson was picked up behind them. The survivors rolled off into shell-holes and D.M. went back to find a dressing for his arm. Annan Ness took command of the company: when he shouted for names, only ten men replied.

Sutherland made for an old pillbox on the line of advance. It was a solid, concrete structure with a narrow passage for a doorway. There were two other men inside – both wounded. He later described what happened next:

We were sitting talking, when a shell came in through the door, killing the other two chaps. It was a most extraordinary sensation. I felt all round for my head and ribs. I groped outside, where there was a pack of wounded and dead men with one fellow doing the bandaging. The concussion rendered me blind for several hours.[41]

A little to the rear, Bobby Johnston could hear the sound of 'heavy musketry' and knew that the battalion was in trouble. His phone lines had been severed by shell-fire and he spent the morning waist-deep in mud, feeling for the breaks. It was raining and a thin gaseous mist clung to the ground. Towards noon, as the sky cleared, he was chased by an aeroplane, which showered him with bullets. He later found a hole in the sleeve of his tunic. He had four signallers left, among them Sgt Bob Davie, a joiner from Temple Park Crescent. At dusk the little party arrived exhausted at HQ.

Bussell was gone – concussed by a shell-burst and evacuated. In command was the adjutant, Bill McCarthy, a 26-year-old regular from Whitley Bay in Northumberland, who had been out since August 1914. Formerly a sergeant in the 2nd Royal Scots, he was commissioned in 1916 and joined McCrae's shortly after High Wood. McCarthy had heard nothing from the attacking companies since shortly after zero; he therefore ordered Johnston to go forward. Leaving Davie in charge of the phones, Bobby took his rifle and an extra bandolier. On the way, he met a stream of walking wounded. They directed him to the railway station, where he found Dick Fox bandaging a comrade in the ruins of the signal box. It was dark now and the rain was getting worse. Random shells were still falling. Taking Fox for protection, he worked his way up to the jumping-off ground. There was a scattering of partially submerged bodies. Close by, they came across a group of 20 men huddled in some shell-holes. They had been counter-attacked but had driven off the Boche and were awaiting orders. Further on, Johnston stumbled into 2/Lt Norman Honeyman, who had been at Gailes with him. Honeyman, a Glasgow accountant, produced 30 men from different platoons. He said he had been halted by the intensity of the barrage and was uncertain whose guns had done the most damage. Moving to the left, Johnston found Ness with his little remnant. Together, they formed a thin defensive screen about 100 yards in front of the original assembly positions. They had two Lewis guns, which Fox stripped and cleaned as the bullets cracked around him. Johnston then made his way back to the right. Honeyman got up to meet him and was shot in the head.

The remains of McCrae's advance companies were finally relieved at first light the following morning. There were seven officers and twenty-seven men. Johnston was incensed and believed that the operation should never have been undertaken. 'The staff work,' he later wrote, 'was inept.'[42]

On 26 October Haig tried again. Two weeks later, the Canadian Corps captured what was left of Passchendaele village. The Flanders offensive slowed to a halt, leaving much of the ridge in German hands. Almost 70,000 British and Commonwealth soldiers were dead; only 5 miles of ground had been gained. The whistles had blown and the season was finally over – or so the Germans thought. Then, on 20 November, Haig unexpectedly moved on the Hindenburg Line. Under cover of a hurricane bombardment, 376 tanks trundled towards the enemy trench-system in front of Cambrai. Five miles were gained there in just ten hours. Beyond lay a further (unfinished) system and open country. Church bells rang in England. Within ten days the Germans had counter-attacked and snatched back most of their losses. Sir Douglas himself explains:

> Apparently our patrols had gone out in the morning, found nothing unusual, then proceeded to breakfast. There seems to have been no warning. The enemy swept through the front held by the left of the 55th Division and parts of the 12th and 20th Divisions. The position rushed is immensely strong, but the defenders seem to have put up little fight. The enemy attacked in great masses, preceded by some '*stoss-truppen*'. Some of the latter were taken prisoner a mile west of Gouzeaucourt! Luckily the Guards Division happened to be near and were marching back to rest with bands playing. They at once faced about and advanced eastwards. Crowds of fugitives were streaming back, some without arms or equipment. By this time the enemy was on the west ridge of Gouzeaucourt, so the Guards at once deployed and, after some heavy fighting, cleared the ridge and re-took the village. If they had not been on the spot, it is difficult to estimate where the enemy would have been checked. The mishap might have spread to a disaster.[43]

It was more than a mishap. It was the promise of a nightmare yet to come.

CHAPTER ELEVEN

'Flowers o the Forest'

On the third day of December in the dying year of 1917 Sir Douglas Haig instructed his commanders to prepare for the possibility of a further offensive. This time the attackers would be German. The collapse of Russia and the closure of the Eastern Front had released a million troops to reinforce the trench-lines in the west. Thus the numerical advantage that the Allies had enjoyed was about to be reversed. By the middle of March 1918 the Germans would have 192 divisions in the field against a Franco–British total of 155. The French were in a parlous state: General Henri Pétain, who succeeded Nivelle as Commander-in-Chief, had warned that a quarter of his 98 divisions were in imminent danger of being broken up for lack of replacements.

Haig's problems were compounded by the reluctance of his political masters to allow him sufficient drafts to make good the losses sustained at Passchendaele and Cambrai. In part, this was his own fault. His keenness to resume the Flanders offensive (together with his confident assertion that he could hold any German attack for at least 18 days) gave Lloyd George the perfect excuse for refusing extra men. They could go when they were needed, and not before. In the meantime, they would be kept well away from GHQ's profligate hands. As a compromise solution to the so-called 'manpower question', the War Cabinet came up with a masterpiece of muddled self-delusion. Extra men, they decided, *could* be provided if they were first removed from existing units. From February 1918, therefore, infantry brigades were reduced from four to three battalions, leaving a surplus of personnel from which new divisions could be built. It took no great genius to foresee the result. With no corresponding reduction in the length of the front, it followed that fewer men would have to hold the same old bit of line. Only it wasn't the same old bit of line. In January, to please Pétain, Haig had extended his front by a full 25 miles across the Somme from St Quentin to beyond the River Oise. The BEF, already stretched, was on the point of breaking.

Haig's counterpart on the other side of the wire was General Erich Ludendorff. Ludendorff, who was effectively his own political master, had a different set of problems. Most of them were called Joe. His advantage would last only as long as it took to train the new battalions of the American Expeditionary Force. By the end of 1917 there were 130,000 'doughboys' in France; by the summer of 1918 the numbers would be overwhelming. For any chance of a decisive victory, therefore, Germany would have to strike early in the spring. But where? His alternatives were limited. Verdun was attractive: a repeat of 1916 would push France out of the war. It would not necessarily, however, have any effect on the British. Ludendorff decided that the defeat of Haig's armies must take priority and chose to focus his assault on the sector between Arras and St Quentin. In a disturbing echo of Sir Douglas's 1916 plan, he proposed to break through in Picardy and roll the British line up to the sea. 'Operation Michael' was approved on 21 January and plans were completed in a matter of weeks. On a combined front of fifty miles, there would be three simultaneous points of attack. In the north, the Seventeenth Army would advance on Bapaume; in the centre, the Second Army would aim for Péronne. Having achieved their initial objectives, they would then swing north-west, encircle Arras and drive the British back to the Channel ports. In the south, meanwhile, the Eighteenth Army would aim for the village of Ham on the Somme and form a protective flank against any French interference. In order to ensure that the momentum of the British retiral was maintained, several further strikes were planned for later on. The scale of these undertakings was enormous. If Ludendorff was throwing his dice for the last time, he was going to throw them hard.

Hard and fast. Since the fundamental requirement of 'Michael' was speed, it followed that Ludendorff could not afford to become bogged down in the sort of grim attritional struggle that bedevilled the British in 1916 and 1917. In order to avoid this, he resorted to the age-old tools of cunning and surprise. Complete concealment of his preparations was impossible. The artillery element, however, was a different matter. Under cover of darkness, 6,473 heavy, medium and field guns were assembled behind the attack front. They had been accurately registered beforehand at special ranges, so as not to betray their presence or position. The resulting bombardment would last for five intensive hours, smothering the British defences with high explosive, shrapnel and phosgene gas. In its wake would come the 'stormtroops' – Haig's '*stoss-truppen*' – trained in the new doctrine of 'infiltration'. Their objectives were depth and continuity of advance: they would bypass strongpoints and stop for nothing. They could even control the creeping barrage by firing signal flares to accelerate its lifts.

There is a clinical sophistication about these tactics that makes the poor old British Tommy seem endearingly naive. SS 135 was reissued in January 1918 as *Training and Employment of Divisions*. In spite of the fact that GHQ knew the Germans were coming, only one side of one page was devoted to defence. The manual envisaged the enemy assaulting with 'masses of troops, pushed forward regardless of loss'. The General Staff's own hard-learned offensive innovations had already rendered this section obsolete; the German methods at Cambrai should have torn it into shreds. Such an attack, it observed, would be bound to fail 'if the defenders remain steady and use their weapons coolly'. They were saying much the same thing before Isandlwana. SS 143 resurfaced in February as *Training and Employment of Platoons*. It contained some useful advice:

> The soul of defence lies in offence; resistance by fire alone may check, but it cannot overthrow the enemy. Commanders must be ready to take the initiative, both to use the bayonet when necessary, and to restore the fight if any part of the position is overwhelmed. Every situation must as far as possible be foreseen and arrangements made in advance so that it may be met *immediately*.

Years later Bobby Johnston would observe that much of the theory in these publications was sound. Some of it was even far-sighted. In practice, however, much of it was fatuous. He quoted the final sentence above. 'Those words,' he added dryly, 'were the first thing that I thought of when the storm broke.'[1]

❋ ❋ ❋

On 25 January 1918 Captain Harry Rawson, the new commanding officer of C Company, wrote to D.M. Sutherland, care of Messrs Cox & Co. in Charing Cross, to solicit his instructions for a stray parcel of first-class cigarettes. Sutherland had multiple shrapnel wounds, the most serious of which was in his jaw, where a piece of shell-casing had lodged below the right ear. He survived an operation at the military hospital in Camiers and spent several weeks recuperating in London. Now, however, he was on the move and Harry knew not where. The matter was urgent:

> I enclose the note which accompanied the cigs. What shall I do with them? Please let me know as soon as you can. How are you getting

on? Hope you are recovering quickly, but not *too* quickly! We are in the front line, but our time is up within a few days and then we go out for a rest. I am afraid we shall see the Kaiser's birthday here. We had a stroke of luck last night. One of my patrols captured a Boche lieutenant who was prying too close to our wire. Great excitement! I had him brought to my dug-out and gave him a whisky. Quite a decent young fellow of 21, a Prussian from Konigsberg. He had come to see if our front line was held.[2]

Rawson was forbidden to divulge the location, but McCrae's were eight miles south of Arras, in a captured portion of the Hindenburg Line, near the town of Croisilles. The front line was formerly part of the German support system and lay at the foot of the forward slope of a modest little ridge. The trenches were deep, well made and protected by 3 successive belts of wire, 9 feet high and 30 yards across. Sadly, these entanglements were also German, so they were situated on the wrong side of the parapet. The British contribution (on the *right* side) consisted of a narrow concertina and a heap of old tin cans. On the opposite side of a shallow valley, 300 yards away, the enemy position climbed to the crest of the neighbouring ridge, cutting through the ruins of the fortified village of Fontaine.

They had been in the sector since November, moving periodically between front line and reserve. Training, refitting and the absorption of drafts continued only as time allowed. Johnston complained that almost all the new men were of poor quality and that some had been in the Army for only three months. One exception was Willie Wilson, Tynecastle forward and founder member of the battalion. Wilson's shoulder – the bane of his professional career – had turned into an unexpected blessing. The recoil of a rifle was apt to throw it out, so he was seldom fit for service overseas. Two weeks with the 13th Royal Scots in April 1917 ended with a dose of trench fever and a boat trip home. This was his first time back and it was hard to come to terms with what he found. 'I think of all the Hearts lads,' he wrote his mother, 'and then I have to think of something else.'

Even without its League stars, McCrae's football team remained all-conquering. Led by Annan Ness, they took the Divisional Cup at Christmas 1917, still wearing the jerseys that Cuthbert Lodge had bought in Ripon. These were finally replaced at Hogmanay by the new manager, Percy Bayliss.[3] Bayliss was a 20-year-old clerk from Finsbury Park, who had overstated his age to join the London Regiment in August 1914. He served in France as a private and was commissioned in the Special Reserve in July 1916. Six weeks later he turned up at HQ and mistook Stephenson (who was having a shave) for an orderly. The two had been something like friends ever since. Steve got a DSO in the New Year honours; Percy – known as

'Bay' – got a belated MC for Cologne Ridge. Following the departure of Bill McCarthy to the Indian Army in November, he was promoted to captain and appointed adjutant – reputedly the youngest in the BEF.

January 25 was Burns Night, and Bayliss was a guest in C Company's little mess dug-out, deep in the bowels of Tunnel Trench on the forward limit of the front line. It was bitterly cold and the duty sections were bundled in their greatcoats. That afternoon he had taken his team to the village of Héninel, in the neighbouring 3rd Division area, to contest the final of the VI Corps Championship against the 2nd Royal Scots. The result was a 1–1 draw and a replay had been arranged for the following week. They were washing down the haggis with a glass of port about 7.30 p.m., when an almighty bombardment began. Rawson ran up the stairs and discovered that they were being 'boxed' in. Shells were landing about 200 yards away on all sides. The barrage lasted for half an hour, at which point he emerged to discover that two of his outpost sentries were missing. Scattered around their position were clusters of stick grenades, tied together with twine, which the enemy had used to blow their way through the entanglements. The battalion had been raided for prisoners. Add the cheerful young Prussian to the equation and it was clear that the Germans were testing their strength.

Two nights later McCrae's were relieved and moved back to the village of Ervillers. Willie Gavin reappeared, along with John Stewart, back in France for the first time since he was wounded at Bois Grenier two years earlier. His right foot had turned septic and it took two operations to save it. He was still limping. On 2 February the Corps Championship was wrapped up with a 5–0 victory in the replay. Murdie McKay, who had rejoined after recovering from his wounds of 1 July, featured in several of the early games but didn't make the final. 'The boys,' he recalled, 'were pleased as punch to do it on the Regiment.' Andy Henderson played in goal, Ness at half-back, and Bobby Wood of Falkirk on the wing. They were the last survivors of the old first eleven.

The battalion was supposed to resume its training programme but ended up providing daily working parties to dig the 'GHQ Line', a new trench system under construction nearby. Haig had been so impressed by the enemy's defensive methods that he circulated a translation of the official manual. Defence in depth was now preferred (especially after Cambrai), but the order to proceed with the necessary work was not issued until 17 December. From Flanders to the Oise, shortage of labour compounded the problem. By February the forward zone was already complete, although in constant need of repair; the battle zone had insufficient strongpoints and redoubts; the rear zone, the last line of resistance, had barely been marked on the ground.

At Ervillers, 34th Division fell victim to the War Cabinet's reorganisation. The 103rd Brigade was effectively disbanded and rebuilt by importing the 1st East Lancs and 9th Northumberland Fusiliers. The 10th Lincolns joined them, leaving 101st Brigade otherwise untouched. The 102nd Brigade, meanwhile, became a composite formation – the so-called 'Tyneside Orphans'. The disruption was appalling. Johnston said that Nicholson and his staff spent most of the month trying to sort out the mess. On 10 February they marched back to Grand Rullecourt, 13 miles behind Arras, for a fortnight of *assault* training. Steve recorded the following in his War Diary:

> The battalion was practised in assuming attack formation and advancing under a barrage, indicated by men carrying flags. Strongpoints were dotted about the area and the initiative of company and platoon commanders was exercised in dealing with these. Following the assault and capture of the final objective, a counter-attack was made by men waving handkerchiefs. This counter-attack was successful and the retiring troops were carried forward by the supports who counter-attacked immediately and restored the line.[4]

The enemy, meanwhile, was practising as well – day and night for weeks on end, over full-scale models of the British positions, under stormtroop instructors and live ammunition of every conceivable calibre. The 111th Infantry Division, earmarked to face Nicholson's battalions, rehearsed its entire assault timetable from start to completion twice. Their barrage was paced at 300 yards every 4 minutes: they called it the 'Hindenburg flat race'.

McCrae's returned to the line on 1 March, taking over their old positions in front of Croisilles. It was strangely quiet. Appearances, however, were deceptive and it gradually became apparent that an attack was imminent. 'No one told us anything,' said Johnston. 'We worked it out for ourselves and then tried to appear surprised when the wisdom came down from Corps.' A German deserter walked into some neighbouring trenches eight days later and informed his captors that the offensive was scheduled to begin on 13 March with an assault on Bullecourt, 400 yards beyond the divisional boundary. Although there was a good chance the man was lying, Nicholson proceeded to strengthen the flank by bringing up a company from his already weak reserve. On the night of the supposed attack, a defensive bombardment was opened on the enemy line.[5] There was no response, no evidence of artillery registration, no sign of movement. 'The Boche were asleep,' said McKay. 'And I wished that I was, too.' After that, there were two further false alarms. Division was getting jumpy and ordered disruptive bombardments to be fired on the enemy positions every morning from 2 a.m. –'counter-preparation', it was called. In the meantime, patrols continued to report nothing unusual and the Colonel went home for ten days leave. Before he left, on 17 March, Stephenson handed the battalion to Alfred Warr with a promise to be back 'before Fritz arrived'.

Nicholson's command was holding the centre sector of the VI Corps front. On the left was the 3rd Division; on the right, opposite Bullecourt, was the 59th. On the night of 20 March the front line was garrisoned by the 101st and 102nd Brigades; the three battalions of the 103rd occupied reserve positions about 6,000 yards to the rear. Nicholson had placed the 102nd on his right: the brigade was numerically weak, but still retained a solid core of Tyneside Scots and Irish. The 101st, on his left, faced Fontaine. Their portion was divided by the shallow Sensée stream. From the north bank, the Suffolks took the line as far as the divisional boundary; from the south, the 15th Royal Scots occupied Tunnel Trench as far as Juno Lane. McCrae's were in Brigade support at Sensée Reserve, a deep and muddy conduit that snaked along for 2,000 yards into Factory Avenue, the main communication trench from the front line to Croisilles.

George Cowan was B Company's duty officer. For a man who had been listed as 'killed in action', he was in remarkably good health. After the relief of Scots Redoubt, the garrison was canvassed for information about casualties. Michael Kelly explained that as he withdrew from Contalmaison, he had heard the distinctive crack of Cowan's rifle in the distance. Looking back towards the village, he saw a khaki figure grappling with some Germans. He was sure that George had not survived. Two days later, on 6 July, a ghost walked into camp at Henencourt and rejoined the remains of his section. He served with some distinction until January 1917, when he left for number 9 Officer Cadet Battalion at Gailes. Cuthbert Lodge testified to his character and he was discharged to a commission in June. He returned to France in September and was posted by good fortune to McCrae's. Held in reserve during the action at Turenne Crossing, he was appointed to command 6 Platoon after Archie Farquharson was invalided home.

Around midnight George was visited in his dug-out by an A Company subaltern, the Reverend Robert Barclay, who believed himself to be the oldest junior officer in France. Barclay, 49, was minister of St Mark's Chapel of Ease in Perth. He had volunteered in January 1916, claiming to be ten years younger, in order to escape the attentions of a parishioner who claimed he was the father of her child. A paternity case followed in the Sheriff Court and the papers had picked up the story. Although he denied the allegation, his defence failed and he faced condemnation and ridicule in almost equal measures. Johnston remembered him as 'a sad sort of fellow'. Cowan poured a whisky and listened to his troubles. At 1 a.m. Barclay departed. As he

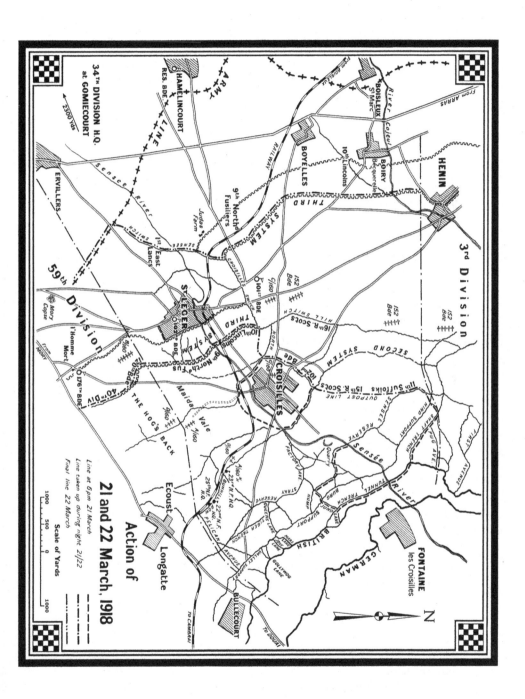

Action of
21 and 22 March, 1918

Scale of Yards

1000   500   0   1000

Line at 6pm 21 March
Line taken up during night 21/22
Final line 22 March

opened the gas curtain, a thick fog loomed up outside. The sentries could see no further than 30 yards. Bang on time, at 2 a.m., the British barrage started; bang on time, at 4 a.m., it stopped. 'Stand to' was at 4.30 and the usual dawn patrols crept out before breakfast. Jimmy Meechan remembered the moment. He was standing, bayonet fixed, with his head above the parapet. Fifteen minutes later the ground was trembling under the most fearsome bombardment of the war. Operation Michael had begun.

The deserter had been telling the truth. The sector held by VI Corps was on the northern extremity of the main German assault. The plan was to break 59th Division around Bullecourt, drive into the exposed flank of the 34th, then swing north-west to threaten Arras. Gas alarms were sounded all along the line as men struggled into their respirators. C Company was about 750 yards behind the rest of the battalion, occupying a line of outposts near the foot of Henin Hill. They were taken by surprise. Phosgene was an *irritant* and could kill several hours after exposure. Jimmy McEvoy remembered being unable to breathe. 'The Germans were using tear gas as well,' he said. 'It got in under your gas-helmet and made you want to take it off to wipe your eyes. Of course if you did that, you were dead.' McEvoy saw Andy Henderson go down and they stumbled off together to the rear. Harry Rawson began the night with 176 men; by dawn he had lost half of them without a bullet being fired.

The bombardment ranged across the British position, picking off strongpoints, HQ dug-outs, and ammunition dumps. By 8 a.m. all but one of the phone lines in the Divisional area had been severed.[6] Half an hour later the mist began to clear and a scene of utter chaos was revealed. Joe Lambert, a 23-year-old undergraduate from London, was in command of B Company. He went looking for 8 Platoon and found 2/Lt George Howie lying in a shell-hole. His head had been blown off. Further along, he met Hamish Mackintosh, who had taken over A Company after Gavin was wounded in October. Mackintosh was an 'original', a bank clerk from Leamington Terrace, who had enlisted in the ranks at Castle Street. He told Lambert that he could find only two of his platoons. While they were shouting at each other, a runner reported that John Stewart had been killed. Barclay was wounded and missing. Shortly after Lambert left, shells started falling on Mackintosh's trench. Concussion blew his respirator off, and a piece of casing lodged itself in his skull. His servant, who was also wounded, helped him off in the direction of the battalion transport lines at Boyelles. The company now passed to 2/Lt Robert Ingles, a 22-year-old insurance clerk from St Boswells. He had one sergeant and no more than a hundred men.

Over at D Company, Willie Gavin was wounded again. His right foot had been broken by a bullet and he had some shrapnel in his thigh. Bobby

Johnston assumed command and moved up into Tunnel to see what was happening. Sandy Lindsay was with him. At 9 a.m. the Germans started cutting their way through the valley entanglements. The 15th Royal Scots opened rapid fire and forced them into shell-holes: they did not continue their attack. At 9.30 the main assault began. About 2,000 yards to the south, the forward defences of 59th Division came under a creeping barrage. Shortly afterwards, they were overrun. The 102nd Brigade, on their left, immediately found its flank in the air. The Germans, however, did not assault them directly, preferring for the moment to advance towards Ecoust and St Léger. The Tynesiders extended their front into Pelican Avenue and waited. Two hours passed before the blow fell: a battalion of Bavarians, pushing through the gap, rushed right onto them, breaking into the front-line system and bombing their way along the trenches. Blocks were raised to hold them but they didn't last for long.

✻ ✻ ✻

Alfred Warr's HQ was in a quarry behind the reserve line. He still had a phone link to Division. Around noon he received a message instructing him to withdraw his three companies from Sensée with immediate effect. It was Nicholson's turn to roll the dice. The front-line battalions of 101st Brigade had not yet been directly attacked. Keeping McCrae's in support of them was like a man with no clothes insisting on wearing his belt, his braces and a knotty bit of string. Warr was ordered to place six of his shattered platoons in Croisilles Switch, west of the village, ready to form a defensive screen facing south if the line broke at St Léger. Robert Ingles's remnant was directed to a ruined factory on the east of Croisilles, ready to support any collapse of the Tyneside position in Pelican. Three remaining platoons were supposed to join up with C Company in the trenches to the east of Henin Hill.

Johnston didn't need an order. Shortly after lunchtime he heard the sound of grenades exploding on his right. Realising the Germans were coming, he ordered a traverse to be pulled down across the trench. When the bombers appeared, he opened fire on them with rifles and a Lewis gun. He thought he was doing rather well, when Lindsay suddenly shouted that the enemy had worked around behind them. He decided to withdraw and headed for the quarry. There was no sign of Warr: instead he found a battery of German field artillery. The gun-teams were dismounted, under shelter, and awaiting instructions. He recalled his reaction:

> My heart jumped into my mouth and I was unable to utter a sound.
> I turned off at full speed across the road and into the brushwood

mud and craters of the Sensée, where the willows gave me some cover. On the other side of the stream was Henin Hill, which was a tangle of old trenches leading up over the crest. I judged I would be safe there. I was followed by my CSM and some 30 men. On the hill we found dozens of soldiers of many regiments all lost in the chaos of battle. There were no officers. No one knew where the Germans were. Our first task was to open fire on any hostiles near the quarry but we could no longer see the guns or horses. I sent runners back over the crest to find someone to tell us what to do.[7]

Minutes later a salvo of shells landed in the trench. Johnston was struck on the knee and thought his leg had been blown off. He was scared to look down. Jimmy Meechan got some shrapnel in his calf and a lump of casing glanced off the back of his head. He could still hop, however, and made it back to a little cart that was loading up with wounded. 'I was glad to be out of it,' he later said.

The race for St Léger, meanwhile, was speeding up. As soon as the extent of the German incursion became apparent, Nicholson had committed his reserve. He brought the East Lancs across to cover 59th Division's flank and ordered the 9th Northumberlands to occupy the wood and high ground south of the village. They arrived at 2 p.m., just as the third line was about to break. Between them, the two battalions were able to stem the advance but the enemy succeeded in gaining a lodgement on the divisional boundary.

The Germans who chased Johnston had fought their way past one of the Tyneside blocks. Violent bombing exchanges were continuing up and down Pelican Avenue and its adjoining maze of trenches. At 2.30 the 15th Royal Scots in Burg Support reported that the position on their right was crumbling. At 3 p.m. they faced about and filed down Factory Avenue to form a defensive flank.[8] At the same time, Alfred Warr spotted a large body of hostile infantry advancing from Ecoust towards Croisilles from the south. He sent Ingles's company to form a screen in front of the village. Ingles was killed soon after but his sergeant took command and drove the Germans into cover. While this was happening the enemy opened an intense bombardment on the Suffolks and the right brigade of 3rd Division. It lasted for thirty minutes, then lifted to the rear as three waves of assault troops rushed the front-line outposts and broke into the northern end of Tunnel Trench. They were held and repulsed but continued to press.

Around 3.30 p.m. the 15th Royal Scots were joined in Factory Avenue by the remains of the 22nd and 23rd Northumberland Fusiliers. The defences to the south had fallen in: the Divisional front now pivoted precariously at right angles. You could almost hear the hinges creaking.

※ ※ ※

Warr's runner to Sensée Reserve did not reach Joe Lambert until 3.35 p.m., by which time the other companies were long gone. Since he wasn't expecting an attack that morning, Lambert hadn't brought his maps. He had never heard of Croisilles Switch, but assumed (not unreasonably) that it would be somewhere near the village. He set off at once, leaving George Cowan and 6 Platoon as a rearguard. Cowan, he said, should await further orders. As Lambert climbed from the trench, he was spotted by three German pilots, who proceeded to strafe him 'all the way to Inverness'. The remaining three platoons followed in sections at two-minute intervals. While they were crossing the open ground west of the stream, a heavy bombardment began. Lambert was knocked down by the concussion: by the time he reached Croisilles, he was shaking. The Switch was on the far side of the village; owing to the barrage, however, he was unable to get through. He took cover in a shell-hole and waited for his charges:

> About 5 p.m. the sergeant of 5 Platoon arrived and reported that he had lost 8 men, including his Lewis gun section and their gun, who were smashed to bits by a shell. About 5.45 No.7 Platoon arrived with about 20 men left and said that the second of the aeroplanes that chased us had been brought down. They also said that the barrage on the road was now impassable and that until it stopped, No.8 Platoon could not move. During this time the road was being heavily bombarded with 6-inch high explosive. I was again practically buried, but dug up unhurt. At 7.15 two Lewis gunners of No.8 Platoon arrived saying that almost the whole platoon had been killed and the remaining few were being shelled intensely in a narrow trench about 300 yards away. It was dusk by now. I had about 45 men left and two Lewis guns.[9]

At 8 p.m. Lambert finally crashed into Battalion HQ. Warr and Bayliss were the only officers left. Ness had disappeared to look for Rawson. The Germans were swarming through the forward zone, bombing their way through the trenches, killing or capturing everything in sight. The force was irresistible. At 9.15 p.m. Nicholson ordered a general withdrawal to a new line of defence. The 3rd Division was still holding its ground, so a new hinge was formed on the left. The front creaked back again. The Suffolks and the 15th Royal Scots retired beyond Sensée to the outposts at the foot of Henin Hill. The 102nd Brigade (commanded by Robin Neeves) spread out along the broken trench that curled behind Croisilles. The Lincolns held St Léger with the 9th Northumberlands on their flank. On the right, the 59th

Division breach had finally been stopped by the arrival of a brigade from GHQ Reserve. Under the circumstances, it was an orderly retiral, executed with no little skill but spoiled by one small act of discourtesy.

No one told George Cowan they were leaving.

❀ ❀ ❀

In the morning the Germans renewed their assault, striking through the mist at the brittle junction between 15th Royal Scots and the Tyneside Brigade. McCrae's were in support, a thousand yards behind, in a fire-trench almost half-way up the slope. 'Hill Switch' was seven feet broad and eighteen inches shallow. The parapet was a two-foot mound of earth.[10] The enemy bombers broke the outpost line and plunged through. At that moment a battery of British 18-pounders opened fire across the hill. The barrage caught the 15th from behind, inflicting heavy casualties. Assailed from all sides by the enemy and shelled from above by its friends, the battalion withdrew to Hill Switch and formed up beside the 16th to prepare for a further attack. While they were waiting, the enemy started bombarding them with 5.9s and shrapnel. At noon the Germans broke through the 102nd Brigade behind Croisilles and came tearing up towards them. Once again, the gunners opened fire; once again the shells fell on their comrades. For half an hour they stood their ground and then the centre collapsed. Royal Scots, Northumberlands, Lincolns and all sorts bolted for their lives. They didn't stop until they reached Boyelles.[11]

The Suffolks, meanwhile, kept their nerve. They turned one platoon to form a defensive flank facing south and resisted all attempts by the enemy to infiltrate their line. Robert Gore ordered Warr to reorganise his men and take them up in support. Warr replied that they were too shaken. Frederick Guard, who had inherited the colonelcy of the 15th, concurred. No one, he said, was going anywhere. Back at Hill Switch, Joe Lambert, who had been knocked unconscious during the bombardment, came round after several hours to find the enemy approaching. There were four men in his traverse and he gave the order to fire, expecting the rest of the company to support him. To his horror, nothing happened: all the other lads were dead or wounded. Lambert and his companions tried to make a run for it but the Germans closed in and forced them to surrender.[12]

The Suffolks fought on until nightfall, retiring towards Henin around 8.15 p.m. On the right, the defence of St Léger had continued until 7 p.m., when a withdrawal was ordered to the third system, west of the village. In two days of bitter fighting, the beleaguered battalions of the 34th Division had been bombarded into fragments and repeatedly outflanked. They now stood at the limit of their battle zone. The line, however, remained intact.

Hoping for Bapaume, or even Arras, the Germans had to settle in the meantime for Croisilles. It was not a fitting prize for all their effort.

McCrae's were relieved during the early hours of 23 March and moved to Armagh Camp at Hamelincourt, about four miles to the rear. Four officers were dead, four wounded and three missing. The number of other ranks killed remained uncertain, but 240 were absent from their companies. At least two-thirds of them were thought to have been wounded.[13] During breakfast these figures were reduced by the sudden appearance of a single subaltern and 27 men. The ghost had returned to the feast. George Cowan heard nothing after Lambert left him at Sensée on the afternoon of the 21st. Around 11 p.m. he wandered up to the quarry to see what was doing. No one was there, so he went back to his platoon. Next morning the enemy stumbled on his position but he beat them off with rifle, bomb and Lewis gun. Shortly after lunch a heavy barrage came down on top of his trench – the guns, so far as he could tell, were British. He decided to retire, and fought his way through the support lines until he made contact with the Suffolks. From there, he led his men back to the third system to be told that the battalion had departed. He doubled off to catch them and was rewarded with the last plate of porridge.

In due course he also got a Military Cross.

❋ ❋ ❋

On the Somme, Gough's overstretched Fifth Army had been pushed back more than twelve miles and counting. South of Arras, however, the advance had been checked. For the next few days Ludendorff tried desperately to resurrect his breakthrough plan. As German pressure continued west of Croisilles, the battered battalions of 34th Division became pawns in a peculiar game of chess. Initially they were marched four miles south to Bucquoy and warned to be prepared to return to the line 'at any moment'. Then they were ordered to entrain at Le Cauroy for the First Army sector at Armentières. Le Cauroy was 16 miles further north and they reached it in stages, bivouacking overnight at Guoy-en-Artois. They were on the platform on 25 March, when orders were received to move to Aix-le-Château, 15 miles to the east, where a despatch rider told Nicholson that the Germans had broken the line and were chasing the entire Third Army back through Doullens. Nicholson deployed his brigades to receive an attack, whereupon it transpired that the fleeing columns were in fact a pair of heavy motor-tractors belonging to the Service Corps. The despatch rider was ordered to the guard-house and (finally) the Division's original movement instructions were reinstated. On 27 March, after a slog of more than 40 miles, they entrained at Petit Houvain for their former haunts at Rue du Bois and Fleurbaix. On 5 April Harry Rawson wrote his father:

> Here we are again after another exciting time. We spent three days in the fight and were then relieved being just about done up. Never had my clothes off for 17 days! We are now away from it in another part of the line. At present my HQ is in a large family vault in a cemetery! Quite a cheerful place. The Hun shells it every day.
>
> We were on the tramp for seven days, but I might say I rode my horse most of the way. Lazy fellow, what? Although we kept the Hun back for three days, we lost most of our kit during the withdrawal. It took me a week before I could buy a toothbrush and some soap, and then I had no towel. Had to use my handkerchief! What a life![14]

Bois Grenier was much changed. The breastworks had been allowed to decay into a poorly wired series of outposts, garrisoned by day and vacated at night. During the hours of darkness, these were protected by 'vigilant patrols'.[15] To the rear stood a series of fall-back positions, somewhat ambitiously described as the Support, Intermediate and Subsidiary lines. Subsidiary turned out to be a soggy ditch. There were no obvious strongpoints. The defensive system (such as it was) covered Armentières itself and extended south-west from the Lys for about 8,000 yards. On the left, north of the river, was 25th Division; on the right, 40th, which had suffered heavy losses in March when it came up to close the Bullecourt breach. Beyond 40th, holding the area around the village of Neuve Chapelle, were two demoralised divisions of the Portuguese Corps. On 6 April two German deserters warned of an imminent attack on this sector. They were treated with suspicion.[16] In fact, as Operation Michael trundled to a halt on the Somme, just nine miles short of Amiens, Ludendorff was preparing to do precisely what they promised.

If Michael was a trench-club bristling with rusty nails, its successor, 'Georgette', was more like a scalpel. It was designed to break the Portuguese, outflank the weak British units to the north and seize the vital rail hub of Hazebrouck. After that, Calais and Dunkirk would surely follow. The attack, scheduled for 9 April, would be preceded by a targeted barrage of such awesome power that nothing underneath it would survive.

On 7 April McCrae's were in Brigade reserve at Erquinghem. Around 8.30 p.m. the enemy opened an intense bombardment on Armentières. They fired around 30,000 shells, most of them phosgene or mustard gas. Casualties were heaviest amongst artillery personnel. The bombardment stopped at seven the following morning; no infantry movement was

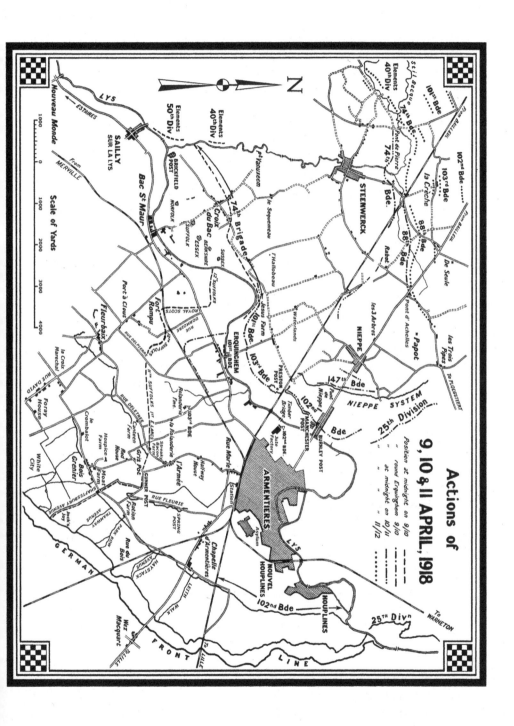

observed and the rest of the day passed quietly. The battalion spent the night shovelling mud near Streaky Bacon Farm and returned to their billets at 2 a.m. At 4.15 they were woken by an almighty crash. Within minutes the shelling was so severe that Stephenson had to disperse his platoons into the surrounding fields. Shortly after 5 a.m. an SOS rocket was sent up by a forward unit of 40th Division, indicating that the enemy was already in or behind their outpost line. Communications were disrupted by the barrage, and for a while no one knew for certain what was happening. At 6 a.m. Nicholson ordered emergency pontoons to be deployed across the Lys. The main bridge crossing at Erquinghem, meanwhile, was to be held at all costs. It was wired for demolition just in case.

At 9 a.m. Nicholson was told that the Portuguese had collapsed. The left brigade of 40th Division had been flanked and hostile troops were pouring in behind it. The 12th Suffolks, in brigade support, had formed a thin screen facing south-west and expected to be attacked at any moment. If they broke, then the 34th was next. He immediately warned 101st Brigade to be ready to move to their assistance. The order reached Stephenson at 9.10. For the next two hours Division kept him waiting. Finally, at 11.20, McCrae's were instructed to proceed to a sunken road in front of the village of Bac St Maur, 4,000 yards downstream. Like Erquinghem, Bac St Maur had a bridge. Stephenson sent Alfred Warr forward to reconnoitre the position, closely followed by Harry Rawson with C Company and George Cowan with D. As they came in sight of the village, there was a sudden explosion. Engineers had blown the crossing. Field-grey figures were spotted on the main road: Bac St Maur had already fallen. Warr was about to retire, when he noticed a single British officer approaching. Bertie Tower, one of Nicholson's staff-majors, had driven down from Division and got stuck on the wrong side of the river. They could still see his car on the opposite bank. Within seconds they started to come under sporadic rifle fire – not from the road, but from the open meadow north of Fleurbaix, where the 12th Suffolks were supposed to be. Grossly outnumbered, Warr fell back on Fort Rompu, where he was joined by Stephenson and the rest of the battalion. The order was given to dig in: as they did so, they were heavily bombarded. 2/Lt Sandy McKay from Bathgate was hit in the legs. His CSM and namesake, James Mackay, a typefounder's foreman from Hill Place, went to help him. A further shell came down and killed them both. Jim was one of the last of the Heriot's originals. After that, men dropped steadily. The German infantry stood back and let the gunners do their work.

Stephenson's right was hanging in the air. The only thing stopping the enemy assaulting his flank from the main road were some friendly machine-guns on the north side of the Lys. But even these were under threat.

Although the bridge at Bac St Maur had gone, the Germans had crossed downstream and elements of 40th Division were fighting a series of desperate rearguard actions to prevent them working their way along the river-bank. If they reached Erquinghem, the 34th would be cut off. Stephenson was ordered to send A and B Companies to cover the village. He could scarcely afford to lose them. At 2 p.m. the shelling subsided and a strong attack was mounted from the south. The battalion withdrew about 200 yards to the Merville–Armentières railway. Reinforced by some Australian tunnellers and a detachment from 15th Royal Scots, the line held. They were, however, short of ammunition. At that point they heard the tooting of a horn. Hurtling down the Rue Dormoire, with shells bursting on all sides, was Bertie Tower's staff car. He'd tramped back to Erquinghem, loaded several crates of S.A.A. and driven back to join the fight. He emerged from the passenger seat with a borrowed rifle, a double bandolier and a bag of Mills bombs. 'Where,' he asked Steve, 'do you want me?'[17]

By late afternoon the river frontage had been pushed back so far that Stephenson's position now resembled one corner of an old-fashioned infantry square. On his left, he remained in touch with the 11th Suffolks. The line then curled east and south beyond Bois Grenier into Shaftesbury Avenue, where units of 103rd Brigade and 40th Division were still holding their ground. Around 5.30 they began to come under heavy fire from Jesus Farm on the opposite bank of the Lys. The farm was directly behind them: it looked as if resistance in the north had finally collapsed. Indeed it had, but not completely: 74th Brigade was attempting to retrieve the situation.

Nicholson had 'borrowed' these three battalions from 25th Division, ordering them to counter-attack the hostiles around Croix du Bac and retake the bridgeheads on the north bank. Stephenson's two detached companies were expected to assist. By 8.30 they had located the enemy and prevented any further forward movement. At about the same time, south of the river, fighting patrols dispatched towards Fleurbaix found the village garrisoned in force. They were chased out and the skirmish turned into a full-scale assault. By midnight the outlook was grim. Steve brought up his last reserve, a company of the 18th NF, and the advance was checked. Murdie McKay recalled: 'They were the divisional pioneers, but if they'd been the Brigade of Guards they would not have got a louder cheer. We were just about done in.'[18]

Two hours later, the 74th recaptured Jesus Farm. The rest of the night passed quietly. At 7 a.m., however, small groups of enemy infantry were spotted in the fields north of Fleurbaix. They were working their way towards the railway, taking advantage of dead ground. At 7.30 a heavy

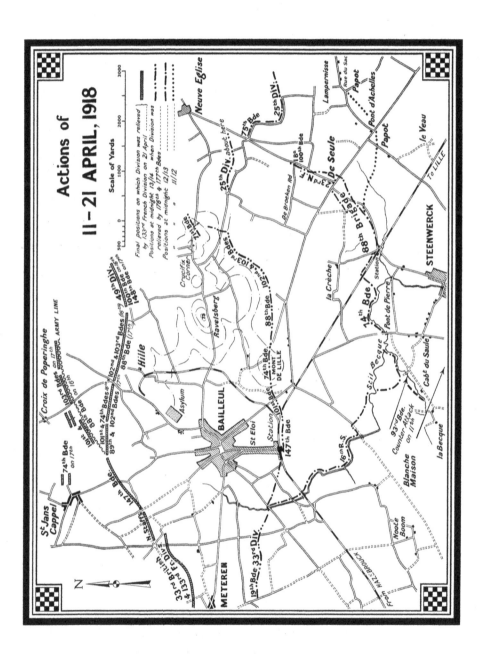

Actions of 11 – 21 APRIL, 1918

Scale of Yards

Final positions on which Division was relieved
by 133rd French Division on 21 April . . . .
Positions at midnight 13/14 when Division was
relieved by 176th & 177th Bdes . . . .
Positions at midnight 12/13 . . . .

bombardment was opened. Shortly after 8 a.m. both sides of the square were assaulted. Harry Rawson was on the corner with 9 Platoon. His sergeant was Andy Robertson, a 21-year-old miner from Motherwell, one of the Scottish Riflemen who had joined the battalion in July 1916. Robertson already had a DCM when he arrived and was awarded the MM after Hargicourt. He was brave, dependable and stubborn. The line held for about an hour but as the pressure mounted, Rawson gave the order to retire. Robertson noticed that the Germans were 'finishing off' the worst of the wounded and shouted a warning for everyone to keep going as long as they were able. They retreated from shell-hole to shell-hole, maintaining a good rate of fire. Suddenly Rawson was hit in the throat. He went down, clutching the wound. The Germans were almost on him: Robertson dashed forward, pulled him to his feet and surrendered.

Alfred Warr's HQ was in a farmhouse on the Rue Dormoire, about 150 yards to the rear. The building was intact and the farmer remained in residence. Around 9.30 Warr gathered 50 men and formed a new line behind the main breach. There was no cover and by 10 a.m. they had been driven back to the farmyard. Fifteen minutes later, they were forced to withdraw to the main building. The Germans brought up their trench mortars and began to dismantle the place. At 10.30 Warr and his companions were captured.[19]

By noon small parties of hostiles were reported on the outskirts of Erquinghem. North of the Lys, meanwhile, the Germans had launched a violent attack on 74th Brigade, pushing it back across the fields in the direction of Steenwerck. The enemy then resumed their advance along the riverbank, driving the defenders before them. Steve saw them break and sent Percy Bayliss across to organise a stand. Bayliss found Tommy Millar in command of the remains of A and B Companies but the two of them could do nothing to restore order. Bayliss discharged his revolver in the air: it was a waste (he later said) of three good bullets. By 2.45 p.m. the Germans were in Steenwerck. To the north, they had already taken Messines and Ploegsteert. There was a narrow corridor of escape but it was shrinking by the minute. Finally, at 3 p.m., Nicholson ordered the evacuation of the south bank. Erquinghem bridge was blown and the pontoon crews stood by.

It took three hours to bring everybody in. The units furthest south had to fight their way back under fire. McCrae's waited till last, harassed by machine-guns, covering each little party in turn. At 6.15 Stephenson finally ordered HQ Company across the river. RSM Ness remained in command of the bridgehead guard, holding off the hostiles with his rifle. Below him was a small boat with a badly wounded soldier. The oarsman had been shot. Jimmy Baigrie dived into the water, swam out with a rope and towed the vessel to safety. At 6.30 Ness withdrew his command, the final pontoon was destroyed and the south bank fell to the Germans.[20]

❋ ❋ ❋

According to the *Field Service Pocket Book*, one man armed with a shovel should be able to dig 30 cubic feet of 'ordinary easy soil' in an hour. Shovels were in short supply on the north bank of the Lys, and the men were obliged to fall back on their portable companion, the 'implement, intrenching, pattern 1908'. By 11.55 on the dark, wet night of 10 April, a new defensive line had been constructed parallel to the river. McCrae's were on the right, occupying the remains of Jesus Farm. Stephenson could find no friendly troops on either flank. Behind him, the 11th Suffolks were in a similar predicament. The line (if line it was) consisted of a series of shallow fire-trenches, incorporating shell-holes, ditches and railway sleepers. Such was the extent of hostile infiltration towards Steenwerck, however, that the position was already untenable. At midnight 101st Brigade was withdrawn almost 2,000 yards to open pasture south of the Armentières–Bailleul railway, where another line (facing south-west) was dug by 5.30 a.m. Shortly afterwards, the enemy mounted a strong attack on 102nd Brigade astride the main Bailleul road. The pressure forced a further retirement to the north-west, falling back on an unfinished part of the old reserve system in front of the village of Nieppe. During the afternoon, German troops began to appear in ever greater numbers from the north-east, where 25th Division was crumbling. By 3 p.m. Stephenson had reorganised his defences to face simultaneous attacks from every direction. The 34th was again in danger of being cut off. Field-Marshal Haig, meanwhile, stunned by the loss of Armentières, Messines and most of his offensive gains at Passchendaele, issued a Special Order:

> Every position must be held to the last man. There must be no retirement. With our backs to the wall and believing in the justice of our cause, each one of us must fight to the end. The safety of our homes and the freedom of mankind depend alike upon the conduct of each one of us at this critical moment.

Of course he was 30 miles *behind* the 'wall' when he wrote it.

By early evening the position at Nieppe had become impossible. Special orders notwithstanding, a general retirement was authorised by Nicholson at 7.30 to new positions beyond Steenwerck. The withdrawal, conducted in darkness under heavy shell-fire, was a nightmare. By 5 a.m. on 12 April, McCrae's had formed a thin screen facing south along the north bank of the

Stil Becque stream. The men had not slept for 72 hours. The day passed quietly but at 5 p.m. a strong attack across the entire Divisional front succeeded in pushing the line back towards Bailleul. Next morning the Germans were reported to be in Neuve Eglise, 6,000 yards to the left rear, and to be massing in front of Oultersteene, 4,000 yards to the right. Oultersteene was only six miles from Hazebrouck. At 3 p.m. they attacked, forcing a further retirement. Percy Bayliss was shot in the arm; Tommy Millar took a bullet in his knee. Steve had 2 officers and around 150 men left. At 2 a.m. on 14 April they withdrew again – to a line directly in front of Bailleul, extending on the left into the high ground around Mont de Lille. Late that afternoon the area was heavily shelled. George Cowan was blown up and concussed; 2/Lt Tom Storer, a Didsbury coal-merchant's clerk, who had been with the battalion since January, was gassed. Bobby Hogg, who had carried Sir George's message to Scots Redoubt, was fatally wounded. As he lay dying, he removed his signet ring and asked that it be sent home to his mother. Robert Gore was gone as well, killed in the cellar of a Mont de Lille farmhouse the previous evening. Stephenson took over the brigade; the remnants of 15th and 16th Royal Scots were combined under the command of David Osborne, a major from the 9th Northumberland Fusiliers. Senior surviving rank in the McCrae's contingent was Regimental Sergeant-Major Annan Buchan Ness.

At 11 p.m. the 34th was relieved by 59th Division. By dawn they had installed themselves in support positions on the forward slopes of a low ridge beside the village of St Jans Cappel. 'For the remainder of the day,' stated the War Diary without a trace of irony, 'battalions were engaged in digging on the new line.' At 4.20 p.m. word was received that the Bailleul defences were under attack. By 6.40 the 59th was retiring in disorder. By 9.50 Bailleul had fallen and the support entrenchments had become the front line. This time Nicholson had no choice. The 34th, he insisted, would remain where it was: there would be no further movement. Not only was Bailleul the last stop on the road to Hazebrouck; it was also the last obstacle in front of the high ground south of Ypres. Beyond were the 'mountains' to the west of Messines Ridge. If the Germans took Mont Noir and Mont des Cats, the Salient would have to be evacuated. For two more days 34th Division stood its ground under constant shelling, sniping and machine-gun fire. McCrae's alone lost 68 more men. Early on the morning of 19 April the battalion was withdrawn to reserve at Mont Noir. At midnight on 20–21 April the 133rd French Division arrived to take over their positions. McCrae's marched back to billets west of Poperinghe. The following evening Harry Rawson died of his wounds on a German hospital train en route to Brussels.[21]

Haig dispatched a telegram, acknowledging 34th Division's contribution to the defence of Armentières and Bailleul. No mention was made of the skill with which the numerous rearguard actions were fought during the long withdrawal to Mont Noir. Had Nicholson sacrificed his command in a pointless stand at Nieppe, there would have been nothing to prevent the enemy pressing north at speed to take the high ground. The General reviewed his exhausted battalions near St Jans-ter-Biezen on 24 April. 'I have always been proud of the Division,' he said, 'but not until recently did I realise how good it was.' John Shakespear later wrote with pride:

> When relieved we had been in action for 12 days. Throughout this period, although heavily attacked from all directions, the 34th Division maintained an unbroken front. No unit, however small, retired until ordered to do so. At times, for hours together, control by Divisional headquarters, brigade and even battalion commanders was impossible, but the steadfastness and gallantry of the men and the initiative of officers and non-commissioned officers never failed.[22]

On 25 April the Germans took Kemmel Hill, south of Ypres. McCrae's moved into the reserve line behind Poperinghe and started digging again. Four days later, hostile troops were standing at the summit of the Sherpenberg, looking down on Dickebusch, a mere three miles away. Ludendorff, however, was finished. That night, with his divisions spent and his guns short of ammunition, he brought Georgette to a close.

McCrae's remained in the Salient for a fortnight, then on 13 May they were bussed back to the village of Bournonville, ten miles east of Boulogne. On 16 May, in an act as unexpected as it was low-key, 34th Division and all its parts were disbanded for want of replacements. As of 9 a.m. that day, at the stroke of a bureaucrat's pen, the 16th Royal Scots were excised from the lists. With unseemly haste, it was announced that most of the remaining other ranks would be sent to the regimental depot as reinforcements, while the officers and NCOs would form a training establishment for the American Expeditionary Force at Alquines. There were perhaps 30 'originals' left, including Willie Duguid. As they formed up for the last time, he had no jaunty air to raise their spirits. Instead he played a slow lament, 'The Flowers o the Forest':

> O fickle fortune!
> Why this cruel sporting?
> Why thus perplex us poor sons of a day?
> Thy frown canna fear me,
> Thy smile canna cheer me,
> Since the flowers o the forest are a wede away.

There was one last distinction. Stephenson had an announcement to make. By order of Major-General Nicholson, RSM Ness was awarded the rare honour of a direct commission in the field. Annan shook hands with the Colonel, looked round at the ghosts and marched the old battalion off to Base. It was not a bit like Princes Street.

❀ ❀ ❀

The 'Advance to Victory' got underway in August. McCrae's were still represented. The remains of the battalion had been posted to the 2nd Royal Scots, and in due course Stephenson was given command of the Dandy Ninth. There were graduates of Heriot's all over the Western Front – too many to mention them all. Jimmy Brown became a gunner in the Tank Corps and managed to set himself on fire. Hugh Somerville from Warrender Park, one of A Company's intellectual sergeants, won two Military Crosses with the Manchester Regiment and befriended a young subaltern called Wilfred Owen.[23] Tom Halliburton, recovered from his wounds, took part in the Battle of Albert. The following extract from the *London Gazette* tells only half of the story:

> 2/Lt Thomas College Halliburton
> 16th Battalion Nottinghamshire and Derbyshire Regiment
> (attached 8th Battalion Royal Berkshire Regiment)
>
> AWARDED THE MILITARY CROSS. For conspicuous gallantry and coolness in the attack on the LA BOISSELLE craters on 24th August 1918. In cooperation with a platoon of a flank company, he led his platoon against the machine-gun posts in the maze of trenches round the craters, rushing them one after another, and greatly assisting in the capture of the main position.[24]

On 1 July 1916 Tom was caught in the entanglements in front of Heligoland with a hole in his face and a 7.9 mm machine-gun bullet lodged in his jaw. He hung on the wire, not daring to move, while number 1 Platoon was cut to pieces around him. His wonderful company was wiped out on the Contalmaison approaches, trying to capture a few hundred acres of scrubby farmland and a village he had never heard of. Two summers later, with the King's commission tucked into his knapsack, they sent him back to the same bloody place and made him do it all over again.

And then there was Crossan. Once his foot had mended, he was posted out to Palestine with the 4th Royal Scots. In December 1917 he was present at the fall of Jerusalem. In April 1918 his battalion arrived in France. On 26

August, during an attack on the village of Hendecourt (just east of Croisilles), he was severely gassed. John Veitch visited him in an Edinburgh convalescent home on the evening of Armistice Day. No Victory trumpets sounded in that grim ward, only the dark, pneumonic rasp of poisoned lungs. Crossan's bed was by a window, looking out over Arthur's Seat. When Veitch asked him what he intended to do when he recovered, Pat replied: 'First I'm going to run up yon wee hill, then I'm going back to play for Hearts.'

Assuming, of course, Hearts would have him.

In the Bois Grenier Line (D.M. Sutherland)

CHAPTER TWELVE

'A great life out there, after all'

In June 1917 John McCartney wrote a short article for the *Sportsman's Gazette*, in which he listed the 16 Hearts players who had volunteered by the first Christmas of the war. Two months later, he expanded this account into a slim pamphlet, entitled *Hearts and the Army*, which was sold for a penny a copy in aid of his 'Footballs for Soldiers Fund':

> In the early days of the war the most virulent, vitriolic and irrelevant attacks were hurled at the heads of the professionals. Their class was anathema to lords, bishops, curates and all grades of professional teachers. Fireside soldiers and critics exhausted their vocabulary of invective. The entire cosmopolitan crew of killjoys were beside themselves. How these parasites find a landing on the bodies of responsible people is one of the Seven Wonders. They are neither fitted for fighting nor willing to fight, but their rudimentary, fragmentary and hearsay knowledge of things has the unfortunate tendency to further distort their limited powers of observation.

McCartney was settling one or two old scores. He'd had a dreadful few years. First, the Kaiser had robbed him of the Championship; then of the 'perfect combination' he had so lovingly assembled. Currie, in particular, was like a son to him. The next casualty was his health. Since Hearts could no longer afford to pay his contracted salary, he generously agreed a substantial pay-cut and took on a second full-time job as manager of the Tivoli picture-house in Gorgie Road. His Tynecastle workload, meanwhile, doubled as he struggled to field a full eleven every Saturday. The Military

Service Acts of 1916 introduced 'reserved' occupations, allowing men with particular mining, shipbuilding or engineering skills to claim exemption from conscription. In industrial Lanarkshire these regulations enabled certain clubs (legally or otherwise) to maintain a first-team squad which differed little from peacetime. With no nucleus of reserved personnel at Tynecastle, McCartney was reduced to searching around for so-called 'soldier footballers' who happened to be stationed locally. The movements of such men had to be monitored, then special permits had to be obtained from the military authorities and the SFA. Since these agreements were only binding for one fixture, the entire process had to be repeated on a weekly basis. The system was utterly impractical, so that subterfuge and pseudonym became an unwanted part of his everyday life. 'It is a fact,' he later wrote, 'that I have left Waverley Station to play a League match in the West without a single player. Men were picked up en route and at Glasgow, Hamilton, etc. to be introduced to each other before kick-off.'

In December 1918 McCartney expanded *Hearts and the Army* into booklet form. *The Hearts and the Great War* incorporated a revised (but still incomplete) 'Roll of Honour', together with biographies and portraits of the dead. There were also extracts from numerous letters of support received at Tynecastle during the course of hostilities – many of them thanking him for his tireless efforts on behalf of a dozen different charities. The football fund (which he ran single-handedly) was the largest of its kind in Britain. He later estimated that from 1914 to 1919 he worked an unbroken sequence of constant 18-hour days. One unfortunate by-product of this over-commitment was the gradual erosion of his influence on the playing side of the club. Elias Furst had brought him to Tynecastle with a promise that members of the board would be discouraged from meddling in team affairs. In April 1918 Furst suffered the second of two wartime heart attacks and his power within the boardroom decreased accordingly. The vice-chairman, William Lorimer (Harry's father), was a sympathetic ally but he contracted influenza that summer, leaving McCartney at the mercy of the 'Three Bills'.[1]

Messrs Brown, Burns and Drummond were directors of the old school. They insisted on joining him on scouting trips and on exercising a veto over signings. Emboldened by a series of petty victories, they then began to extend their interest into the dressing-room. McCartney found himself being offered gratuitous advice about particular players. Favourites emerged; alliances formed; cliques began to undermine what he once described as the 'Musketeer Spirit' of the 1914 side. Matters came to a head during the summer of 1919 over new contracts for the surviving McCrae volunteers. Briggs had already retired from competitive football, but five others remained available. Pat Crossan (who was still far from well) and

Willie Wilson were signed at once; Bob Preston took time to consider. The board, however, was unwilling to sanction funds to employ the unproven Annan Ness or Jamie Low. In Low's case they preferred to persevere for another year with the old warhorse Geordie Sinclair. McCartney stated boldly that he had built one Championship team and (given the chance) was quite capable of building another. The directors were not prepared to take the risk. When the new season started in 1919, the local press observed that Hearts were most unlike themselves. 'There is a slowness about the side,' observed the *Evening News*, 'and a want of understanding. Things may improve over time, but for the moment the old stamp is sorely lacking.' In September the manager dipped into his bottomless trunk of whimsical stories to provide the *Evening Dispatch* with a telling quote:

> 'When I started out in life, I was convinced that the world had an opening for me.'
> 'And had it?'
> 'Yes, I am now in a *hole*.'

On 17 October McCartney resigned his position, complaining of 'two minds at work in the selection of the team'. Prompted by the *Evening News*, the board issued a brief confirmatory statement, citing 'questions of policy'. There was not so much as a 'thank you' for nine momentous years of loyal service.

❈ ❈ ❈

Cast your mind back to Cologne Ridge in August 1917. One of the lads wounded during the assault on that bleak hillside was Andrew Riddell, a 27-year-old sniper from Peaston Farm, near the East Lothian village of Ormiston. Riddell was shot in the stomach and lay out in the rain for two days before he was picked up by a stretcher-party. He returned to France in 1918 and was badly concussed when a shell exploded directly above his head. Two men on either side of him were killed. 'I'm not supposed to be here,' he used to tell friends after the war. People thought he was joking.

After his discharge, Riddell found employment as a commercial traveller. In April 1919 he looked on with interest (and perhaps a little envy) as McCrae's officers gathered for a grand dinner at the North British Hotel in Princes Street. Both colonels attended, along with Herbert Warden, Dick Lauder and around 30 others.[2] The evening was a qualified success: everyone enjoyed it but expressed the opinion that there was something missing. That 'something' was the rest of the battalion. It was agreed that there would be no more 'officers' nights'; henceforth the reunions would be open to all ranks. This of course implied the compilation and upkeep of a roll of names and addresses, the formation (in effect) of a 'McCrae's Association'. The task was by no means simple and would require the attention of a permanent organising secretary. Private Riddell was unanimously volunteered. On 15 December the first Reunion Dinner of the 16th Royal Scots was held at the Victoria Hall in Leith Street. Bob Martin took the chair. Most of the hundred or so diners had not seen each other since Bécourt Wood on the night before the Push. Many were surprised to find that a particular pal was still alive. Roast beef was followed by plum pudding, coffee, speeches and port. Martin was prevailed upon to give the boys a song. 'Bazentin' was an old trench favourite he had written during the winter of 1916/17. As his audience beat their fists slowly on the tables to simulate drumfire, Bob's deep, soulful voice recalled another time and place:

> Did ye stand wi McCrae on the German hill?
> Did ye feel the shrapnel flyin?
> Did ye close wi the Hun, comin in for the kill?
> Did ye see your best friends dyin?
>
> Well there's those that will say that they stood wi McCrae.
> And there's those mair content just tae think it.
> Now we each rise and stand for the Toast tae the Deid,
> All those lads never able tae drink it.
>
> McCrae's Battalion!

It was after midnight before they dispersed, vowing to return the following year. Two further bits of business were settled that evening – firstly, the formal establishment of the 16th Royal Scots Association (with Riddell as honorary secretary); and secondly, the passing of a resolution to secure the creation of a 'fitting' memorial. The idea was D.M. Sutherland's. Twin cairns would be erected – one in Edinburgh, the other in the rebuilt village of Contalmaison. These would carry identical bronze plaques, incorporating the city crest, the regimental badge and a brief history of McCrae's. Each year, on 1 July, a party of local schoolchildren would make the pilgrimage to France to lay wreaths in honour of those who had sacrificed their lives. In the spirit of friendship, a similar party from Contalmaison would be invited to make the return journey. A new Edinburgh tradition would be founded, as unique as the battalion itself, and last as long as men of goodwill were prepared to keep it going.

Goodwill, however, was in short supply in the chambers of Edinburgh

Corporation. When Sir George and his Memorial Committee submitted their proposals for support and funding, they were dismayed to be told that neither would be forthcoming. Bearing in mind that McCrae's was the 2nd Edinburgh City Battalion and that Edinburgh owed an unacknowledged debt of gratitude to the original volunteers, this was just insulting. McCrae's had done the city proud, but the city didn't know it. No one who had stayed at home throughout the late hostilities had the slightest notion of the horrors of trench warfare. Carried along by a censored press that was never anything less than optimistic about the Allies' prospects, that described 1 July 1916 as 'a day of broad success along the line', the Edinburgh public and their elected representatives remained in a deep state of blameless ignorance. Thousands of local men had been killed since 1914, and thousands more wounded, but family grief was *private*. It crossed the landing to a neighbour, it whispered up and down the common stair, but it seldom reached beyond the outside door. Even after 1 July the suspicion that something dreadful had happened was never officially confirmed. It was weeks before the relevant casualty returns found their way into the papers – and when they did, they were staggered to minimise their impact. Thus McCrae's roll of wounded from the battle was published anonymously over five days in mid-August, with the names of the missing withheld for a fortnight. The roll of killed did not appear until September – concealed within several separate regimental lists. It took a further six months for the War Office to announce that the missing were actually dead. The same procedure was followed with the 15th Royal Scots, so that while Edinburgh undoubtedly knew that the two City battalions had fared badly, there was nothing (other than the conflicting accounts of returned convalescents) to suggest that 1 July 1916 had been the capital's blackest day since Flodden.

The public said, 'This awful war,' but no one knew *how* awful. The advance on Contalmaison was a tragedy untold. 'It is gratifying to note,' observed the *Evening Dispatch* with the offensive nine days old, 'that the Edinburgh battalions have performed well in the Push. Sgt Roddy Walker, the former Hearts back, has been recommended for the Victoria Cross.' The news (which wasn't even true) was met with quiet satisfaction, but no one saw poor Roddy's wounds or heard him weeping softly for his dead brother.

The civilian population had been utterly misled. 'People who told the truth were likely to be imprisoned,' wrote Siegfried Sassoon ten years later, 'and lies were at a premium.'[3] The press portrayed the conflict as a justified crusade, in which daring young subs laughed carelessly before nipping across no man's land to bomb old Billy Boche, while wounded Tommies regaled waiting reporters with cheerful tales of shrapnel and tin helmets. It was absurd. Denied any realistic account of conditions at the front, civilians were able to congratulate themselves on their own patient tolerance of what *The Times* called 'our grim domestic hardships' – an attitude returning troops found difficult to swallow. Hardship, they muttered bitterly, was not a petrol shortage or a scarcity of potatoes. Hardship was soaking waist-deep in some stinking shell-hole with your best pal lying dead beside you. But they never said as much out loud: the gap in understanding was too great. Sassoon again: 'Any man who had been on active service had an unfair advantage over those who hadn't. And the man who had really endured the War at its worst was everlastingly differentiated from everyone except his fellow soldiers.'

A battalion daughter told me that her father, normally a warm and cheerful man, suffered an annual 'depression' which culminated in him locking himself for several hours in the front room of the family's Stockbridge flat. She was certain he was crying but no one had the nerve to ask him why. Yes, she said, it *was* around the beginning of July, and how on earth did I know? This lady, who was in the fullness of her 70s, had never heard of Scots Redoubt. For many, the 'Land fit for Heroes' turned out to be a cold wilderness of ignorance and incomprehension. The true purpose of the commemorative proposals, therefore, went far beyond the ceremonial. Once established, they would have been the means for a diminishing handful of survivors to convey something of their wartime experience to a wider community that at times seemed both bewildered and bored by the fierceness of their pride. John Veitch: 'We were not looking to be thanked or admired. All we wanted was a bit of understanding.'[4]

This was the problem when McCrae's approached the council. The submission that the city might care to recognise their sacrifice was made to a group of middle-aged and elderly gentlemen who had spent the preceding five years in a different world. There was no common ground. Indeed the veterans' decision to initiate the matter themselves (rather than waiting politely to be asked) may even have been interpreted as a presumptuous and unwanted reminder of a time that would be better forgotten – except for when Remembrance Day came round. 'As if we could pack up our memories in some old chest with our medals and dig them out just once a year,' wrote Pte Rab Gordon in 1964. 'After the war we were told that a daily service would not be practical and of course we deferred to that opinion. But later on, we heard about the Menin Gate and thought: "If the Belgies can do it, why can't we?" After all, they were our boys. What would it have cost? I think the powers-that-be just lacked the will. They didn't have to fight, so they didn't really care.'[5]

In the face of widespread civic indifference, the association now tried a change of approach. Since their appeal to the Corporation's conscience had failed to impress, perhaps an appeal to its pocket might succeed. There remained the matter of the Provost's own battalion, the 1ˢᵗ Edinburgh City, sponsored by the late Sir Robert Inches. Surely the capital was obliged to commemorate their efforts. If all parties were agreed, perhaps some *joint* commemoration might be adopted – a statue, a plaque, or something less expensive. The suggestion that Princes Street be renamed 'McCrae's March' apparently went down like a lead observation balloon. When Sir George tried to shame the council by announcing that the Tyneside battalions were proposing to place a substantial memorial close to the Bapaume road at la Boisselle, he was all but ignored.[6] This was the final straw: at their next reunion, in December 1920, the 16ᵗʰ Royal Scots resolved to go it alone. A 37-strong Memorial Committee was appointed with McCrae as chairman. Donald Gunn, who was gassed at Croisilles, agreed to serve as honorary secretary. The rest of the members were battalion veterans like D.M. Sutherland, Jim Davie and Sandy Yule; battalion friends like Leishman, Rawson, McCartney and Furst; and battalion bereaved like Sir Richard Mackie (Nap Armit's father-in-law), Alice Ross (Peter's widow), Walter Coles (Lionel's father) and Sir Richard Lodge. Five days before Christmas Sir George sent out the following dispatch:

> The 16ᵗʰ Battalion The Royal Scots was raised in Edinburgh in December 1914. It took part in the famous forward movement on the Somme on July 1ˢᵗ 1916, and from that date it was constantly in or near the front line, until it had been so shattered that it could no longer exist as a unit. Eight hundred members of the Battalion sacrificed their lives in the War and we feel sure that neither Edinburgh nor Scotland would be willing to see these brave men pass away unrecorded. As a fitting memorial, it has been agreed to erect a tablet on the wall of St Giles Cathedral. In order that the memorial may be worthy of those whom it commemorates, it is desirable to raise a sum of £1,000. We respectfully appeal for the support of the survivors of those who served or were trained with the Battalion; of the relatives of the fallen; and of all friends in Edinburgh and elsewhere who wish to express their appreciation of these men who fell in the service of their country.[7]

This was not the favoured cairns. The committee had costed that proposal and found it too expensive. Indeed McCrae was concerned that even the tablet might be beyond them. A thousand pounds was a substantial sum. Most of the veterans had little in the way of savings, while the families of the dead were struggling on a pension that James Hogge had lately denounced as 'insufficient for survival'. Sir George (who was far from wealthy) opened the fund with a donation of £25, which was immediately matched by Bill Robertson. James Cormack of Glencairn Crescent, who had equipped the 1914 pipe band, gave the same. Sir Richard Mackie pledged ten pounds, Walter Coles and Harry Rawson five apiece. Bob Martin and Willie Gavin stumped up four guineas between them; McCartney and Furst managed two. Sandy Yule scraped together five shillings, and so on down the pennies to the final widow's mite. It took 14 months to fill the coffers, then in February 1922 local sculptor Pilkington Jackson was commissioned to execute the carving. Sir Robert Lorimer, the noted architect, volunteered to supervise the installation and by November the work was complete. On Sunday, 17 December McCrae's returned to George Street one quarter of their mobilisation strength. A damp wind stirred the Colour as they marched towards the west. They turned down Hanover Street, then climbed the Mound to Parliament Square and filed slowly into the High Kirk. By 3 p.m. they were seated. As the bells struck the hour, Jimmy Black signalled to the organist, who responded with the first psalm sung the night before the Push:

> God is our refuge and our strength,
> In straits a present aid,
> Therefore, although the earth remove;
> We will not be afraid.

There followed a prayer for the dead, whose families took an honoured place among the congregation. Six councillors, in scarlet robes, sat hidden in a corner. According to ancient tradition, the Colour was passed into the care of the church. Donald Gunn observed that 'the old flag looked strangely new as it was borne beneath the overhanging lines of dusty, ragged and shell-torn standards overhead; but none, one felt, represented sterner fields or celebrated more honourable service'.

Then, on the north wall of the Albany aisle, the tablet was unveiled. Cut from rose-coloured limestone, it depicted the armoured figure of St Michael astride the dying Prussian dragon. General Sir Francis Davies, who performed the ceremony, was the Army's senior officer in Scotland. He had brought two letters to read. The first was from Sir William Pulteney, former commander of III Corps:

> I hope that whoever unveils the memorial will allude to the magnificent work the battalion did at the first great Battle of the Somme, when they held on to the position on the Boisselle–Contalmaison road. It enabled many subsequent advances to be made on the left flank which would otherwise have been made very difficult and more costly. Please remember me to all those who

served under me and tell them how I look back with pride on their loyalty and courage.[8]

The second note came neatly typed from Kingston Hill in Surrey. It was signed 'Earl Haig of Bemersyde, F.M.':

> I much regret that it has not been possible to join you in the tribute you pay today to your fallen comrades. I am the more thankful to Sir George McCrae for giving me the opportunity to express by letter my own sense of gratitude to the officers and men of the gallant battalion he so loyally helped to raise.
>
> To all ranks of the Army I commanded, I owe a debt which I can never sufficiently acknowledge. Yet, as a Scotsman, I may be allowed a kinsman's sympathy with those who mourn our Scottish dead; and as the responsible commander of our Army in its first great offensive battle, I can pay a special tribute to a Scottish regiment which on 1st July 1916 suffered such heavy loss and served its country so well.
>
> It is surely of our country's service that we must think on an occasion such as this. To have served our country truly and well is the best reward for our own efforts; the thought that they died in that service is the highest consolation for the loss of our comrades and friends.[9]

'Consolation,' answered Jimmy Black before the benediction, 'is the hardest thing to find – concealed, as it often is, by bitterness and pain. I have lost count of the number of times I have been asked, "Where, minister, is my consolation? Where is the good? Why did he die?" As one who was there – a phrase much used by the pompous, but I *was* there, so you will forgive me its use . . . As one who was there, I would say only this. Yes, service to the country was important. And service to the Lord. But there was another service – narrower, perhaps, and more selfish – and that was service to our comrades in the field and to our loved ones at home. It was God and Country that took us out to France, but it was loyalty to our pals that made us fight. And so my consolation lies in knowing that these men died for their friends and with their friends, keeping each other company like good comrades in death as in life. They died in the belief that they were doing right and I am proud to say I served beside them.'

Then as the final blessing echoed from the pulpit, Willie Duguid piped up 'Dark Lochnagar'. And as the tears were dabbed away, a lone bugler sounded the 'Last Post' followed by 'Reveille' as the ghosts of the battalion stood at ease.[10]

After the service a small party of C Company veterans, led by Sir George, collected a wreath from the public cloakroom and walked down Victoria Street into the Grassmarket. They marched past Hunter's Close and the old Castle Brewery, through the West Port to Morrison Street. Five minutes later, they arrived at Haymarket, opposite the railway station, where earlier that year a large stone memorial to the Heart of Midlothian fallen had been unveiled before a crowd of 40,000 by Robert Munro, Secretary of State for Scotland. The monument, surmounted by a handsome clock, was paid for by club supporters, on whose behalf the board had presented it to Edinburgh Corporation. Plain but imposing, it occupied the centre of a busy junction and was a fitting reminder of the old team's dreadful loss.[11] McCrae and his companions had taken part in the ceremony. Today's visit, however, was a private affair, unheralded and simple, to honour just the 16th Royal Scots dead: Boyd, Currie, Ellis, Gracie, Wattie and all those others less well known but every bit as worthy. The Colonel bowed his head in silent prayer, laid the wreath, saluted and withdrew. Murdie Mckay walked back into town with him and noticed that his pace had greatly slowed. The long, purposeful stride of 1914 had been replaced by a statelier step that at times seemed almost hesitant. 'Sir George's physical decline,' the obituaries would later claim, 'can be traced back to his service in the War.'

For once the papers almost had it right.

✳ ✳ ✳

On 14 December 1916, three days after finally conceding defeat in the campaign to retain his battalion, McCrae was formally promoted to the rank of brigadier-general. On 15 December the Edinburgh press reported him 'on duty at the War Office' and about to return to France 'in an administrative capacity'.

We know tantalisingly little about these few weeks in Sir George's career. There was apparently a view in Whitehall that his unique experience might be usefully deployed in France – in the same way, possibly, that Eric Geddes, the civilian railway expert, had been drafted into GHQ to address the transport crisis of early 1916. McCrae was one of the most able civil servants of his generation, a gifted organiser, who could spot incompetence a mile away. He was also a decorated veteran with two years' service at the sharp end of the Western Front. Who better to identify and deal with the many petty logistical complaints that infuriated soldiers in the line – the chronic shortage (for example) of dischargers for rifle grenades, spare parts for Lewis guns, clean receptacles for water, or fuel for trench-braziers. The list went on forever: there was a shrewd suspicion in the trenches that no one beyond five miles of the front had a clue that such problems existed. The newspapers' certainty, however, turned out to be misplaced, for on 3 January 1917 it was announced that he would be leaving the Army in order to resume his duties at the Local Government Board. He stepped down with a full colonelcy and the 'heartfelt thanks' of the War Cabinet. Lloyd George sent his warmest regards, as did Asquith, Bonar Law and Winston Churchill. Evidently he had not been forgotten.

The middle of January found him back in George Street, staring at the wreckage of his earlier reforms. Many of his best appointees had gone off on active service, leaving their positions to be filled by older men whom he had long since marked down as unsuitable. The Board had suffered something of a relapse and though there was little prospect of effecting a cure while hostilities continued, he did make a start by recruiting young invalided officers and NCOs in an effort to halt the decline with an infusion of khaki initiative. 'Progressive thinking,' he told *The Scotsman*, 'is what we need to prepare our towns and cities for the troops when they return. The problems we face in housing and public health have been too long neglected. They will not stand another decade of reports and well-meaning words. It is deeds that are required.'

This was vintage McCrae, harking back to his pre-war concern for working-class housing conditions. 'A national disgrace,' he called them at the beginning of 1914; and now, some three years later, things were worse. 'No new buildings have been erected,' he observed, 'so to the evil of insanitary dwellings has been added greatly increased overcrowding.' The Royal Commission on Housing in Scotland was due to conclude within months and he made his feelings known to its members; but other than that, there was nothing he could do. Constrained by military priorities and lack of funds, the Board's wartime remit amounted to little more than maintenance of essential services. Peace, perhaps, would bring the cash to act. In the meantime they would simply have to wait.

And in the meantime, there was also the battalion – old now and bloodied and bolstered by drafts, but still his 'boys'. He felt a terrible nostalgia for the trenches. 'You have no idea how much I miss you all,' he wrote D.M. Sutherland to congratulate him on his mention in despatches. 'It is a great life out there, after all.'[12]

Nights were the worst. He dreamt by star-shell. Sitting in his dug-out; hot tea, dry socks and the Padre duetting with Bob Martin. 'If you were the only girl in the world.' Sgt Currie was handing him a small box. He woke with a start, opened his bedside drawer, took out a watch and read the inscription: 'To Colonel Sir George McCrae on the occasion of his birthday. From the officers and men of C Company, 16th Royal Scots, August 29th 1915.' It was a grand timekeeper. Once it measured barrage and bombardment; he had worn it by his heart at Scots Redoubt. Now it nestled in his waistcoat, saw him onto trains and into dinner. It sat on his desk as he searched the casualty lists for familiar names and scribbled off battalion correspondence – 'Any gossip you can send me would be welcome.' And on the eleventh day of the eleventh month of 1918 it counted down the seconds to the last eleventh hour. When he snapped the cover shut, the war was over.

✳ ✳ ✳

On 16 August 1919 Heart of Midlothian defeated Queen's Park by three goals to one in the first home fixture of the peacetime League campaign. Alan Morton was on the wing for the visitors but even a half-fit Paddy Crossan had his measure. Seated in the stand were around a hundred survivors of the original applicants for the Hearts Company, who had recently received a complimentary season-ticket from the club. On the inside-cover, below their name and regimental number, was some typical McCartney prose:

> Voluntarily these men went forth to fight for King and Country. The gloomiest hour in the Nation's history found them ready. As Pioneers in the formation of a brilliant Regiment, sportsmen the world over will ever remember them. Duty well and truly done, they are welcomed back to Tynecastle.

The Colonel was unable to attend. On 1 July he had become chairman of the new Scottish Board of Health, recently formed by the joining of the Local Government Board with Sir James Leishman's National Health Insurance Commission. McCrae was busy preparing to implement the first great piece of post-war social legislation, the 1919 Housing Act, which was due to come into force on 18 August. During its Parliamentary passage, he had criticised the Bill severely. 'Quite inadequate,' he called it. 'Incapable of meeting a grave and dangerous situation.' The Act provided for the construction of 115,000 new houses in Scotland, but even the conservative Royal Commission had concluded that at least 236,000 were required. Moreover the government had agreed after long discussions with the local authorities to subsidise all expenses incurred over the amount of one penny on the municipal rates. This, according to McCrae, was 'financial insanity'. Unless the local contribution were larger (25 per cent, for example, as the original Bill had proposed) there would be no incentive to economy. Construction costs would soar, fewer houses would be built and the scheme would ultimately collapse.

And that's precisely what happened. A house that might have cost £300 to build in 1914 cost £1,000 by 1920. To protect itself, the Treasury introduced new financial regulations – which caused further delay, increased costs even more and retarded the construction programme to such an extent that *The Scotsman* calculated that it would take at least 20 years for 1919's modest building target to be met. Indeed the rate at which new houses were appearing was barely fast enough to cover the loss of older, uninhabitable dwellings that were being demolished under the legislation's slum-clearance provisions – which themselves were grossly underfunded. In 1914 McCrae had suggested £60,000 per annum as a likely minimum sum to tackle this problem. Five years on, and with the problem so much worse, the government saw fit to offer *half*.

Sir George had hoped that the Housing Act (which impinged upon every conceivable aspect of public health) would enable him to preside over something of a social revolution in Scotland. In December 1918 he stated that the prospect of British troops coming home to tenement slums that were no better than the trenches and dug-outs they had left across the Channel was 'more shameful than any civilian could know'. The Act's effective failure – a failure he foretold – was both a bitter disappointment and a key factor in his decision to leave the Board and stand again for Parliament.

His chance came in October 1922, when Bonar Law's dominant Conservatives withdrew from the coalition that had governed the country since May 1915. Lloyd George duly stood down as Prime Minister, whereupon Bonar Law assumed the premiership and called a general election for 15 November. The previous election (in December 1918) was the first fought under the new Representation of the People Act, which had doubled the number of eligible males and extended the franchise to all women over the age of 30. As a result of these changes, the electorate was now predominantly working-class: seven Scottish constituencies returned Labour candidates to Parliament that year – including Central Edinburgh, where William Graham defeated his coalition Liberal opponent by a narrow 364 votes. Graham was a moderate, who had spoken on behalf of the 'patriotic worker' at several of McCrae's recruiting meetings in 1914. In another time, his natural home would have been the Liberal Party; in 1922 he found himself standing on an extremist platform that advocated nationalisation of key industries and the establishment of a Socialist state. 'Mr Graham,' observed the *Evening Dispatch*, 'is clearly ill at ease in the company of many of his followers.'

McCrae was persuaded to contest the seat on behalf of the National Liberals. A pact was agreed with the Unionists, allowing him a clear run against Graham. He made it plain that if elected, he intended to serve as an 'independent' and to concentrate his efforts on the creation of a more effective Housing bill. 'It is typical of Sir George,' declared *The Scotsman* 'to go where he believes his duty lies. There is no thought of self here, for he has given up a senior position with a comfortable competence for life. He moves ahead, but boldly, into an uncertain future. We wish him well.'

Three weeks' campaigning just wasn't enough, and he fell short of Graham's total by 3,505 votes – victim of a national swing from Liberal to Labour that left the former with 117 seats and the latter (with 142) as the second party in the land. It was not a clean contest and Graham had to apologise for the organised disruption of McCrae's public meetings by some of the more militant Labour supporters. A whispering campaign spread a vicious rumour that Sir George had been directly responsible for the loss of his battalion on the first day of the Somme, and that having issued the fatal order, he had sat out the advance several miles to the rear. Donald Gunn was furious and penned a long letter to the *Evening News* in defence of the old man:

> Of all the senseless yarns that any ex-infantryman could swallow, there surely can be none more ignorant than the suggestion that war losses can be attributed to individual battalion commanders in any big attack. The offensive on the Somme was not organised by any one battalion commander; it was thought out by the best military brains on the Western Front. Corps Commanders, Divisional Generals, Brigadiers and Colonels all took their orders from people 'higher up'. Failures, and there were many on the 1st of July, could not be blamed on individual battalion commanders any more than on an individual lance-corporal.
>
> The 'C.O.', like the rest of the boys, carried his life in his hands for days on end. Battle headquarters was simply a dug-out, made the reverse way, with the door gaping towards the enemy. Here, the 'C.O.' ran the show; here was the new British front line, of which domestic followers of the big battle would read in the official communiqués. When Sir Douglas Haig said his troops had penetrated so many miles on the outskirts of Contalmaison, let Edinburgh folks understand that Edinburgh and district boys travelled farthest. Our colonel was in command of a wide expanse of front and was right amongst his men when we were relieved late on the night of the 3rd. Was this a pleasurable occupation for a man over military age who could certainly have chosen the comforts of home over a miserable meal in a shell-swept trench surrounded by a ruthless enemy?
>
> Of course our colonel got the DSO and any man of the 16th who

appeared on that hurried parade in Henencourt Wood, whence we marched for a well-earned rest, must have felt a thrill of pride when Sir George was singled out by the Army Commander and, in full view of the assembled troops, English, Scottish and Irish, congratulated on the splendid achievement not of the division, not of the brigade, but of the 16th Royal Scots.

McCrae was beaten but not bowed: more than 9,000 people had placed their cross next to his name. He resolved to stand again at the earliest opportunity – which arrived in November 1923, when Stanley Baldwin, who had replaced the ailing Bonar Law as Prime Minister in May, announced that he would go to the country on 6 December in search of a continued Conservative mandate. On 19 November Sir George accepted the nomination as the Liberal candidate for Falkirk and Stirling Burghs, where a further agreement had been struck with the Unionists to allow him a clear run at the sitting Labour MP, Hugh Murnin. Once again, the contest was marked by what the press described as 'Socialist disturbances', notably in Falkirk, Stirling and Grangemouth, where he was subjected to a torrent of humourless verbal abuse. This time he was ready and deflected the barbs with all his old wit, winning round a considerable number of Labour supporters in the process. It was a close finish, but he edged home by 156 votes and took up his place on the back benches when Parliament reassembled in January 1924.

Baldwin was still Prime Minister – but just only. The Conservatives now had 258 seats, a reduction of 87. Labour and the Liberals had improved their position to 191 and 158 respectively. If Baldwin was to retain power he would need to secure substantial Liberal assistance, but it was not forthcoming. In the crucial division on a motion of 'no confidence' the Liberal leaders voted against the Government and therefore allowed Ramsay MacDonald to form the country's first Labour administration. Against both his principles and his better judgement, Sir George had gone along with those leaders – effectively voting away his seat, for he knew that a minority Labour government could not last long and in the ensuing election his failure to support Baldwin would be remembered by his Unionist constituents. And he was right. Nine months later, MacDonald fell from office when the Liberals refused to support his policy on Russia. The election campaign was dominated by speculation about the imminent dangers of Bolshevism; Labour lost 40 seats, the Liberals 119 – leaving the Conservatives with a majority of more than 2 to 1 over all the other parties. Sir George was defeated by 1,924 votes and immediately announced his political retirement. It was a cruel way to go.

This, however, was not the end of his public career. In February 1925 he resigned from the Liberal Party in order to devote his energies to the housing question.[13] In October he moved into a new home at Tantallon Terrace in North Berwick, taking the name *Torluish* with him. Shortly after Christmas, he suffered a debilitating stroke. Confined to his bed for several months, he was unable even to write. On 24 June 1926 his spinster daughter Gladys copied the following note for D.M. Sutherland:

> The fates have been very unkind. I cannot tell you what a blow it was when I was told I would not be able to be with the old battalion on their visit to the Somme. Please convey to all ranks my deep regret that I am unable to travel with them on their pilgrimage. I will be most interested to hear an account of your doings when going over the ground which we know so well and where the 16th covered themselves with glory. I was never prouder of the battalion than on that famous day. My thoughts will be with you.

He had waited until the last possible moment – two nights before embarkation. The tenth anniversary pilgrimage was to have been the highpoint of his year. A memorial statue to the 34th Division had been placed near la Boisselle and he was scheduled to lay a wreath. That task would now be performed by Bob Martin. D.M. tried to sweeten the pill with a string of cheery postcards ('intelligence reports', the Colonel called them), and took time on his return to write a long, descriptive letter. Sir George replied that he wasn't yet 'quite right', but hoped to have recovered sufficiently to make a short crossing the following summer. 'You may pass the word that I am looking for companions.'

He refused to give up on a cairn for Contalmaison and felt that the civic conscience might yet be pricked if a party of battalion orphans were to join the next pilgrimage. 'I'm told the public wishes to forget the War,' he continued, 'but before they cast it fully from their minds, let them first be informed what took place near that shattered village whose name means so much to us and so little to them. I do not think they will be so ready to forget once they have the facts. Let a dozen local children place their tributes beside those of their young French cousins and soon the *Dispatch* will be asking "Where is our Memorial?" There is no surer way of producing movement in those grey council chambers than to redden a few faces. We must get this matter settled, for the shame is all the city's and I cannot rest while such a state prevails.'

Before Sir George could act he suffered a second attack. He battled back and May 1928 found him in defiant mood. 'This time,' he assured Sutherland, 'I intend to put it all behind me. You may count on me for the next reunion.'

December 14 was the day. He awoke that morning determined to attend but felt unwell while dressing. The venue was the Royal Scots Club in Abercromby Place, which had opened in 1922 as a retreat for former members of the regiment. He had made an appointment there for lunch and arranged for the use of a room to rest during the afternoon. His main problem, however, was getting into town. A telegram went in his place, the words as sad as they were short: 'Heartfelt apologies for my absence. Warmest thoughts are with you all tonight.' On 21 December he wrote Bob Martin. The hand was steady, if a little squint. 'The men must be thinking me a useless article. My promises have come to naught once more, but I did so want to get along to see you all.'

Next morning came yet another bumper letter from D.M., enclosing an account of the reunion and a souvenir menu signed by the lads. Sir George wrote back, apologising for being such a 'nuisance' and hoping that he would soon be well enough to travel. The following week brought many more notes, all wishing him the best for a full recovery. On the evening of 26 December he took a bundle of these into his study to look at before he retired. The room was snug, furnished as a library, with a pair of padded chairs beside the fire. It was his habit to sit late, reading or listening to the wireless through his headphones. The threadbare tartan rug that kept him warm on active service was tucked around his knees. There were old familiar faces in the coals. At 11.30 Gladys came in to get him up for bed. He was sound asleep. She pressed his shoulder. There was no response. He died shortly after midnight.

✳ ✳ ✳

'You might have thought the King had passed away.' I lost count of the number of people who told me that. The capital was draped in mourning black. There was a feeling of shock, for all through his illness the *Torluish* despatches remained optimistic, hinting at an eventual return to the public domain. Sir George seemed indestructible. Among the many tributes in the local and national press was the following passage from the leader column of the *Evening News*:

> The Great War roused McCrae to martial action. His raising of the 16th Royal Scots (McCrae's Battalion) was a swift, dramatic stroke. The men flocked to his standard. Famous footballers left their training quarters for the billets and the parade ground. The voluntary principle was splendidly maintained through those amazing days and a stalwart leader marched proudly at the head of a battalion that was a credit to Edinburgh. The moral left by this

273

life is the old classical adage that the Gods sell everything for hard work. Sir George was always a trier. He was never discouraged by transient failure. He kept at it and won through. He was kindly and genial. There was nothing of the stern martinet about him. To the working classes he was a real comrade, and to the cause of democracy he was always true.

On the afternoon of 28 December, the Colonel finally caught his Edinburgh train. From Waverley the coffin was conveyed to Piershill Barracks, where an honour party from the 1st Royal Scots was waiting to see it through the night. Around 7 p.m. Sandy Yule turned up with a small group of 16th veterans. After a short but civil exchange, the regulars withdrew to the guardroom in search of their officer. Ten minutes later a captain appeared, flanked by two burly corporals. Sandy and his mates would not be moved. It was 10 a.m. next day before the enemy was sighted again, approaching in force across the parade-ground. McCrae's stood to their positions. There was a sharp knock at the door. Sandy asked the soldiers what they wanted. The provost sergeant cleared his throat. 'We've brought you in some breakfast,' he said quietly.

Then the gun carriage arrived, drawn by four black horses. A Union flag was draped across the coffin. On top were laid the Colonel's medals, his sword and the battered glengarry he had worn at Scots Redoubt. It was raining now, a cold persistent drizzle. At 12.30 p.m. they set off for Lady Glenorchy's Church in Roxburgh Place, where Sir George was an elder – the battalion's official chapel during its Edinburgh days. As the cortège emerged into Portobello Road, another 50 veterans fell in behind; by the time they reached Abbeyhill, the followers exceeded 200. All along the route, the pavements were blocked by people dressed in mourning. In the Canongate there was barely room to pass. They climbed into the High Street and turned left onto South Bridge. John Veitch recalled the silence. 'It was eerie,' he said. 'There was nothing but the horseshoes and the trundle of the wheels. I never even heard a cough.' At Lady Glenorchy's the family was waiting. Herbert Warden helped to carry the coffin inside.

The service was conducted by Jimmy Black. Afterwards the coffin was replaced on the gun carriage and the cortège set off for Grange Cemetery along Nicolson Street, Clerk Street and Newington Road. It was the best part of two miles and every inch was crowded. One estimate put the total at well over 100,000 souls. Sir George was laid to rest beside his wife while a piper played 'The Flowers o the Forest'. It wasn't Willie Duguid. Two days later, at Bangour Hospital, Duggie died, aged 53, of general paralysis related to his wartime tribulations. He was latterly employed as a messenger; the money was poor and his wife couldn't afford a headstone. On 5 January 1929 he was buried at Piershill in an unmarked grave.[14]

❈ ❈ ❈

The Great War continued to claim its victims long after the Armistice. With a little help from cruel fate. Jimmy Crawford, wounded in the hip near Contalmaison, died of septic poisoning in March 1919. He was still only 21. Five months later Joe Jardine, the Colonel's servant, died of gas-related pneumonia. Jim Steuart died in May 1920 of a brain haemorrhage resulting from his Arras wounds. He had been suffering from blinding headaches and the military doctors insisted his complaint was imaginary. In November 1921 Bob Bird, the only member of the Cow-punchers to come home unscathed, was crushed during an underground accident in his Addiewell shale pit. He died two weeks later at Edinburgh Royal Infirmary. Robert Husband, the battalion's Transport Officer, died of a stroke in 1923. He was 29. Ralph Armstrong, a B Company subaltern who married John McCartney's daughter in 1915, died insane in July 1925. He was wounded in the face in 1916 and never recovered. Bob Mercer died of heart failure in April 1926 while making a guest appearance for Hearts at an exhibition match at Selkirk. He had been severely gassed in 1918 with the Royal Garrison Artillery. Although he returned to Tynecastle post-war, he was (said the *News*) 'no more than a ghost of his former self'. Donald Gunn died on 14 May 1930 – the same day as Charlie Robertson. Crossan held on till 1933. He had finally married Alice seven years earlier after what he claimed was 'the longest engagement in Scottish history'. After leaving Hearts, he bought a public house in Rose Street and proceeded to ruin it by standing drinks for his numerous friends. A factor was brought in to steady the ship and Pat was just starting to prosper when the chlorine caught up with him. Pulmonary tuberculosis was diagnosed and he died that April at Southfield Sanitorium in Liberton. The funeral was not quite on the Colonel's scale but the turn-out was spectacular. The handsomest man in the world might just have been the best-liked one as well.

McCartney was already away. He had succumbed to diabetes in January. After leaving Tynecastle (where he was succeeded by his son Willie), he was lured out of retirement by Portsmouth. When he arrived at the club, it was struggling in the Third Division; he left it, seven years later, in the First. A short spell with Luton Town was ended by illness and the amputation of his right leg. He returned to Edinburgh, where he bolstered his meagre savings by contributing a regular column to the *Daily Express*. In 1930 he wrote and published the first history of the Scottish League and became a familiar figure on the correspondence pages of Scottish newspapers under the pseudonym 'Sir Gorgon Zola'. He continued to watch Hearts but had to pay at the turnstile: a complimentary season-ticket was apparently out of the question. The board didn't even offer him a benefit match.

McCartney's 1914 'family' was cursed. Seven of them, including Alex Lyon (Duckworth's assistant) died in the war. Duckie himself never recovered from the pneumonia contracted on one of Fred Muir's abominable marches: he passed away in August 1920. Crossan and Mercer are mentioned above. Peter Nellies, the vice-captain, died in a motorcycle accident in 1930. Harry Graham was finally beaten by his asthma in 1940. Annan Ness died of cancer in an Edinburgh nursing home two years later. Bob Preston moved to Northern Ireland, where he ran a pub in County Antrim. He died in May 1945. Norman Findlay, the reserve goalkeeper, never did get to France. He was a carpenter to trade and late in 1916 he was released from the Army to work in a Newcastle shipyard. He moved to Isleworth in Middlesex post-war and found a job repairing barges on the Thames. He died in 1949, two months before Elias Furst.

Alfie Briggs recovered from his wounds but never played football again. In his spare time he did a bit of scouting for Partick Thistle. His only vice was a weekly pools coupon. He suffered spells of black depression, especially around 1 July and Remembrance Day. When he died in 1950, he still had two machine-gun bullets lodged near his spine. Harry Lorimer went to his funeral. Harry remained blissfully married to Isabella until his death in 1953.[15] Isa survived until 1980 and continued to talk to him every day. Willie Wilson remained with Hearts until 1923. Following his retirement he ran a sweetie shop in Bristo, then moved to Stretford in Manchester to work at his trade as a tinsmith. He died shortly after Hearts won the Scottish Cup in 1956.

Passed over by the Hearts directors in 1919, Jamie Low was snapped up by Newcastle United and became a star of their great team of the '20s, playing regularly alongside the peerless Hughie Gallagher. In 1930 he returned to Elgin and took over the family net-manufacturing business. His only son, David, was posted missing while serving with the Manchester Regiment in Singapore in 1942. Jimmy died in 1960. Jim Frew joined Leeds United after the war. His career was curtailed by injury and he opened a sports outfitters in the town, combining the business with a second career as a trainer. He climbed through the ranks to become the FA's chief coach in West Yorkshire and helped Jack Charlton (among others) to make his first move into management. He died in 1967. Wattie Scott became a publican in Edinburgh and achieved brief fame in 1974 when he was hailed as Tynecastle's oldest surviving player. He died the following year, still full of tales of Crossan and McCartney and the season that they should have won the League. The last survivor was Bob Malcolm from Loanhead, who wore Harry Wattie's jersey several times. Bob had a short spell with Airdrie after the war, then returned to the Burghlee coal pit. He died in 1979. Of Teddy McGuire, nothing is known: he disappears in 1918 and is never seen again.

❈ ❈ ❈

In July 1936 twenty former members of McCrae's Battalion travelled to France for the twentieth anniversary of the first day of the Battle of the Somme. A commemorative photograph was taken on the edge of the great crater at la Boisselle.[16] It was the summer of the Berlin Olympics; Hitler was in his ascendancy and war clouds were again gathering over the shattered Continent. Alfred Warr died in September following an operation at Middlesex Hospital on the duodenal ulcer that had troubled him since his imprisonment. Three years later the activities of the 16th Royal Scots Association were suspended 'due to the *resumption* [author's italics] of hostilities'. Some of the lads tried to re-enlist: most made it only so far as the Home Guard. John Wilson, one of Duggie's side-drummers, was 46 but looked much younger. He marched into the recruiting office in Cockburn Street, claimed to be 37 and was accepted at once. That winter was bitterly cold; he contracted pneumonia while stationed on the Forth island of Inchcolm and passed away in the hospital at Edinburgh Castle on 6 February 1940. He is the only McCrae's veteran known to have died on active service in the Second World War.[17]

Gerald Crawford, absurdly busy till the end, died in 1942. His symphonic poem was finished but has never been performed. Archie Ewing died of coal-gas poisoning in his Rankeillor Street flat in January 1944. Almost completely blind and suffering from depression, he took his own life. Seventeen suicides have been identified among battalion veterans in the thirty years after 1918: there were probably more.

Andrew Whyte died on 8 May 1945 – 'Victory in Europe Day'. He was still employed at the Royal Infirmary. Herbert Warden died in 1946, a respected solicitor and loyal supporter of the Scottish Limbless Ex-Servicemen's Association. George Cowan worked as a Hoover agent in England and America. He died in 1947. Jimmy Black became minister of St George's West in Edinburgh and held generations spellbound with his sermons. In 1938 he was appointed Moderator of the General Assembly, in which capacity he had occasion to visit Germany. Appalled by the treatment of the Jews, he returned home and denounced the Nazi regime at every opportunity. In 1942 the King invited him to serve as one of his personal chaplains. He died in October 1949; *The Scotsman* carried the following 'appreciation':

How he will be missed in this city that he loved. That familiar
figure with its buoyant, eager step; the striking face crowned with
the gleaming white hair; the instant greeting of a truly friendly
spirit; the boyish zest and characteristic gestures. Here was a
personality vivid and powerful, and it is not easy to think of him as
gone from our midst. But we remember gratefully how much he has
given, and still more how much cannot be taken away.[18]

Andrew Riddell also died that autumn. His place as honorary secretary of
the Battalion Association was taken by Sandy Lindsay, who was now the
clerk of works at Fettes College. One of Sandy's first duties was to
announce the death of Arthur Stephenson, who passed away after a game of
bowls in March 1950. In 1919 Steve had returned to Rhodesia; initially he
tried his hand at farming but gave that up in 1925 to join the police. In 1930
he became general manager of the Native Labour Association and
commanded a division of the East African forces during the second war. He
maintained an irregular correspondence with D.M. Sutherland and wrote
that he hoped to make an appearance at the 1954 reunion. That dinner went
ahead without him but drew a record attendance of 127 veterans and 10
guests — a tribute to 12 months of arm-twisting and detective work by
Lindsay, who pulled out all the stops to counter the increasing effects of
illness and death. Fred Muir's name was scored from the list in 1953. He
had spent 30 years as a traffic manager in Burntisland shipyard.

Bob Martin died in 1961 after a decade of painful arthritis. Bill
Robertson, Dick Lauder and Willie Gavin followed in rapid succession.
George Blaney, the battalion bard, died in Glasgow in 1963. He had been
discharged as an invalid and never worked again; indeed he spent much of
the remainder of his life in bed, where (among other things) he
manufactured wooden doll's houses which were sold to Lewis's department
store to defray the domestic expenses. After his death, dozens of notebooks
were destroyed: just a fragment of his output has survived.

Michael Kelly died in 1964 in his daughter's home at Maryfield. Jimmy
Moir, who almost died in 1916, held on till 1965 – as did Fraser MacLean
and Jimmy Brown. Brown had a spell in America between the wars and
visited California. If he is to be believed, Clark Gable, Jimmy Stewart and
Errol Flynn blew a collective sigh of relief when he decided not to remain
in Hollywood. 'I had offers,' he said mysteriously. 'But I was wanting
home.'[19] MacLean, it transpired, had brought some souvenirs back from
France. While clearing out his Fairmilehead bungalow, his son-in-law
discovered a selection of live shells and other assorted projectiles. The
Army was summoned and removed the cache to South Queensferry, where
a controlled explosion sent shock waves through much of west Edinburgh.

In June 1967 former teacher Jimmy Wood died at the Royal Edinburgh Hospital for Mental Disorders in Morningside. There were bars on the window of his room. He had been ill since 1916, when he was blown up during a German bombardment near Armentières. Occasionally he was allowed out to visit his sister; her daughter recalls a gentle old man who brought along a gramophone to play his favourite records. Six months later Donald Munro died in Wales. He had been partially blind since he was gassed with Stephenson at Poelcappelle in 1917. Sandy Lindsay followed him in 1969. After his death, the complete written records and photographic archive of the 16th Royal Scots Association were accidentally destroyed.

Sandy Yule survived until 1970. He worked mainly as a commissionaire after the war, including a memorable spell at Tynecastle during the glorious '50s. No one there remembers him today. That same year saw the deaths of Willie Redden, Tom Teviotdale and Tommy Millar, who had helped each other crawl to safety in front of the Quadrangle machine-guns in July 1916. Redden died at home with his daughter beside him; Millar (who had become one of Britain's most respected general surgeons) died on holiday with his wife in Oban. Teviotdale died of malnutrition and neglect at his flat in the Edinburgh district of Sciennes. He never married and had no substantial family.

In May 1972 the 46th Annual Reunion Dinner took place at the Royal Scots Club. Only 28 members were fit to attend and they reluctantly decided that it was no longer possible to carry on. Some minor offence was caused by the *Evening News*, when its thin coverage of the occasion twice described McCrae's as the 'Hearts Battalion' – an expression not used once in 60 years. On behalf of his comrades, John Wylie (one of the lads lifted by Sandy Yule in Sausage Valley) wrote a letter to the editor, pointing out the error and explaining that the battalion was a broad church which was composed of players and followers of many different clubs and (for that matter) many different sports. His objections were not published and he did not receive a reply.[20]

In September 1972 Jim Davie died at Matatiele, near the town of Kokstad in Natal. After recovering from his wounds he had enrolled at Edinburgh University, where he joined the Athletic Club and became a member of the same mile relay squad as Eric Liddell. Following graduation he returned to South Africa to take over the family farm and kept in touch with the battalion through Arthur Stephenson. When the Colonel died, nothing more was ever heard. D.M. Sutherland (who missed the last reunion) passed away at Plockton on 20 September 1973 in his 91st year. In 1933 he was appointed head of Gray's School of Art in Aberdeen and in 1936 he was elected to the Royal Scottish Academy. Throughout his long life, he retained the same kindly modesty that endeared him to his friends in the battalion. He was a wonderful teller of tales. Even today his reputation as a painter continues to grow. In 1916 Bob Martin asked him what he would like to be remembered for. D.M.'s reply was typical: 'Nothing in particular,' he said. 'It would be nice just to be remembered, full stop.'

Percy Bayliss died in 1974. After demoblisation he dipped his toe into every conceivable kind of business. In 1937 he was manufacturing sectional wooden buildings at Rainham in Essex. The venture failed; had he kept it going until the war, military contracts would have made his fortune. In 1939 he re-enlisted and was sent to France to guard German prisoners. He returned home via Dunkirk, having become attached to a unit of the Middlesex Regiment during the chaos of evacuation. He was later posted as a staff colonel to the Middle East Supply Corps in Iraq, where problems developed due to food and other materials being diverted onto the black market. When Percy intervened, he became so unpopular with the local merchants that a price was placed on his head. He never expected to make it to 50.

In November 1975 former private Tom Litster passed away in Toronto. He emigrated after the war, worked as a travelling salesman in the Maritime Provinces and was eventually promoted to vice-president of the company. He was wounded in the shoulder and the heel near Croisilles and required continual treatment to his foot for the rest of his life. He never complained. The day before he died, he told his daughter: 'Weep no tears for me, lassie. Every day since 1918 has been a gift.'

The last of the survivors were dropping from the twig – John Veitch, Jimmy McEvoy, Murdie McKay and Jimmy Baigrie; Frank Weston and Andy Ramage, who shared the same shell-hole for nine days and nights and travelled together to the final reunion; Ned Barnie, who was the first Scot and the oldest person ever to swim the English Channel both ways. Leslie Kitton died in 1983. Having recovered from his wounds of 1 July, he transferred to the regular Army and secured a commission in the Beds and Herts Regiment. His 'Kitchener' engagement finally ended in 1946, when he retired to rear pigs and poultry at an old rectory in Kent. Donald McIntosh, the battalion's youngest volunteer, died in Toronto in 1990. One February evening that same year, Bobby Johnston was listening to the wireless at his retirement home in Bournemouth. Around 7 p.m. the telephone rang. He later told his son Gordon that it was someone from McCrae's. Gordon thought the old man had finally lost his marbles. No, insisted Bobby, the chap must have been in the battalion because he knew *everybody*. In any case he promised to call back, so the mystery would eventually be solved. Two nights later I rang again. It was the start of an unexpected friendship that lasted till he passed away in 1991.

❋ ❋ ❋

Cuthbert's uncle, Sir Oliver Lodge, the brilliant physicist and mathematician, believed that past and present coexist in the same place, separated only by the mysterious fourth dimension known as Time. If he was right, then even as you read these final words, there's a strange man following a marmalade cat all the way to Morningside.

McCrae's Battalion? You couldn't make it up.

16TH BATTALION
THE ROYAL SCOTS ASSOCIATION

CHAIRMAN
CHAS. S. ANDERSON

HON. SECRETARY AND TREASURER
ALEX. LINDSAY
9 Davidson Road, Edinburgh, 4

COMMITTEE
ANDREW F. ALLAN
GEORGE NESS
ROBERT PURDOM
JOHN W. REID
WILLIAM YEAMAN
ALEX. YULE

16th (S) Bn. THE ROYAL SCOTS
THE ROYAL REGIMENT

31st Annual

Reunion Dinner

IN

THE ROYAL SCOTS CLUB
ABERCROMBY PLACE, EDINBURGH

ON

FRIDAY, 13th DECEMBER, 1957
6.45 p.m. for 7 p.m.

Menu

Cream of Tomato Soup

Steak Pie

Mashed Potatoes

Carrot and Peas

Trifle and Ice Cream

Coffee

Toast List

The Queen
"LEST WE FORGET"

THE BATTALION — WILLIAM E. BARNIE
Reply — ROBERT GORDON

THE COMMITTEE — J. W. MOIR
Reply — SANDY YULE

THE CHAIRMAN — WM. S. GAVIN

ARTISTES — A. F. ALLAN

Chairman
T. McW. MILLAR, F.R.C.S.E.

Menu card for the 1957 Reunion Dinner

Postscript and Acknowledgements

This book was 12 years in the making. I have been told on numerous occasions that the tale of how *McCrae's Battalion* came to be written is worthy of a volume on its own. (I fear that some folk have a rather romantic notion of the rigours of historical research.) A brief explanation of why the work took so long may be of interest, none the less.

Sir George's desire to establish a permanent element of pilgrimage as part of the commemorative effort was borne of much more than a post-Edwardian love of sentiment and ceremony. The Colonel was wise enough to see that once the Great War generation had passed on, there would be no one left who knew what really happened. It was incumbent, therefore, on the survivors to ensure that necessary steps were taken to prevent the story of the 16th from slipping into the past. The creation of a unique and 'living' memorial would have been the foundation upon which much else could be built – an archive, a photographic record, newspaper articles, a dedicated book; an ongoing interest in the battalion that would effectively keep it alive for subsequent generations and serve as a 'fitting' tribute to the lads who had sacrificed their lives. 'Fitting' was one of his favourite words.

Sadly the High Kirk plaque was as far as matters went. St Giles Cathedral is an important building but it is not well frequented by the general public. Placing the memorial on a dark interior wall has turned out to be a little bit like storing it in a dusty old attic. No one in the city knows it's there. The battalion's Edinburgh cairn (and its Contalmaison twin) would have been impossible to miss. D.M. Sutherland also favoured a witty and innovative addition in the form of a life-size bronze of a 'loafing' private to be placed somewhere in the High Street at pavement level ('not on a plinth or a pylon'), where he would become a familiar and 'weel-kent'

282

face. Crossan and Brown were suggested as models, along with Murdo McLeod ('Scotland's Strongest Man') who was killed at Wood Alley. Again the proposal came to nothing.

By 1990, when I began this project, the memory of McCrae's was hanging from the cliff-top by its elderly fingertips. *Nothing* had survived; indeed Sir George himself might never have existed. None of the Edinburgh libraries, archives or museums had a single relevant item. Nor did any national institution – including the Regiment itself. The Royal Scots own archive is substantial. Unfortunately the 'Service' battalions have been badly neglected, so that very little material survives from these units. In the case of the 16th, this translates into one solitary photograph: there are no letters, personal diaries or other information relating (for example) to its raising. The regiment has retained a copy of each battalion's daily Intelligence Summary or 'War Diary', but these (like the originals in the Public Record Office) are 'weeded' versions from which 'Part Two Orders', (most) Operation Orders and (almost all) appendices have been removed. Instead of a sheet of foolscap typescript for each day, we are left with perhaps half a dozen lines. McCrae's diary was compiled by Bill Robertson, Bill McCarthy and Percy Bayliss. It is an above average specimen, but still (for the most part) no more than a thin guide to geographical movement and commissioned comings and goings. A vast volume of historically valuable paperwork was simply thrown away.

There was a similar problem at Tynecastle. This is not unrelated to McCartney's early departure after the war. Most of the thousands of letters received during the conflict were addressed directly to the manager, so he took them with him when he left. Decades of neglect by consecutive boards simply helped the process along, so that all that now survives from 1914 is one obscure (and quite misleading) entry in the boardroom minutes. During the late 1960s the club stopped organising the annual Armistice Day ceremony at its Haymarket memorial, passing their responsibility to the local representatives of the Salvation Army. Attendances dwindled alarmingly. By the 1970s only a very few wreaths were being laid: among others, those of Celtic, Hibernian, the SFA and the Scottish League disappeared around this time. On one memorable occasion, Hearts themselves forgot to send a tribute. The occasion has since been rekindled, but still leaves much to be desired. What used to be a simple Church of Scotland service of remembrance now resembles nothing so much as a meeting of the Band of Hope, complete with cymbals and trombones.

The problem at the outset, therefore, was how to conjure a book out of nothing. It occurred to me that there *was* a vast archive of research material out there – if it could only be assembled. The key was the nominal roll. The original battalion lists were destroyed immediately after the war; while platoon and company roll-books from the active service period were routinely discarded when the information they carried became outdated, that is when all the names had been scored through with blue indelible pencil. If, however, a nominal roll of the original battalion could somehow be *reconstructed*, it might be possible to trace the families of the members and (by so doing) gather their memories, their letters, their photos or whatever else they might have preserved.

This was the starting point. A tentative 'block' of regimental numbers was identified from the 'Killed' lists in *Soldiers Died*. The gaps were then slowly 'filled in' by searching the War Office casualty returns which appeared daily in *The Scotsman* until early 1918. These listed casualties in various categories, including 'Missing', 'Wounded', 'Shell-Shocked' or 'Prisoners of War'. Publication of the same information continued until well into 1919 under the War Office's own imprint. Contemporary Rolls of Honour and Rolls of Service for schools, churches and businesses were also consulted. Finally the Great War medal entitlement rolls at the Public Record Office added a few unwounded survivors who had otherwise slipped through the net. By the end of 3 years, almost 1,200 of the battalion's original 1,392 members had been identified by name. The problem now was to learn a bit about them and (if possible) identify their next of kin. Over a hundred newspapers in the UK and beyond carried appeals for information. Their assistance was invaluable:

Aberdeen Evening Express; Advertiser (Adelaide); *Advertiser* (Midlothian); *Aldershot News; Ashbourne News; Aussie Post; Australasian Post; Ayr Advertiser; Ayrshire Post; Bedfordshire Times; Belfast Morning News; Birmingham Evening Mail; Border Telegraph; Brechin Advertiser; Camberley News; Cambridge Evening News; Cape Times* (South Africa); *Countryman* (Australia); *Courier-Mail* (Brisbane); *Cumberland News; Cumnock Chronicle; Daily Record* (Glasgow); *Delta Optimist* (Canada); *Dumfries Courier; Dumfries and Galloway Standard; Dundalk Democrat; Dunfermline Press; East Fife Mail; East Hants Observer; Eastern Evening News* (Norwich); *Edgeware and Mill Hill Times; Evening Chronicle* (Newcastle); *Evening Herald* (Dublin); *Evening News* (Edinburgh); *Evening Press* (York); *Evening Telegraph and Post* (Dundee/Fife); *Evening Times* (Glasgow); *Express and Echo* (Exeter); *Falkirk Herald; Farmer* (Zimbabwe); *Farmer's Weekly* (South Africa); *Fife Free Press; Globe and Mail* (Toronto); *Hemel Hempstead Gazette; Herald* (Zimbabwe); *Herald Sun* (Melbourne); *High Wycombe Leader; Home Front* (South Africa); *Inverness Courier; Irish News; Jersey Evening Post; John o' Groat Journal; Kent and Sussex Courier; Kilmarnock Standard; Kokstad Advertiser* (South Africa); *Lancashire Evening Post; Lancaster Guardian; Life and Work; Liverpool Echo; Lothian Courier; Mississauga Booster* (Canada); *Mississauga News* (Canada); *Manchester Evening News; Motherwell Times; New Zealand Farmer;*

News Guardian (Whitley Bay); *News Post Leader* (Blyth); *North Delta Sentinel* (Canada); *North Devon Gazette*; *North Devon Journal*; *Northern Echo*; *Orcadian*; *Otago Daily Times* (New Zealand); *Oxford Mail*; *Peebleshire News*; *Perthshire Advertiser*; *Press and Journal* (Aberdeen); *Quebec Chronicle Telegraph*; *Saskatoon Sun* (Canada); *Scottish Sunday Express*; *Selby Chronicle*; *Selby Times*; *Sheerness Times Guardian*; *South Australian Weekly News*; *Southern Reporter*; *Spectator* (Canada); *Stanmore Observer*; *Sunday Post*; *Surrey Comet*; *Surrey Advertiser*; *Surrey County Magazine*; *Sutton Borough Guardian*; *Uttoxeter Advertiser*; *Wallingford Herald*; *Waterford News and Star*; *Wellington Evening Post* (New Zealand); *West Australian*; *West Australian Mining Chronicle*; *Weston Mercury*; *Willowdale, Scarborough and North York Mirror* (Canada); *Windsor Express*; *Yorkshire Evening Press*.

❋ ❋ ❋

The cooperation of the following libraries and other assorted institutions is also gratefully acknowledged:

Aberdeen Central Library; Advocates Library; Airdrieonians FC; Albion Rovers FC; Alloa Athletic FC; Alloa Library; American Battle Monuments Commission; Army Records Office; Australian Consulate (Edinburgh); Australian War Memorial; Ayr Library; Bathgate Library Headquarters; Bedford Local Archives; Belfast Central Library; Berwick Library; Blyth Spartans AFC; Borders Regional Library; Boroughmuir School; British Legion; British Library Newspaper Collection; British Limbless Ex-Servicemen's Association; Camberley Information Centre; Canadian High Commission; Carlisle Library; Central Regional Council Archives; Chartered Society of Physiotherapy; City of Sunderland Central Library; Commonwealth War Graves Commission; Coventry City FC; Craigton Cemetery Company; Cumnock District Library; Dalkeith Library; Daniel Stewart's and Melville College; Dumfries Archive Centre; Dumfries Library; Dundalk Library; Dundee District Archive; Dundee FC; Duns Library; Edinburgh and District Trades Council; Edinburgh College of Art; Edinburgh Central Library (Edinburgh and Reference Rooms); Edinburgh City Museums; Edinburgh University Library (Medical Archivist/Special Collections); Eton College; Everton FC; Faculty of Advocates; Family Record Centre, London; Galashiels Library; George Watson's College; General Register Office, Dublin; General Register Office, Northern Ireland; General Register Office, Scotland; George Heriot's School; George Heriot's Trust; Glamis Castle; Glasgow University Archives; Grampian Regional Archives; Gray's School of Art; Greenock Morton FC; Haddington Library; Hawick Library; Heart of Midlothian

FC; Heriot Watt University Archives; Highland Regional Council Archives; Imperial War Museum; Irish Record Office; King's College London/Liddell Hart Centre; Kirkcaldy Central Library; Leeds Library; Leith Public Library; Liverpool FC; Liverpool Record Office; Mexican Embassy, London; Midlothian Local Studies Centre; Mississauga Library; Mitchell Library, Glasgow; Morningside Cemetery Company; Mount Vernon Cemetery; Motherwell Museums and Heritage Service; Musselburgh Library; National Archives of Canada; National Library of Scotland; National Maritime Museum; National Register of Archives (Scotland); Newcastle United FC; North Yorkshire County Library; Old Gala Club; Orkney Archives; Oxford University Archives; Penicuik Library; Perth Library; Piershill Cemetery Company; Public Record Office, Kew; Queen's University, Belfast; Raith Rovers FC; Riksarkivet, Oslo; Roslin Library; Royal Consulate General of Norway; Royal College of Surgeons, London; Royal College of Surgeons, Edinburgh; Royal (Dick) Veterinary College Library; Royal Infirmary of Edinburgh; Royal Military Academy, Sandhurst; Royal Scots Club; Royal Scots Regimental HQ; St Andrew's University Library; St John's College, Waterford; Salvation Army; Scottish Football League; Scottish Hockey Union; Scottish National Portrait Gallery; Scottish National War Memorial; Scottish Record Office; Scottish Reformation Society; Scottish United Services Museum Library; Shetland Archives; Skattedirektorat, Oslo; South Leith Church; Strathclyde Police Personnel Department; Sutton Borough Heritage Department; Thomas Alleyne's School; Trinity College, Dublin; Tunbridge Wells Library; World Ship Society.

❋ ❋ ❋

The descendants of more than a thousand of the men who served in McCrae's have now been traced. Ultimately, most of them were found by using the 'statutory' records of births, deaths and marriages at the General Register Office in Edinburgh and the Family Record Centre in London. It was a slow and laborious task, lightened only by the keenness of people to cooperate once they knew what I was doing. Elderly spinsters climbed the ladders to their lofts for the first time in years to search for the biscuit tin that might contain a long-forgotten studio portrait of a young man in khaki. So far as I am aware, there were no serious casualties, although one redoubtable old lady nearly blew her foot off when she found her father's revolver. A 'nice young policeman' got a cup of tea and a Mills bomb when he turned up to take it away. Letters, diaries, postcards and photographs began appearing in welcome profusion and I am reliably informed that the resulting archive now makes the 16th Royal Scots (by some distance) the best-recorded battalion of the Great War. It was originally my intention to close with an alphabetical list of all those individuals who were kind enough to help. Since the total climbed past 3,000, however, this has become impractical. Many of the battalion relatives and other contacts have become friends. To all of them, I extend my thanks, my best wishes, and the earnest hope that they will consider this volume worthy of its subject. One day, hopefully far off, I may bump into Mr Muir and I wouldn't like to think he'd be unhappy.

I am also grateful to Andrew Swanston, Toby Long and David Archibald of 'Photo Express' for the skill with which they handled many hundreds of precious and delicate photographs. They, too, became friends over the years; Toby introduced me to Photoshop and collaborated in the design of the jacket. He deserves the credit for all the clever bits: I was merely looking over his shoulder. The 'poster' of Sir George on the front of the jacket evolved over time from the half-tone image on a 1914 recruiting card; the *pickelhaube* figure on the dedication page was drawn by Fred Bland, who was killed near Albert in June 1916. Fred is also responsible for the cartoons on pages 8 and 12. I take the blame for everything else.

Finally, I owe an incalculable debt to Margaret Alexander, who acted as an unpaid assistant, sounding board and general dogsbody throughout the course of this endless project. I have long since lost count of the number of telephone messages she took while I was wandering around the country and of the number of families she befriended and sandwiches she made. She died within sight of the finish, just as the final chapter got underway. This is her book as well.

Thanks, Mum; I couldn't have done it without you.

Appendix 1

16ᵀᴴ ROYAL SCOTS, DECEMBER 1914

(a) 16th Royal Scots: other ranks by *Age on Enlistment*

Ages	Number of Men	No. of Men as % of 1,009	%age projected to battalion (1,347 men)
15 and under	4	0.40	5
16 to 18	145	14.37	194
19 to 23	419	41.52	559
24 to 28	228	22.60	304
29 to 33	105	10.41	140
34 to 38	76	7.53	102
39 to 43	21	2.08	28
44 to 48	11	1.09	15
Total	1,009	100	1,347

Data for this table was compiled by checking the birth certificates of 1,009 original members of the battalion. Rounded figures for each year of age are as follows (extrapolated in bold): 15 (4/**5**); 16 (14/**19**); 17 (42/**56**); 18 (89/**119**); 19 (87/**116**); 20 (112/**150**); 21 (93/**124**); 22 (78/**104**); 23 (49/**66**); 24 (66/**88**); 25 (56/**75**); 26 (46/**62**); 27 (28/**37**); 28 (32/**43**); 29 (30/**40**); 30 (21/**28**); 31 (16/**21**); 32 (16/**21**); 33 (22/**29**); 34 (24/**32**); 35 (21/**28**); 36 (10/**13**); 37 (10/**13**); 38 (11/**15**); 39 (6/**8**); 40 (6/**8**); 41(6/**8**); 42 (0/**0**); 43 (3/**4**); 44 (0/**0**); 45 (1/**1**); 46 (2/**3**); 47 (3/**4**); 48 (5/**7**). It will be seen that most of the volunteers fell into the age group 18 to 22: this was a *young* man's battalion.

(b) 16ᵗʰ Royal Scots: all 45 'original' officers by *Age on Enlistment*

18 (2); 19 (1); 20 (7); 21 (3); 23 (3); 24 (3); 25 (4); 28 (2); 29 (5); 30 (3); 31 (1); 32 (3); 34 (3); 36 (1); 37 (2); 41 (1); 54 (1).

On Sir George McCrae's instructions no one under the age of 16 was permitted to remain in the battalion. Birth certificates of all suspicious cases were checked within days of mobilisation, and around 30 youngsters dismissed 'with the City's thanks'. Such thoroughness was far from uniform in the New Army. From the table, it would seem that no more than five boys slipped through the net. The identities of four of them have been established and, in fairness to the recruiting clerks, at least three of them looked substantially older than their true age. At the other end of the scale, several men *under* stated their age in order to enlist. The names of the youngest and oldest volunteers are given below:

Name	Address/Occupation	Date of Birth	Age*
Alfred Donald McIntosh	14 Salisbury Street/schoolboy	7/10/99	15/54
James Alexander Hutcheson	81 Henderson Row/schoolboy	13/7/99	15/143
Cecil Dunbar Nisbet ★★	33 Hillside Crescent/schoolboy	8/4/99	15/234
Charles Hastings Hyslop★★	60 Montgomery Street/schoolboy	17/3/99	15/261
George McCrae	61 Grange Loan/civil servant	29/8/60	54/90
Norman Joseph Blair	8 Prospect Terrace/compositor	25/12/65	48/330
William Richard Littlejohn	33 Dean Park/shoe-maker	3/4/66	48/241
James Thomson	197 Dalry Road/oatmeal miller	28/11/66	48
Patrick Courtney	Anisfield Mains, Haddington/cattleman	2/12/66	48/13
Philip Ovenstone	8 West Newington Place/bookbinder	11/12/66	48/4
John Witherspoon★★	105 St Leonard's Street/housepainter	27/5/67	47/187
Robert George Rae Miller★★	3 Tower Street, Selkirk/commissionaire	30/5/67	47/184
Edwin A. Hart	18 Lothian Street/umbrella-maker	24/12/67	47
Gerald Walker Crawford	21 Windsor Street/consulting engineer	3/9/68	46/91
David Brabner★★★	7 (a) Leslie Place/plasterer	18/8/68	46/43

*Age on *date of enlistment* – years and days.

★★ **Cecil Nisbet** was killed in action on 1/7/16, the battalion's youngest fatality. He has no known grave and is therefore commemorated on the Thiepval Memorial. **Charlie Hyslop** died on 12/9/18 of wounds received while serving with 13th RS. He is buried at Noux-les-Mines Communal Cemetery Extension, near Bethune. **Jock Witherspoon** was the oldest wartime fatality. He was gassed in 1917 and died of heart failure on 2/5/18, having recently been discharged from the Labour Corps. He is buried at Newington Cemetery in Edinburgh. **Robert Miller** was the oldest man to lose his life while serving with McCrae's. He was killed in action on 29/5/16 (see Chapter Seven) and is buried at Albert Communal Cemetery Extension.

★★★**Archie Brabner**, David's only son (born 1/10/99), tried to volunteer with him. He was turned away. In June 1915 he tried again, claiming to be 20, and was accepted. He served briefly with his father in C Company but was left at Heriot's with the reserve when McCrae's went to Ripon. He joined the battalion in France and may have been present on 1 July when his father was killed. He was wounded late in 1916. Transferred to the Scottish Rifles, he was promoted to sergeant and died of wounds on 26/4/18. **William James Rankine** of 60 Strathearn Road (born 12/5/00), also tried to volunteer in November 1914. He claimed to be a dental student and member of the Officer Training Corps. He was turned away, but succeeded with the same story in June 1915. Unlike Brabner, he accompanied the battalion to Ripon. In September 1915 he was transferred to the 34th Division Cyclist Corps and accompanied them to France in January 1916. He served abroad until September 1916, when his parents secured his discharge. He re-enlisted in January 1918 and was commissioned as a Flying Officer in the Royal Naval Air Service.

(c) 16ᵗʰ Royal Scots: other ranks by *Civilian Occupation* (based on 1,084 of the 1,347 'original' volunteers)

Accountants (3); agricultural student (1); architects (2); architectural sculptors (3); art college lecturer (1); art college student (1); asylum attendants (3); auctioneer's clerks (2).

Bakers (13); bank clerks (16); barmen (6); biscuit maker (1); blacksmiths (6); boilermakers (4); bookbinders (11); booksellers (1); boot operator (1); boots (1); brass finishers (2); bricklayers (3); brickworks contractor (1); butchers (12); butler (1).

Cable greaser (1); can/pipe-maker (1); cattleman (1); carter (1); cello player (1); Chamberlain's clerk (1); chauffeurs (3) chemical engineer (1); chemical worker (1); chimney sweep (1); civil servants (4); chromo-lithographer/engraver (1); chef (1); clerk typists (2); cloth lappers (2); coalmen (2); coal miners (59); colour grinder (1); cook (1); coopers (7); coppersmith (1); commissionaires (2); commercial travellers (9); consulting engineer (1).

Delivery boy (1); dental student (1); distillery workers (4); drapers (5); draughtsman (1); dyer (1).

Electrical engineers (7); electric lamp trimmers (3); engineer's driller (1); engineer's fireman (1); explosives makers (2).

Factory workers (3); farmers (7); farmer's labourers (6); fish-market salesman (1); flour miller (1); footman (1); foundryman (1); fruit rancher (1); furniture salesmen (2).

Gamekeepers (5); gardeners (10); gas-fitter (1); glass blowers (4); glazier (1); golf-club maker (1); GPO parcels clerk (1); GPO sorters (3); GPO postmen (7); greenkeepers (2); grocers (30); groom (1); ground-nut planter (1).

Hairdressers (8) ham curer (1); Higher Grade students (21); hotelier (1); house factor (1); housepainters (16).

Ice-skating instructor (1); insurance clerks (14); insurance agents (5); iron-dresser (1); ironmonger's assistants (9); ironmoulders (5); ironworks fitters (3).

Janitor (1); jewellers (2); joiners/cabinet-makers (28); journalist (1).

Labourers (29); law apprentices (2); law clerks (11); librarians (5); lithographer's draughtsman (1); locomotive engine cleaners (2); lorrymen (2).

Maltmen (4); marine engineer (1); market gardener (1); mechanical engineers (16); mercantile clerks (89); messengers (2); ministers of the Kirk (3); monumental sculptor (1); motor-bus driver (1); municipal clerks (2); music hall artiste (1).

Newsagent (1); nurseryman (1).

Oatmeal miller (1); oilworkers (4); organ builder (1); ornamental wood-carver (1).

Paper cutters (3); paper-makers (14); paper rollers (2); paper ruler (1); paper-mill electrician (1); paper-mill firemen (3); park-keeper (1); pawnbroker's clerk (1); pharmacist (1); photo-engraver (1); piggery manager (1); plasterers (2); plumbers (16); plumber's merchant (1); police constables (5); porters (7); pottery worker (1); power-loom tenters (11); printer/compositors (39); printer/letterpress (10); printer/lithographers (9); printer/monotype operators (5); printer/linotype operators (4); printer/stereotyper (2); printer's artist (1); printer's colour etcher (1); printer's labourers (2); printer's machinemen (15); professional golfer (1); professional footballers (30); publisher (1).

Railway servants (7); railway stokers (3); railway surfacemen (2); railway-engine driver (1); railway-wagon examiners (2); restaurateur (1); roadman (1); rubber planter (1); rubber-workers (10).

Saddler (1); Salvation Army officer (1); saw-maker (1); scavengers (4); schoolmasters (18); scientific-instrument maker (1); seaman (1); seedsman (1); self-employed shopkeepers

(8); shale miners (18); Sheriff's clerk (1); shipbuilder's platers (2); shipbuilder's riveter (1); shipwright (1); ship's officer (1); shoe-makers (6); shoe repairer (1); shop assistants (52); slaughtermen (2); solicitors (7); stableman (1); stationers (2); steelworker (1); steel pattern-maker (1); stone sawyer (1); stonemasons (13); storeman (1); stoker (1); surveyor (1).

Tailors (6); tailor's cutters (3); telegram boy (1); telephone operator (1); tile fixers (3); tinsmiths (2); training college students (10); tram-car motormen (2); typefounder's foreman (1).

Umbrella maker (1); upholsterers (8); undergraduates (26).

Valets (2); van-man (1).

Waiters (3); warehousemen (18); watch-makers (2); wire-makers (2); wood sawyer (1).

(d) 16ᵗʰ Royal Scots: all 45 'original' officers by *Civilian Occupation*

Advocate (1); agriculture students (2); apprentice solicitors (2); architect (1); art college lecturer (1); bank clerks (3); civil servant (1); Chamberlain's clerk (1); company directors (2); electrical/ mechanical engineer (1); factory manager (1); insurance clerks (2); insurance inspector (1); hospital clerk (1); law clerks (2); medical students (2); mercantile clerk (1); ministers of the Kirk (2); photo process engraver (1); rancher (1); rubber planter (1); schoolmasters (3); shipping clerk (1); solicitors (3); surgeon (1); trainee civil servant (1); trainee stockbroker (1); undergraduates (3); veterinary student (1); Writer to the Signet (1).

(e) 16ᵗʰ Royal Scots: *Marital Status* (based on 1,049 of the 1,347 'original' volunteers)

175 other ranks were married – 16.7 per cent of the sample. Applying this percentage to the entire battalion produces a total of around 226. In January 1915, at a recruiting meeting at Leith Docks, Sir George McCrae stated that a higher than intended proportion of his volunteers were married. He put the number at 'more than two hundreds', so the above figure is fairly reliable.

Seven of the battalion's original 45 officers were married.

Appendix 2

16ᵗʰ Royal Scots – 75 football clubs known to have contributed members, December 1914.

Armadale; Arniston Rangers; Bathgate; Bo'ness; Bonnyrigg Rose Athletic; Boroughmuir School; Broughton Higher Grade School; Broxburn Shamrock; Broxburn United; Civil Service Strollers; Colinton Wednesday; Cowdenbeath; Crossgates Thistle; Cupar Violet; Dalkeith Thistle; Dunfermline Athletic; Eastern; East Fife; Edinburgh Corinthians; Edinburgh & Leith Fish Trades; Edinburgh & Leith Postmen; Edinburgh Nomads; Edinburgh Renton; Edinburgh Union; Edinburgh University; Falkirk; Fisherrow Shop Assistants; Gala Fairydean; Heart of Midlothian; Hearts of Beath; Heriot-Watt Training College; Hibernian; Inverkeithing United; Kinleith Thistle; Kinneil Ramblers; Kirkcaldy United; Ladybank Violet; Leith; Leith Ivanhoe; Leith Police; Leith Provident; Leith Shop Assistants; Leith Wednesday; Leslie Hearts; Linlithgow Rose; Loanhead Mayflower; Moray House; Mossend Burnvale; Musselburgh Athletic; Musselburgh Juniors; Newtongrange Star; Niddrie Bluebell; Peebles Rovers; Penicuik Juniors; Pharmacy United; Portobello Thistle; Pumpherston Rangers; Raith Rovers; Rosewell Rosedale; St Bernard's; St Cuthbert's Athletic; St Leonard's United; Saughton Athletic; Shaftesbury Juveniles; Shandon Athletic; Tranent Juniors; Tynecastle Wednesday; Valleyfield Athletic; Vale of Grange; Vale of Leithen; Wallyford Thistle; Warrender; Wemyss Athletic; West Calder Hearts; West End Athletic.

Appendix 3

Survey of clubs in the First and Second Divisions of the Scottish Football League with players serving in the armed forces or engaged in government service. (Compiled April 1915 by William McAndrew, League secretary.) 'Government service' was a pre-conscription euphemism for employment in shipyards, mines, munition or engineering works.

Club	Armed Forces	Government Service
Aberdeen[1]	14	1
Airdrie	1	0
Ayr United	5	8
Clyde	8	5
Dumbarton	5	0
Dundee	8	0
Falkirk	10	3
Hamilton	0	4
Heart of Midlothian[2]	16	0
Hibernian	2	1
Kilmarnock	5	6
Greenock Morton	5	3
Motherwell	0	5
Partick Thistle	1	8
Queen's Park[3]	26	6
Raith Rovers	7	2
Rangers	2	6
St Mirren	9	5
Third Lanark	4	2

[1]   Mostly Reservists and Territorials in Gordon Highlanders.
[2]   Four of Hearts' remaining players were employed as miners, including one man judged unfit for military service.

[3]   A gentlemen's amateur sporting club. The secretary seems to have responded with the number of *members* who had enlisted. Queen's figure would exceed 100 by the end of the year.

Glasgow Celtic declined to take part in the survey, stating that all their signed players were sole-supports, engaged in Government service. Celtic's 'poor recruiting record', as the *Glasgow Herald* called it, drew considerable attention throughout 1914 and 1915, particularly in relation to the records of Greenock Morton and Clyde, and that of the club's own supporters, who had enlisted in their thousands.

Appendix 4

Letter from John McCartney, Secretary/Manager of Heart of Midlothian Football Club to Frederick Charrington, founder and proprietor of the Tower Hamlets Mission for Hungry Men and Women. (Written at Tynecastle Park, Edinburgh, on 29 December 1914.)

Having conducted a vitriolic campaign against the 'moral scourge' of professional football since the outbreak of war, Mr Charrington seized the festive moment to allow certain leading clubs the chance to 'redeem themselves' by contributing funds to his mission for the London poor. McCartney plainly relished the opportunity to communicate with the Fiend:

> Sir – I am at a loss to understand why you should address your appeal to anyone connected with football. You have heaped ignominy and calumny, both in speech and writing, quite sufficient to throttle the sources that hitherto have contributed liberally to all philanthropic works. It is a disgrace that needy and worthy objects have to suffer through the conduct of misguided and ill-informed crusaders.
>
> The thousands of pounds raised annually through football on behalf of charitable institutions would be diverted if all agencies were of your particular brand. It is quite impossible for any sane person, fully acquainted with football matters, to take up a position similar to yours. The thinking public will not tolerate any self-appointed moralist or censor whose main aim is to advertise his own personality. Your protest against professional footballers, directors, shareholders and followers is one of the foulest slanders ever laid against any section of the community. If, sir, you ask for bread and receive a stone; if you pester His Majesty the King, General French and Admiral Jellicoe etc., and receive snubs, you must blame only yourself. These high officials have more important business. Failing your return to the normal, I am afraid it will be necessary for you to adopt the garments with which you would so readily adorn footballers, and go and join the gallant Pankhursts.

Such elegant derision. Charrington, however, was undeterred. He continued his crusade, encouraged by a growing split in the game's own ranks. The conference of the four home associations, held in London in the wake of Forsyth's revelations, produced two distinct camps. The Scottish representatives were in favour of continued cooperation with the military authorities. They had given their word (they repeated yet again) to abide by War Office policy; if the War Office now believed that some conciliatory gesture was required from football, then the SFA was bound to comply. Tennant made it known that suspension of international fixtures and cup-ties would suffice in the short term; the SFA duly agreed. The English representatives, however, were having none of it. Football, they insisted, must proceed unrestrained. Seven hours of bitter argument was ended by the adoption of a compromise resolution, suspending internationals for the duration of hostilities. This was insufficient for the Scots, who repaired immediately to Whitehall to assure officials of their support for the abandonment of cup-ties as well.

Relations between the two associations now deteriorated rapidly. The Scots were vilified in London for dissociating themselves from the conference vote; the English were condemned in Scotland for their 'selfish stupidity'. The English League made matters worse by announcing that if the FA were to abandon the Cup, they would purchase their own trophy and play for that instead. Unsurprisingly, on 7 December the FA Council voted firmly against abandonment; while, a fortnight later, the SFA voted narrowly *for*. Then on 15 December, even as McCrae's were mobilising, the FA hosted a grand public meeting at Fulham Town Hall to inaugurate England's response to Sir George's campaign. The 17th Battalion of the Middlesex Regiment was intended by its raising committee to be a 'Footballers' Legion'. Around 35 first-class professionals enlisted on the first day (including the old Hearts wing-half Bob Dalrymple of Clapton Orient); however, the momentum was not sustained. By the time the battalion was officially completed (in March 1915), it was estimated that only about 100 footballers of any note had joined – the point being, of course (though Charrington would not concede it), that most professional players without some civilian trade had already volunteered.

The sinking of their flagship signalled the end of English football's resistance. They had not the nerve to start another season with 'business as usual'. The 1915 Cup final, in which Sheffield United defeated Chelsea 3–0 before a crowd of 50,000, was held at Old Trafford in Manchester – as far away as possible from its Crystal Palace home (which the Admiralty had commandeered for training purposes). Arrangements by then were well in hand for drastic changes when football returned in the summer. For the duration of hostilities, the game would be reorganised on a regional basis with players paid only travelling expenses. The 'emergency competitions', as the press quickly dubbed them, bore little resemblance to the pre-war leagues: effectively, professional football had been suspended. Mr Charrington had won.

But only in England. North of the border, the Fiend was repulsed. As James Hogge later put it, Heart of Midlothian had 'saved the game's good name'. With the stipulation that all players must be engaged in other work through the week and accept no more than one pound for each Saturday appearance, the leagues would thus continue as before.

Appendix 5

Heart of Midlothian Football Club Roll of Honour, 1914–18.

1. McCrae's Battalion

James Boyd — Killed in action, 3 August 1916.
Alfred Ernest Briggs — Wounded in action, 1 July 1916; discharged invalid.
Patrick James Crossan — Wounded in action twice; gassed; discharged invalid.
Duncan Currie — Killed in action, 1 July 1916.
Ernest Edgar Ellis — Killed in action, 1 July 1916.
Norman Findlay — Discharged to trade, September 1916.
James Hearty Frew — Transferred 1st Lowland (City of Edinburgh) RGA, 1915.
Thomas Gracie — Died in service, 23 October 1915.
James William Hazeldean — Wounded in action, 1 July 1916; discharged invalid.
James Low — Commissioned 6th Seaforth Highlanders; wounded in action twice.
Edward McGuire — Wounded in action, 1 July 1916; discharged invalid.
Annan Buchan Ness — Twice wounded; commissioned 16th RS; Lt 9th RS.
Robert Malcolm Preston — Transferred HLI; wounded in action.
Henry Benzie Wattie — Killed in action, 1 July 1916.
William Rose Wilson — Transferred 13th RS; returned to 16th RS; wounded in action.

2. Other units

John Allan — 9th RS. Killed in action, 22 April 1917.
Colin Douglas Blackhall — 1st Lowland (City of Edinburgh) RGA.
James Gilbert — 1st Lowland (City of Edinburgh) RGA.
Harry Nicol Graham — Gloucester Regiment; transferred to RAMC.
Charles Hallwood — RE.
James Macdonald — 13th RS.
John Mackenzie — 1st Lowland (City of Edinburgh) RGA.
Robert Watt Malcolm — RS; transferred to MGC.
John Martin — 5th RS; twice wounded in action; discharged invalid.
Robert Mercer — 1st Lowland (City of Edinburgh) RGA; gassed; discharged invalid.
George Miller — 9th RS; wounded.

Neil Moreland	8th HLI; transferred to 7th RS; wounded in action three times.
George Leckie Sinclair	RFA; injured on service; discharged.
James Hodge Speedie	7th Cameron Highlanders; killed in action, 25 September 1915.
Philip Whyte	Gloucester Regiment.
John Wilson	9th RS; wounded in action twice.

3. Roll of Dead

John Allan	Killed in action on 22 April 1917.
James Boyd	Killed in action on 3 August 1916.
Patrick James Crossan	Died on 24 April 1933.
Duncan Currie	Killed in action on 1 July 1916.
James Duckworth	Died on 25 August 1920.
Ernest Edgar Ellis	Killed in action on 1 July 1916.
Thomas Gracie	Died on 23 October 1915.
Alexander Slight Lyon	Died on 14 February 1915.
Robert Mercer	Died on 23 April 1926.
James Hodge Speedie	Killed in action on 25 September 1915.
Henry Benzie Wattie	Killed in action on 1 July 1916.

Crossan is buried at Mount Vernon Cemetery in Edinburgh; Duckworth at Cathcart Cemetery in Glasgow; Gracie at Craigton Cemetery in Glasgow; Lyon at Dalry Cemetery in Edinburgh; Mercer at Haddington Churchyard in East Lothian. Duckworth and Lyon contracted their illnesses while accompanying McCrae's Hearts players on route marches and manœuvres during the winter of 1914–15.

Boyd, Currie, Ellis and Wattie are commemorated on the Thiepval Memorial to the Missing, near the village of Thiepval in France; it is likely that Currie is one of the 'unknown soldiers' at Gordon Dump Cemetery, near la Boisselle. His body was buried beside Lionel Coles in the original battlefield plot, which was close by. When Gordon Dump was formally laid out, Coles was reinterred; presumably Duncan isn't far away. The remains of Boyd and Ellis were found and buried in 1916 and 1917 respectively; subsequently, however, the locations of their graves were lost. No trace of Wattie has ever been found. Speedie is commemorated on the Loos Memorial at Dud Corner Cemetery, Loos.

John Allan is commemorated on the Arras Memorial at Faubourg d'Amiens Cemetery, Arras. He was 30. McCartney signed him from Tranent Juniors in 1915 as cover for Mercer. A joiner to trade, he lived with his parents at 10 Springwell Place in Edinburgh. On 5 June 1917 his father received official notice that he was missing; a member of his platoon had seen him wounded, but there was no further news.

Notes

Unless stated otherwise, all letters are from the author's collection.

ONE: 'THIS VERITABLE CURSE'

[1] Recruiting figures for Edinburgh (published periodically in local newspapers) broadly follow the national trend. For a month-by-month breakdown of national enlistment totals, see *General Annual Reports of the British Army (including the Territorial Force from date of embodiment)*, *1st October 1914 to 30th September 1919*. P.P. 1927, XX, Cmd. 1193 – Table 1(b), page 60.

[2] *Ministry of National Service, 1917 to 1919. Report on the Physical Examination of men of Military Age by National Service Medical Boards from November 1st 1917 to October 31st 1918*. P.P. 1919, XXVI, Cmd. 504. 'Of every nine men of military age in Great Britain, on average three were perfectly fit and healthy; two were upon a definitely infirm plane of health and strength, whether from some disability or some failure of development; three were incapable of undergoing more than a very moderate degree of exertion and could almost (in view of their age) be described with justice as physical wrecks; and the remaining man [could be described] as a chronic invalid with a precarious hold on life.' (The age-group under consideration here was 18 to 50.) See also J.M. Winter, 'Britain's "Lost Generation" in the First World War' in *Population Studies*, Volume 31, 1977; and Denis Winter, *Death's Men* (Penguin 1979).

[3] *The Times*, 17 November 1914. The last seven words seem oddly out of place. Letters and reports alleged to come directly from the front at this time should be treated with caution. On 10 August the government established an 'Official Press Bureau' under the self-willed F.E. Smith (later Lord Birkenhead), Unionist MP for the Walton Division of Liverpool. The Bureau was given two main responsibilities – to release material furnished by the Admiralty/War Office, and to censor material gathered independently by the nation's newspapers. In effect all war-related press cable messages going to, from, or through London were diverted to the Bureau by the Post Office or the cable companies. Submission of other war-related material remained *voluntary*, but those editors or proprietors who published without authorisation were subject to prosecution under the Defence of the Realm Act. On 30 August *The Times* carried a dispatch from correspondent Arthur Moore headlined 'Broken British Regiments', which described the appalling losses sustained during the retreat from Mons. The following day Kitchener issued a stiff rebuttal through the Bureau, explaining that these losses (in guns and men) had already been made good by reinforcement and that the BEF once more stood ready to receive anything the Germans cared to throw at it. The Bureau itself added a curious disclaimer, pointing out that dispatches from private correspondents in France

or Belgium were bound to be unreliable since the said correspondents were permitted nowhere near the actual fighting. The ensuing row in Parliament over the right of newspapers to truthfully report the war was only eased when it emerged that the desperate picture painted by Moore had persuaded a swarm of additional volunteers – 30,000 men in 2 days – to besiege the nation's recruiting stations. Moreover, Smith himself had approved publication – with this very aim in mind. Lord Kitchener, he said, had asked him to use his position to assist in recruiting. Smith also readily admitted *embellishing* Moore's copy in order to influence waverers to enlist. In the last week of September he resigned from the Bureau, volunteered for active service, and accompanied the Indian Corps to France as its Intelligence and Recording Officer. In May 1915 he returned home to take up the post of Solicitor-General in the first coalition government, and later became one of the fiercest critics of Sir Douglas Haig's command. See *Memorandum on the Censorship. P.P.* 1914–1916, XXXIX, Cmd. 7679; and *Memorandum on the Official Press Bureau. P.P.* 1914–1916, XXXIX, Cmd. 7680.

⁴ Comparative table of selected peacetime/wartime match attendances, produced by the FA in November 1914 in defence of continuation. (Figures in thousands.)

	17 November 1913	7 November 1914	21 November 1914
Chelsea	35	25	15
Newcastle United	25	20	8
West Bromwich	35	14	10
Grimsby	9	7	8
Gillingham	6	6	3
Crystal Palace	10 ·	7	8
Brighton	6	5	3
Total	126	84	55

⁵ 2/Lt Arthur Herbert Rosdew Burn was killed in action on 29 October 1914. Colonel Burn had already visited France himself – as a member of the King's Messenger Service, attached to GHQ.

TWO: *'AULD REEKIE, WALE O ILKA TOWN!'*

¹ Chambers, *Traditions of Edinburgh* (Edinburgh, 1931).
² Cockburn, *Memorials of His Time* (Edinburgh, 1946).
³ Stevenson, *Edinburgh: Picturesque Notes* (London, 1879).
⁴ Robertson and Wood, 'The Old City Debt' in *Castle and Town* (Edinburgh, 1928).
⁵ The *Evening Dispatch* informed its readers that 'Sgt Baker fought with the Scots Guards at Paardeberg.' No explanation was offered as to the cause of the quarrel.
⁶ The journalist was Donald Gunn of *The Scotsman*, soon to be a CQMS in McCrae's Battalion. Gunn told his wife, who passed the anecdote on to their son.
⁷ Later the Ramsay Technical Institute in Portobello Road.
⁸ Sir George McCrae, *Mine Own Romantic Town*. Autobiographical fragment, written (apparently) after his retirement. (Author's collection).
⁹ Established as a charitable school for children of the poor by the Edinburgh Education Society around 1807. One of the early subscribers was James Hope, WS, father of John.
¹⁰ Sir George McCrae, *Mine Own Romantic Town*, op. cit.
¹¹ George McCrae, 'The Old City Debt – Report by the City Treasurer' (Edinburgh, 1895).
¹² 'The 6ᵗʰ Royal Scots'. (Author's collection).
¹³ Public Record Office, WO32/11242. McCrae to Seely, 16/11/13. A little-known problem thrown up by the Territorial annual camps was the disappearance of many soldiers at the end of the first week, and the arrival of many others at the start of the second. Trade holidays were to blame. Commanding officers, therefore, seldom got the chance to work with their entire battalion.
¹⁴ McCrae to Seely, 26/11/13.

THREE: *'WHITE FEATHERS OF MIDLOTHIAN'*

[1] Lockhart, *The Life of Sir Walter Scott* (Edinburgh, 1893).

[2] At least two other local sides would later follow this lead. Leith Ivanhoe and Edinburgh Waverley were clearly inspired by the Bard, while I recall many years ago at Hampden Park overhearing a venerable ancient in a maroon scarf remark that Hearts should change their name to *Old Mortality*. (The hyphen in Mid-Lothian appears in the club's 1914 letterhead but it had vanished from common usage long before.)

[3] The northernmost pitch was said in to have been 'over and beyond' what used to be the north terracing, which would place it partly in the grounds of the present Tynecastle School. (*Evening News*, 13/2/15).

[4] Tom Campbell and Pat Woods, *A New History of Celtic* (Edinburgh, 1996).

[5] Isa Brindley, daughter of 20053 Pte Sam Brindley. Sam was a founding member of 'Ye Olde Hearts Association' and a particular chum of Walker's.

[6] Heart of Midlothian Football Club Limited – Memorandum and Articles of Association, April 1905.

[7] McCartney later pinned up a newspaper portrait of himself in the dressing-room, as a joke at Crossan's expense. 'Never rely on good looks,' he wrote underneath.

[8] Not Busby, Renfrewshire, as the sports papers claimed. Mauchline is McCartney's own stated birthplace.

[9] William J. Melvin, Gunner, RFA 1917–19, saw Mercer play many times. He told me: 'Think of Alan Hansen crossed with Richard Gough.' Willie wanted to join McCrae's in 1914, but he was too young. After the war he helped found crack Edinburgh juvenile side, Ashton FC, and was responsible for discovering Willie Woodburn of Rangers and Scotland.

[10] William J. Melvin again. He thought Wattie a better player than Alex James.

[11] As Duncan arrived, his brother, Bob, departed: the entire Currie family were footballers.

[12] The Brazilians seem to have been unaware that Walker had retired. There was some talk of his being persuaded to return for the trip.

[13] The second was apparently Chelsea.

[14] Conversation with Walter McKenzie Scott.

[15] Heart of Midlothian FC Ltd. Minute Book No. 5 – minutes of board meeting, 19 September 1914.

FOUR: *'IF IT'S FOOTBALL THAT YOU'RE WANTING . . .'*

[1] Sir John Murray of Broughton, *Memorials*, ed. R.F. Bell (Edinburgh, 1898)

[2] Conversation with Walter McKenzie Scott.

[3] *Evening News*, 3 September 1921. (McCartney family cutting book).

[4] *Saturday Post*, 11 November 1916. Wattie's nephew, Hildred ('John') Wattie told me that his father said 'it was all arranged. The players had already been approached in advance.'

[5] Conversation with Jane Lorimer, daughter of 19271 Cpl Harry Lorimer. Scott's account agreed. He told me that Gracie had sworn him to silence and added that most of the players knew about Sir George's appeal long before the manager or board.

[6] Heart of Midlothian FC Ltd Minute Book No. 5 – minutes of board meeting, 23 November 1914.

[7] *Evening News*, 3 September 1921. (McCartney family cutting book).

[8] Not to be confused with 'The Historic Sixteen', McCartney's romantic term for the *total* of Hearts players on military service by the end of 1914.

[9] Army Council Instruction 471, 1 March 1916.

[10] Conversation with George Hogg, nephew of Peter Nellies. Harry Lorimer also told his daughter: 'We were waiting on Bob to join us when he was fit.' Scott told me about the rheumatic fever himself. He persisted in his efforts to enlist, including a second try for McCrae's. In December 1915 he was finally accepted for the RASC but was considered unfit for overseas service. He was discharged through ill-health in January 1919. Graham was conscripted in August 1916 and sent to the Gloucester Regiment. During initial training his asthma found him out, and he was transferred to the RAMC, where he served as a dental

mechanic in the Middle East. Neither Aitken nor Bryden were conscripted for military service. See also Chapter One, note 2.
11 Recruiting Card, November 1914. (Author's collection).
12 Edinburgh and District Trades Council – Minute Book, 1914/15.
13 McCartney to Harry Lorimer, December 1920.
14 Hearts weren't first. Supporters of West Bromwich Albion had already filled a company of the 5th South Staffordshires, a local Territorial battalion.
15 The others were Elias Furst, James Campbell of the Trades Council; Rev William Lindsay of Chalmers Church in the West Port; John Clark, headmaster of Heriot's; Mr W.L. Stephen, and Mr J. Lumsden.
16 19376 Pte Henry Scott Swan – discharged 8/4/15 (flat feet).
17 Conversation with Walter McKenzie Scott. See note 10 (above).
18 Crossan's intervention on the Mound became something of a legend among a certain generation of Hearts supporters. It is the only battalion anecdote I have ever heard in general circulation. Scott told me that the Colonel was not pleased.
19 Directors' Admission Card. (Author's collection.)
20 Conversation with Kelly's daughter, Mary Cairns.
21 Conversation with Hawthorn's son, George.
22 Conversation with Jane Lorimer.
23 The 17th Battalion of the Middlesex Regiment. See Appendix 4.
24 Mobilisation postcard. (Author's collection.)
25 Conversation with 19944 Cpl John Veitch.
26 'Colonel Sir George McCrae' sheet music and lyric handbill. (Author's collection.)
27 'Hey, Billy boy'. (Author's collection.)
28 George Heriot's Trust – Minutes of Meetings of Governors, November–December 1914.
29 Harry to Isa 18/12/14.
30 19646 Pte Andrew Reid Smith of Auchtermuchty in Fife.
31 The tale of the Colonel's Christmas dinner and of the mysterious arrival of Jock that night was told to me independently by several unacquainted daughters of older members of the battalion. These girls heard the story at the time, directly from their fathers. The minister's bizarre letter was quoted in the *Evening News*.

FIVE: *'MARCHING WI GEORDIE'*
1 Muir PRO WO97/5557.
2 Muirhead PRO WO97/5557; Neill PRO WO97/5582; McManus – discharge papers; Purcell – 'Small Book'. Muir quote: Lt R.W.F. Johnston. Note also the little-quoted War Office instruction of 1914 that permitted New Army battalions to enlist ex-warrant officers for Home Service *only*. These men were used as drill instructors, passing on their experience to Kitchener's green NCOs. (Army Order 315, 1914).
3 See Appendix 1 – 16th RS by *Age*, *Occupation* and *Marital Status*.
4 Gunn to his wife.
5 Warden to friend 5/1/15.
6 *Evening News*, 13/2/15.
7 D.M. Sutherland to friend (undated).
8 Conversation with Veitch.
9 Harry to Isa 18/12/14.
10 General Staff, War Office, *Infantry Training 1914*.
11 *Evening News*, 13/2/15.
12 Warden to wife 23/1/15.
13 *Evening News*, 13/2/15.
14 Campbell is buried at Piershill Cemetery; David Welch (mentioned earlier) is buried at Morningside.
15 PRO WO 364, Ewing's record file; Donald Gunn's recollections.
16 19858 Pte Robert MacMillan record file (Ministry of Defence); Warden letters.

17 MacLean to Dr Donald McIntosh 30/4/15.
18 *The Chequers: A Year Book of the 34th Division*, 1952. It was named after the division's distinctive chequer-board 'identification', designed by Inky Bill at Perham Down.
19 Sandy Grosert left around this time. He transferred by request to a motorised section of the Machine-Gun Corps and was later commissioned in the 6th Gordons. In 1917 he was awarded the Military Cross.
20 'McCrae's Own Farewell to Auld Reekie'. (Author's collection).
21 Duguid discharge parchment (Author's collection); Chalmers Hospital Minute and Record Books, 1914.
22 'McCrae's Own'. (Author's collection).
23 18756 Pte Arthur Grant from North Berwick was a professional golfer in Monte Carlo before the war. McCrae took lessons from him at Heriot's.
24 Conversation with Isa Brindley.
25 McCartney to Harry Lorimer, December 1920.
26 19740 Sgt Gerald Crawford to sister 29/6/15.
27 19445 Pte James Crawford to mother, June 1915.
28 19532 Pte Tommy King to mother, 20/6/15.
29 Tommy King to mother, 26/6/16.
30 18889 L/Cpl David Philip – undated but post-war.
31 19054 L/Cpl John McParlane to wife, 14/7/15.
32 18801 Pte Thomson Bonar to mother, 20/6/15.
33 19374 Pte Harry Sutherland. (Galloway collection).
34 Conversation with 19053 Pte James McEvoy.
35 D.M. Sutherland to mother, June 1915.
36 D.M. Sutherland to mother, 1/7/15.
37 Thomson Bonar to mother, 10/7/15.
38 Letter from unknown 4th RS officer. (McCrae family).
39 D.M. Sutherland to mother, early July 1915.
40 19040 L/Cpl Andy Henderson, undated cutting. (McCrae family).
41 Speedie to McCartney, undated cutting. (McCrae family).
42 *The Chequers*, 1948.
43 Conversation with Veitch.
44 Conversation with 29601 Pte Tom Hunter, 15th R.S.
45 Conversation with Veitch.
46 Leishman to McCartney, 25/10/15. (Heart of Midlothian FC)
47 Conversation with McEvoy.
48 18925 Pte James Steuart to brother, 7/12/15.
49 Steuart to sister, 13/12/15 and 15/12/15.
50 *The Weakly Rumour*. (Author's collection).
51 *The Weakly Rumour*. (Author's collection).

SIX: *AN AWFUL BIZ*
1 Sgt Crawford to sister, 10/1/16.
2 Kitchener embarkation paper.
3 Diary of 19697 Cpl Tom Young.
4 Warden to wife, 15/1/16.
5 Sgt Crawford to sister, 26/1/16.
6 Sgt Crawford to sister, 1/2/16.
7 Armit to Dr Robertson, 2/2/16
8 MacLean to Dr Donald McIntosh, 2/2/16.
9 Bob Martin to D.M. Sutherland, undated but post-war.
10 18871 Pte James Muir to parents, 20/1/16.
11 18980 Cpl Alfred Briggs to McCartney, 16/2/16.
12 18998 Pte Patrick Crossan to McCartney, February 1916.

13 James Crawford to mother, 17/2/16.
14 Armit to Dr Robertson, from undated cutting. (McCrae family).
15 MacLean to Dr Donald McIntosh, 24/2/16.
16 *Evening News*, 10/3/16.
17 19711 Pte Ernest Becker, undated transcript.
18 19035 Pte Harry Harley 15/3/16; 19939 Pte John Thomson, 9/3/16.
19 *The Chequers*, 1940–41.
20 Briggs to McCartney, 14/3/16.
21 Ness to McCartney, 19/3/16.
22 19816 Pte Florance Kelly, 24/3/16.
23 Ness to McCartney 2/4/16.
24 War Diary, 23ʳᵈ Infantry Battalion, Australian Imperial Force (Australian War Memorial).
25 Warden to wife, 11/4/16.
26 Sir George McCrae recollection in *The Scotsman*, 28/12/28.
27 Warden to wife, 11/4/16. Ingouville-Williams watched the bombardment from a distance. When the shelling stopped, he rushed down to see if he could help. Sir George was mentioned in despatches for supervising the evacuation. With his usual modesty, he insisted that the credit belonged to Warden.
28 Conversation with Veitch; Moir in the *Weakly Rumour*.
29 Warden to wife, 14/4/16.
30 Rawson to uncle, 17/4/16.

SEVEN: *'MY LITTLE ALL TO MOTHER, WITH BEST LOVE'*
1 'Geordie McCrae'. (Author's collection)
2 19112 Pte Harry Wattie to mother 7/5/16. (Wattie family).
3 Warden to wife, 10/5/16.
4 King to parents, 23/5/16.
5 D.M. Sutherland to mother, 24/5/16.
6 McCrae to Leishman, late May/early June 1916.
7 Warden to wife, 27/5/16.
8 D.M. Sutherland to mother, 28/5/16.
9 Crawford to sister, 28/5/16.
10 Warden to wife, 29/5/16.
11 Conversation with Crighton family.
12 PRO WO 158/233: 'Plan for Offensive by Fourth Army.'
13 GHQ to Rawlinson, 12/4/16 in Edmonds, *Military Operations*, France and Belgium, 1916, vol. I, Appendix 9.
14 PRO WO 158/233: 'Memorandum by Rawlinson' 19/4/16.
15 GHQ to Rawlinson in Edmonds, *1916*, vol. I, Appendix 11.
16 Edmonds, *1916*, vol. I, Appendix 17. (SS 109).
17 19711 Pte Ernest Becker – diary.
18 19409 L/Cpl Robert Armour – diary.
19 'Fourth Army Tactical Notes', in Edmonds, *1916*, vol. I, Appendix 18. See also SS 106, 'Notes on the Tactical Employment of Machine Guns and Lewis Guns.' (War Office, 1916).
20 'Further Examination of Robert Kirchstetter . . .' General Staff, III Corps, 5/6/16. (Author's collection).
21 Soldier's Pay Book for Use on Active Service (Army Book 64).
22 McIvor, McNulty wills. (SRO).
23 Black to wife, 18/6/16.
24 'On Seeing a Staff Officer Drive Past a Royal Scots Burial Party', 23/6/16 (Author's collection)
25 21200 L/Cpl Primrose Fairweather to sister, 24/6/16.
26 PRO WO 95/2432 – General Staff, 34ᵗʰ Division: 'Report on the Raid carried out by the 26ᵗʰ N.F.'
27 Steuart to father, 26/6/16.

28 18874 Pte Cecil Nisbet to mother, 24/6/16; Fraser MacLean to Dr McIntosh, November 1915, for 'twins'.

29 Conversation with McEvoy.

30 PRO WO 95/2432 – General Staff, 34th Division: Report of Millar's patrol.

31 Ross to Mrs Wood; Ross to Mr and Mrs Watt, 30/6/16.

32 Steuart diary, 30/6/16; Buchan to mother, 29/6/16. Jamieson will (SRO).

33 16th RS 'Timetable of Events' July 1st to 4th 1916, transcribed by Andrew Riddell. (Author's collection).

34 Edmonds, *1916*, Chapter XII; General Staff, War Office, Field Service Pocket Book, 1914, Chapter 7.

35 Edmonds, *1916*, Chapter XV, endnote.

EIGHT: *'A TALL, GREY-HAIRED SOLDIER'*

1 McParlane at 1936 reunion of 16th Royal Scots.

2 McEvoy at 1954 reunion.

3 18787 Sgt Charles Anderson at 1954 reunion.

4 Conversation with 19061 Pte Murdo McKay, MM.

5 PRO WO 95/2432 – General Staff, 34th Division: Report of officer i/c Smoke Screen, 101st Brigade.

6 *The Chequers*, 1953. For the 15th RS, see their War Diary (with the Regiment) and D. Nott, *Somewhere in France* (Adelaide 1996), which is based on the letters of Captain Lewis Nott, the battalion's adjutant.

7 18907 Pte Francis Scott. Letter 16/7/16, in C.S. Tait, *Stones in the Millpond* (Shetland, 2001).

8 Conversation with Tom Hunter.

9 The sometimes florid *Pipes of War* has the pipe-sergeant wrestling with a German and then fighting on with a rifle 'until overcome by his wounds'. The account used here is Anderson's own, taken from the *Evening Dispatch* of July 1916. His pipes had silver mountings and had travelled on several Polar expeditions, including that of Scott to the Antarctic; they were destroyed during the action and he was able to save only one small piece of tartan from the drones.

10 Riddell timetable, op. cit.

11 Steuart, letter to father after the action.

12 18982 Pte James Brown at 1954 reunion.

13 19877 Sgt James Mowatt, MM, at 1954 reunion.

14 Campbell to Becker family, 24/8/16.

15 Lt Stewart Bryce to Primrose Fairweather's sister, 28/9/16.

16 19068 Pte James Miller to Alexander McGregor, 21/7/16. 'Stevie' was 19101 Pte Alexander Stevenson, an apprentice printer from Beaverbank Place. He was killed in 1917.

17 19985 Cpl Robert Stewart at 1954 reunion.

18 Riddell timetable.

19 It was the opinion of McCrae's Old Comrades' Association that Kelly should have been awarded the Victoria Cross for his gallantry. There were no commissioned witnesses, however, so he received no recognition. I was told the story independently by several veterans and battalion relatives. When I finally met Michael's daughter, Mary, I was astonished to be presented with the flag.

20 Lt Wilfred Lodge, 15th RS. Letter 5/7/16 to father, in M. Lodge, *Sir Richard Lodge* (Edinburgh 1946).

21 Riddell timetable.

22 PRO WO 95/2432: War Diary, General Staff, 34th Division. See also *The Chequers*, 1940/41.

23 PRO WO 95/2455: War Diary, 101st Infantry Brigade, January 1916–June 1917.

24 101st Brigade War Diary; Riddell timetable.

25 Davie lost out on a fair bit of schooling during the family's travels. He was 20 years old when he finally left Stewart's in June 1914.

26 Riddell timetable; conversation with McEvoy. McCrae was an excellent shot. At the opening

of the Heriot's miniature rifle-range in 1914, he hit five central bulls out of five. During the period of his command, the 6th RS took a particular pride in their musketry.

[27] Neeves to Lt. Col. John Shakespear, 22/12/29. Robin's correct name was 'Horace'; in civilian life he was a Post Office telegram messenger and wore a red waistcoat as part of his uniform. *Robin* Red-breast.

[28] Riddell timetable. In *The Thirty-Fourth Division 1915–19* (London, 1922) Lt-Col. Shakespear states that 'orders were received' for the operation on the redoubt. This is based on a mis-reading of 34th Division Operation Order 18 (PRO WO 95/2455) which relates to actions in the early hours of 3 July. In fact *all* offensive operations at Wood Alley/Scots Redoubt were mounted on the initiative of (firstly) Robson and Brown, then (later) McCrae and Temple. Shakespear also states that carrying parties arrived 'before noon' in time to re-supply Robson and Hamilton's bombers. In fact the carrying-parties arrived shortly before 12 *midnight*, fully 12 hours later.

[29] There are inconsistencies between the War Diaries of 34th Division General Staff and 101st Brigade (see above) on the timing of the alleged fall of Heligoland. Division says 5.30 p.m.; Brigade says notification was 'received' at 11.15 p.m. Armit could not have mounted his 8 p.m. attack unless his rear was at least partially secure. When he arrived at the redoubt, he reported that Heligoland had been cleared at 6 p.m. We know, however, that fighting continued well into 3 July.

[30] *The Chequers*, 1940–41.

[31] PRO WO 95/2455: 34th Division Operation Order 18.

[32] PRO WO 95/2455: 101st Brigade Operation Order 38.

[33] Brown at 1954 reunion. Aitchison was killed on 23/8/18 with the 2nd R.S. He was 25.

[34] Crawford to sister, 24/7/16.

[35] PRO WO 95/2455: 34th Division Operation Order 19; 101st Brigade Operation Order 39.

[36] Sutherland 'diary', 4/7/16.

[37] Veitch at 1954 reunion.

[38] Riddell timetable.

[39] The Official History's 'abnormal' statement of McCrae's losses remains uncorrected to this day. (See Edmonds, *1916*, vol. 1, page 380). In 1969, during the preparation of *The First Day on the Somme*, Martin Middlebrook surveyed all of the then available records for 1 July in order to produce a definitive appendix identifying 32 'Battalions Suffering More than 500 Casualties'. The 16th Royal Scots are absent from the list. In fact, with 12 officers and 573 men, they should be in 11th place, beside the Accrington Pals. A total of 4 officers and 225 other ranks were killed; 2 officers and 7 other ranks were captured; 6 officers and 341 other ranks were wounded. All have been identified by name. Of the latter, 27 died of their injuries before the end of the war. As a proportion of those engaged, casualties amount to 72 per cent. The list of dead (including deaths from wounds) comes to 31 per cent. Note that the casualty return quoted in Shakespear is even less accurate than Edmonds. Note also that fewer than 400 of the men who went over the top with the battalion on 1 July 1916 remained alive in 1919.

[40] Veitch at 1954 reunion.

[41] Shortly after Stephenson's funeral in March 1950, his son, Mike, was told this story by Sir Harold Cartmel-Robinson, CMG, OBE, who served as a captain in 58th Brigade R.F.A. Cartmel-Robinson was a colleague of Steve's before the war in the Northern Rhodesian Native Labour Bureau and they remained close, lifelong friends. In 1945 he became Chief Secretary of the colony, acting briefly as Governor in 1946. I have spoken to several people who knew him, and all testified to his absolute honesty and straightness of character. Haig did travel down to Querrieu on the afternoon of 1 July: it's in his diary. The visit, however, is not mentioned in many (if any) commonly available contemporary accounts. There is a rather vague reference to it in Edmonds, 1916, Vol. 1, page 481, which was published in 1932, but this would hardly be required reading in the wilds of Northern Rhodesia. Note also that from surviving records of Haig's comments that day, he laid particular emphasis on the importance of enveloping Fricourt and securing advances south of Mametz Wood. Stephenson's division had attacked just north of the village.

[42] 19646 Pte Andrew Reid Smith.

43 Wilfred Lodge to father, 5/7/16 (see above).

NINE: 'SUCH A WALL OF STEEL AND SHELL'
1 One of the subs in 9ᵗʰ KOYLI at this time was Basil Liddell Hart. See (for example) B. Bond, *Liddell Hart – A Study of his Military Thought* (London, 1979).
2 *Dunfermline Press*, July 1916.
3 Barbara Buchan to John, 14/7/16.
4 Conversation with Christina Harley.
5 Ness to McCartney, 20/7/16.
6 *The Chequers*, 1940–41.
7 Cpl George Simons recovered from his injuries. He was posted back to France in early 1917 and sent to the 11ᵗʰ RS. Shortly afterwards, he was awarded the MM for rescuing a comrade from a burning hut. On 12/10/17 he was killed in action near Poelcappelle. He is buried in the local cemetery. ('Dod' is the familiar form of 'George'. Members of the 16ᵗʰ sometimes referred to the Colonel as '*Auld Dod*'.)
8 PRO WO95/2455: Manuscript memo from Mangles to GOC 101ˢᵗ Brigade.
9 PRO WO95/2455: 101ˢᵗ Brigade Operation Order 43.
10 PRO WO95/2455: 101ˢᵗ Brigade Operation Order 44; 34ᵗʰ Division Operation Order 36.
11 PRO WO95/2455: Gore to 34ᵗʰ Division.
12 Margin note in Arthur Stephenson's copy of Shakespear.
13 Conversation with Tommy's sweetheart, Mary McDougall, who kept him alive in her memory.
14 Sutherland's younger brother, Duncan, died with the York and Lancs Regiment in November 1944.
15 Nicholson to HQ, III Corps, 18/8/16. (McCrae family papers.)
16 Margin note in Stephenson's copy of Shakespear.
17 Nicholson quoted in Shakespear. He wrongly states that 1ˢᵗ Division captured the Intermediate.
18 In chapter ten of his classic autobiographical account of the war, *A Passionate Prodigality*, Guy Chapman notes the distrust that infantrymen felt towards the staff. 'There was fierce resentment,' he wrote, 'when brass hats descended from their impersonal isolation to strafe platoon or company commanders for alleged shortcomings in the line.'
19 Stewart and Buchan, *The Fifteenth (Scottish) Division, 1914–19* (Edinburgh, 1926).
20 PRO WO339/69872: Sir George McCrae's record file. Back in the UK, his illness was more accurately diagnosed as typhoid. PRO WO339/18945: William Robertson's record file.
21 PRO WO339/18924: Nap Armit's record file.
22 Steuart to sister, 27/11/16.
23 He was appointed acting *Divisional* commander for the last week in October. Nicholson was on leave.
24 Conversation with Paddy Crossan junior.
25 *The Chequers*, 1928–29.
26 Stephenson to Shakespear, 4/1/29.
27 'The Soldier's Return', written in 1793.

TEN: 'THE OFFENSIVE SPIRIT'
1 Letter to D.M. Sutherland, 28/3/50.
2 19858 Pte Robert MacMillan record file (Ministry of Defence).
3 Steuart to father, 26/2/17.
4 Steuart to father, 9/5/17.
5 Edmonds, *Military Operations, France and Belgium, 1917*, vol. I, page 182.
6 Steuart diary, April 1917. The prisoner was a private in the 25ᵗʰ Reserve Infantry Regiment. The German report on the raid explains that there was another captive: Warrant Officer Schneider managed to escape in no man's land.
7 PRO WO95/2455: 101ˢᵗ Brigade War Diary, 7 April 1917.
8 Steuart diary, 9/4/17.

9   Arthur Rose was invalided home at the end of 1916. The commanding officer of 15th RS during this action was Cuthbert Lodge's 24-year-old brother, Wilfred, lately promoted to temporary *lieutenant-colonel*. He was invalided home in August 1917. The remains of two members of the 15th RS killed during the advance on Point du Jour, were discovered on the hillside in spring 2001. Willie Gunn from Edinburgh and Archie McMillan from Armadale were buried in the nearby military cemetery in the summer of 2002.

10 Gavin was awarded the MC. One of the guns was 'claimed' for Edinburgh. It still hasn't turned up.

11 PRO WO95/2455: 101st Brigade War Diary, 9 to 14 April 1917. Early on 10/4/17 Pte James McKenna died at Point du Jour of wounds sustained the previous day. 'Jake', a 22-year-old baker with the West Calder Co-op, played at wing-half for Mossend Burnvale. In 1914 he had a trial for Hearts and was expected to join them the following year. He is buried at Bailleul Road East Cemetery, St Laurent-Blangy.

12 *Soldiers Died in the Great War 1914–19* is the official list of dead. It was compiled in 80 parts and published in 1921. Part 6 is devoted to the Royal Scots. McCrae's columns contain the names of 66 'killed' for 9/4/17, a figure which includes most of the 'missing' as well. Few men (if any) were captured that day. Analysis of War Office casualty returns in *The Scotsman* suggests a total of around 220 wounded.

13 Cowan to father, 13/4/17. When Steve forwarded his name for a gallantry award, he was thinking in terms of the Victoria Cross – Stephenson letter to Cowan 16/5/17. (Both Cowan family). Comrie's first MC came on the recommendation of Sir George, following the trench-raid of 23/11/16.

14 Martin to D.M. Sutherland, 28/3/50.

15 PRO WO95/2455: 101st Brigade narrative of operations – 11th Suffolk Regiment.

16 PRO WO95/2455: 101st Brigade narrative of operations – 10th Lincolnshire Regiment

17 PRO WO95/2455: 101st Brigade War Diary 28/4/17; conversation with 19950 Pte George Watson. MacRae got a bar to his MM for this action. Armstrong was awarded the MC; Rhind received a 'Card of Honour' from Nicholson.

18 Lyon diary. (Mary Strathmore).

19 PRO WO339/78125: Henderson's record file.

20 PRO WO339/59654: Howat's record file.

21 Pte Robert Alexander MacMillan is buried at Rœux Cemetery. The battalion's losses in the attack eventually worked out at 59 other ranks killed, 44 captured and around 160 wounded. One officer, 2/Lt Alex Brown, an Edinburgh advocate, was killed. Three were wounded, including the artist Alick Sturrock, who commanded D Company. Six were taken prisoner.

22 PRO WO95/2455: 101st Brigade War Diary; 101st Brigade narratives. Alfred Warr's personal account.

23 Shakespear, *The Thirty-Fourth Division 1915–19* (London, 1922)

24 Conversation with Robert Johnston.

25 Johnston diary.

26 Johnston diary.

27 PRO WO95/2456: 101st Brigade War Diary 25/8/17.

28 Johnston diary.

29 The other dead officer was 2/Lt James McHoul, a grocer from Duntocher.

30 Henderson to brother, 6/9/17.

31 It is likely that Lodge and Martin are still in their dug-out. Neither man is known to be buried in any cemetery: they are commemorated on the Thiepval Memorial to the Missing.

32 Conversation with Isa Brindley.

33 Conversation with 42280 Pte James Meechan. Gavin was six foot one; Meechan five foot four.

34 D.M. Sutherland to mother, 12/10/17.

35 The were suede shoes. He eventually produced a fine pair of handmade knee-length boots.

36 All of the men killed in this incident are buried at Solferino Farm Cemetery, near Brielen.

37 Johnston diary.

38 Sutherland to mother, 18/10/17.

39 PRO WO339/69782: Randle Evans record file.

[40] PRO WO339/69782: Randle Evans record file.

[41] Sutherland to mother, 24/10/17 and PRO WO95/2435: 34th Division War Diary. Both the Divisional diary and that of 101st Brigade (WO95/2456) indicate just how little information was filtering back from the line of advance. Neither Division nor Brigade had the slightest bit of control. This was a shambles. In *The Thirty-Fourth Division*, John Shakespear states that 'what we were to do, and when and where we were to do it, was the subject of numerous and contradictory orders – the fact being that our fate depended on the success or reverse of operations then pending, in which the Boche had a good deal to say.'

[42] Johnston diary. Bobby got an MC for his efforts. He saw to it that Davie and Fox (and Bob Liston, another of his signallers) received MMs. During the day a fair number of stragglers appeared – mostly members of Sutherland's missing platoons. The final casualty total for 22 October was 58 killed, 47 captured and about 120 wounded. Seven officers were wounded, including Randle Evans, the only commissioned rank captured that day. Six officers were killed, including George Adam, who kept a grocer's shop in Abbeyhill. George was wounded on 1/7/16 as a lance-corporal in A Company. When he returned to his old platoon as an officer in September 1917, there wasn't a single 'original' left.

[43] R. Blake, ed., *The Private Papers of Douglas Haig 1914–1919* (London, 1952)

ELEVEN: *'FLOWERS O THE FOREST'*

[1] Conversation with Robert Johnston.

[2] Rawson to D.M. Sutherland, 25/1/18.

[3] The old jerseys, together with boots and other kit belonging to the dead and wounded players, were lost near Croisilles during the German offensive. The Battalion 'Shield', which was engraved with a record of sporting distinctions, is also missing.

[4] War Diary, 16th (Service) Battalion The Royal Scots, 23/2/18. (Regimental HQ.)

[5] PRO WO95/2436: 'Action of the 34th Division in the Battle of the Sensée River.'

[6] PRO WO95/2456: 'Report of German Attack on 101st Infantry Brigade.'

[7] Johnston diary.

[8] WO339/37807: Record file of Lt A.T. McLaren, 15th RS; PRO WO95/2456: Attack Report, op. cit.

[9] Lambert diary.

[10] PRO WO95/2456: Attack Report, op. cit. 'It wasn't dug; it was *scraped*,' said Meechan.

[11] PRO WO95/2456: Attack Report, op. cit. It is plain from certain passages in *The Thirty-Fourth Division* that Shakespear had seen this report. He chose, however, to omit the revelations about 'friendly' fire, preferring to blame the carnage on 'the enemy's gunners, informed by an air scout'. This was probably intended as a kindness to the families of men who died that day.

[12] Lambert diary and PRO WO339/11916: Lambert record file.

[13] Analysis of *Soldiers Died* and contemporary War Office casualty lists has now produced precise figures for the engagement of 21–23 March. 138 men were wounded and 35 were captured. Only 27 were killed. This would suggest that the battalion held together remarkably well under the circumstances. Apart from Lambert, one other officer was captured: Percy MacAndrew, a 28-year-old builder from Lauder Road, got lost on the morning of the 22nd and was picked up by the Germans while looking for HQ.

[14] Rawson to father, 5/4/18.

[15] PRO WO95/2456: 101st Brigade War Diary, 1/4/18.

[16] PRO WO95/2456: 101st Brigade War Diary, 6/4/18.

[17] S.A.A. is the common abbreviation of 'Small Arm Ammunition' and normally refers to .303 calibre cartridges. James Baigrie told John Veitch that Tower joined C Company in the firing line and remained there until evening. After dark he drove back to Division to report to Nicholson but returned to rejoin the garrison at Rue Dormoire before morning. Tower died on 22/8/18 of wounds received in action while commanding the 4th Royal Fusiliers. He is buried at Bellacourt Military Cemetery, south of Arras.

[18] Conversation with Murdo McKay.

[19] Enraged by the havoc wrought on his home, the farmer later alleged that eight British officers

had forced him down to the cellar at gunpoint and hidden while the fighting continued outside. His account, however, does not fit with the known facts. Nor does it explain why the men in question should have been so keen to take him with them. Two of the officers were seriously wounded (one unconscious); three had been decorated for gallantry in the field and Warr was commended by both Stephenson and Nicholson for his bravery during the action. After the war he remained one of the most popular and respected members of McCrae's Old Comrades Association. The farmer's accusations are referred to in the file of 2/Lt Herbert Tonathy in the Public Record Office – WO339/99920. The statements of the other named officers have also been checked. They were given independently and are consistent with the actual events. None of the officers, incidentally, spoke French.

[20] CSM James Baigrie was awarded the MM for this action. The withdrawal order from XV Corps was received by 34th Division HQ at 10 a.m.; Nicholson decided on 3 p.m. as the start time for the operation. Notification didn't reach 101st Brigade until 12.45 p.m.; Stephenson was informed at 2.55 – giving him a remarkable five *minutes'* notice. Shakespear stated in *The Thirty-Fourth Division* that a company of 18th NF formed the bridgehead guard and finally retired 'after 5 p.m.' Stephenson's War Diary (written on 24 April) gives the details for McCrae's and the time of 6.30. Shakespear was referring to the *second* last pontoon, slightly further west. That bridge was destroyed early to prevent it falling into enemy hands. Two platoons (one 18th NF, one 4th West Ridings) were just about to cross it when it blew. The last unit of 34th Division to leave the south bank was a small party of the 10th Lincolns, which crossed the stone bridge at Pont de Nieppe (west of Armentières) at 8.27 p.m. See the Lincolns War Diary in PRO WO95/2457.

[21] The Battalion War Diary is understandably vague about losses sustained during the actions on the Lys, stating a simple total of '13 officers; 554 other ranks'. Analysis of *Soldiers Died* and War Office casualty lists, however, produces the following. Two officers were killed; ten were wounded. Two of the latter were captured and died of their injuries; a further two were captured and survived. In addition, 2 *unwounded* officers were captured, making a total of 14 – one more than the War Diary. The figures for other ranks are 110 killed in action; 18 died of wounds; 70 captured and around 370 wounded. The last man to die while serving with McCrae's was Cpl James Dickie, a 24-year-old post office clerk from Easter Road, who was killed by shell-fire on 17 April. He enlisted with his brother, Frank, at Tynecastle in December 1914. The last McCrae original to lose his life *during the war* was William Mackie, a 24-year-old hairdresser from Murdoch Terrace, who died at home on 7 November of wounds received near Bailleul in April. William was a Hearts ticket-holder.

[22] *The Thirty-Fourth Division*, page 244.

[23] Hugh is the mysterious 'Captain Somerville' mentioned in Dominic Hibberd's excellent *Wilfred Owen – The Last Year* (London, 1994).

[24] *London Gazette*, 1 February 1919.

TWELVE: *'A GREAT LIFE OUT THERE, AFTER ALL'*

[1] Conversations with Jane Lorimer and Laura Bade. Laura was the daughter of John McCartney's son (and Tynecastle successor), Willie.

[2] This was Stephenson's only appearance at a reunion. For the rest of his life, he had to be content with descriptive letters from Bob Martin and D.M. Sutherland.

[3] Sassoon, Siegfried, *The Complete Memoirs of George Sherston* (London, 1937).

[4] Conversation with Veitch.

[5] Gordon at 1964 reunion. Buglers from the Ypres Fire Brigade have sounded the 'Last Post' at the Menin Gate Memorial to the missing every evening in peacetime since 11 November 1929.

[6] The 'Tyneside Memorial Seat' at la Boisselle remains one of the most poignant and impressive memorials on the entire Western Front.

[7] McCrae letter and subscription intimations, 20/12/20. In the absence at that point of any official lists, the figure of 800 dead was no more than an estimate. In fact, at least 1,400 officers and men lost their lives while serving with the battalion – including 422 'original' members. Incidentally, anyone who doubts the niggardliness of the post-war Town Council would do

well to examine the official Edinburgh War Memorial outside the City Chambers. It is (by some distance) the meanest specimen to be found in any major municipality in Great Britain. It is entirely out of keeping with the scale of the city's sacrifice and simply reeks of parsimony and ignorance. The veterans were ashamed of it.

8   Pulteney letter, 14/12/22.

9   Haig letter – undated but mid-December 1922 (Royal Scots Regimental Museum). According to a note from Sir George to Donald Gunn (26/11/22), Haig was originally invited to perform the unveiling in person. He declined, citing other commitments.

10 16th Royal Scots Memorial Unveiling and Presentation of Colours: 'Order of Service'. (Author's Collection). It was November 1925 before the Edinburgh and Manchester contingents of the Provost's Battalion were able to unveil their memorial. Desperately short of funds, and having suffered a similar series of official rebuffs, they also settled for a tablet in the High Kirk. Fittingly, it was placed directly beside McCrae's. Jimmy Black again presided and an honour party from the 16th were the principal guests.

Attendant to the publication of the first edition of *McCrae's Battalion*, the Contalmaison element of the post-war commemorative proposals was resurrected. Working from a simple D.M. Sutherland sketch, I drew up plans for a 14-foot-high cairn to be erected on open ground beside the rebuilt village church. The cairn – constructed from Scottish stone, quarried near Elgin – will carry a four-foot-square ornamental bronze plaque, telling the battalion's story for generations to come. Two substantial 'supporting' plaques will record the unique contribution of Heart of Midlothian Football Club and the sacrifice of the 15th Royal Scots. A committee has been formed to raise funds to finance this project – which is said to be the Western Front's most ambitious memorial undertaking since the highpoint of such schemes in the 1920s. It is intended to complete the work over the summer and autumn of 2004, in time for unveiling on 7 November.

11 Elias Furst was so unwell that he had to watch the proceedings from the upper floor of a nearby house.

12 McCrae to D.M. Sutherland, 5/1/17. The letter closes dryly: 'I hope the RSM has not blown his head off, or any other body's' – a reference to Fred Muir's recent attendance at a bombing school.

13 McCrae to Asquith 5/2/25.

14 Duguid's resting place remains unmarked; however, thanks to the kindness of Sarah Innes, daughter of William Berry Robertson, plans to construct a commemorative marker on the plot are finally afoot. By the end of 2004 the Pipey will have his headstone.

15 Their bungalow home at 44 Mountcastle Crescent was called 'Harribelle'.

16 For long enough this enormous hole was simply called 'New Crater'. At some point, veterans and historians began referring to it as 'Lochnagar' – after the front-line trench where the tunnelling started.

17 Neil Moreland, the old Hearts centre, remained in the Territorials after 1918. In 1939, aged 46, he was mobilised for the second time in his military career. Fortunately, he was not sent overseas.

18 *The Scotsman*, 21/10/49.

19 Conversation with Violet Walker, daughter of Frank Harkness, who was killed on 1/7/16. Jimmy used to visit her family fairly regularly – always arriving just in time for tea.

20 This misleading and offensive epithet has occasionally resurfaced – mainly from within the club itself. Heart of Midlothian FC's grasp of its own history leaves much to be desired.

Select Bibliography

BOOKS AND ARTICLES

Anon., *List of British Officers taken prisoner in the various Theatres of War between August 1914 and November 1918 – Compiled from Records kept by Messrs. Cox & Co.'s Enquiry Office* (London, 1988)

Anon., *9th Royal Scots (T.F.), B Company on Active Service, February–May 1915* (Edinburgh, 1916)

Anon., *Notes on Trench Routine and Discipline – By a Second in Command* (London, 1916)

Armit, Captain Napier, ed., *The Weekly Rumour – Magazine of the 16th Royal Scots* (Edinburgh, 1915)

Becke, A.F., *Order of Battle of Divisions* – 8 volumes (London, 1937–1945)

—— 'The coming of the creeping barrage' in *Journal of the Royal Artillery*, 58 (1931–1932)

Bewsher, Major F.W., *History of the 51st (Highland) Division, 1914–1918* (Edinburgh, 1921)

Birchall, Captain A.P., *Rapid Training of a Company for War* (London, 1915)

Blake, Robert, ed., *The Private Papers of Douglas Haig* (London, 1952)

Brelsford, W.V., *The Story of the Northern Rhodesian Regiment* (Salisbury, 1954)

Brophy, John and Partridge, Eric, *The Long Trail – Soldiers' Songs and Slang 1914–1918* (London, 1969)

Bryant, Peter, *Grimsby Chums – The Story of the 10th Lincolnshires in the Great War* (Hull, 1990)

Chambers, Robert, *Traditions of Edinburgh* (Edinburgh, 1931)

Chapman, Guy, *A Passionate Prodigality* (Leatherhead, 1993)

Charlton, Peter, *Pozières 1916 – Australians on the Somme* (London, 1986)

Cockburn, Lord, *Memorials of His Time*, ed. W. Forbes Gray (Edinburgh, 1946)

Cooper, Duff, *Haig* (London, 1935 and 1937)

Croft, Lt.-Col. W.D., *Three Years with the 9th (Scottish) Division* (London, 1919)

Daiches, David, *Edinburgh* (London, 1978)

Dallas, Gloden and Gill, Douglas, *The Unknown Army* (London, 1985)

Dann, H.C., *The Romance of the Posts of Rhodesia, British Central Africa and Nyasaland* (Zimbabwe, 1981)

Dewar, George and Boraston, Lieut.-Col. J.H., ed., *Sir Douglas Haig's Despatches, December 1915–April 1919* (London, 1919)

Dunn, Captain J C., *The War the Infantry Knew 1914–1919* (London, 1997)

Edmonds, Sir James E., *Military Operations: France and Belgium, 1914*, vol. I (London, 1933)

—— *Military Operations: France and Belgium, 1914*, vol. II (London, 1925)

—— *Military Operations: France and Belgium, 1916*, vol. I and maps and appendices (London, 1932)

—— *Military Operations: France and Belgium, 1917*, vol. II (London, 1948)

—— *Military Operations: France and Belgium, 1918*, vol. I and maps and appendices (London, 1935)

—— *Military Operations: France and Belgium, 1918*, vol. II and maps (London, 1937)

Ellis, Edna, *A Ripon Record 1887–1986* (Chichester, 1986)

Ewing, Major John, *History of the 9th (Scottish) Division* (Edinburgh, 1919)

—— *The Royal Scots 1914–1919*, vols I and II (Edinburgh, 1925)

Falls, Captain Cyril, *Military Operations: France and Belgium, 1917*, vol. I and appendices (London, 1940)

Farrar-Hockley, A.H., *The Somme* (London, 1964)

—— *Ypres 1914: Death of an Army* (London, 1967)

Ferguson, Niall, *The Pity of War* (London, 1999)

Gammage, Bill, *The Broken Years – Australian Soldiers in the Great War* (London, 1982)

Griffith, Paddy, *Battle Tactics of the Western Front* (London, 1994)

Hart, B.H. Liddell, *History of the First World War* (London, 1972)

Hankey, Lord, *The Supreme Command 1914–1918*, vols I and II (London, 1961)

Henniker, Col. A.M., *Transportation on the Western Front 1914–1918* (London, 1937)

Henry, Fred, *Ships of the Isle of Man Steam Packet Company* (Glasgow, 1967)

Imperial War Graves Commission, *Cemetery Registers, France and Belgium 1914–1919*

Imperial War Graves Commission, *Memorial Registers, France and Belgium 1914–1919*

James, Brigadier E.A., *British Regiments 1914–1918* (Heathfield, 1998)

—— *A Record of the Battles and Engagements of the British Armies in France and Flanders, 1914–1918* (Aldershot, 1924)

Keegan, John, *The First World War* (London, 1999)

Lewis, Cecil, *Sagittarius Rising* (London, 1983)

Liddle, Peter H., ed., *Passchendaele in Perspective – The Third Battle of Ypres* (London, 1997)

Lodge, Margaret, *Sir Richard Lodge – A Biography* (Edinburgh, 1946)

Longworth, Philip, *The Unending Vigil – A History of the Commonwealth War Graves Commission* (London, 1985)

Lynch, Michael, *Scotland – A New History* (London, 1993)

McCartney, John, *The 'Hearts' and the Army* (Edinburgh, 1917)

—— *The 'Hearts' and the Great War* (Edinburgh, 1918)

—— 'The Hearts Roll of Honour' in *The Sportsman's Gazette*, June 1917

—— *The Story of the Scottish Football League* (Edinburgh, 1930)

McCrae, George, *The Old City Debt: A Report by the City Treasurer* (Edinburgh, 1895)

Mackie, J.D., *A History of Scotland* (London, 1966)

Marwick, Arthur, *The Deluge* (London, 1991)

Maurice, Maj.-Gen. Sir Frederick, *The Life of General Lord Rawlinson of Trent* (London, 1928)

Mead, Gary, *The Doughboys – America and the First World War* (London, 2001)

Middlebrook, Martin, *The First Day on the Somme – 1 July 1916* (London, 1984)

—— *The Kaiser's Battle* (London, 1983)

Miles, Captain Wilfred, *Military Operations: France and Belgium, 1916*, vol. II and maps and appendices (London, 1938)

—— *Military Operations: France and Belgium, 1917*, vol. III (London, 1948)

Nott, David, *Somewhere in France* (Adelaide, 1996)

Prior, Robin and Wilson, Trevor, *Command on the Western Front* (Oxford, 1992)

—— *Passchendaele – The Untold Story* (London, 1996)

—— 'Summing up the Somme', in *History Today*, November, 1991

Richter, Donald, *Chemical Soldiers* (London, 1994)

Rorie, Col. David, *A Medico's Luck in the War – Reminiscences of RAMC Work with the 51ˢᵗ (Highland) Division* (Aberdeen, 1929)

Ross, Captain Robert B., *The Fifty-First in France* (London, 1918)

Sandilands, Brig.-Gen. J.W., *A Lancashire Brigade in France* (London, 1919)

Sandilands, Col. J.W. and MacLeod, Lieut.-Col. Norman, *The History of the 7ᵗʰ Battalion of the Queen's Own Cameron Highlanders* (Stirling, 1922)

Seton, Col. Sir Bruce and Grant, Pipe-Major John, *The Pipes of War – A Record of the Achievements of Pipers of Scottish and Overseas Regiments 1914–1918* (Glasgow, 1920)

Shakespear, Lieut.-Col. John, *The Thirty-Fourth Division 1915–1919* (London, 1922)

—— ed., *The Chequers – A Yearbook of the Thirty-Fourth Division* (Nottingham, 1924–1968)

Smout, T.C., *A History of the Scottish People 1560–1830* (Glasgow, 1977)

—— *A Century of the Scottish People 1830–1950* (London, 1997)

Spiers, Edward M., *Haldane: An Army Reformer* (Edinburgh, 1980)

Steuart, Daniel Rankine, *Bygone Days* (Edinburgh, 1936)

Stevenson, Robert Louis, *Edinburgh: Picturesque Notes* (London, 1879)

Stewart, Lieut.-Col. J. and Buchan, J., *The Fifteenth (Scottish) Division, 1914–1919* (Edinburgh, 1926)

Tait, Christian S. *Stones in the Millpond – Reflections on the First World War* (Lerwick, 2001)

Taylor, A.J.P., *The First World War* (London, 1981)

Ternan, Brig.-Gen. Trevor, *The Story of the Tyneside Scottish* (Newcastle, 1919)

Terraine, John, *Douglas Haig – The Educated Soldier* (London, 1990)

—— *The Western Front* (London 1970)

Thomas, Captain T.C., *With a Labour Company in France* (Birmingham, 1919)

Thomson, Lieut.-Col. R., *History of the Fifty-Second (Lowland) Division* (Glasgow, 1923)

Various, (school magazines) *Boroughmuir School; Broughton School; The Herioter; The Merchant Maiden; The Merchistonian; The Student* (Edinburgh University); *Stewart's College; The Watsonian.*

War Office, *Soldiers Died in the Great War 1914–1919* (London, 1921)

—— *Officers Died in the Great War 1914–1919* (London, 1919)

Winter, Denis, *Haig's Command – A Reassessment* (London, 1991)

—— *Death's Men – Soldiers of the Great War* (London, 1979)

Winter, Jay, *Sites of Memory, Sites of Mourning – The Great War in European Cultural History* (Cambridge, 1998)

Winter, J.M., 'Britain's Lost Generation in the First World War' in *Population Studies*, vol. 31, November 1977

Wolff, Leon, *In Flanders Fields* (London, 1959)

NEWSPAPERS AND JOURNALS

Alloa Journal; Alloa & Hillfoots Advertiser; Ayr Advertiser; Ayrshire Post; Berwickshire Advertiser; Border Telegraph; Border Standard; British Medical Journal; Burnley Express & Advertiser; The Cairn; Caithness Courier; Carlisle Journal; Cumberland News; Cumnock Chronicle; Daily Record; Dalkeith Advertiser; Devon Valley Tribune; Dumfries & Galloway Standard; Dundee Advertiser; Dunfermline Press; East Fife Mail; Edinburgh Evening Dispatch; Edinburgh Evening News; Falkirk Herald; Fife Free Press; Fifeshire Advertiser; Evening News (Glasgow); Evening Times (Glasgow); Glasgow Citizen; Glasgow Herald; Glasgow News; Hamilton Advertiser; Haddingtonshire Courier; Hawick Advertiser; Hawick Express; Inverness Courier; John o' Groat Journal; Labour Standard; Leith Observer; Leven Advertiser; Linlithgowshire Gazette; London Gazette; Luton News; Midlothian Journal; Motherwell Times; Municipal Journal and Public Works Engineer; North British Rubber Company News; Northern Whig; Orcadian; Orkney Herald; People's Journal; The Post; The Phonographer and Shorthand Students' Magazine; Punch; Ross-shire Journal; Saturday Post; Scots Pictorial; The Scotsman; Scottish Typographical Journal; Southern Reporter; Sporting Post; Strathearn Herald; Sunday Post; Sunderland Daily Echo; The Thistle; The Times; Weekly Record; West Lothian Courier.

ROLLS OF HONOUR, 1914–19

Aberdeen University (Aberdeen, 1919)

Bertrams Ltd (Edinburgh, 1919)

Carlisle Grammar School Memorial Register (Carlisle, 1924)

Clan MacRae Roll of Honour and Service (Aberdeen, 1923)

City of Edinburgh (unpublished, 1920)

City of Glasgow (Glasgow, 1920)

Commercial Bank of Scotland (Edinburgh, 1921)

County of Peebles (Peebles, 1920)

Dean and St Cuthbert's UF Church: Remembrance Album (Edinburgh, 1919)

Dunfermline High School (Dunfermline, 1920)

Edinburgh College of Art (Edinburgh, 1919)

Edinburgh Corporation (Edinburgh, 1920)

Edinburgh Typographical Society, Case Room, 1914–1917 (Edinburgh, 1917)

Edinburgh Typographical Society Service Roll, 1914 and 1915 (Edinburgh, 1914 and 1915)

Edinburgh Writers to the Signet and Apprentices (Edinburgh, 1920)

George Stewart & Son Ltd (Edinburgh, 1920)

George Heriot's School (Edinburgh, 1921)

Glasgow High School (Glasgow, 1921)

Hawick and the War (Hawick, 1919)

Inland Revenue (Scotland) Land Valuation Department (Edinburgh, 1920)

John Ker Memorial Church (Edinburgh, 1920)

Leith Town (Leith, 1919)
Merchiston Castle School (Edinburgh, 1921)
Moray House Training College (Edinburgh, 1920)
National Bank of Scotland (Edinburgh, 1922)
Parish Church of St Cuthbert Roll of Service, July 1915 (Edinburgh, 1915)
Parish of Corstorphine (Edinburgh, 1920)
Parish of Currie (Edinburgh, 1919)
Parish of Newbattle (Edinburgh, 1920)
Penicuik and Glencorse in the Great War (unpublished, 1919)
Royal High School of Edinburgh (Edinburgh, 1920)
Scottish Co-operative Wholesale Society (Glasgow, 1919)
Shetland's Roll of Honour (Lerwick, 1920)
Thomas Nelson & Sons (Edinburgh, 1917)
Tweeddale Book of Remembrance, vols I and II (Peebles, 1921)
Union Bank of Scotland (Edinburgh, 1922)
University of Edinburgh (Edinburgh, 1921)
University of St Andrews (Edinburgh, 1920)
Watsonian War Record (Edinburgh, 1920)
William Younger & Co. (Edinburgh, 1920)

WAR OFFICE MANUALS ETC.

Assault Training, September 1917 (SS 185).
Bayonet Fighting – Instruction with Service Rifle and Bayonet, 1915.
Bayonet Training, 1916.
Field Service Manual – Infantry Battalion (Expeditionary Force), 1914.
Field Service Pocket Book, 1914.
Fourth Army – Tactical Notes (General Staff, May 1916).
Index to Maps of Belgium and France – Scale 1/100,000 (General Staff, 1916).
Infantry Training, 1914.
Instructions for the Training of Platoons for Offensive Action (SS 143), February 1917.
Instructions for the Training of Divisions for Offensive Action (SS 135), December 1916.
King's Regulations and Orders for the Army, 1912.
Manual of Military Law, 1914.
Musketry Regulations, Part I, 1909.
Notes on Company Training (General Staff, September 1914).
Notes on the Tactical Employment of Machine Guns and Lewis Guns (General Staff, March 1916).
Notes on Trench Warfare for Infantry Officers (General Staff, March 1916).
Notes on Trench Warfare for Infantry Officers– Revised Diagrams (General Staff, December 1916).
Organisation of an Infantry Battalion and the Normal Formation for the Attack (General Staff, April 1917).
Questions a Platoon Commander Should Ask Himself Before an Attack (General Staff, July 1917).
Tactical Employment of Lewis Guns (SS 197), January 1918.
Training and Employment of Divisions, 1918 (SS 135), January 1918.
Training and Employment of Platoons, 1918 (SS 143), January 1918.
Training of Divisions for Offensive Action (SS 109), May 1916.
War Establishments of New Armies, 1915.

OTHER SOURCES

Alexander Cowan & Sons Ltd – Wage Books, October 1914–September 1918.
Alexander Cowan & Sons Ltd – Register of Members and Directors, 1914–1935.
Annual Reports of the Registrar General for Scotland 1914–1919.
Army Council Instructions, 1916–1918.
Casualty Lists of 16th (Service) Battalion The Royal Scots, 1916–1918 (compiled by the author).
Census of Scotland, 1911: Report of the 12th Decennial Census of Scotland.
Chalmers Hospital Minute Books, December 1914.
Chalmers Hospital Record Books, December 1914.
Confirmations and Inventories, 1915 to 1928 (Scottish Record Office).

City of Edinburgh Valuation Rolls, 1913–1923.
City of Glasgow Valuation Rolls, 1911/12–1919/20.
County of Midlothian Valuation Rolls, 1913–1920.
Dod's Parliamentary Companion for 1914.
Edinburgh & District Trades Council – Minute Books of Executive Committee, 1912–1920.
Edinburgh Corporation – Minutes of Meetings, 1914/15.
Edinburgh Typographical Society: Index of Members, 1904–1914.
—— Minute Books of Press and Machinemens' Section, 1912–1920.
—— New Members' Entry Books, 1901-1920.
—— Register of Case Department Employees, 1911.
Fasti Ecclesiae Scoticanae: The Succession of Ministers in the Church of Scotland from the Reformation, vol. VIII 1914–1929; vol. IX 1929–1954; vol. X 1955–1975.
First World War Medal Roll (Public Record Office).
First World War Service Records – Other Ranks, WO 363 and WO 364 (Public Record Office).
First World War Service Records – Commissioned Ranks, WO 338 and 339 (Public Record Office).
George Heriot's Trust – Minutes, 1914–1915.
General Annual Report of the British Army 1913–1919 (P.P. 1927, XX, Cmd. 1193).
Heart of Midlothian Football Club – Boardroom Minutes, March 1914 to February 1919.
Heriot-Watt Training College: Principal's Record Books, 1914–1915.
Imperial War Museum 1/10,000 Trench Map Archive on CD-Rom.
Medical Directory; Medical Register.
Membership Books, The Royal Scots Club, 1923–1980.
Memorandum and Articles of Association – Heart of Midlothian Football Club Ltd, 1905.
Ministry of National Service. Report on the Physical Examination of men of Military Age by National Service Medical Boards from November 1917 to October 1918. (P.P. 1919, XXVI, Cmd. 504).
Monthly Army List and Supplements, 1914–1919.
National Census: 1861, 1871, 1881, 1891, 1901 (General Register Office).
Navy List, 1910–1918.
Newsplan: Directory of Newspapers in Scotland.
Nominal Roll of 15th (Service) Battalion The Royal Scots, 1914 (compiled by the author).
Nominal Roll of 16th (Service) Battalion The Royal Scots, 1914 (compiled by the author).
Parliamentary Debates, Fifth Series, Vol. LXVIII, House of Commons, Session 1914–1915, vol. I.
Parliamentary Registers of Electors for Edinburgh, 1910 to present (includes Leith after 1920).
Parliamentary Registers of Electors for County of Linlithgowshire, 1914/15, 1920.
Post Office Directories: Edinburgh & Leith 1910–1975; Glasgow 1913–1921.
'Regimental Dead' registers (General Register Office).
Report of the Committee on the utilisation of Edinburgh Castle for the purposes of a Scottish National War Memorial (Edinburgh, 1919).
Soldiers' Attestation and Discharge Documents, 1883–1913 (Public Record Office).
Soldiers' Wills, 1914–1918 (Scottish Record Office).
Scottish National War Memorial – 'Regimental Dead' books 1914–1919.
University of Edinburgh Matriculation Albums and Graduation Books, 1910–1915.
War Diaries: 16th Royal Scots; 15th Royal Scots; 2nd Royal Scots; 9th Royal Scots (Regimental HQ).
War Diaries: 101st Brigade; 102nd Brigade; 103rd Brigade (Public Record Office).
War Diary of 23rd Australian Infantry Battalion (Australian War Memorial, Canberra).
War Diary of 23rd Manchester Regiment (Public Record Office).
War Diary of 34th Division General Staff, January 1916 to August 1918 (Public Record Office).
War Diary of 34th Division Adjutant and Quartermaster General (Public Record Office).
War Diary of 34th Division Artillery (Public Record Office).
War Office – Weekly Casualty Lists, March 1916–February 1918 in *The Scotsman.*
War Office – Weekly Casualty Lists, numbers 1–65: 7 August 1917 to 29 October 1918.
War Office and Air Force – Weekly Casualty Lists, numbers 66–83: 5 November 1918 to 4 March 1919.
War Office – Ordnance Survey maps of France and Belgium: 1/40,000 and 1/100,000.
War Office – Trench Maps: 1/5,000, 1/10,000 and 1/20,000.

Index

Adamson, A.G. 22
Ainslie, Sgt John 149
Aitchison, Pte George 173–4
Albert 137–8, 140, 143, 147, 150, 177
Allan, Pte John (9th RS) 298
American Expeditionary Force 233, 254
Amiens 118, 134, 137, 140, 153, 178
Anderson, Pte Alfred 192
Anderson, Sgt Charles 156, 158
Anderson, Pipe-Sgt David (15th RS) 156–160
Anderson, Pte John 141
Anderson, Lord 54
Armadale 86, 110
Armentières 119–20, 124, 195, 245–54
Armit, Napier 93, 115, 121–2, 162, 166, 169, 171, 179, 190, 192
Armstrong, 2/Lt Bernard 212
Armstrong, 2/Lt Ralph 275
Arras 200–210, 233, 235, 237
Asquith, Rt. Hon. Herbert Henry 51, 77–8
Australian Expeditionary Force 130–132, 187, 189, 194, 202

Baigrie, Sgt James 251–2, 280
Bailleul 195, 197–8, 205, 209, 252–4
Baird, 2/Lt James 221
Baldwin, Rt. Hon. Stanley 271
Bapaume 136, 139–40, 145–46, 185, 205, 233, 245, 263
Barclay, 2/Lt Robert 238, 240
Barnie, Pte Edward 280
Bathgate 73, 86, 125, 161, 248
Baxter, 2/Lt Andrew 229
Bayliss, Capt. Percy 235–6, 251, 253, 280, 283
Bazentin-le-Petit 184–186, 188–189
Becker, Pte Ernest 125, 162
Bécourt 150, 154, 158, 176, 183, 185
Bethune, Piper Murdo 162
Bibby, Capt. James (27th NF) 166, 168
Bird, Pte John 165

Bird, Pte Robert 275
Bishop, Pte Alfred (15th RS) 163, 167
Black, Capt. James 111, 122, 155, 158, 168, 181, 202, 264, 265, 277–8
Bland, Pte Fred 149, 287
Blaney, Pte George 89, 103, 148–9, 192, 278
Bois Grenier 120, 122, 124, 196, 216, 246, 249, 256
Bonar, Pte Thomson 108, 109
Boulogne 118, 182, 202, 254
Boyd, Archibald 69, 78
Boyd, Pte James 69, 78, 186, 195, 197, 298
Brabner, Pte David 289
Brabner, Pte Archibald 289
Briggs, Cpl Alfred 68, 73, 105, 123, 126–7, 156, 161, 174, 183, 276
British Army
  Armies: Third 204–5; Fourth 134, 145, 153; Fifth 223–4, 245
  Corps: III 135, 144, 147, 179, 193, 264; VI 209, 238, 240; XVII 204, 211; Canadian 205, 209, 230
  Infantry Divisions: (3rd) 238, 242–3; (4th) 209; (8th) 135; (15th) 194–5; (19th) 135, 170, 172, 175, 185–8, 194; (21st) 167,174–5, 178–9; (23rd) 176, 187, 189; (24th) 246; (25th) 249, 252; (33rd) 185; (35th) 228; (37th) 183; (40th) 246, 248–9; (51st) 185, 212; (59th) 238, 240–4, 253; Indian Cavalry 185
  Infantry Brigades: (101st) 112, 162, 184, 187–9, 195, 212, 220, 238, 241, 252; (102nd) 112, 158, 162, 167, 238, 241, 252; (103rd) 112, 167, 212, 237, 238, 249
  Infantry Battalions: Royal Scots (2nd) 255; (4th) 35–6, 48, 50, 110; (5th) 35–6, 183; (6th) 35–6, 50, 183; (7th) 35, 103–4, 110; (9th) 35; (11th, 12th,

13th) 41; (15th) 106, 158, 160–1, 169, 209–10, 212, 214–15, 220, 228, 238, 241, 242, 244
  Infantry Regiments: Cameron Highlanders 72; East Lancs 170, 174, 242; King's Own Yorkshire Light Infantry 178, 181; King's Royal Rifle Corps 189–90; Highland Light Infantry 183; Lincolnshire 106, 158, 160, 162, 175, 176, 212, 220; Manchester 228–9; Middlesex 296; Northumberland Fusiliers 112, 127, 150, 162, 169, 237, 242, 249; Royal Fusiliers 17; Royal West Surrey 23; Scottish Rifles 183; Shropshire 186; Suffolk 106, 162, 169, 187–9, 190, 212, 244, 248, 252; Warwickshire 186
Brodie, Sgt John 124–5
Brodie, Deacon William 30, 46
Brown, Pte James Stirling 84–5, 108, 156, 161, 173–4, 278
Brown, Capt. Osbert (11th Suffolks) 166, 190–2
Brown, Pte Alexander 143
Brydie, Pte William 148
Bryson, Pte James 291
Buchan, John (uncle of SGM) 46
Buchan, John (author) 77
Buchan, John, Pte 152, 182
Buchanan, Lt Fred 166, 167–8
Bullecourt 205, 238, 240–6
Burns, Robert (poet) 30, 62, 80, 200, 236
Bussell, Major Thomas 225–30

Cambrai 205, 231–2, 234, 236
Cameron, CSM Angus 186
Campbell, Duncan 15, 22, 25–6
Campbell, James 79
Campbell, L/Cpl John 100
Campbell-Bannerman, Rt. Hon. Sir Henry 49–51

317

Castle Brewery 88–105
Cawley, L/Sgt Thomas 187
Charrington, Frederick Nicholas 21–2, 24, 295–6
Chemical Works *see* Rœux
Churchill, Winston 77, 267
Cockburn, Pte George 161
Cockburn, Lord 30–2
Cockburn, Pte Peter 161
Coles, Capt. Lionel 93–4, 126, 155, 159, 163, 165, 182
Cologne Ridge *see* Hargicourt
Contalmaison 144, 146–7, 153, 163–5, 167, 174 181–2, 184, 260, 272, 282
Cowan, Capt. Alexander Comrie 196, 208, 210
Cowan, 2/Lt George 165, 238, 240, 245, 277
'Cow-punchers' *see* Mossend Burnvale
Craig, James (architect) 30
Cranston, Lt-Col. Sir Robert 44
Crawford, Sgt Gerald 83–4, 105–6, 120, 122–3, 125, 141, 175, 202, 277
Crawford, Pte James 123, 275
Crichton, Pte John 159
Crighton, Pte James 143
Croisilles 235–45
Crombie, 2/Lt William 159, 161
Crossan, Pte Patrick 66–7, 78, 80, 83, 105, 123, 156, 164, 181, 197, 256, 258, 275, 298
Currie, Sgt Duncan 68–9, 73, 148, 164, 182, 298

Davie, Lt James 169, 174–5, 179, 221, 263, 279
Davie, Sgt Robert 230
Dawson, Percy 66, 69
Deans, Pte Walter 141–2
Defoe, Daniel 29
Dods, Pte James 164
Dougan, Pte John 149
Downie, Pte Harry 159
Doyle, Arthur Conan 38, 77
Duckworth, James 96, 276, 298
Duguid, Pipe-Major William 103, 116, 122, 156, 162, 254, 274–5
Dumaresq, Captain Reginald (101st MGC) 172
Duncan, Sgt John 129–30
Dunfermline FC 86
Duns 86

Edinburgh: 46, 56–7, 129; history of 28–36; spies in 45; War Memorial 260–3
Edinburgh City Battalions *see* McCrae's Battalion, Provost's Battalion
Edinburgh & District Trades Council 77, 79
Edinburgh Nomads FC 83, 202
Edinburgh Territorial Force Association 40–2, 43

Ellis, Pte Ernest 73, 105, 164, 222, 298
English Football Association (FA) 16, 20–1, 296
English Football League 16, 18–19, 20, 26–7, 296
Erquinghem 126, 127, 195, 246, 248–9, 251
Evans, Capt. Randle 228–9
Ewart, Gen. Sir John Spencer 104
Ewing, Sgt Archibald 100–1, 105, 123, 149, 277

Fairweather, L/Cpl Primrose 150, 159
Falkirk FC 71, 82, 96, 236
Farquharson, 2/Lt Archibald 228
Farrow, Pte Adolphus 221
Fergusson, Robert (poet) 30
Findlay, Cpl Norman 73, 105, 276
Fitton, Brig.-Gen. Hugh 106, 119
Flett, Lt Arthur 209
Ford, Patrick 80
Forsyth, Thomas (Airdrieonians FC) 15, 16, 25
Foster, Pte Magnus 152
Fotheringham, Pte George 229
Fox, Cpl Richard 218, 230
French, Field-Marshal Sir John 23, 52
Frew, Pte James 73, 98, 276
Fürst, Elias 60–1, 64, 66, 73, 80, 263

Gallipoli 110, 114, 130, 183
Gavin, 2/Lt William 149, 210, 211, 222, 228, 241, 278
Gibb, Pte Robert 229
Gibbon, Pte Michael 82
Gill, L/Cpl Christopher 192
Gilmour, Capt William, MD 130, 181, 195, 208
Goodall, Pte Charles 121, 192
Gordon, Pte Robert 262
Gore, Brig.-Gen. Robert 153, 187–8, 192, 195, 197, 203, 253
Gough, Gen. Sir Hubert 223–4
Gourlay, Pte John 229
Gracie, Cpl Thomas 70, 73, 74, 105, 109, 114, 298
Graham, Harry 67, 76, 276
Graham, William, MP 269–70
Grange Cemetery 11, 51, 274
Grant, Sir Ludovic 79
Green, Sgt Alfred 178
Grosert, Pte Alexander 82
Gunn, CQMS Donald 94, 98, 124, 263, 270, 275

Haig, Field-Marshal Sir Douglas 133–4, 144, 201, 223, 230–1, 232, 252, 265
Haldane, Richard 50–2
Halliburton, Pte Thomas 159, 255
Hamilton, 2/Lt George 170, 217
Hargicourt 218–22, 236, 259
Harley, Pte Harry 125–6, 161, 182

Harrison, Capt. Alfred (15th RS) 111, 209
Hawthorn, Pte James 85, 164
Hazebrouck 119, 133, 246, 253
Hazeldean, James 110, 127, 156, 164, 174, 183
Heart of Midlothian FC 39; formation and development 54–61; John McCartney 64–9; players' enlistment 73–6, 81–2; Roll of Honour 297–8; War Memorial 266
Heart of Midlothian, The (novel by Sir Walter Scott) 35
Henderson, L/Cpl Alex 82
Henderson, Sgt Andy 82, 222, 240
Henderson, 2/Lt George 214–15
Hendry, Capt. James 94, 186, 195, 197
Heriot's School 88–105
High Kirk (St Giles Cathedral): service of commemoration 264–6
High Wood 185, 189, 193
Hill, Sgt Thomas 186
Hindenburg Line 204–5, 217, 231, 235
Hogg, James (author) 30, 178
Hogg, Pte Robert 168, 253
Hogge, James, MP 80, 83, 178
Honeyman, 2/Lt Norman 230
Hope, Charles (Lord Justice-Clerk) 31
Hope, John (lawyer and Volunteer) 34
Hope 2/Lt John A. 229
Howat, 2/Lt William 215
Howie, 2/Lt George 240
Hunter, Pte Thomas (15th RS) 160
Husband, Lt Robert 112–13, 275
Hyslop, Pte Charles 289

Inches, Robert Kirk 36–7, 41, 42–3
Ingles, 2/Lt Robert 240–242
Ingouville-Williams, Maj.-Gen. E.C. 113, 126, 190
Intermediate Trench 186–95
Izatt, Pte David 86

Jack L/Cpl David 151–2
Jamieson, Pte James 152
Jardine, Pte Joseph 169, 275
Joffre, Gen. Joseph 23, 200
Johnston, Pte George 164
Johnston, 2/Lt Robert 217–18, 220–1, 226, 230, 241–2, 280
Jollie, Pte James 125
Jolly, Sgt John 161–2
Jones, Sgt George 160, 163

Kay, Pte Andrew 129
Kelly, Pte Florance 127–8, 162
Kelly, Cpl Michael 85, 165, 174, 179, 183, 278
King, Pte Thomas 106, 137, 196–7
Kinnaird, Lord 21
Kitchener, Lord 39–40, 40, 52, 117, 146, 299

Kitton, 2/Lt Leslie 153, 159, 280
Koerber, Pte John 129

La Boisselle 139–78, 255, 263, 272
Lady Glenorchy's Church 274
Laing, Pte Alexander 164
Laing, Pte John 164
Lambert, Capt. Charles ('Joe') 240, 243, 244
Lauder, Major Richard 93, 119, 150, 278
Lavery, Pte William 82
Law, Rt. Hon. Andrew Bonar 77, 267, 269, 271
Leishman, Sir James 59–60, 74, 114, 263
Leitch, Archibald 69
Lewis, Pte Fred 161
Lindsay, Sgt Alexander 187, 241–2, 278–9
Linn, 2/Lt Peter 229
Litster, Pte Thomas 280
Lloyd George, Rt. Hon. David 77, 200–1, 232, 267
Lodge, Lt Cuthbert 53, 94, 166, 168, 179, 221
Lodge, Sir Richard 52, 263
Lodge, Lt Wilfred (15th RS) 52–3, 179
Lody, Carl Hans 45
Logan, Sgt James 82
Lonsdale, Sir John 77–8
Lorimer, Harry 75, 85, 89, 95, 105, 276
Lorimer, William 73, 258
Low, Cpl James 68, 70, 73, 105, 259, 276
Lyon, Alexander 98, 276, 298
Lyon, Capt. Michael C.H.B. 196, 214

Macdonald, Capt. John 196, 210
Macdonald, Rt. Hon. Ramsay 271
Mackay, Hugh 79
Mackay, CSM James 248
Mackenzie, Lt James 184, 190, 192, 194
Mackintosh, Capt. Hamish 240
MacLachlan, 2/Lt Alastair 186, 195
MacLean, 2/Lt Fraser 102, 108, 115, 122, 124, 142, 159, 278
MacMillan, Pte Robert ('Hamlet') 101, 127, 202, 204, 216
MacRae, Sgt Finlay 179, 221
Malcolm, Robert 73, 97, 99, 276–7
Mangles, Lt-Col. R.H. 187, 190
Mark, Pte William 179
Marshall, Pte John 164
Martin, Sgt James 187
Martin, Sgt James T. 221
Martin, Capt. Robert 122, 202, 210–11, 217, 260, 278
McAra, Pte John 124
McArthur, L/Cpl William 85–6, 179, 192
McCarthy, Capt. William 230, 283
McCartney, John 61–70, 73–6, 80, 105, 129, 222, 257–9, 275–6, 295–6

McCrae, Capt. George (son of SGM) 51, 53, 110
McCrae, Lt.-Col. Sir George: biographical details 46–52, 59, 268–75; raising of 16th RS 49, 72–7, 80–4, 88–90; bombarded at Foray House 130–1; on Somme 138–41, 150, 156; Scots Redoubt and Wood Alley 168–71, 172, 175–7, 179; Intermediate trench 187–94; leaves 16th RS 195, 197–9, 266–8; 16th RS Memorial 263–4
McCrae, Kenneth 51, 53, 74
McCrae, William 51, 53
McCrae's Battalion (2nd Edinburgh City): raising and Hearts enlistment 72–8; further recruitment 78–86, 103; billeting and uniform 87–90; structure and training 92–8; France (Jan–April 1916) 117–32; arrival in Albert sector 134–8; Somme front 138–40, 147–54, 158–67; Wood Alley and Scots Redoubt 168–78; Intermediate Trench 186–95; Arras and Rœux 204–16; Hargicourt 219–22; Passchendaele 224–30; Croisilles 235–45; Armentières (April 1918) 248–54; reunions and Old Comrades Association 259–66, 279
McDougall, Sgt William 179, 220, 221
McEvoy, Pte James 114, 126, 151, 171–2, 206, 280
McFarlane, Sgt William 163, 179, 183
McGhee, James 64, 67
McGrouther, L/Sgt William 229
McGuire, Pte 'Teddy' 110, 127, 156, 164, 183
McIntosh, Pte Donald 280
McIvor, Cpl David 124, 147, 163
McKay, 2/Lt Alexander 248
McKay, Pte Murdo 161, 164, 174, 280
McKeen, Pte John 148
McLaren, Duncan, MP 32–3, 35, 48, 56
McLay, Sgt George 82, 229
McLean, Pte Donald 148
McLeod, Pte Murdoch 101
McManus, CSM Thomas 91
McMichael, 2/Lt William 127, 161
McNulty, Pte Andrew 147–8
McParlane, L/Cpl John 107–8, 128, 155–6
Meechan, Pte James 222, 225–6, 240, 242
Mercer, Robert 64, 71, 275, 298
Millar, 2/Lt Thomas 143, 151, 163, 183, 217, 251, 253, 279
Miller, Pte James 164
Miller, Lt Jock 131, 168, 196

Miller, Pte John 148
Miller, Sgt Robert 142, 289
Miller, Pte Thomas 148
Milligan, Pte Jeremiah 221
Moir, Lt James 128, 216, 278
Mont Noir 253–4
Moreland, Neil 39, 67
Morrison, Pte John 82
Morton, Pte James 86
Mossend Burnvale F.C. 85, 275
Mowatt, L/Sgt James ('Jerry') 229
Muir, RSM Frederick 91, 168, 177, 179, 278
Muir, Pte James 123
Muirhead, CSM John 91, 162, 187
Munro, Lt Donald 153, 172, 176, 210, 279

Needham, Capt. E.J. 170–1
Neeves, 2/Lt Horace ('Robin') 167, 168, 170, 173
Neill, Sgt Cecil 91
Nellies, Peter 64, 68, 276
Ness, CSM Annan 71, 73, 98, 100, 127, 129, 156, 173, 183–4, 186, 222, 230, 251, 255 259, 276
Nicholson, Maj.-Gen. Cecil Lothian 184, 187, 193–5, 212, 254–5
Nicol, Robert 46–8
Nisbet, Pte Cecil 150–1, 289
Nisbet, Pte Herbert 176
Nivelle, Gen. Robert 200–1, 211, 232
Norrie, Pte Alfred 206
North Berwick 272

Osborne, Major David (9th NF) 253
Owen, Wilfred 255

Pagan, Capt. Gavin (15th RS) 214, 216
Palmer, Pte Thomas 84, 208
Passchendaele 224–30, 232
Penicuik 86, 92, 97–8
Penman, Pte Thomas 129
Pétain, Gen. Henri 232
Peters, Pte George 128
Philip, L/Cpl David 107
Philp, Piper George 190
Philp, Pte Thomas 192
Piershill Barracks 274
Poelcappelle 225–6
Poperinghe 223, 253–4
Porteous, Acting RSM James (15th RS) 172
Porter, Pte William 82
Powburn 35, 56–7
Pozières 140, 144, 187
Preston, Pte Robert 73, 105, 276
Price, Charles, MP 79, 80
Pringle, 2/Lt Robert 160
Provost's Battalion (1st Edinburgh City) 41–4, 86, 148, 155, 160, 263
Pulteney, Gen. Sir William 135, 147, 179, 184, 194, 264
Purcell, CSM Daniel 91, 192
Purdie, Thomas (poacher) 55

Purdie, Thomas (HMFC) 55–7

Queen's Edinburgh Rifles 34

Raith Rovers FC 82, 126, 161, 229
Ramage, Pte Andrew 165, 181–2, 280
Rankine, Pte William 289
Rattray, Pte John 82
Rawlinson, Gen. Sir Henry 143–5, 153–4, 185
Rawson, Harry (chairman TFA) 41–3, 70–1, 89, 263
Rawson, Capt. Harry 94, 127, 132, 163, 183, 197, 234–5, 246, 251, 253
Redden, Pte William 164, 183, 279
Reilly, Pte Frank 82
Rhind, Sgt William 212, 229
Riddell, Pte Andrew 259–60, 278
Ripon 105–8
Roberts, Lord 17, 112
Robertson, Sgt Andrew 251
Robertson, CQMS Charles 131–2, 172, 176
Robertson, Capt. William, VC 41, 81
Robertson, Capt. William Berry 93, 168–9, 202, 278, 283
Robson, Lt Leonard (15th RS) 166, 168–9, 170, 174, 214, 216
Rœux 211–216
Rosebery, Lord 38, 52, 57–8
Ross, Charles 57
Ross, Capt. Peter 83, 94, 126, 152, 156–7, 161–2, 182
Ross, William 57
Royal Scots Club 273, 279
Russell, 2/Lt George 127, 165, 167
Russell, Pte Robert 121–2

St Léger 241–44
St Omer 118, 123, 128, 132, 202
Sassoon, Siegfried 261–62
Scots Redoubt 168–77, 262
Scott, Sgt Frank 158, 159
Scott, Pte Jimmy 82, 161
Scott, Walter McKenzie 71, 76, 83, 276
Scott, Sir Walter 31, 36, 46, 55
Scottish Football Association (SFA) 15–16, 22, 25–6, 56, 57, 296
Scottish Football League 58, 70, 293–4

Seely, Col. John 51–2
Shakespear, Lt-Col. John (18th NF) 197–8, 254
Simons, Cpl George 186
Sinclair, George 39, 64, 70
Sloan, L/Sgt William 162
Smart, L/Sgt David 158, 159
Smith, Drummer William 161
Smith, Pte John 181
Somerville, Capt. Hugh 255
Speedie, Pte James (7th Camerons) 67, 72, 110, 113
Spence, Pte William 151
Sponder, Sgt William 215–16
Steele, L/Sgt Wilbert 164, 182
Stephenson, Lt-Col. Arthur 178, 180–1, 193, 196, 198, 226, 252, 278
Steuart, Pte Jim 114, 150, 152, 161, 183, 196, 204, 205–6, 208–9, 275
Stevenson, Robert Louis 31
Stewart, 2/Lt John 124, 236, 240
Stewart, Cpl Robert 164–5
Stewart, 2/Lt Tom Grainger 184
Stocks, Major Harris (15th RS) 160, 163, 167
Storer, 2/Lt Tom 253
Strathclyde, Lord 79
Sutherland, Pte Alexander 192
Sutherland, Capt. D.M. 94, 108–9, 137, 141, 160, 176–7, 190, 225, 226–7, 229, 263, 279–80
Sutherland, Pte Harry 108
Swan, Pte Harry 82

Tait, Pte John 162
Taylor, Pte Frank 124
Temple, Major Richard (27th NF) 167, 168
Terrett, Tom 87
Teviotdale, Cpl Thomas 164, 183, 279
Thomson, Pte John 126, 162
Thomson, Cpl William 159
Thomson, Pte William 148
Thurburn, 2/Lt Erik 209
Tod, 2/Lt Russell 125
Todd, Pte James 82, 126
Tower, Major Bertie 248, 249
Turenne Crossing 228, 238
Turnbull, Pte William ('John McLeod') 148
Turnbull, Pte William 109

Urmston, Lt-Col. Archibald (15th RS) 111–12, 156

Veitch, Cpl John 95, 112, 118, 154, 172–3, 177, 192, 256, 280
Vignoles, Major Walter (10th Lincolns) 126
Volunteer movement 34–5

Walker, 2/Lt Norman 127
Walker, Robert ('Bobby') 58–9, 66
Walker, Sgt Roddy (15th RS) 110, 261
War Office 18, 22, 25, 43, 86, 104, 109
Warden, Major Herbert 43, 71, 93, 96–7, 118, 119, 125, 130–1, 136, 141, 142–3, 168, 172, 179, 277
Warr, Major Alfred 93, 104, 173, 214, 225, 241, 251, 277
Warren, 2/Lt Matthew 128
Watson, Pte George 229
Watson, 2/Lt John 208
Watt, Pte Edward 151–2
Wattie, Pte Harry 66–7, 73, 75, 80, 105, 135–6, 148, 156, 164, 298
West, Sgt Archibald 186
Weston, Pte Frank 165, 181–2, 280
Whyte, Capt. Andrew 93, 153, 160, 163, 277
Wilson, Drummer John 277
Wilson, Robert 59
Wilson, Pte William R. 67, 73, 105, 110, 235, 259, 276
Winning, Pte Walter 128
Witherspoon, Pte Jock 289
Wood, Pte Frank 151
Wood, Pte James 279
Wood, Pte Robert 82
Wright, Sgt John 208
Wylie, Pte John 159, 279

Young Scots Society 37
Young, Cpl Thomas 118
Ypres 13, 23, 101–2, 119, 140, 200, 202, 223–4, 226, 253–4
Yule, Sgt Alexander 87, 156, 159, 161, 183, 263, 274, 279